Land of Women

ALSO BY LISA M. BITEL

Isle of the Saints: Monastic Settlement and Christian Community in Early Ireland

Land of Women

*Tales of Sex and Gender
from Early Ireland*

LISA M. BITEL

Cornell University Press

Ithaca and London

First published 1996 by Cornell University Press.

Printed in the United States of America

∞ The paper in this book meets the minimum requirements
of the American National Standard for Information Sciences—
Permanence of Paper for Printed Library Materials, ANSI Z39.48-1984.

Library of Congress Cataloging-in-Publication Data

Bitel, Lisa M., 1958–
    Land of women : tales of sex and gender from early Ireland / Lisa M. Bitel.
        p.   cm.
    Includes bibliographical references and index.
    ISBN 0-8014-3095-X (alk. paper)
        1. Women—Ireland—History—Middle Ages, 500–1500.   2. Women in popular culture—
    Ireland—History.   3. Sex role—Ireland—History.   4. Women in literature.   5. Ireland—
    Social life and customs—To 1500.   I. Title.
    HQ1147.I73B57   1996
    305.4'09'02—dc20   95-39296

To Peter: *Cride é,*
daire cnó,
ócán é,
pócán dó.

And to Nick, one of our products

An cheist—"Do chara, do namhaid, agus ceann urraí an ti?"
An freagra—"Do mhadra, do bhean, 's do bheithíoch!"

Question: Who are your friend,
your enemy, and the head of the house?
Answer: Your dog, your wife, and your beast!

—Tory Island proverb

Trí shórt ban nach féider le fear a dtuiscint:
bean óg, bean mheánaosta, seanbhean.

Three kinds of woman that man cannot understand:
A young woman, a middle-aged woman, an old woman.

—modern Irish triad

Contents

Illustrations

Preface

This book takes an unromantic approach to the history of early medieval Ireland. I do not seek heroines or golden ages of powerful queens, nor have I tried to describe what daily life was like for women in the distant Ireland before the Norman invasions. Instead, I confront a larger historical problem: how to reach the women of a society where men dominated formal culture and where all the written evidence about women was produced by a small group of literate men—in the case of early Ireland, mostly by monkish men vowed to a religion that has always been ambivalent toward the female sex. The book explains what men in early Ireland thought about women, how men and women interacted, and how gender ideologies and important forms of gender relations influenced each other. In short, the book represents an attempt to sketch the gender system of a society long dead.

When I engage the early Irish texts, I feel a little like Clifford Geertz blundering into the midst of the Balinese cockfight. When the anthropologist watched the cocks tearing at each other and Balinese villagers' reactions to the fight, he was able to use the event as a meeting place of his notions about his host society and that society's own representations of itself. But Geertz could share the intuitions, jokes, and camaraderie of Balinese men. I am separated by almost impenetrable screens of time and gender from the men who composed the documents that confine early Irish women. I have attempted to understand the Irish literati's questions about their women (what are they? what should they do? what should I do with them?) while still remaining responsible to my own audience's concerns (what was the status of women in early Ireland? how were women then different from women now? what can they tell us about ourselves?). Like every good historian, I have also endeavored to tell my readers more than they want to know. Most histories of women in medieval Europe—and many other inquiries into gender—treat traditional problems of marriage, the public/private and nature/civilization debates, and female pollution. I have let the documents carry my inquiry into other areas, too, attempting an *histoire problème* where my questions meet those of the early Irish literati.

As a storyteller, I have tried to arrange my answers in an entertaining narrative. Fortunately, the Irish literati were themselves excellent tale-tellers who recorded many stories of men and women courting, fornicating, loving, procreating, conversing, doing business, and quarreling, which I have repeated in this book. But in this study of men and women, I have also tried to remember that every time I rehearse the words of an ancient scribe, every time I approach a text produced by a man from long-ago Ireland, I myself am conducting gender relations. My interpretation of men's stories of women's lives has become its own story of Tír inna mBan, the Land of Women. Let the reader beware.

Friends, colleagues, and organizations have helped with this book. For reading portions of the manuscript and offering criticisms I must thank Ann Schofield, Robin Stacey, Mary Odem, Patrick Ford, Penny Johnson, Katherine Gill, Mary McLaughlin, John Carey, Fergus Kelly, Patrick Geary, Jo Ann McNamara, and John Ackerman. The manuscript readers for Cornell University Press and Joseph F. Nagy struggled through the entire manuscript. Peter Mancall heroically read every draft; he also offered company in the field, constant support, and invaluable advice. In addition, I obtained valuable references and ideas in conversation or correspondence with Máirín Ní Dhonnchadha, Chris Lynn, Máire Herbert, Dorothy Africa, Caroline Bynum, Dáibhí Ó Cróinín, Nancy L. Wicker, James Brundage, Thomas Fanning, Joseph Eska, students of my "Women in Barbarian Europe" course (especially Daphne Young), the audiences of papers given at Harvard University, UCLA, and the University of Kansas, and at meetings of the New England Historical Association and the American Historical Association. Financial support for my research and writing came from the National Endowment for the Humanities, the American Philosophical Society, the Irish-American Cultural Institute, Coláiste na hOllscoile, Gaillimh, and the General Research Fund and the Hall Center for the Humanities, both at the University of Kansas.

Portions of the manuscript have been previously published in an earlier form. Chapter 2: " 'Do Not Marry the Fat Short One': The Early Irish Wisdom on Women," *Journal of Women's History* 6/7 (1995), 137–59. Chapter 4: " 'Conceived in Sins, Born in Delights': Stories of Procreation from Early Ireland," *Journal of the History of Sexuality* 3 (1992) (© 1992 by the University of Chicago, all rights reserved). Chapter 6: "Domestic Economies and Gender

Ideology in Early Ireland," in Steven Epstein and Samuel Kohn, eds., *Portraits of Medieval and Renaissance Living: Essays in Memory of David Herlihy* (Ann Arbor, Mich., 1996).

Finally, the book owes its ultimate inspiration to my teacher, David Herlihy. David's last works on women and the family in medieval Europe and his interest in his Irish heritage sent me to the Land of Women.

LISA M. BITEL

Lawrence, Kansas

Abbreviations

ALI   W. N. Hancock et al., eds. *The Ancient Laws of Ireland*. 6 vols. Dublin and
       London, 1865–1901.
AU   Seán mac Airt and Gearóid Mac Niocaill, eds. *The Annals of Ulster to A.D.
       1131*. Dublin, 1983.
CA   Kuno Meyer, ed. and trans. *Cáin Adamnáin: An Old-Irish Treatise on the
       Law of Adamnan*. Oxford, 1905.
Can. Hib.   Herrmann Wasserschleben, ed. *Die irische Kanonensammlung*. Leipzig,
       1885.
CG   D. A. Binchy, ed. *Críth Gablach*. Dublin, 1941.
CIH   D. A. Binchy, ed. *Corpus Iuris Hibernici*. 6 vols. Dublin, 1978.
Cormac, *Glossary*.   Kuno Meyer, ed., *Sanas Cormaic*, in *Anecdota from Irish
       Manuscripts* IV, ed. O. J. Bergin et al. Dublin, 1912.
DIL   E. G. Quin, gen. ed. *Dictionary of the Irish Language,* compact ed. Dublin,
       1983.
ÉC   *Études Celtiques*.
FO   Whitley Stokes, ed. *Félire Óengusso Céli Dé*. London, 1905.
JCHAS   *Journal of the Cork Historical and Archaeological Society*.
JRSAI   *Journal of the Royal Society of the Antiquaries of Ireland*.
MGH   *Monumenta Germaniae Historica* (Hanover, 1828–).
PHCC   *Proceedings of the Harvard Celtic Colloquium*.
PL   J. P. Migne, ed. *Patrologia Latina*. 221 vols. Paris, 1844–64.
PRIA   *Proceedings of the Royal Irish Academy*.
RC   *Revue Celtique*.
SEIL   Rudolf Thurneysen, D. A. Binchy, et al. *Studies in Early Irish Law*. Dublin,
       1936.

UJA   *Ulster Journal of Archaeology.*

USMLS   Ulster Society for Medieval Latin Studies.

VT   Whitley Stokes, ed. and trans. *The Tripartite Life of St. Patrick and Other Documents Relating to the Saint.* London, 1887.

ZCP   *Zeitschrift für celtische Philologie.*

Land of Women

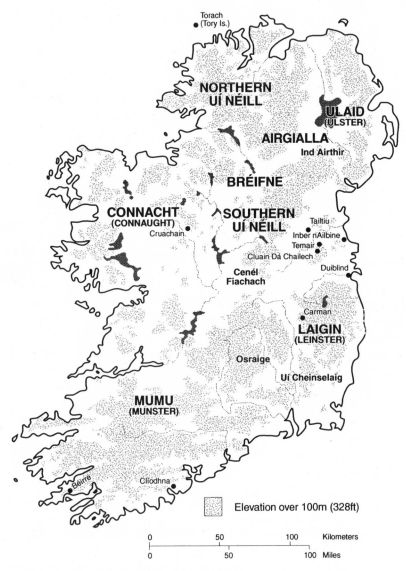

Torach
(Tory Is.)

NORTHERN
UI NÉILL

ULAID
(ULSTER)

AIRGIALLA

Ind Airthir

BRÉIFNE

CONNACHT
(CONNAUGHT)

Cruachain

SOUTHERN
UI NÉILL

Tailtiu

Inber nAilbine

Temair

Cluain Dá Chailech

Duiblind

Cenél
Fiachach

Carman

LAIGIN
(LEINSTER)

Osraige

Uí Cheinselaig

MUMU
(MUNSTER)

Béirre

Clíodhna

Elevation over 100m (328ft)

0   50   100   Kilometers

0   50   100   Miles

Places and population groups mentioned in the text.

1

The Texts and the Tellers of Women's Tales

The women of early Ireland are gone. So are their masters and guardians, the men with whom they lived, slept, and struggled. No trick of the light or lilt of the voice should lead us to think that the people of early medieval Ireland resembled their descendants. Too much has happened since their time: the birth of the republic, the tragedies of civil war and famine, the centuries of oppression by penal laws and English occupation, the reorganization of Catholic Christianity, the waning of traditional culture. The language they spoke was different not only from the English predominant now but even from today's endangered Gaeilge. Nature and the numinous permeated their conceptions of the world, but no longer much influence ours. The fundamental ways in which men and women practiced love, marriage, family, friendship, and hatred were all profoundly unlike our ways.

Gaelic revivalists a hundred years ago leapt the gulf between their century and the pre-Norman period with gullible ease. They found what their patriotic, romantic hearts sought in early Ireland, when Celts bravely repelled Vikings and Normans had not yet invaded Irish shores. In the same spirit that inspired Prince Albert's affection for the statue of Boadicea, fighting queen of the Britons, by Westminster Bridge, Irish folklorists, poets, and playwrights idolized Maeve, Grania, and golden-haired Deirdre as stern and gorgeous mothers of the modern Irish. Convinced that early Ireland had been a golden age in every way—even proud of its barbarous violence—they touted it also as a Celtic paradise of warrior queens and fairy women, unique in ancient Europe.[1] The singular status of Irishwomen was proven to revivalists when they remembered that Ireland had always been a woman in the minds of the poets. Sometimes desirably fertile and sometimes wasted by her conquerors, sometimes staunch and sometimes fickle, she was lover and mother and always feminine. Róisín Dubh and Cathleen Ní Houlihan were only modern names for the island once called after the goddesses Ériu, Fotla, and Banba.[2]

Celticists and other students of myth have also delighted in the strong female characters of Irish sagas and king-tales, identifying them as long-lost goddesses of pagan times.[3] Circling around in their arguments, they have seen the goddesses as archetypes for real women with sexual, martial, and sacral powers over men. Even recently, scholars continue to be seduced by the hero-ines of early Irish texts. "We must ask," wrote the Celticist Proinsias Mac Cana, "whether a society which in its literature attributes such independence to its women characters as does much of early Irish literature would on the other hand deny it or rigidly curtail it in real life."[4]

Historians who study the laws of early Ireland have added seemingly trust-worthy detail to this charming picture of warrior women and influential queens. The seventh- or eighth-century divorce laws, which allowed some women to leave their husbands and take their property with them, only lend substance to the vision of Medb, the sexy leader of Connacht's armies, who strode from the twelfth-century manuscript of the earlier saga *Táin Bó Cuailnge* (Cattle raid of Cuailnge). As Cú Chulainn, the hero of the *Táin*, became the symbol of the new republic—his famous statue adorns the General Post Office in Dublin, site of the Easter Rising—so Medb became the darling of Irish historians and Celticists. "We need not doubt that there were many like her in real life," declared Donnchadh Ó Corráin in his study of women's legal status. According to Ó Corráin, only the coming of retrograde Norman laws quashed the flowering of gender symmetry, so rare among early medieval Europeans.[5] Yet the romance of Medb and the Ériu of poems reveal little about the real women who once walked the hills and fields of Ireland, as historians are eventually coming to see.

Dreamy visions of the Celtic twilight are finally giving way to critical analyses of the formal social, economic, and political roles of women in Ireland. Still, most of these, like historical surveys of women in other early European societies, misinterpret the premodern world in two fundamental ways. First, they focus on women at the expense of the other half of the human population. While enlightening us about the experience of women and the influence of elite ladies, the result has too often been specialized information discrete from traditional, mainstream historiographical concerns, or studies of marriage and family under the guise of women's history. Second, and more problematic, many of these histories have synthesized the written sources in an effort to recreate a mythical single status or common experience for women of a particular society, rather than try to recognize and accommodate contra-dictions in the texts or to view the tensions among different kinds of texts in

Queen Medb, Frontispiece from Tom Peete Cross and Clark Harris Slover, *Ancient Irish Tales* (New York, 1936).

a larger social-cultural milieu. To avoid these misinterpretations, I have taken on a twofold task: to present the multitudinous ideas and experiences of gender by both men and women, sensitive to the kinds of questions the early Irish themselves had about women, and to tell lively stories of women in an almost forgotten place and time.

The history of ideas, attitudes, culture, and social processes is what my doctoral adviser once called "soft" history, history without facts. In order to envision the people who had the ideas and held the attitudes, I begin with some hard data about the land of Ireland, the size and distribution of its population in the early medieval period, and the general situation of women described in material terms and in the traditional historical terms of their legal status. Then I describe the men who wrote women's stories and the nature of their texts before starting an informed excavation of the documents in which the women of Ériu are buried.

Women's Spaces

Although the women of Ireland have changed over the nine centuries since the early medieval period, the island itself has not altered in shape or size. It still lies at the edge of the known world, as Saint Columban was fond of describing it, washed by the constant rains of a western maritime climate and warmed by the Gulf Stream. But the land looks much different now than it did in Columban's time, when it had more trees but far fewer people. About 32,600 square miles in area, Ireland hosted a population of between a quarter and half a million by 1100.[6] The Irish built no cities; the Viking ports that later became towns remained camps and villages until the Normans arrived in the 1170s. Men and women gathered at monasteries, king's forts, mills, and fairgrounds, but they lived on farms, isolated or in small clusters, as we shall see in more detail later. It was a land of farms and forts, hills and fields, woods and wastes. The good soil was parceled out among free families, who passed it on to their children if they could. The unfree rented small tracts of ground or lived with their masters. The wilderness belonged to grazing animals, bandits, the *fiana* (mercenaries), and religious hermits.

The documents supply all sorts of information about the society that the early Irish constructed for themselves, if little about the physical world in which they built it. In 1954, one historian characterized the society as "tribal, rural, hierarchical and familiar," a generalization that still holds good, with some qualification.[7] Kinship was one of its fundamental organizing principles. Society was tribal in that people formed political solidarities based on kinship, both real and fictive. The rest of this book treats the complexities of this rural, tribal, familiar hierarchy, and the ways that women moved through it.

To find the world that was "familiar" in a more common sense—in the sense of the ways and places of normal life, where women went, and what they looked upon day after day—we have to look elsewhere than on dusty pages. The women of early Ireland hover in the historical record without a sturdy material anchor, for whereas monks left behind the stones of their churches, women's houses and workplaces are gone from the landscape, with only a few exceptions. Although some forty thousand walled enclosures (raths, or ring forts) have been spotted by aerial photographers, no one knows for sure whether most of them were medieval, early medieval, iron age, or even earlier. From among these enclosures, archaeologists have excavated only about two hundred probable early medieval house sites. Yet, if the population approached a quarter to a half million, somewhere around fifty thousand houses must have existed at any one time.[8] In northeastern Ulster, for example, most of the remaining raths were probably built between 650 and 950 C.E.—but that is three long centuries of people moving in and out of homesteads.[9] It has been impossible, so far, for the experts to figure the density of coeval buildings, the nature of related agricultural and economic activity, or even the size of buildings within the enclosures. It is difficult to prove that enclosures were occupied for any length of time. In short, a cautious archaeologist cannot adduce any relationship between the ruins that remain.[10]

To a less wary historian, however, what little is left in wood and stone and bone hints at a society that was infused with intimacy, physical and social. We know, at least, that habitations were small. People dwelled in tight little groups in tiny houses sometimes protected by ditches and walls, which were probably placed near other such islands of life.[11] The foundations of excavated early medieval house sites average six or seven meters in diameter, which means that the families occupying them had only three hundred to four hundred square feet in which to maneuver. In the middle they set up their hearths, often stone-lined, over which the cookpot hung on a hook and stake. Along the windowless walls they arranged their beds (*imdae,* pl. *imdada,* in the literature), sometimes partially hidden by woven screens.[12] Although the material remains refuse to tell how many people occupied this simple space, elsewhere in barbarian Europe an ordinary household consisted of five or six people.[13] This small group, crammed into its tiny shelter, ate, slept, had sex, and relaxed together in one room, under one roof. The women also did much of their daily work there, spinning, weaving, cooking. In bad weather—of which there is plenty in parts of Ireland—they had nowhere else to go.

The five or six people who lived in a house were probably a family. A free woman usually lived with her male partner (not always a legal husband), a few children, possibly a foster child or a servant, and maybe a more distant kinsperson or two. Perhaps a couple lived with one or the other's parents.[14] The seventh- and eighth-century legal tracts suggest that a normal household

DEER PARK FARMS Glenarm County Antrim

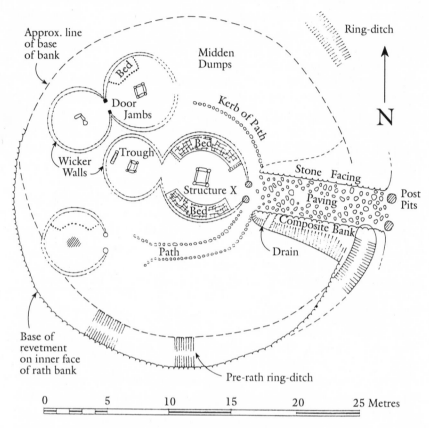

Layout of enclosed farmstead at Deer Park Farms, County Antrim, from Chris Lynn, "Ulster's Oldest Wooden Houses," in Ann Hamlin and Chris Lynn, eds., *Pieces of the Past: Archaeological Excavations by the Department of the Environment* (Belfast, 1988), 46. Reprinted by permission of the Department of the Environment for Northern Ireland.

consisted of a *gelfine,* a three-generational family unit.[15] But unless its members had a terrible survival rate, three generations were too many for one house of the kind dug up by archaeologists. In some enclosures two or more small households lived in adjoining buildings. At Deer Park Farms, a uniquely preserved seventh- to tenth-century site, three or four houses stood within a twenty-five-meter enclosure at any given time over its four centuries of use. Extra houses were added or allowed to collapse as the number of inhabitants increased or decreased. More than thirty dwellings have been found at different levels of the site. When children of the original family grew up and married, they may simply have built a house next door; in one case, the family just added a circular addition to an original house, creating a backhouse that turned an 0 into an 8.[16]

Expansions and improvements to the enclosure walls at Deer Park Farms hint that its inhabitants became well enough off to support not only several nuclear groups within the enclosure but also families of lower status who served them and may have lived at related settlement sites.[17] Someone, probably clients and tenants, had to dig the ditches and build the main enclosure. Whereas the free and noble lived within the banks and ditches of their ring forts, the others inhabited unprotected houses, now completely lost. Archaeologists are just beginning to recover human space from the landscape that has absorbed it, and the houses of the working poor have largely eluded the spade, just as their lives remained hidden from the pens of the early medieval literati.

The upland site at Ballyutoag, County Antrim, offers one exception. The remains of twenty-three unenclosed houses, which were probably coeval (two of the houses have been carbon-dated to the seventh or eighth century), composed a village of some kind, but whether a permanent settlement or a summer encampment in the high pastures its excavators cannot say. If all the houses were occupied simultaneously, however, approximately a hundred people lived at Ballyutoag.[18] And although no material finds suggest that villages were common or that people lived in the crowded population islands so familiar from Carolingian documents, the evidence does hint that sites like Ballyutoag cannot have been so rare. Isolated souterrains (storage tunnels), surviving without any other remains, probably once protected the goods of unenclosed houses, which were far more common than the modern landscape is willing to show.[19]

All the evidence of archaeology, scant though it be, suggests that a woman in early Ireland ordinarily moved within a small space and a small group. Travel out of the enclosing walls of a homestead was dangerous and difficult, doubly so for women; the documents take it for granted that a woman risked assault and murder when she left home to go any distance. Normal social roles and relationships, regulated by laws and described by narratives, all took place within the intimate bounds of a few neighboring enclosed farms. When women occasionally burst out of those bounds, according to the literati of early Ireland, havoc ensued.

Women's social roles encircled them as protectively and restrictively as walls of mud and wood. A woman's life began in her parents' home, though she might have left it before her teens in order to be fostered by a set of surrogate parents. Fosterage was vocational training: upper-class girls learned to sew and spin and manage a noble household, and girls of lesser status spent their late childhood and adolescent years serving their betters. After fosterage, when she reached the appropriate age (defined by the laws as fourteen but probably higher in practice), a free woman expected to move in with a man and begin her own family.[20]

A woman did not necessarily marry in what came to be the official Christian sense. Early Irish laws recognized nine kinds of legal unions between a man and woman, any of which were normally negotiated by the couple's families.[21] The most prestigious was a "union of joint property" (*lánamnas for comthinchuir*) concluded by two people of free birth and some wealth; the most dubious was a union by rape or a union of two insane people.[22] In practical terms, though, a woman entered one of three basic kinds of relationships: official marriage as a *cétmuinter* (literally "chief wife"), a looser contractual tie in which she was an *adaltrach* (literally "adultress," a secondary wife), or concubinage, formal or informal.[23] One way or another, most women, free or semiservile, expected to find a man and produce babies. This was the culmination of their vocational training and the goal of their kinfolk.

A woman moved from the guardianship of her father to that of her mate. If she had neither father nor legal husband, she belonged to someone else. A legal tract on honor price (*díre*) clearly defined women's legal and social position:

> Her father has charge over her when she is a girl, her husband when she is a wife, her sons when she is a [widowed] woman with children, her kin when she is a "woman of the kin" (i.e. with no other guardian), the Church when she is a woman of the Church (i.e. a nun). She is not capable of sale or purchase or contract or transaction without the authorization of one of her superiors.[24]

Given the dialectic in many Irish laws concerning specific rights of women, the extreme position of the *díre* text cannot be safely taken as anything but a seventh- or eighth-century legal ideal. Nevertheless, the principles articulated by the tract represent all Irish—and, indeed, all barbarian—laws. Women's legal definition derived from that of their kinsmen; women were socially and

---

Reconstruction of an early Irish settlement system from Matthew Stout, "Ringforts in the South-west Midlands of Ireland," *PRIA* 91 C 8 (1991), 239. According to Stout's scheme, derived from the legal tracts, the *aire forgill* and *aire déso* represent lords who gave fiefs of land to freemen (*ócaire*) in return for rents and services; the *bóaire* represents freeholders in free clientage to the same lords. Settlement of unfree clients is not represented. Reprinted by permission of the officers of the Royal Irish Academy.

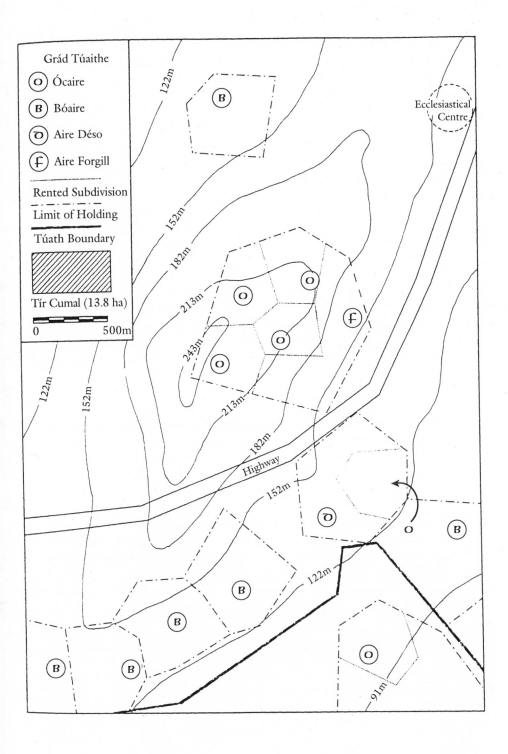

122m

B

Ecclesiastical
Centre

152m

182m

213m

Ó

Ó

243m

Ó

F

Ó

Ó

213m

122m

152m

182m

Highway

152m

Ō

O

B

122m

B

B

B

B

B

Ó

91m

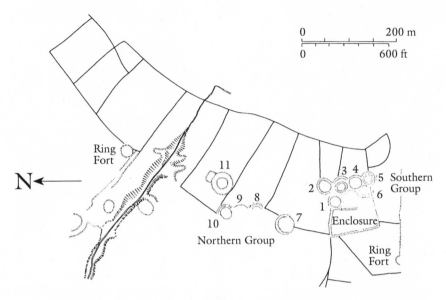

0 |———————————| 200 m

0 |—|—|—|—|—|—| 600 ft

Ring Fort

N←——————

11

10

9 8

Northern Group

7

2

3 4

1

6

5 Southern Group

Enclosure

Ring Fort

Related farmsteads at Cush, County Limerick from Nancy Edwards, *The Archaeology of Early Medieval Ireland* (Philadelphia, 1990), 55. Reprinted by permission of B. T. Batsford, Ltd.

thus legally inferior; and women had few or no independent legal rights.[25] In almost all public legal processes, a woman needed a man to act for her. She could not swear an oath, make a contract, or own family land entirely on her own. The assumption of the lawyers, who made special provisions for women and the other disenfranchised, was that free males, and particularly the heads of families (*cenn fine*) acted for their dependents in legal disputes.[26] Canonists decreed that no woman but a virgin abbess could act as surety or guarantor; most women, with idiots and outsiders, were not allowed to bear witness because of their innate inability to act like grown-ups. A *banfiadnaise*, woman witness, was by nature *éccoitchenn eisinnraic*, partial and unworthy.[27] Most women could not even conclude a contract to hire a *brithem*, jurist, to negotiate for them.

These stay-at-home legal incompetents were the real Medbs of early Ireland, and yet even the laws themselves were full of contradictions, suggesting that women had more room to maneuver than the *díre* text or the mean huts of archaeologists would permit. Those historians who tout women's high status in early Ireland often point out that the divorce laws, composed by the same class of jurists as more restrictive texts, seem quite liberal; they allowed free women to get rid of cranky, insane, or sexually inadequate husbands.[28] For every law circumscribing women there was another that allowed them considerable lib-

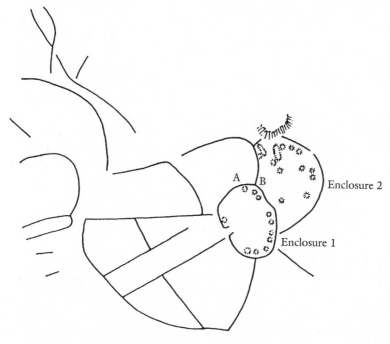

Related farmsteads at Ballyutoag, County Antrim from Edwards, *Archaeology of Early Medieval Ireland,* 55. Reprinted by permission of B. T. Batsford, Ltd.

erties. What is more, contradictions in the laws of status and contract did not diminish over the centuries; throughout the Middle Ages, women's legal disenfranchisement was mitigated by other, more flexible rules.[29]

The rest of this book will demolish the model I have just constructed of women marooned on their walled islands, hedged about with coercive laws. Women in early Ireland were no goddess-queens, but neither were most of them prisoners or slaves. They were participants in the culture, members of society, players in politics, and partners in the economy. They were not social or political equals of men, but equality was not a concept comprehensible to the early Irish. Early medieval European societies assigned to women a limited set of roles to play, but women in Ireland, as elsewhere, colluded in creating and maintaining those roles, as well as subverting them. Literate men recorded a profusion of ideas about women, positive and negative, about which women had their own ideas and to which they responded with their own strategies. In order to grasp the relation between the texts, which contain men's diverse thoughts about women, and the varied experience of women in early Ireland, we must come to know this literate male elite and its texts.

The Tellers of Women's Tales

The literati of early Ireland wrote of women and female characters in saints' lives, poems, sagas and myths, gnomic texts, histories, chronicles, genealogies, folktales, theological tracts, and extensive ecclesiastical and secular laws, among other texts. All these offer evidence—straightforward, concealed, and merely incidental—about women and about gender relations. Scholars began to record their texts before 800 C.E. Most of the legal tracts, canons, penitentials, and many vitae were written in the seventh and eighth centuries, and quite a few of the sagas exist in essentially eighth- or ninth-century forms.[30] Some of the texts are more exactly datable, and a few can be assigned to authors, but most are anonymous and only roughly datable.[31]

Celticists, who make the language and structure of the documents intelligible to historians, used to think that many of these works originated as oral compositions, passed from pagan druids and poets to the Christian scribes who faithfully and uncritically penned them.[32] Many scholars are still searching for the ancient core of stories and laws. When the language of a tale mixes old and new forms or when a vita of Brigit melds saint and goddess, the only explanation seems, to some, to be the persistence of a pre-Christian tradition.[33] To other Celticists and historians, however, it has become clear that the intellectuals of early medieval Ireland were no more or less astute than modern academics. They recognized archaic linguistic forms and employed them for an antiquarian feel to their texts. They repeated old stories for sheer pleasure, not because they still revered the gods hidden in the plots. They rehearsed ancient laws in the same way that we preserve our legal precedents, modifying and changing rules where practice made necessary. Most important, they knew a pagan concept when they saw one and used it only when it suited them. The men who produced the texts were writers, intellectuals, and artists highly conscious of their own authorial voices, not simply scribal automatons. Their scholarship was on the cutting edge and much in demand among their continental colleagues.[34]

Recruited from the nobility and infused with the values of that class, the literati were conscious of themselves as an intellectual elite modeled on the Levites of the Old Testament.[35] They categorized themselves in four kinds: *ecnae* or *fer léigind,* a scholar of Latin learning (Latin *sapiens*); *brithem,* who kept the laws; *senchaid,* a genealogist or historian; and *file,* a poet and storyteller.[36] Any of the four could be layman or cleric, but all were trained in monastic communities, and most probably remained resident there. The *Triads,* a gnomic text of the ninth century, referred to three monastic communities famous as schools for jurists, one school for historians, and one for Latin learning, but training in all branches of learning must have occurred at many more monasteries.[37] Annalists recorded the deaths of men who were *file* and monk, jurist and monk, scholar and monk.[38] Legal tracts equated the grading of poets with that of churchmen.[39] One tract cited the privilege of the bishops of Ard Macha to keep their own scholars, jurists, and poets. Another described the monastery of Túaim Drecain, where there were "scol léigind ocus scol fénechais ocus scol filed," schools of Latin learning, law, and poetry.[40] Hence, Donnchadh Ó Corráin and Kim McCone, among others, have argued convincingly for a "mandarin caste" of clerics who produced all the extant texts, secular and ecclesiastical.[41]

Nonetheless, although the literati may have been a homogeneous class, they did not always successfully articulate a coherent agenda in their texts. McCone has suggested that the learned elite produced literature of, by, and for the monastery, largely dependent on biblical models for texts as well as for everyday life.[42] But the Christianity of early medieval Europe was not in the nineteenth-century style of religion suggested by McCone. People visited the sacred space of Christian churches and cemeteries for a variety of purposes; the general population may have been familiar with the rudiments of Christian theology, and clerics enjoyed a fair amount of prestige in barbarian societies, but the pervasive Catholic mentalities and rituals of post–Vatican I Europe simply did not exist.[43] What the Irish called *monachi*, monks, were neither the cloistered brethren of the later medieval Continent nor the hip and secularized Jesuits of the mid-twentieth century nor even necessarily praying men with tonsures. Even the literati, while they may have been Christian, were not necessarily all devout. Not every writer of saga employed explicit sexual references for purely allegorical or didactic reasons. Not every jurist placed the interests of ecclesiastical communities first.

In fact, the literati disagreed about everything, including women. The laws of property represented several different, conflicting opinions on various subjects, for instance, and many saints' lives existed in contradictory versions that were either more or less orthodox. Writers adapted royal histories to favor this or that family. Canonists and jurists constantly feuded over the status and privileges of the lay community vis-à-vis clerics. The learned elite, for all its shared training and status, was, after all, just men in a severely localized world, with personal loyalties to kin, neighbors, and nearby lords.[44]

It is not surprising, then, that the literati also disagreed about women. It is astonishing, however, that among a literati so addicted to categorization and detail, no early Irish writer articulated a definition of woman or defined the ultimate dichotomy of human society: man-woman. Jurists methodically listed such arcane items as the seven binding and nonbinding contracts, the seven kinds of boundary markers, the seven reasons for divorcing a husband. Churchmen, aiming to destroy the enemy by naming it, produced exhaustive definitions of sexual sins, sins of assault and murder, sins of theft, of gluttony, of gossip. The tellers of tales named genres of sagas and stories. Glossators specified, one by one, the Latin terms of the Psalms. Grammarians defined parts of speech. But none of these men thought to note down what, exactly, a woman was or how, precisely, men and women regarded one another.

Did no one need to know? Or was no one able to tell? Dry vellum could never reveal what a man felt when he woke on a raw morning to find his lover curled against him, her arm wrapping his chest, her breath warm on his back. Laws or penitentials were not the proper genre to describe the sinking of a man's heart as he headed home from a rough day in the fields to find the same smelly, bad-tempered bitch waiting to curse him. No medieval writer— and few modern—could capture the drama of a father's first glimpse of his squalling daughter, or the last sight of her when, all grown up, she left with another man. And what of all the other women who passed through men's lives, talking to them, touching them, ruling or serving them, running to or from them, sighted in the distance or just drifting as phantoms through their imaginations?

In early Ireland, the literati defined women not directly, not as independent entities, but in relation to themselves. Women existed for every man as lover, wife, mother, daughter, kinswoman, or stranger. All men, even the most withdrawn of scholars or celibate of Christian clerics, knew women as extensions of themselves. Hence men's literature—which is to say, probably all texts written in early Ireland—spoke of women only in relation to its other messages, for although vitae and related texts suggest that some religious women were literate, no evidence exists to prove that women produced any of the extant documents. The style, structure, and purpose of different genres of texts helped determine their presentation of women. Some texts buried information about women deep below their surfaces. For example, the extensive body of secular laws rehearsed the different statuses and legal capacities of women, but the tedious details of oaths and property rights concealed contradictory assumptions about women's capabilities, character, and relations with men. Canons of the eighth century described Christian marriage, the rights of widows, and the duties of nuns—all of which added up to a concept of the Christian woman. But the woman in the canons was not the same as the woman found in penitentials and saints' lives. Like the proscriptive texts, narratives and poems offered various female characters. A parade of voracious Amazons, passive sex kittens, androgynous prophetesses with otherworldly powers, and goddesses passed through the cattle-rustling epic *Táin Bó Cuailnge*.

Between different texts, the tensions are even more apparent. Legal definitions of women as wards of men seem irreconcilable with the fierce women warriors of literature. The misogynist equations of women with sexual sin, so popular in the saints' lives, simply have no relevance for the women we can find in mundane legal rules, the women who went about their everyday work of cooking, tending their children, keeping tame animals and small gardens, weaving, and sweeping their muddy huts. Hidden behind the contrasting images of women found in all these kinds of evidence we may hear men's differing opinions and confusion about what women were and how men should deal with them.

But sounding through the confusion are certain persistent themes, hints at constant values, and devotion to enduring principles that allow us to outline some coherent ideologies. The texts assumed a social hierarchy based on blood and wealth, with women, children, foreigners, and slaves languishing at the bottom. They assumed the dominance of Christianity, despite its variety of practice and interpretation. They also took for granted certain ideas about the nature and character of women, the social roles appropriate for them, and the parameters of relations between men and women, although they rarely stated any of these notions explicitly. And their implicit assumptions about women coincide with other evidence for social structures often enough that we may identify the literati's gender ideologies with those of the social and political elite who controlled the land, wealth, and other souls of early Ireland.

I use the early Irish texts to define the dominant gender ideologies of the society, as well as the major types of gender relations and the most important social roles created for and by women, but I do so with two reservations. First, I have tried to be cautious in synthesizing such a variety of texts and genres. The bountiful canon of early Irish texts provides tempting but dangerous evidence for what Annalistes might term the *longue durée* of early Irish life. The evidence is dangerous because scholars cannot date or assign authors to most of the texts; many of the genres are highly formulaic; and many of the early medieval texts were revised and redacted throughout the Middle Ages. My assumption in using this evidence is that the literati maintained a fairly comprehensive familiarity with the major genres but that, when possible, texts should be assigned to a more specific chronological and regional context. I also assume, however, that texts roughly datable to the same century or two can be cautiously analyzed as representative of the literati's ideas over longer periods.

This assumption is corollary to a much more important supposition: that the rural organization of European economies, the local social and political structures of Ireland, and the increasingly formalized theology of the church ensured that some broad outlines of women's experiences, although varying and shifting in subtle ways, remained much the same throughout the early Middle Ages. Most women lived with men, bore children, kept house, struggled to survive, and were disenfranchised. Indeed, these remained the most basic conditions of life for women in premodern Europe.

My second reservation concerns ideology—or, rather, ideologies—a term that most conveniently describes the confused, often conflicting collection of beliefs and attitudes toward, and the customs and traditions of, gender expressed in the variety of Irish texts. Ideology also appropriately suggests, with Gramscian connotations, some purpose of dominance on the part of the literati and those they represented, which underlay even the most tension-filled documents.[45] And anyone who thinks that the early medieval literati did *not* presume dominance of one small social group over other groups is falling easy prey to anachronism; they were always boosters of the sociopolitical elite, of which they themselves were bona fide members. The concept of ideologies can help us understand the connection between the diverse representations of women in early Irish sources and the various experiences of women in a culture where they lacked high status or formal authority.

Such an approach also allows for an appreciation of women's participation in the culture and the possibility that women had their own discrete ideologies. Women left no texts to tell their own stories, but they may well have infiltrated the writings of men, sometimes colluding in the dominant messages of a document, but other times causing a tension among the words which betrays real-life conflict.[46] If jurists argued over women's property rights, it was because some women held and used property in defiance of some formal laws, often with men's collaboration. If saga writers depicted women eloping with handsome warriors, it was because some young women and men rejected the marriages planned for them, arranging their own loves and rendezvous. With effort, then, we may be able to hear the faint echo of women's own voices calling from the documents with self-definitions and outlining survival strategies.

If all this methodological talk suggests that early Ireland witnessed a war between the sexes, it also hints at regular parleys and truces. What the texts reveal are several well-defined, well-articulated social roles for women—lover, wife, mother, economic partner, holy woman, warrior woman—each with its own behavioral code and symbolic meanings. Yet the texts also repeatedly announce the variations on these roles, the violations of their boundaries, and a mind-bogglingly wide and subtle range of relations between real men and women. From the fiercest misogyny of gnomic tracts to the equitable collaboration of husband and wife within the domestic economy, early Ireland hosted a set of gender relations every bit as flexible and complex as our own. This is what most modern historians, out to prove the power or oppression of medieval women, and Celticists, with their eyes rapt on Medb, have often failed to see.

I have laid out the book in nine chapters covering the pre-Norman period, from roughly 700 to 1100. After this introduction, the first section (Chapters 2–5) analyzes the major social roles of women in early Ireland and recreates several related gender ideologies culled from different genres of men's texts. In particular, these chapters focus on sex, love, marriage, and motherhood. The second section (Chapters 6–8) treats the economic strategies that women developed and the social networks they constructed in the face of restrictive social roles and a misogyny derived from both continental Christian and native Celtic traditions. In the conclusion (Chapter 9) I use images of violent and powerful women to answer the larger question of why the gender ideologies of premodern Europe diverged from the reality of gender relations, why men's texts depicted women so negatively when men and women interacted in a variety of ways, positive and negative. The book's structure parallels my own archaeology of the sources. The first chapters, like the first layer of sources, reveal the stated aims and attitudes of the medieval authors. As I dig deeper, I try to excavate the underlying assumptions of the authors' explicit messages. At even lower depths, I am mining for gold, tunneling to the Land of Women.

2

The Wisdom on Women

arly medieval Europeans, including the early Irish, never both-
ered themselves with formally articulated definitions of the
sexes and genders. By and large, these are modern concerns,
answers to the questions of historians and other social scientists. The clerics of
Gaul did have one lively discussion in 585 as to whether women could rightly
be included in the expansive term *homo,* which they took to mean "human."
This, however, was technically a grammatical debate over Genesis, rather than
a patriarchal investigation of gender.[1]

Nonetheless, the problem of woman—who she was, what she was, where
she belonged—was one that long annoyed churchmen throughout Christendom.[2] In cultures so obsessed with precise calculations of social status,
constantly worried about reproductive success, often openly appreciative of
sexual pleasures, and ambivalent—at best—toward women, it was inevitable
that men and women should wonder about the ways of getting together and
getting along and, in the process, about each other's nature.

Even if they found answers, we will never recover most of them, since at
least 99 percent of the European population had neither impetus nor opportunity to record their ideas. But we do know what a tiny group of educated
men in Ireland thought about women. In particular, three genres of early
Irish texts, all written at about the same time (700–900 C.E.), posed a series
of interrelated questions about the nature and behavior of women. Two of
these genres—laws of status and contract, and wisdom texts—organized their
questions in the form of categories and hierarchies of women, men, and other,
less familiar beings. The third, secular narratives about otherworldly women,
offered images of women clearly informed by the concepts also found in laws
and gnomic literature.

Considered together, as they were meant to be, these documents read like a long man-to-man conversation about women. The texts resonated with one another; one set the questions, a second answered and posed new questions, taken up by yet another text. Thus, a reader of any single discussion of women already held assumptions about them which he had gathered from others of these sources. Together, writers of these three kinds of texts suggested that women were different from men in crucial ways, not only physically but intellectually, emotionally, and spiritually. The sources hinted that sometimes women were more like other nonhumans, such as animals or supernatural beings, than like men. Women were not simply other but often otherworldly; they were not composed of rejected elements of manliness or traits derivative of the male sex but were actively, mysteriously, and intentionally both like and unlike men.

In fact, the Irish evidence makes a point vital for the understanding of all early medieval considerations of woman and what she was. The Other is too simple, foreign, and logical a paradigm for what early medieval Europeans (both men and women) saw when they observed the females around them.[3] Any woman was, at once, both human (*homo*), just like man, and yet a multiplicity of ever-changing Others. What is more, this was just one of many competing concepts of woman and femaleness embedded in a particular set of gender ideologies; other ideologies, articulated in other texts (or not written at all) must have existed simultaneously. Hence, the complexity of the early Irish debate over women in the three genres selected here is surprising not because of its many conflicting opinions, but because of the few coherent themes that repeated throughout different kinds of documents.

The very chaos of educated men's thoughts shows that it was not so much the clash of discordant European cultural traditions (such as Christian versus classical, or imported continental versus native Celtic) that caused their disputes over woman. Nor did any progressive development or historical decline in women's status make men change their minds. It was simply the nature of the relation between ideologies and gender interactions that kept the men of medieval Europe wondering, guessing, and arguing.

For although early Irish definitions of the creature woman influenced the behavior of both sexes, these concepts were themselves rooted in social experience. The debate over woman's nature helped confine real women to traditional social roles, exclude them from formal politics, and deprive them of property—all on account of their theoretical inferiority. It is essential to keep in mind the basic inequality imposed on women in early medieval European societies such as Ireland, but it is equally important to recognize the strategies by which women accommodated, maneuvered, and resisted such inequality, often with men's help. The plain fact that many men and women interacted amiably every day of their lives, despite patriarchal custom and the dominance of misogynist ideas in the written literature, best prepares us for the tumbled confusion of the literati's debate over woman.

How could a man decide which woman to marry, which to do business with, which to pray to, which to avoid altogether if he could not guess her type and nature? Men needed to know. To protect themselves, men had to predict the behavior and understand the character of women. Still, as the literati themselves sometimes acknowledged, their desperate efforts were doomed from the start.

Are Women Human?

Early Irish laws were jurists' notebooks rather than enacted legislation. Like the barbarian codes of the Continent, they contained precedents and guidelines for negotiating civil disputes.[4] Jurists based their decisions not only on points of evidence and precedence but also on questions of social status; the more important a litigant, the more witnesses or oath helpers he could summon to his support and the more weight his case carried. Hence, one of the gender-related issues addressed by early Irish jurists was women's status. Specifically, the laws measured women against a legal norm of the free adult male. The tracts, both early medieval texts and later glosses and commentary, treated women indirectly in discussions of marriage, property, and status.[5] Behind all the mundane problems of dowry exchange, divorce, inheritance, and contract lay two broad impressions. First, women were born legally genderless and only later acquired their femaleness. Second, by developing into females, women became legally and socially less than men, which is to say, not fully human.

Every free child was born of equal value among the early Irish because, at least in theoretical legal terms, everyone was born without gender. Until the age of seven, all children's honor prices (*lóg n-enech, eneclann,* or *díre,* the material value set upon a person for legal purposes) were relatively high; one tract valued children and adult clerics at the same rate.[6] At age seven a boy or girl child became worth only half of his or her father's honor price, but at fourteen, the "age of unfosterage" (*áes díailtri*) or legal age of adulthood, a boy gained the full status of his class and merited full honor price, although his legal rights remained restricted until later in life.[7] A girl, however, remained worth only half of her father's honor price until she married, when her honor price became half that of her husband.[8] In purely legal terms, then, a human child became a man or woman (*ben,* pl. *mná*) at age fourteen. Unlike the case in some Germanic law codes, according to the Irish, when a girl developed the physical characteristics of a woman and the ability to reproduce, she became socially less valuable than the legal standard, the free adult male.[9] Once she had become a female, a girl or woman was always defined socially in relation to her male guardian and always retained a legal value of, at most, half of her guardian's honor price.

Although legal worth had a social and political basis, Irish concepts of human physiology justified women's legal inferiority. Women remained less valuable than men because they failed to develop not only socially but physiologically. The Irish literati, along with many early medieval writers (influenced indirectly by Galenists), considered women's bodies to be poor, less valuable copies of men's.[10] This is one reason that the only extant Irish medicolegal tracts — *Bretha Crólige* and *Bretha Déin Chécht* — placed different value on men's and women's bodies. These eighth-century tracts, which focused on legal compensation for injuries, accorded women and children less medical attention than men, just as they gave noble patients more compensation than ailing peasants. Doctors were to feed women patients, for example, half or less of the rations prescribed for men, on the specious assumption that women required and deserved less food than men.[11]

The only exceptions to this hierarchy of bodies were nursing women and fertile women. According to a gloss on *Bretha Crólige,* nursing mothers were one of four kinds of women accompanying the injured party who had to be cared for legally and materially during his convalescence even though they themselves had not been injured (the others were the wife of the attending physician and chaperones to convalescing women or women replacing the victim at work.)[12] The tract also ordered extra compensation for injuries inflicted on a woman "in the proper periods" for conception and for a man whose wife was injured during those same proper periods.[13] A woman whose body could produce children defied the standard legal categorization as an inferior human specimen, according to the medicolegal tracts; in physiological terms, then, a woman's sexual and reproductive nature made her the exception.[14]

Women were not the only legal group classed by lawyers as incompetent according to physiological criteria. Others who had never fully metamorphosed into adult male humans or who had degenerated from the adult male norm also had limited legal rights and social status. A woman's connection (*lánamnas*) with her husband was legally identical to the contractual relationship between a child and his or her parent, a foster child and fosterer, a woman and her brother, a student and his tutor, or an unmarried woman and her male protector.[15] Responsibilities within these relationships, which were clearly modeled on parent-child ties, were mutual, but the adult male partner was legally and socially superior. According to this categorization, then, women and children shared the same pitiable condition: they had not, or had not yet, grown into men. In this same legal class were unfree tenants and clients, social outcasts and criminals, political hostages, slaves, and all sorts of idiots, dotards, fools, and madmen.[16] Peasants and idiots may have developed male bodies but their minds never became fully adult, fully male, fully human.

Irish jurists inserted women into their legal hierarchy in two ways. First, they treated women only in relation to their men. Second, they explained women's status and rights by analogy to other underdeveloped humans. With such methods, early Irish lawyers constructed the definable and controllable creature, woman.[17] From a legal perspective, early Irishwomen behaved predictably only when they behaved like men—more specifically, preadult men, criminal men, insane or outcast men, but men nonetheless. Legal writers could categorize women so efficiently, however, by representing them as passive participants in specific legal situations engineered by men. Whenever women acted outside the law or lawyers' constructs of the childlike woman, women became less categorizable and controllable. For example, women deserved no honor price, and thus no place in the legal hierarchy, when they stole, satirized others, eloped, betrayed men, lied, behaved violently, or refused hospitality.[18] In taking such aggressive action women behaved not like children or fools, but like total outsiders to the community and its laws, like bandits, foreigners, or even animals.

Still, that laws existed for such aberrant situations suggests that women could defy legal typologies and still remain members of early Irish communities. Even lawyers themselves had to admit, by their efforts to explain exceptional legal situations, that some women claimed an existence outside strict legal definitions. When women chose to make their own marriage contracts or run away from home, they resisted efforts to categorize and control them; and when men avoided strict laws of patrilineage by giving land to their daughters, or when they allowed women to choose their own husbands, participate in legal contracts, or take part in economic transactions, they aided and abetted women. In other words, some women and even some men may have accepted women's feminization at age fourteen—with its negative legal consequences—as a positive development, rather than abnormally arrested physical development. Lawyers could do nothing to change this attitude.

Within the confines of their texts and typologies, lawyers would not even formally recognize women who completely evaded legal categories. Laws did not seek to regulate the kinds of actions taken by the aggressive women so familiar from other kinds of texts, such as sagas and saints' lives. The warrior queen who flagrantly practiced adultery and the spell-casting hag who tried to destroy her stepchildren were beyond the grasp of jurists. Legal writers must have known these stories but found them to be incompatible with, and irrelevant to, legal typologies.[19]

The jurists' aim was to set the legal standard for human beings and to measure all who could not or would not develop into a free adult male in relation to him. The only literary connection between the women defined by legal theorists and the more frightening and exotic women of other genres is a ridiculously simple idea: women may have begun life as men did, fully physiologically and legally human, but they ended up physically, mentally, and quite willfully not like men.

What Are Women Like?

The disturbing assumption of legal writers that women, like idiots, never attained their full human potential raised questions taken up by other early Irish writers. If women never became men, what did they become? That is, if they were not like men, what were they like? The ninth-century *Triads* text (*Trecheng Breth Féne,* literally "A triad of judgments of the Irish"), one of several gnomic or wisdom tracts popular in early Ireland, provided no simple answer but did reveal a couple of basic convictions about the nature of woman.[20]

The *Triads* never typologized women but instead categorized some characteristics of women and their experience. The "three drops of a wedded woman," for instance, were drops of blood, tears, and sweat; that is, a good wife was a virgin at marriage, willing to suffer and work hard to support her husband and children.[21] A wife's three best virtues were a steady tongue, a steady virtue, and a steady housewifery.[22]

Beyond offering such homely aphorisms, however, the *Triads* explained what or whom women were like. First, ideally, a woman was an inevitable and ubiquitous feature of every man's life, like a lord or a piece of land. The three misfortunes for a normal householder were proposing marriage to a bad woman, serving a bad lord, or bargaining for bad land, whereas the three lucky breaks for a farmer were a good woman, a good lord, and good land.[23] Like land, most of which was inherited, and a lord, with whom an ordinary farmer made a contract for life, marriage to a woman was unavoidable and usually lifelong for the average free or semifree layman. And as with land and lord, a householder could do little to improve a bad wife. For better or worse, wife, land, and lord defined the contours of many adult male lives.

Second, according to the *Triads,* women were also like animals. When a man lent either a woman or a horse, he had to expect it to be used by the borrower. Like a fine horse or a swift dog, a beautiful woman was one of the "three glories of a gathering" and the property of her master.[24] On the other hand, like the grin of a hound at a man's throat, worse than sorrow was the smile of his woman after she had slept with another man.[25] But like a cow's udder, a woman through her womb was one of "three renovators of the world."[26] Whether positive or negative, a woman's physical characteristics—sexuality, beauty, fertility—linked her to dogs, horses, and cows.[27] Yet even the most domestic of animals could not always be relied upon; dogs could turn on their masters, horses could be ridden by others, and cows would wander or go dry.[28] The *Triads'* author was pointing out that something in their unmanly natures could cause animals and women to stray from men's expectations and betray their needs.

These two fundamental characteristics of women—their inevitable ubiquity and their animal natures—also appeared in the legal text the *Heptads*. Its author (or authors) likened women to animals, possibly because their sexuality seemed so similar. For example, neither a jealous wife nor a domestic beast was liable for certain assaults. Animals that had just given birth or were in rut were assumed to be potentially vicious and violent.[29] Like an amorous ram or a cow just calved, a chief wife (*cétmuinter*) was potentially dangerous to her husband's secondary wife, his concubine, or his other women. Wives had no rutting season, although ideally they were frequently pregnant or newly delivered; but the lawyers' assumption was that women were always on the verge of assault against those who threatened the objects of their sexual or maternal interest. Of the seven bloodsheds that required no formal legal compensation, besides the jealous *cétmuinter*'s assault on an *adaltrach* (secondary wife), the others included only those committed by a legally incompetent fool or by men whose job it was to shed blood; for example, physicians and warriors were not liable.[30] Although a woman's legal incapacity resembled that of a fool, the *cétmuinter*'s excuse for assault was clearly sexual. No man was exempted for a crime of passion; no woman was exempted for any assault *except* her instinctive attack on a female competitor for her husband's sexual attentions.[31]

We cannot take the analogy any further than Irish legal theorists themselves did. Women should be "feared like beasts," according to *Tecosca Cormaic*, another wisdom text from the eighth century, because they were "capricious beasts."[32] Yet the medicolegal literature showed that women were human, if defectively so. Women were only *like* animals; they were not actually beasts. And being like animals, women shared the qualities that made beasts unlike the male human norm.

Some secular narratives from roughly the same period as the laws and *Triads* repeated the theme of the animal woman but gave it a different twist that sheds further light on the association. The tales classed women and beasts with another nonhuman, the supernatural inhabitant of the otherworld (called in Old Irish *síd,* meaning both the burial mound, the traditional entrance to the otherworld, and the otherworld itself).[33] In fact, the nexus of three symbols—

woman, animal, otherworld—informed several genres of early Irish literature. This is not to say that the only images of women in secular narratives were animal images; a splendid variety of females crowded the tales and sagas as well as religious narratives such as saints' lives, and they carried a profusion of symbols and meanings. Nor did the literati believe that only women were animal-like or that only women were associated with the supernatural or that all women were actually escapees from the otherworld. Both male and female characters shed human shape for animal or bird form, and vice versa; Lí Ban, for example, doffed her bird suit to flagellate the lovesick Cú Chulainn, and a certain Dobarchú became an otter for his sins.[34] Many male heroes in medieval sagas and stories wandered in and out of the otherworld, either on foot or by boat.[35] Chthonic deities disguised as supernatural champions rushed from the otherworld to aid their human kin, as Lug came to his son Cú Chulainn, and hapless adventurers accidentally landed their boats on its shores.

Nonetheless, early Irish writers used both otherworldly shapeshifters (humans who could change into bird or animal form) and female characters (and often female shapeshifters) to represent all that was most unreal and inhuman about this world and the other. These literary similarities functioned like gnomic or legal analogies of women and animals. No one really expected his wife to go to sleep as a human and wake the next morning barking and hungry for bones. Instead, the comparison enlightened men in their hunt for understanding of the foreign gender: to be female was to be both otherworldly and beastly. Storytellers were able to explain otherwise incomprehensible femininity if they could evoke by it the mysteries of the otherworld. At the same time, the unreality of the otherworld became more accessible in terms of both the feminine and the beastly, as well as through its other traditional, formulaic attributes.

To begin with, tale-tellers characterized the otherworld, above all, by unreality. Instead of a natural world alive with vegetation, rinsed by the perpetual rains of Ireland, and blessed by the occasional smile of the sun, the otherworld was an artificial place in two senses: it constituted an alternative reality, and it existed primarily in literature.[36] It lay either in manuscript pages or beneath lakes and burial mounds, lit by crystal and constructed of precious metals; or it was an Edenic paradise aflourish with exotic flora and fauna and utterly without weather.[37] Food always appeared magically and abundantly there, instead of having to be won from the parsimonious landscape of the real world. Time passed along different trajectories for otherwordly residents and their human guests.[38] In such a setting, men and women were bound to be more beautiful than humans, more erratic, and more generous. They appeared and disappeared without warning, which indicated that their bodies were not built of the same flesh and bone as human bodies. What is more, their moral composition was completely inhuman; they were, as Proinsias Mac Cana has shown, without sin. Like dogs or other beasts, they coupled when they felt desire and exchanged mates freely.[39]

The artificiality, beauty, and amorality of the otherworld was best exemplified by its female citizens in their interactions with mortal men. In early Irish narratives, only men were tempted to leave reality for the otherworld; mortal women never strayed into another reality (unless they were *mná síde,* women of the otherworld, disguised as humans).[40] Men usually went because *síd* women enticed them, often visiting their victims in bird or animal form.[41] In *Aislinge Oenguso* (The dream of Oengus), the hero followed a siren who called to him from a dream; in *Serglige Con Culainn* (The sickbed of Cú Chulainn), Cú Chulainn chased birds who turned into otherworldly women; in *Echtra Nerai* (The adventure of Nera), Nera accidentally stumbled into the otherworld and stayed because he found a wife there.[42] In several tales, the citizens of some otherworldly islands were all females who were so happy to receive mortal men into their paradise that they took such human adventurers captive.[43]

The women of the otherworld were alluring because of their unearthly beauty, their promiscuity, and their power over men. They could extract men from the coils of social networks and responsibilities and carry them off to a neverland of structureless pleasure.[44] They were just as abundant in exaggerated charms as the otherworld itself, and their loveliness was artificially formulaic.[45] Étaín, mother of Mess Búachalla in *Togail Bruidne Da Derga* (Destruction of Da Derga's Hostel) was paradigmatic: her clothing was of silk embroidered with gold and adorned with precious jewelry, her hair was yellow-gold and elaborately coiffed, her skin—which she showed quite a bit of, judging by the description of thigh and breast offered in the tale—was white as fresh snow, her teeth pearly, and her eyes hyacinth blue. She was, as the tale said, "the fairest and most perfect and most beautiful of all the women in the world."[46] Étaín represented all that was most typical, tempting, and fearful in the otherworld: she was without ugliness, morals, or human purpose. Once an ordinary man ventured into the clutches of such a bombshell, he never freed himself of her influence; in fact, he was lucky to escape with his life.[47] The actions of *síd* women could not be measured by normal human standards but operated according to their own antilogic. The otherworldly women in these tales represented an alternative, nonhuman reality, something no humans, especially no male humans, could ever fully participate in even when it operated to their advantage.

The women of the *síd* were doubly alien in the literature of early Ireland. They were reversible tropes. As female characters they signified all that the unhuman otherworld could perpetrate, for good or evil, upon humans. As otherworldly characters interacting with humans, they showed how tangential the cognitive world of women was to that of men. Both mortal women and *mná síde*, women of the *síd*, were in many ways closer to beasts and birds and more exotic creatures than they were to men. Women of sagas could turn themselves into swans and heifers, but try as they might, they and their real-life sisters could never become what was most human. They could never become men.

What Is the Best of Women?

The tellers of tales and the *Triads* explained to men that women were like dogs and the shapeshifting, two-timing females of the otherworld. This explanation left most men in a somewhat uncomfortable position since, as the *Triads* suggested, women were an inevitable feature in men's lives. Men were born of them and had to marry them to produce more men. Further, men occasionally found pleasure in the company of women and even had a disturbing tendency to fall in love with women, as many stories, happy, tragic, and matter-of-fact, recounted. If women were unavoidable, then men had to domesticate their mysteries.

Writers of *tecosca* (instructions) approached the problem of women's nature with their own typologies of good and bad women. Some of these wisdom texts were simply lists of aphorisms. Others were admonitory texts in the tradition of the *speculum principum* so popular throughout early medieval Europe. Based on Solomon's proverbs for his son, these "mirrors of princes," set in the mouths of paternal advisers, sought to articulate the duties and correct behavior of a new ruler.[48] Several of the *tecosca* included passages on women, similar to but not derived from the catalogs of women, their vices, and their virtues popular in late antiquity.[49]

One unusual *tecosc,* the eighth- or ninth-century *Senbríathra Fíthail* (Advice of Fíthal), considered women in the context of advice from wise man to royal pupil about how to live a prosperous, virtuous gentleman's life. Learning how to deal with women was clearly an important part of the process, for one long section of the tract treated the problem of wives and how to select them. The *Senbríathra* seemed at first to propose a handy guide to the identification of worthy women. However, the text's underlying message was darker and more complicated than a simple *vade mecum* to the tangled paths of gender relations.

The section on wives began when Cormac mac Airt, king of Ireland and pupil of the druid Fíthal, the text's wise narrator, asked his teacher, "What is the keystone of husbandry?"[50] Fíthal responded, "A good wife."[51] But this was not enough for Cormac, who demanded that his tutor describe the best and worst of women. Fíthal replied with a seemingly straightforward typology of good and bad women, each of whom could be handily identified by easily recognizable characteristics. The good woman had common sense, prudence, modesty, excellent Irish (or well-spokenness), delicacy, mildness, honesty, wisdom, purity, and intelligence. The bad woman was characterized by wretchedness, stinginess, vanity, talkativeness, laziness, indolence, noisiness, hatefulness, avarice, visiting, thieving, keeping trysts, lustfulness, folly, and treachery.

The two lists did not derive directly from any textual precedent. The Old Testament Proverbs, for example, praised an industrious woman but said nothing of wealth or nobility or good Irish.[52] Earlier *tecosca,* canons, and laws each offered a different list of the evil woman's characteristics, none of which closely resembled the bad woman of the *Senbríathra.*[53] The sole criterion for evaluating a particular trait, as Fíthal did, was whether or not it made a woman a desirable wife. It would have been quite handy to have a wife who spoke well, one who could charm guests with her honeyed tongue or haggle with tradesmen, whereas a lazy, noisy, or violent wife—not to mention a wife who made trysts with other men—would have presented problems for a young prince.

The passage on women's characteristics comes at the end of the section on wives in *Senbríathra Fíthail* and seems to constitute the author's last word on the subject of women. But in fact, earlier in the text, the narrator, Fíthal, further divided good and bad women into subcategories. It was possible, Fíthal claimed, to detect a woman's nature before marrying her. Her looks gave her away as soon as one laid eyes on her.[54] His pupil and any canny man were to avoid not only the fat, short one, but also the slender, short one with curling hair; the fair, tall one; the dark-limbed, unmanageable one; the dun-colored, yellow one; the black, swarthy one; the white-faced, boisterous one; the slender, prolific one who was lewd and jealous; and the evil-counseling, evil-speaking one.[55] The very worst wife was a whore (*bé cairn*), whom only a fool would marry.[56] A man could, however, count on a successful union with the "tall, fair, very slender ones" (*na móra finda forsiunga*)—obviously a subtle distinction between this and the undesirable "fair, tall one" (*in find fotai*)— and the "pale, white, black-headed ones" (*na bána gela cenduba*).[57] Best of all was a virgin, particularly if she were a "noble wellborn beautiful woman with good manners and needlework" ("as í in ben ṡáer ṡochinéilech ṡochruid co ndegbésaib ocus co lámthorad").[58]

Yet, in spite of his precise description, the author of *Senbríathra Fíthail* acknowledged that his typology had little to do with flesh-and-blood women. For one thing, the narrator admitted in the text that the ideal wife might be difficult, if not impossible, to find. When Fíthal's charge asked what he should do if he could not hold out for an ideal woman, Fíthal responded: "Take them in spite of their defects, however they look, for there will be no choice at all if they are not taken in spite of their faults."[59] In other words, categorizing women was ultimately useless because the model woman may not really exist; most women had flaws; and anyway, the faults of some women were not dire enough to prevent a man from marrying one of them.

Further, the author contradicted himself by creating alternative typologies within the text itself. His main scheme divided women into bad and good wives, distinguishable by looks. But he went on to say that the best woman was a virgin and the worst a prostitute; appearance had nothing directly to do with this twofold typology. Whereas a bad-natured woman might make life unpleasant for her husband—the evil-counseling woman might give him wrong advice, the trysting woman might cuckold him—the promsicuous wife permanently decreased a man's status in the community by bearing children of uncertain paternity. By such a deed, his wife threatened the status and property of his entire family.[60] Other passages suggested still more ways of distinguishing among women, for example, by fertility or wealth.

In the end, for all his seeming wisdom, the narrator could not provide a single foolproof method for categorizing and evaluating women. The author of the *Senbríathra* must have realized as much when he advised taking a wife no matter what her perceived physical and character flaws. As he must have known all along, none of the advice about women in this seemingly sensible text was genuinely trustworthy.

Comparison of *Senbríathra Fíthail* with other *tecosca,* in particular *Tecosca Cormaic* (Advice of Cormac), helps explain *Senbríathra*'s ambivalent message about women. *Tecosca Cormaic,* for example, displayed none of the uncertainty toward women found in *Senbríathra*. Its narrator declared: "I distinguish between women but I make no difference between them."[61] Whereas Fíthal divided women into a confusion of categories, Cormac refused to notice any variety among women because he simply could not. He could define them only by their negative attributes, the most despicable being that women were, by nature, not men. In a haphazard list of accusations that defy categorization, Cormac denounced women as chronically dissatisfied, bad-tempered, untrustworthy, wanton, manipulative, ambitious, greedy, arrogant whiners.[62]

Yet, like Fíthal, Cormac offered no real help to the young men he purported to advise. The *tecosca* merely warned of women's faults, so that men did not fall prey to women, and hence to their own innate weaknesses. For although the literati stereotyped women's perceived vices, these vices remained beyond the ability of men to prevent or even to comprehend fully. Why on earth would a woman be bitter and haughty, as *Tecosca Cormaic* charged, when a man declared love for her? Why would she ignore her husband's affection but leap at sex with the first virile lout to happen along? Why steal from, lie to, and slander her male protectors and guardians and give away their secrets? And why be gorgeously attractive but misery to marry and live with? Whereas legal tracts described women who failed to become men in terms of social inferiority, and secular narratives understood women as unmale and inhuman by nature, *Tecosca Cormaic* accused women of refusing, from pure malice, to behave like, and thus to become, men.

Yet, when they rejected the good advice of *tecosca,* women adhered to an etiquette of their own, a protocol of contrariness which the *tecosca,* as well as laws and stories, actually set down for them. By elaborating the vices and follies of women in such poetic detail and by juxtaposing the unpredictability of women to the familiar and positive characteristics of a good ruler, the *tecosca* formally defined women's behavior and nature. The wisdom on women was this: women would always do exactly what men did not expect them to do. They might suddenly transform themselves into otherworldly queens and carry their lovers off to paradise. They might reveal themselves as greedy, talkative, vicious adulteresses. Or they just might settle down to a comfy life of hardworking matrimony. A man never knew. This is why *Senbríathra Fíthail* offered so many competing typologies of women. Women even refused to fit into neat gnomic categories in manuscripts, just as some refused to conform to legal categories. The behavior of women, and thus descriptions of it, defied any kind of definition. If women had represented a simple submale other, the literati might have expressed it more easily. But for the writers of gnomic tracts, women could be defined only by their multiplicity and ultimate undefinability.

Where did that leave poor fictional Fíthal and his real-life followers, who only wanted to get on with a daily life that necessarily included those wily creatures? The literati disagreed. Wisdom texts advised men to do everything from marrying women to beating them. Secular tales described men who lost themselves in the arms of blond *síd* women, but also heroes who subjugated women by the sword. Lawyers admitted that men and women involved themselves in all sorts of social and economic transactions but insisted that women be reminded of their inferiority and kept under strict control.

It was left to men who supposedly viewed the world in more rigidly dualistic and moral terms to propose a stop-gap solution to the problems raised by other literati. And unlike writers of other kinds of texts, they addressed the offenders directly.

Are Women Redeemable?

Religious writers struggled with the same need felt by secular writers to know the nature of woman, but like authors of laws, narratives, and wisdom literature, they too were clerically trained and hence subject to the same ideological confusions and discrepancies that plagued all thinking men in early Ireland. If anything, they were even more tainted by a long tradition of ambivalence toward women which had arrived in Ireland in the baggage of Christian missionaries.

The opportunities of religious authors for straightforward treatments of the creature woman were few. The Irish did not produce as much theology at home as their pilgrim brothers—Sedulius, Eriugena, and others—did on the Continent. No native Irish Jerome described a virginal ideal; no Irish Augustine expounded upon wives, no Irish Isidore etymologized the names of woman. On the other hand, Irish prayers to the Virgin Mary and to Saint Brigit suggest that clerics could envision females of great power and sanctity.[63]

Hagiographers, too, provided saintly prototypes for Christian women, but as we shall see in later chapters, the saints were exceptional exemplars, practicing manly asceticism and determination. Nor were they all flawless, abstract objects of prayer; Íte, for example, was a cranky old crone who cracked jokes at the expense of novice monks and Fáenche was a tough woman who took no nonsense from her highly confused brother, Saint Énna. In sum, hagiographers created a whole gallery of women whose portraits were didactic, ornamental, or incidental; they were sometimes meant to be taken as honest role models, sometimes meant to warn women, and sometimes simply meant for entertainment or to add color to a dry vita. From these portraits we can deduce much about women's lives in early Ireland, but we cannot extract a coherent theme regarding women's nature or behavior.

Only canonists and penitentialists gamely responded to the question of women in direct, practical, moral terms. They agreed that, although women were determined to be unlike men, men had to persuade women to redeem themselves by becoming less like animals, less like themselves, and more like men. This was a well-worn theme of the church fathers.[64] Women could never actually become men, of course, as the bishops gathered in Mâcon in 585 had decided. Most Christian writers of the Continent agreed, although some later theologians, including expatriate Irishmen, continued to wonder whether women might lose their female characteristics and arise as males on Judgment Day.[65] But the end was not so nigh; hence, in the context of these general propositions, posed by contemporary saints' lives, orthodox theology, and secular texts that defined women as undefinable, Irish writers of canons and penitentials created an agenda for the rare woman who wished to counter her inscrutable nature and become more manly.

Like secular laws, to which they were intimately related, the canons were practical documents written to help Christians in specific situations. The main body of Irish canons was collected and copied down by two monks in about 725, soon after the period when secular laws first began to be recorded.[66] They shared the laws' purpose of assisting community leaders, in this case clerics, to regulate daily interactions of all kinds. Their emphases were similar, although not identical, to those of the secular laws. They treated matters of status, property, and contract, along with problems of Christian behavior and ritual.

The canons, however, assumed a different set of priorities for the community and imposed a blatant morality on human activity which was lacking in the laws. For instance, the canonists wrote many pages on the classes and duties of religious professionals—from bishop to lowly monastic porter—and reorganized the elaborate social hierarchies of the laws into one simpler tripartite typology: clerics, laics, and nonbelievers. Within this simple hierarchy, practicing laics ranked above sinners, the celibate above the carnal, and men above women. Penitentialists, writing in the seventh and eighth centuries, provided a manual for climbing up the hierarchy. Canonists mediated among the different ranks of Christians, trying to create guidelines for every believer's life; they treated such matters as the consecration and use of sacred space, the identifying uniform of religious professionals, and the religious and legal aspects of marriage, among others.

The canons defined women, as did secular laws, exclusively in the context of the hierarchy. Canonists articulated a subhierarchy of gender most explicitly in their discussion of Christian marriage, for like the author of *Senbríathra Fíthail* and despite their pleas for religious virginity, canonists assumed that marriage was inevitable for most ordinary men and women. They cited Paul to prove that women should be subordinate to men, and Augustine by way of Isidore to describe the fundamental differences between spouses and between the sexes generally. Men, who derived their name (*vir*) from the word "power" (*virtus*), were by nature bellicose, hardworking, and protective. Women (*mulier*) were named from their softness (*mollitia*), and were thus fragile, weak, humble, and submissive.[67]

Whereas the canonists' chapter on marriage, among others, established a gender hierarchy, the chapter "De quaestionibus mulierum" suggested a canonical typology of women. Unlike the typologies found in other kinds of texts, the canonists' schedule of women assigned a moral value to all females, as well as males. Nuns topped this female hierarchy, followed by penitent widows who took the veil. Beginning with the chapter's first section, on the benefits of virginity, the canonists defined all women according to whether or not they practiced sexual intercourse. To do so lowered a woman's status since virginity was the "eliminator of vices" and "conqueror of lust." Although virgins were automatically able to practice all sorts of other virtues, however, not every woman could remain a virgin; the canonists quoted Jerome quoting Christ, "Not everyone can follow the Word, but only those to whom it is granted by my father."[68]

Although canonists established that virgins were the best Christian women, professional virgins were not to criticize women who languished lower on the Christian hierarchy.[69] In canonical theory, married Christian women were less perfect than lifelong celibates, but some wives were better than others. A woman who entered marriage still a virgin ranked the highest among wives, according to Irish canonists and their sources, Jerome and Augustine (echoing, without the needlework, Fíthal.)[70] The worst kind of Christian wife, the kind that could be divorced without recrimination from the community, was a drunken, irascible, extravagant, quarrelsome, gluttonous, abusive woman who was not a virgin—in short, one much like the women of *Tecosca Cormaic*.[71] But even this sort of woman was better than one who commited abortion, infanticide, or other crimes against the church.[72]

Yet, no matter how pious the nun at the top of the moral hierarchy of females, she and all her sisters were by nature less than righteous men. Canonists assumed in proper orthodox fashion that all Christians achieved their rung on the hierarchy by good works; men and women were created as potentially perfectible Christians and when they strayed into sin and slipped down the hierarchy it was a result of their own spiritual ineptitude. Monks and clerics could fall, just as laymen or -women could; however, Irish and continental theologians alike knew for a fact that women were more prone to stumble than men. As the first woman, Eve, lamented from a Middle Irish poem:

> I am Eve, great Adam's wife,
> I that outraged Jesus of old,
> From my children Heaven I stole,
> By right 'tis I should have gone on the Tree . . .
> I that plucked the apple
> Which went down my narrow gullet;
> For that, all the days of their lives
> Women will not cease from folly.[73]

In keeping with the gender ideology of Christians on the Continent, Irish clerics associated women by nature with sex, pollution, and sin, and cautioned holy men to keep away from all of these.[74] One ninth-century poem, supposedly penned by the abbot Daniel Úa Liathaide of Lis Mór, depicted a female confessant trying to seduce her soul friend, Daniel, even as she recounted her other sins to him. He knew better, though, advising her to "be not on the chase after what is not good, Since the Prince will put thee to death; Dread thou, [as] I dread Christ without sin, Whose malediction I do not risk, O woman!"[75] That the poet assumed any advice to a female soul friend must come as a rebuke to attempted seduction gives a good idea of his attitude toward women. According to canonists, clerics who lived or associated with women other than their close kinswomen were liable to the same kind of trouble, for a relationship with any other woman was absolutely *nefas*, forbidden and disastrous.[76] Authors of religious works were convinced that even the holiest nun could easily fall from grace and end up at the bottom of the Christian ladder, sometimes bringing an unwary man with her. There she could be spotted by her tendency to be corrupt, garrulous, fickle, untrustworthy, and burdensome—that is, again, everything *Tecosca Cormaic* warned about in women.[77] That is why even nuns were not allowed to enter the most sacred of Christian spaces, the oratory of a church, for fear that their sinfully female natures would pollute it.[78]

Women could, however, come close to manly perfection if they abandoned their femaleness. Unlike other kinds of writers, canonists approached the problem directly, advising women rather than reviling them or lamenting about them. As the canons put it, only women who realized "the fragility of their sex" could work hard enough to combat their own weaknesses.[79] Women who wished to climb the Christian hierarchy had to act more like men, who were not associated with sex, sin, and the body as women were. Both canonists and the seventh-century penitentialists gave practical instruction in how to become a manly woman. Some of their advice applied to all men and women; every genuine Christian was to adhere to orthodox doctrine and practice, including fasting as well as abstaining from sex in certain seasons and on certain feast days.[80] But professional religious men and women had higher responsibilities, such as maintaining complete chastity. The greater part of the penitentials focused on violations of this particular duty, assigning the heaviest penances to clerics and laymen who fornicated with nuns and produced children, material evidence of their sins which shamed the entire community.[81] The penitentialists paid hardly any attention to the sexual offenses of nuns; they normally assigned penances only to the impregnators of nuns, not to the women themselves. It seems that nuns were as prone as the rest of womanhood to the polluting sins of sex and were therefore, like animals and jealous wives, partially excused the act.[82]

The idea that the best Christian was a nonfemale—either born a man or become manlike through her efforts—was obvious from other ecclesiastical sources, and both canonists and penitentialists must have had this in mind when promoting the nun's life. Several of the most famous early Irish female saints refused to behave as women were supposed to, although they remained fiercely female in other ways. Saint Íte, for instance, advised Saint Brénainn the wanderer never to trust a woman. Saint Íte also fasted until her body was wasted to bloodless, androgynous bones.[83] Other nuns also proved their sanctity by destroying what secular texts took for their most feminine characteristic, their physical beauty; whereas the otherworldly women of secular tales were perfectly beautiful, women of the Christian vitae were often purposely hideous. Saint Brigit, one of the more traditionally feminine of saints, went so far as to gouge out her own eye when threatened with marriage.[84] Men saints who wished to avoid the advances of the other sex maintained their physical attractions but prayed to God, who, in response, turned the women's carnal love into unthreatening spiritual affection. But the holiest of women mutilated their bodies or fasted until they eliminated all outward signs of their reproductive capacities and the beauty that marked their femininity.[85]

Nonetheless, once they had aged past genderless childhood, the only way for women to become fully immune to the physical world was to leave it, as canonists and theologians across Europe advised.[86] Women were to depart not for the *síd* but for the Christian otherworld. The best Christian woman was a dead one—spiritually, if not physically. Canonists ordered women who took the veil to obey without question the orders of their pastor, never dressing to attract attention, and to live, in short, "as if dead."[87] Early Irish saints' lives added vivid illustrations of this canonical admonition. Many episodes described young women who chose simultaneously to marry Jesus and die, avoiding the physical pollution of sex and marriage with a carnal spouse and setting an excellent example for other young virgins who, presumably, were to interpret the stories in a symbolic sense.[88]

Virginity was itself a liminal state between life and death. In many cultures, women who reject normative roles of marriage and childbearing in order to deny their sexuality occupy a position on several kinds of boundaries; they are more than girls but less than women, less than alive but more than dead.[89] This can be a powerful place from which to interact with other members of society, as Íte and her saintly sisters demonstrated, but it is not normally a woman's place.

"When is a woman redeemable?" asked the religious literati. When, they answered themselves, she is not a woman but instead manly, virginal, dead, or all three. This ecclesiastical agenda would have presented a problem for early Irish men and women had most of them taken it for their own. If women became less womanly, amputating from nature and spirit what made them female, even destroying their identifying physical characteristics through self-mutilation and self-denial, they would have eliminated a fundamental tension that held society together and enabled it to reproduce itself. Even the literati had to admit that men needed their women. No Irish utopian vision of heaven or the otherworld excluded women. Even monastic communities, the closest earthly approximations, where canons and penitentials were composed, included servant women and the wives and lovers of clerics. And the most misogynist typology of women never suggested shunning women altogether or sending them away; beat them, scourge them, be wary and mistrustful of their unpredictable behavior, ordered the author of *Tecosca Cormaic,* but never try to do without them. The penitentialists, who constantly nagged ordinary Christians about their sexual misconduct, suggested just how seriously men and women took the ecclesiastical ideal of the virtuously manly woman: not very seriously at all. It seems that the sexes colluded in ignoring the canonical plan for women.

Why Do Men Need to Know?

Fortunately, women perversely persisted in being women. The author of *Tecosca Cormaic* warned of their iniquities, but women continued to be greedy, talkative, untrustworthy, lustful, and sexually available. Lawyers insisted that women were socially less than men; yet some women refused to act within the bounds of law. Sagas and stories about otherworldly temptresses continued to seduce male audiences. And despite the demands of clerics that females become males, both secular and religious women continued to disobey canons and laws, consort with men, and reenact the Fall. This was reality at odds with the ideologies expressed by men's typologies of women. Why else would such various sources constantly repeat their questions about women?

If women wished to be other than men, even other than human, men had to figure out how to react. The problem informed a thousand daily encounters between ordinary men and women in early Ireland. When a man chatted with his wife or daughter, ran into his kinswoman, met up with a female neighbor or a strange woman, he wondered if he should be friendly, hostile, indifferent. Should he seek out the companionship of women or avoid them? Value or fear them? Most men probably did not consciously ask themselves such questions on a regular basis, but the literati, prone to such absurd speculation, did the asking for them.

The ideological responses of the literati to the question of women were various. Both practical (by their standards, if not ours) and outlandish, they were sometimes contradictory and yet sometimes pointed to a relatively coherent cultural definition of the creature woman. The learned elite was convinced that it could answer men's questions about the opposite sex. Further, the literati tried to persuade other men that these questions had to be answered for society to run smoothly, for marriages to succeed, for householders to produce the next generation, for farmers to bring in harvests, for warriors to win battles, and for kings to prosper. The texts suggested—no, positively insisted—that a formal gender ideology was a necessary tool for men's survival.

Among a perplexing variety of motives for this insistence, two were repeated in the texts again and again, as we shall see in the next few chapters. First, the need for coherent gender ideologies derived partially from the society's obsession with its collective reproduction and survival. To create and maintain an orderly, prosperous society, men needed cooperative women—hence, the necessity of determining the behavior, character, and very nature of the opposite sex. Second, the need for men to know women also had to do with the definition of the male gender. In early Ireland, women could, with great effort, make themselves act like men, but men rarely imitated women. The sagas were full of references to the feminine counterparts of male professionals: *ban-file*, female poet; *ban-láech*, female warrior; *ban-sáer*, female craftsman; *ban-liaig*, female physician. But since no categories existed for women other than in relation to men, and since they had no formal identity except their gender function alone, no masculine counterparts to the "female-man" existed.[90] What is more, these were exceptional women, not everyday wives and neighbors. Ordinary women were no more likely to take up doctoring or soldiering than they were to shift shapes or hop a chariot to the otherworld.

The wisdom texts, narratives, and secular and ecclesiastical laws all suggested that men needed to know about women in order to avoid becoming like them. To become like women was also to become socially inferior, beastly, otherworldly, to adopt all the other faults that Cormac found in the despicable sex. Women's flaws caused laws to malfunction, communities to fall apart, and alternative realities to creep into this knowable world. When extraordinary women crossed gender boundaries, they became better humans, but for men, the crossing could only be disastrous, a demotion, and completely taboo.[91] In fact, according to men's sources, men and women conspired together to keep the boundaries of gender identity intact. Women not only refused to turn manly but helped men avoid turning womanly.[92]

Together, male authors of many different kinds of early Irish texts articulated their wisdom on women. Their definition of women as undefinable became the basis for the competing gender ideologies that informed the early medieval sources. As a result, participants in these ideologies were left with two compelling problems, which demonstrate exactly how far from reality men's ideas about women could stray. First, without formal definitions for women, men had to conceptualize the other sex in terms of desirable social roles. They thought of women as sexual partners, birth givers, and kinswomen, but rarely as beings with an inherent identity unrelated to that of men. Analysis of these predominant social roles for women forms the basis of the next several chapters.

Second, in their man-to-man talk of women, the literati suspected that women did not even care that they were unlike men. The laws and *tecosca* suggested that women intentionally violated rules of male behavior. The ecclesiastical legislation showed women how to be manly if they wanted to improve themselves. Surely, if women persisted in being nonmale, they had their own unsettling, damning reasons for doing so.

One tale, *Scéla Muicce Meic Dathó* (The tale of Mac Dathó's pig) depicted a woman who thoroughly understood and resisted the typologizing of *Tecosca Cormaic* and similar texts. When the hero of the story, Mac Dathó, got himself in a bind by promising his famous greyhound to two different kings, he became desperate with worry because he feared that warriors of either or both kings would destroy him. His perceptive wife noticed Mac Dathó sulking and chided him for not eating, sleeping, or telling her his problems. "Sleeplessness has come to Mac Dathó's house," she observed; "he would have advice but he speaks to no one." Mac Dathó responded rudely with an aphorism straight out of *Tecosca Cormaic*: "Do not give your secret to a woman. A woman's secret cannot be kept; no treasure is given to a slave."[93] But she would take no nonsense: "Though you tell it to a woman, no ruin results; what your mind cannot grasp another's can." Eventually she advised him to offer the dog to both parties and let them kill each other for it. Mac Dathó admitted that his wife gave good advice, but the storyteller was not so generous, for when Mac Dathó followed her suggestion, the disastrous result was a battle that demolished his property and retinue, not to mention the dog.[94]

Nonetheless, the tale suggested, at the very least, that women were wise to the more critical typologies of their sex, and if they were wise, then women did indeed willfully maintain their difference. Not only otherworldly and legally marginal women but all women chose to be womanly (in the early Irish sense), to defy definition, and to behave in a way that was annoying and unpredictable to men—or so men told other men. For as Fíthal acknowledged in *Senbríathra*, the men of early Ireland really had "no choice at all" either among or about women. They could categorize and typologize in innumerable manuscripts, and they could try to subordinate and restrict women in real life, but they could never force women to become other than women.

3

The Canon of Coupling

ary as they were of women, the men of early Ireland still lusted after them and fell in love with them, though lust and love were not necessarily related. No man was immune. Even the margins of monastic manuscripts bore the lyrical jottings of romantic clerics. "Happy those who have their sweethearts in a long-prowed boat," mused one, "rowing off high and proud, having abandoned their country." Another reflected more cynically, "I do not know who Etan will sleep with, but I do know that Blonde Etan will not sleep alone." A third celebrated the joys of love and companionship: "A blessing from me on glorious Eithne, daughter of Domnall who casts a spear, with whom, after searching through a poisonous town, I have drunk a stream of mead that was load enough for thirty-two wry-necked hauliers."[1]

How did men and women cope with the necessities of coupling, physically and emotionally? We can only guess the strategies of amorous women for attracting and keeping men (although the literature gives hints), but the literati offered explicit, if conflicting, advice to lovelorn and sex-hungry men. Jurists and canonists, for example, assumed that love, lust, and passion had little to do with the marriage and concubinage relationships that they called *lánamnasa cumtusa comperta*, "unions of partnership for the purpose of reproduction." Lawyers guided a young man's family through the complicated rituals that formalized such unions. The man's family was to confer together, select one from a list of potential brides, negotiate with her family, trade some property, and announce a liaison of one kind or another. Whether or not love or good sex resulted was of no concern to the legal writers, who viewed affection as a lucky side effect of a union aimed at creating social solidarity and a new generation, and sex as a means to the end of legitimately produced children.

Historians, either ignoring their own romantic experience or revealing a lack of it, have tended to accept the legal picture of gender relations as accurate and thorough, accusing all medieval marriages of lovelessness.[2]

Yet there must have been more to coupling, even legal coupling, than the sensible alliance of two people as represented in secular and ecclesiastical legislation. Although not every culture considers sexual intercourse, passion, formal heterosexual unions, and reproduction to be part of the same conceptual package, the Irish clearly perceived such a possibility. They also conceived of many other, wilder combinations, too, not all of which were legitimate or happy. In the narrative sources of the same period as the laws, men and women sometimes obeyed but as often disobeyed or ignored community sanctions and formal laws in order to pursue an object of desire or, possibly, even what we self-satisfied moderns call love.

Contrary to the passive subjects depicted in the laws, the Irish men and women of "love" stories (I use the term warily) were no passionless, law-abiding dreamers longing for abduction, seduction, or delirious rendezvous. Instead, they were aggressive and destructive seekers of the other sex. Cú Chulainn, one of the most virile warriors of early Irish literature, fell sick with desire when supernatural blond beauties lashed him provocatively with a horsewhip, so that he almost lost his beloved wife by his infidelity. Deirdriu, whose story enchanted Yeats and Synge, committed suicide over a love affair, but not before she caused deadly mayhem among the Ulstermen. All sorts of other loves, obsessions, and sex appeared in various combinations in the sources: brief encounters, disastrous adulteries, betrayals, rapes, and happy marriages. Sometimes one kind of union turned into another.

All these couplings implied either a disregard for laws or different sets of rules and guidelines which contradicted the laws and canons. If jurists idealized the docile union of men and women wrought by their kin groups in a solid marriage alliance, writers and audiences of love stories celebrated the erotic collision of two sexually charged individuals—individuals who sometimes represented grand concepts and ancient convictions in these distinctly mythological or allegorical tales but who were, nonetheless, men and women aflame with sexual passion. The most profound point of disagreement among the literati was over women's roles in the process of coupling. According to some, women sat by and were traded, loved, or sexually sated, but never placed in control. Other writers knew that women were the real erotic arsonists.

Storytellers must have been aware of the laws when they initiated the textual foreplay that gave so many tales their momentum and hurled a hero and his woman together in a rash or illicit sexual encounter. They may not have been writing what they saw, but they were seeing beyond the laws. Narratives may not have been closer to social reality than legal tracts, but the tales did expand the range of models for sexual and affective interactions.

Read together, these different kinds of texts, produced for unrelated purposes but recorded by the same literate class, reveal the common assumptions about coupling among the early Irish. We must approach the laws conscious of the literature, and vice versa, as the early Irish themselves were. For only at the intersection of laws and romances, at the point of both harmony and dissonance in these related documents, can we possibly grasp the reality of coupling. Then it becomes obvious that, despite their discord, laws and stories shared assumptions: that one man and one woman needed to join together in intimate union; that this need sometimes conflicted with the demands of families and communities. All the texts concurred that, for better or worse, when the lovers came together, like spark and kindling, neither was the same again. The couple changed in ways social, cultural, and physiological, producing a fire that sometimes warmed and comforted their kin and allies and sometimes caused a devastating social conflagration.

For the historian sifting through the ashes of these ancient passions, the problem of coupling in early Ireland has three parts: the different meanings for men and women; the nature of the perceived transformative effects on the larger society; and most important, the connection between the reality and the fiction of narrative and law.

The Rules of Coupling

On the subject of coupling, legal writers told a story of social alliance, property exchange, and procreation. To canonists and *brithemoin* (legal professionals), the love and passion of courtship were mostly fictional embellishments of what was an orderly social and political process. Courtship resulted in formal legal relationships that included but were not limited to marriage and concubinage.[3] The main legal problem with affective coupling was that it inspired disorder. For one thing, passion caused men and especially women to defy the wishes of their families and select their own mates. For another, passion led to sex, sex created babies, and babies became heirs to property, the main concern of jurists. Or else, which worried jurists even more, the babies did not become heirs, depending on the exact nature of the relationship between their parents. Coupling thus had to be bound by formal laws, both religious and secular in a Christianizing society, of betrothal, marriage, and inheritance. Finally, sex itself caused all sorts of trouble for the body and soul of both women and men, as we shall see in the next chapter. The aim of the rule makers, then, was to build legitimate procreative couples while limiting the ill effects of this most powerful social union.

Lawyers and, to a lesser extent, canonists accomplished this goal primarily by ignoring what they perceived as the most unstable element in the process: women. Unlike the bold, exquisite beauties who often dominated the narrative romances, women in the rules of coupling played a minor role. This was a bias of a secular law code that assigned full legal status only to free adult males and of church laws that considered the sexes to be spiritually but not socially equal. In the formal process of coupling, women had only to give passive consent by maintaining their virginity until betrothal and by remaining monogamous thereafter. Theoretically, they took no part in the choice of spouses or the negotiation of families. As one law put it pragmatically, "At a proper age a girl should be betrothed to God [as a nun] or to a man," and that was that.[4] Thus, rather than direct negotiation between lovers, legal coupling consisted of bargaining between men.[5]

The laws did not describe how men brought a man and a woman together. Instead, they treated the final outcome of the process: the different kinds of legal relationships created between men and women and, in particular, the economic consequences of the unions. The terms of legal contracts suggest that by the seventh or eighth century, when the laws were first recorded, the ideal process of coupling between members of the socio-political elite was quite complicated, consisting of a series of negotiations and exchanges. The guardians of a nubile freewoman, defined as a girl of fourteen or older, were to meet with a prospective groom and his guardians to negotiate a contract.[6] What preceded the meeting, the laws did not say. Did she catch his eye at market, or did he drop by to chat her up while she helped in the garden? Or did one of them hear gossip about the other, as so often happens in the narratives, and instantly fall in love?[7] Presumably in the small rural communities of early Ireland the pool of spouses was well known to all; even outsiders would have had some sort of link to the community, probably kinship, clientage, or political alliance. Discussion of various candidates for marriage probably took place privately among families before they got down to bargaining.[8] Parents and other concerned kin must have analyzed the candidates' property, status, and character.[9] The groom, and perhaps informally the bride, may have added words about the looks or reputation of the proposed spouse, also important in narratives of love but unmentioned in the laws. And at least for clerics, master craftsmen, and poets, the bride's virginity was a matter of concern; indeed, canonists insisted that both man and woman be virgins at any marriage.[10]

Once the two parties had approached each other, they were to hammer out the details of the exchange at a meeting where witnesses from both sides affirmed the terms of the contract (*airnaidm*).[11] Ideally, at least in the very early Middle Ages and among the prosperous, the two families formalized the union by trading property. The bride went to the groom's family in return for a marriage payment or bride-price (*coibche*) for her folks, although already by the early Middle Ages the payment could also be bestowed on the bride herself.[12] But the formal direction of *coibche* to her kin indicates the marginal role taken in the formal bargaining by the bride herself. The groom may also have given either the bride or her family a *tinnscra* or *tochra,* once payments for removing the bride from her kin group but later simply gifts for the bride or equivalent of *coibche.*[13]

After the initial exchange of property, the couple was officially betrothed. Ideally the groom acquired his bride's legal guardianship, although the laws allowed for many exceptions when her status or wealth differed from that of her mate-to-be, or when the union was less formal.[14] In medieval and early modern Europe, betrothal might have lasted for some time. The Merovingians occasionally left their fiancées alone for years before consummating the marriage.[15] Theoretically, a betrothed woman was to remain chaste for her groom during the wait, no matter how long. This was Luaine's sad fate in the story of her betrothal to King Conchobar mac Nesa of Ulster; she died of shame while biding her time as a betrothed woman (*bé urnadma*) after three satirists tried unsuccessfully to seduce her.[16] Less honorable men and women were not so true to their vows, however, according to the canonists; officially, the act of sex while betrothed was adulterous unless committed with one's betrothed, when it was still frowned upon by clerics but probably quite common.[17] Moreover, the groom, if he were prosperous and important enough, might already have a wife, concubine, or some other kind of sexual partner; further, not all unions followed betrothals.

Eventually, the betrothal became a union (*lánamnas*) of marriage or concubinage after an additional exchange of property, or else it just lapsed into permanence when the couple moved in together.[18] The bride usually brought some property with her, depending on whether she was a primary wife or some sort of secondary spouse or concubine, although it was not officially a dowry in the Roman sense.[19] Her contribution to the union differed not only according to her own status but also according to the wealth and status of the groom. All these prestations were negotiable terms in the contract, providing a little more flexibility for the parties to come to an agreement.

Although these were business deals, the community probably helped to celebrate formal marriages, if not the less formal but legal kinds of *lánamnasa* such as concubinage or temporary liaisons, with feasts as well as some sort of public ceremony. None of the narratives depicted a wedding celebration, Christian or otherwise. Yet the very word for marriage in Old Irish—*banais,* from *ben,* "woman" and *feis,* "a sleeping with" or "a feast"—suggests a celebration.[20] Further, the eighth-century canonists, arguing from Augustine, insisted on a public announcement, presumably accompanied by a Christian ceremony, by which the whole community acknowledged the couple's union.[21] At least one late vita refers to a wedding ring worn by a wife.[22] These signs were meant not only to legitimate the contract but also to warn everyone against trying to rupture the union.

Even if the betrothal or marriage ceremony was a churchman's dream, disregarded by ordinary farmers and warriors, it is hard to believe that the dull and public business of marriage contracts should have no connection with the mad fusion of hearts and bodies that occurs in the secular narratives. Yet, on the surface, nothing but very basic resemblances linked the sensible exchange of property and persons that appeared in the laws and canons with the wild coupling found in romances and other stories. True, both representations followed strict, if quite different, guidelines with the aim of joining a man and woman in some sort of long-term relationship. Both involved the couple's kin and community in the process, for better or worse. Both allowed a man to be attached to several women at once, although only the narratives permitted the same to women. And occasionally, love stories described behavior that legal tracts help us elucidate. Beyond these broad similarities, the legal paradigm for coupling seems to have come of a different culture—or, perhaps, a different literati—from the narrative paradigm.

Jurists and canonists purposely recounted a story different from the tales of storytellers. Lawyers were concerned with property and inheritances, taletellers with entertainment, as well as more Lévi-Straussian issues such as alliance and domination. To grasp the significance of the jurists' very consciously limited depiction of coupling, we need to look at the stories they did *not* tell, found in other extant sources concerned with the mingling of men and women.

Tochmarca *and* Aitheda

Unlike legal writers, who described the results of complex negotiations between the families of two nubile people, the composers of love stories were interested in the dynamic process by which a woman and a man joined together. The action of love stories followed a familiar pattern. A man and a woman saw or heard about each other, met, fell in love, negotiated a relationship, consummated their union, and experienced the social effects of it. In both of the two most prominent types of formal love stories, *tochmarca* (courtships) and *aitheda* (elopements), the action ended, one way or another, not after the couple had sex but with its meaning for others in the community.

Once the courting hero had knocked off a few heads and negotiated his way into the heart of his favorite maiden, or once the eloping jezebel had finally persuaded her man into the forest, the story still needed a proper finish.

Nonetheless, coupling provided one of the dramatic high points of every tale of courtship or elopement. One marvelous image from the tenth- or eleventh-century tragic tale of Baile Binnbérlach and his darling Ailinn showed how intimately lovers and their histories were identified. Trees planted on the unfortunate sweethearts' graves grew into likenesses of their heads; when cut down, the trees were carved into wooden tablets upon which poets inscribed "the vision-tales and feasts and loves and wooings" of Ulster and Leinster.[23] While passion remained the point of their tales, however, storytellers expressed no single paradigm for romantic coupling. Their stories sent additional messages about social relationships, the proper roles of men and women, and various other important subjects, just as lawyers and canonists used the rules of coupling to make multiple statements about social and political order.

In particular, *tochmarca* and *aitheda* depicted alternative behavioral guidelines for women. This is not to say that storytellers were consciously challenging the laws or their organizational purposes; narratives simply recorded other ways in which men and women might join together and laid greater emphasis than laws on the role of women. In both elopements and courtships, women were not the passive objects of exchange found in most legal paradigms. On the contrary, a *tochmarc* told a story of active negotiation between a woman and a man, sometimes leading to her willing abduction and often to their marriage. An *aithed* usually recounted a woman's seduction of a man. Although many stories and poems treat love and sex, *aitheda* and *tochmarca*, elopements and courtships, are the only two formal genres of early Irish narratives that announced a focus on love. According to the tale lists compiled by Irish scribes before the tenth century, there were twelve important *aitheda* and thirteen *tochmarca* known to every good professional storyteller. Both of these genres occasionally overlapped with others; tenth-century and later lists also mentioned *serca*, love tales, some of which were identical with elopements and wooings. A competent tale-teller included these adventures in love and physical attraction among his usual stock of yarns, along with cattle raids (*tána*), frenzies (*baili*), visions (*aislingi*), and other types of stories.[24]

However, although love stories described alternative roles for women, the tale-tellers did not necessarily endorse them unreservedly. Whereas the lovers in *tochmarca* usually concluded a successful union, *aitheda* generally ended tragically for both man and woman. Still, the literati did not use these parallel genres simply to condemn women aggressive in love, for the stories were also similar in significant details. In examples of both kinds of stories the passion between man and woman was mutually uncontrollable and the pain and pleasure of inevitable love shared equally. Also, in both courtship and seduction, men and women took turns playing passive and aggressive roles. The different messages of the genres had less to do with the balance of power within a sexual relationship than with the relation of lovers to the surrounding community, for both *aitheda* and *tochmarca* described illegal, (initially) illicit, or unorthodox love, in the sense that the lovers themselves tried to control the coupling. Whether initiated by man or woman, both courtships and elopements were usually accomplished by the illegal means of seduction or abduction. Thus, at the same time that they delighted their audiences with love and adventure, the storytellers of *tochmarca* and *aitheda* were advancing the possibility that the legal process was not the only way in which women could find men and men their women. Storytellers reminded their audiences of what they already knew: that women were not always the legally passive objects of men's exchanges and alliances.

The *tochmarca* made up one of the most pleasant of early Irish literary genres. Heroes and heroines usually survived the stories unharmed and, after a series of exciting mishaps and daring feats, ended in each other's arms. Courtship tales varied widely in details. Some featured otherworldly men and women, some dealt with humans. Most courtships led to legitimate unions of marriage, but a few did not. Some tales were melodramatic; others were humorous. The tales generally emphasized the mutual affection of the protagonists, but a few also described relationships based on nothing more than ungovernable lust. And although characters in these stories behaved in larger-than-life ways, they are far more familiar and probable to modern readers than the emotionless couples depicted in the laws.

One of the more charming *tochmarca* is the ninth- or tenth-century *Tochmarc Becfola,* in which the heroine actually enjoyed two courtships.[25] The tale began when Diarmait mac Aeda Sláine, king of Temair, encountered a bejeweled woman driving her chariot at Áth Truim; the circumstances betrayed her to the audience, if not to the gullible Diarmait, as an otherworldly visitor. They engaged in some sexual punning. She said she was looking for some seed-wheat and he responded, "If it be the seed of this territory that you desire, your destiny does not lie beyond me." She negotiated a bride-price with him, settling for the nominal gift of the little pin from his cloak. The reason seems to have been that she refused to tell her name—another hint that she came from beyond Ireland—and thus associate herself with a particular family.[26] Diarmait's people decided to call her Becfola, "little value," after the paltry bride-price.

Although Diarmait was the tale's hero, he came off as more dupe than lover. Becfola began her married career by trying to seduce Diarmait's foster son and political hostage, Crimthann mac Aeda, arranging a tryst for the next Sunday at Cluain Dá Chaileach. Becfola tripped off to her rendezvous unaware that Crimthann had thought better of seducing his fosterer's wife. Meanwhile, en route, Becfola and her female attendant were ambushed by wolves and the attendant killed.

Then began the second courtship. Becfola happened on a lone warrior in the woods. His appearance marked him as a fellow denizen of the otherworld. Although he remained silent, Becfola followed him to a bronze boat and thence to an otherworldly island, where he entered a hostel, fed her, and took her to bed. But the warrior offered no conversation and no sex. Only the next day, after he won a bloody battle against his uncle's sons, did he reveal his identity: he was Flann úa Fedaich, fighting his kin for his inheritance, the island. Flann promised to take Becfola as his companion once he had won his island and made himself worthy of her. Becfola returned to Diarmait, arriving at the exact moment she left on Sunday morning, another signal that unearthly powers were abroad. Eventually, Flann appeared at her door, wounded but victorious after eliminating all his rival kin, and they left together. Kindly clerics explained the situation to the confused Diarmait who took his mate's departure stoically and seemed more disturbed that the clerics had violated the sabbath by traveling on Sunday.

Several conventions of romantic courtship appeared in this *tochmarc*. The most important was the frank negotiation between potential partners in love, the purpose of which was to lay down the preliminary terms of the relationship. The parties entered negotiation with equal status, although what they offered and demanded differed. Becfola's beauty, wealth, and obvious nobility were her best assets, and she aggressively led off the bargaining with Diarmait by demanding the highest quality returns: the best "seed-wheat" in Ireland. But Becfola could offer no name and made no claim to a prestigious kin group to back her personal qualities, nor did she misrepresent her (possible lack of) virginity. Diarmait made his own status clear by offering the best seed around, referring not only to sexual prowess but also to his aristocratic lineage, to be continued in his future progeny. The balance of the deal weighed in Diarmait's favor, and Becfola came to terms by accepting the meager bride gift of a pin. Becfola's second negotiation with Flann followed a similar if abbreviated pattern. Becfola demonstrated her willingness to sleep with him by following Flann home to bed; Flann laid down the honorable condition that only once he had won his inheritance would their status be equal—she was, after all, wife of the king of Temair—and their union consummated.

Such stories show that, in effect, literary courtship consisted of negotiation between two individuals. Of course, in this particular tale, as in many *tochmarca,* the characters were not ordinary citizens; Becfola and Flann came from another time and space, and Diarmait was a legendary king of Ireland.

No early Irish reader of *Tochmarc Becfola* would have expected these people to adhere to normal behavioral conventions, just as modern audiences grant all sorts of moral leeway to characters in novels and films. This tolerance may well have contributed to the story's finale; since, as we have already seen, other-worldly women followed mysterious rules of conduct, Becfola's chutzpah in chasing Crimthann and Flann practically before Diarmait's eyes brought her no retribution. But not every *síd* woman's story ended so happily; in *Aided Muirchertaig Meic Erca* (The death of Muirchertach mac Erca), for instance, the negotiation and consummation of Muirchertach's marriage to Sín allowed her to destroy him mercilessly, after which she died of grief.[27]

Whatever else the characters' actions may have meant to early Irish audiences—allegories of sovereignty being only the most obvious—the courtship of Diarmait and Becfola was in its crudest reduction as simple for the early Irish to understand as it is for us: a man and a woman who desired each other determined together the balance of property and status within their relationship. What is more, once they began negotiating, man and woman were briefly of equal status until the relationship was agreed upon. Each had the same rights to make, accept, and reject demands. No parents, kinsmen, or friendly advisers intruded on this intimate bargaining, although such negotiation was contrary to the whole force of law, for legally, families guided the mating of their children and determined the terms of formal unions. In story, even when the lovers adhered to the laws of betrothal, or when the guardians of the woman tried to exert some influence, the couple still initiated the affair and the heroine and hero won each other through direct negotiation.

In some *tochmarca* it is simply unclear whether the guardians of hero or heroine were present, since the narrator focused exclusively on the lovers' negotiations. In *Tochmarc Luaine,* for example, after King Conchobar of the Ulaid (Ulster) heard a poem about the "exquisitely lovely, nubile, yellow-haired, well-renowned, very modest, very noble" Luaine, he fell instantly in love (*serc*) and rushed off to speak with her. As a result of their meeting, Luaine was betrothed to Conchobar and her bride-price settled. Although the language suggests a formal legal negotiation, whether or not Luaine's guardians were also present is simply not mentioned. The tale had an unhappy ending, but not on account of any irregularity in the lovers' negotiation.[28]

In other tales the lovers conducted their negotiations in total defiance of the heroine's guardians and the laws of betrothal and marriage. When Cú Chulainn courted Emer in *Tochmarc Emire,* he met her inappropriately where she sat among her foster sisters working embroidery.[29] In this place of women, the most manly of men made sexual jokes with Emer. Catching sight of her breasts, he sighed, "This plain is beautiful, a plain for resting spears on." But it was she who controlled the negotiation, announcing her own value as a virgin and setting him feats to accomplish before she would let him approach her plain.[30] However, her foster sisters tattled to their fathers who, in turn, informed Emer's father, Forgall Manach, that a fearsome warrior had been to visit. Forgall realized it was Cú Chulainn who came to woo his daughter without permission. Forgall tried to prevent the match because, according to the storyteller, he feared Cú Chulainn's ferocity and believed that the hero would cause his death. But the lovers were wise to Forgall's perfectly legitimate objections to their negotiations. Eventually, Cú Chulainn completed his lover's tasks, returned for his woman, and caused much mayhem and bloodshed—including the death of Forgall—before the two settled down and sealed their bargain.

Within the logic of *tochmarca,* a woman's guardians represented the legal intervention of kin which jeopardized the negotiation between two lovers. *Táin Bó Fraích* (The cattle raid of Fráech) told the story of Fráech, son of the otherwordly Bé Find, who heard of the beauty of Finnabair, daughter of Ailill and Medb of Connacht. He came with an impressive retinue to court her but first tried to persuade her to run off with him. Finnabair had actually begun the affair by letting her attraction to him be known and then agreeing to meet him secretly at a riverbank, but she stoutly refused to elope and told him to ante up a proper bride-price. "I won't elope because I am the daughter of a king and queen. You are not so poor that you couldn't get me from my family." Finnabair had no qualms about revealing her desires and acting on them, despite her parents, but she knew well the disaster that followed elopement. Ailill and Medb tried everything to prevent the match (for reasons unclear in the tale),[31] demanding an outrageous bride-price, attempting to ambush Fráech, and even condemning Finnabair to death. In the end, however, thanks to Finnabair's clever negotiating and Fráech's otherworldly connections, the lovers triumphed over her contrary parents.[32]

In other tales, however, hostile, interfering parents were more justified in resisting their daughters' courtship. In the late medieval *Tochmarc Delbchaime* (which appears as *Echtra Airt* in the early medieval tale lists), the hero Art mac Cuinn fought not only giants and monsters to win his woman but also her mother, Coinchend Cendfada, who had the strength of a hundred and the habit of impaling the severed heads of her daughter's suitors on stakes. After dispatching Delbchaem's parents, Art negotiated a union with his mate, giving her all her parents' property, and they cheerfully consummated their union.[33] Folklorists might point to all sorts of deeper themes present in *Táin Bó Fraích, Tochmarc Delbchaime,* or *Tochmarc Emire,* for instance, the obvious oedipal connotations or the generational cycle of destruction and renewal evident in the grooms' murder of their intended in-laws.[34] However, these other meanings do not obviate the importance of suspicious parents as obstructions to the extralegal, personal negotiations of lovers.

Husbands were at risk, too, of losing their wives or their lives. In the ninth-

or tenth-century story of Fothad Canainne's death, Fothad and Failbe Flann dickered their way to an understanding despite Failbe's marriage to Ailill mac Eochain. Failbe demanded a bona fide bride-price (*tintscrae*), and with good grounds, according to the sympathetic storyteller: "Fothad was better-looking than Ailill but Ailill's wife was lovelier than the wife of Fothad."[35] Despite all the laws against adultery, then, not even legitimate, noble, and blameless husbands could interfere in the negotiations of two determined wooers, as the complex *Tochmarc Étaíne* also showed. This is a composite of three separate stories concerning the lovers Étaín and Midir. In the first episode, Étaín married Midir, but another of Midir's wives was jealous and transformed Étaín into a marvelous fly. In the second part of the story, Étaín was reborn and married to Eochu, king of Temair, unsuccessfully courted by his brother Ailill who was sick for love of her, and finally, in the third section, approached again by her true love, Midir. At first Étaín refused to negotiate with Midir. Although he claimed that she was once his wife in another life, she took a practical attitude, arguing that she had no reliable information about his family and would not (unlike Becfola) trade in a perfectly good king of Temair for an unknown. But Midir later successfully wooed Étaín with a love poem, begging her to come away to the otherworld, "where there is neither mine nor yours" and where his supernatural origins and her past were merely terms in the lovers' bargaining:

> Woman, if you come to my bright people,
> You will have a crown of gold for your head;
> Honey, wine, fresh milk to drink
> You will have with me there.[36]

Étaín relented, agreeing to take Midir if he could win her from her husband. But they did not include Eochu in the negotiations and neither of them approached Eochu directly. Midir eventually tricked the king into giving up Étaín. He presented Eochu with fifty Étaín look-alikes from which the king, like a contestant on some perverse game show, was to choose the real Étaín. Poor Eochu chose his daughter by Étaín instead, which choice eventually led to incest, attempted infanticide, and another king-tale.[37]

In the eyes of the early Irish, it took only two people to make a *tochmarc*. In courtship stories, a man and a woman met, fell in love, and privately negotiated their worth to one another, haggling over property, family, her chastity, and his strength and virility. They formed a lasting relationship of equals based on mutual attachment, despite any rights of kin, guardian, or legal spouse to take part in the process. Although most *tochmarca* included otherworldly elements—lovers from the *síd*, monsters, magical adventures—their depiction of courtship represented a familiar backdrop upon which the dramatic feats of heroes were played. The process itself was strikingly repetitive and straightforward. By and large, these enterprising couples were successful in their literary context not because they possessed special powers but because they came to an agreement and legitimated their illegitimate union by forcing its public recognition.

Tochmarca presented a different story of courtship than did the laws and canons, particularly in their description of women's active participation in negotiation. The *aitheda,* elopement tales, took the point of contention with laws even farther, endowing women with a more aggressive role than the *tochmarca*. Although in both kinds of tales a man and a woman found mutual passion, defied the laws of sexual union, and formed a relationship, there was one crucial difference: men engineered courtships, but women caused and controlled elopements. As a result, instead of living legitimately ever after, the lovers in *aitheda* often ended up dead.[38]

The whole idea of the lovers' secret elopement from their kin and communities seems to have connoted disorder and violence to the early Irish. Wooers of *tochmarca* negotiated a stable union and created a normal household; even Becfola briefly became a royal housewife. Eloping men and women, however, were forced to flee fatal opposition to their covert union and live like animals beyond the bounds of society in the forests, on unsettled islands, or abroad. A story from the eleventh- or twelfth-century *dindsenchas* (place-name tales) recounted how the ancient rulers of Ireland had tried to prohibit elopements in order to bring about a general peace, proclaiming:

> Men may not enter the company of women,
> Women may not enter the company of handsome men
> In case an elopement should result (may it not be heard of)
> Even though it should be with a second partner or [create a] second
> household.[39]

That is, even when lovers were adults with full legal capacity under little or no official control of guardians, they still were legally prohibited from running off together because of the violent opposition their union would surely provoke.

Although storytellers practiced a certain disregard for the laws of coupling and envisioned women taking part in the process, they also warned of the danger of allowing females to initiate it. In stories, women who instigated illicit unions selected the wrong mates and caused disaster. The *aitheda* were violent tales with obvious moral lessons for lovers. In the Middle Irish story of Diarmaid and Gráinne (which probably derived from an earlier original), countless men were wounded and killed, along with the hero himself, because the wife of Finn mac Cumaill tricked Diarmaid into abducting her.[40] Similarly, in the *Aithed Ruithcherni re Cuanu Mac Cailchíne* (Ruithchern's elopement with Cuanu mac Cailchín), of which only fragments remain, the protagonists' elopement is but one event in an extended and bloody feud among the nobility of Munster over kingship of the province.[41]

Neither Gráinne nor Ruithchern appears to have committed a worse offense than some women courted in the *tochmarca*. All the heroes and heroines of *tochmarca* and *aitheda* suffered uncontrollable desire for what might seem unsuitable mates, including married women. They all, men and women alike, defied the opposition of kin or community, and they all broke laws in order to consummate their yearning. Yet the storytellers allowed Becfola and Flann to settle down on their island, whereas Diarmaid and Gráinne did not survive their *aithed*. If Diarmaid had seduced Gráinne, rather than Gráinne dragging Diarmait off to the woods, the story might have ended differently.

Nothing makes this likelihood clearer than the most poignant of elopements, that of Deirdriu with Noísiu mac Uislenn (also called *Loinges Mac nUislenn,* Exile of the sons of Uisliu).[42] From the start of this roughly eighth-century tale it was obvious that the heroine brought trouble on herself, her lover, his people, and the entire province of Ulster not because she fell in love with Noísiu but because she acted on her passion. The tragedy was set in motion early in the tale, while Deirdriu was still only a potential trouble-maker safe in her mother's womb. The men of Ulster were feasting while Deirdriu's pregnant mother doled out the drink; the opposite of Cú Chulainn among the embroideresses, she was a woman in the most womanly condition intruding upon men's comradely space. As she crossed the floor, her womb shrieked—fairly ominous as omens go—which the druid Cathbad interpreted as imminent catastrophe for the Ulstermen. He announced its source to be "a woman with twisted yellow tresses, green-irised eyes of great beauty, and cheeks flushed like the foxglove." This "fatal woman" would be the cause of "harsh hideous deeds . . . and little graves everywhere."[43] The Ulstermen sensibly demanded that the baby be killed, but their king, Conchobar mac Nesa, had her brought up in seclusion until she was ready for his bed.

One day, though, Deirdriu saw her foster father skinning a calf on the snow and a raven drinking its blood. She told her companion, a sour old female satirist, that she could love a man with coloring like that: hair like the raven, cheeks like blood, skin white as snow. The satirist mentioned that such a man happened to be staying up the road at Conchobar's fort. Deirdriu slipped out to initiate a courtship, an action that would have been legitimate even in a *tochmarc*. She wandered among Noísiu's cows, pretending not to notice him. Noísiu showed interest. "That is a fine heifer going by," he said.[44] They exchanged a little sex talk in cattle metaphors, but Noísiu rejected Deirdriu's advances for fear of Conchobar. Deirdriu seized control of the negotiations by grabbing Noísiu's ears and threatening to satirize and publicly shame him (presumably by spreading rumors about his lack of virility) if he would not run off with her, and Noísiu was caught. For the rest of the tale the lovers, along with Noísiu's brothers and followers, fled Conchobar's men until finally, through treachery, Noísiu was murdered before Deirdriu's eyes on the green outside Conchobar's fort. Conchobar took Deirdriu away, as he had always planned, but she would only sing laments for Noísiu. When Conchobar threatened to give her to Noísiu's murderer, she killed herself by leaping from a chariot to dash out her brains on a rock.[45]

Deirdriu, though pitiable, was nevertheless guilty in the teller's eyes. The men of Ulster referred to her as a "bad woman" for causing the exile of their best warriors, for annoying their king, and—so was the implication—for destroying the most sacred of male bonds through her sheer sexuality.[46] Her only vices seem to have been her beauty, which she was born with, and her impetuous love for Noísiu, which the teller sympathetically presented as genuine and deep, as her laments showed:

> I loved the modest mighty warrior,
> loved his fitting firm desire,
> loved him at daybreak as he dressed
> by the margin of the wood. . . .
> I don't sleep now,
> nor redden my fingernails.
> What have I to do with welcomes?
> The son of Indal will not come.[47]

If Deirdriu died and caused the murder of Noísiu, it was partly because she also brought about their love and elopement in the first place. The heroines of *tochmarca* were just as beautiful as Deirdriu and loved their men as just wildly, but they did not usually choose their men, seek them out, and force them to elope.

Two kinds of extralegal coupling appeared in the formal love tales. Neither adhered to legal norms or custom, although courtships led to legitimated unions and *aitheda* led to trouble. The thematic difference between the two tales derived from the depiction of their heroines. The *aitheda* featured uppity women who seized control of a love affair, turning private passion into public event and thus driving men to kill each other.[48] On at least one level, the literati's message appears obvious: sexually aggressive women threatened men and the society that men had engineered.[49]

In other kinds of tales besides *aitheda*, however, women initiated sexual encounters without killing themselves or their lovers, or if a few men died for love of them, they themselves were none the worse for it. In *Serglige Con Cu-lainn* (The wasting sickness of Cú Chulainn), for example, the otherworldly temptress Fand reduced Cú Chulainn to a moaning mess for love of her; then she enticed him to the otherworld, where they enjoyed a fortnight's affair before his wife, Emer, won him back.[50] Granted, Fand did not get her man permanently and she suffered emotionally, but neither of the lovers died or was even much damaged, despite Cú Chulainn's sadomasochistic lashing. Each returned to his or her respective spouse. Possibly Fand incurred no blame because, like Becfola, she operated according to unearthly rules. Still, despite the heavy mythological connotations they carried, women like Fand made the entirely human decision to ignore laws of coupling, which, anyway, contained no provisions for seduction by *mná síde,* "women of the otherworld."

Medb, heroine of the *Táin Bó Cuailnge, Cath Bóinde,* and a series of related tales, seems to have been entirely exempt from the consequences of her own sexual advances and adventures. She lent out her "friendly thighs" whenever it benefited or pleased her.[51] In fact, the last of Medb's many husbands was her own foster son, whom she raised until she could seduce him.[52] The parallel with Conchobar, who unsuccessfully tried to raise Deirdriu to be his lover, could hardly be coincidental. Granted, their stories had different morals and functions; still, apparently the literati's censure of the middle-aged Conchobar in a similar situation did not apply to Medb. She, like Fand, may have been beyond the reach of mortal moralists.

Even the Christian literati could be sympathetic to aggressive adulteresses and fornicators in the right circumstances. The tenth-century tale of Liadain and Cuirithir told the story of fruitless negotiation and broken vows. Two professional poets, one a woman named Liadain, met while touring the country. Cuirithir asked her to sleep with him; she refused for, it appears, professional reasons, agreeing to rendezvous after her tour. She seems to have had second thoughts, though, for when Cuirithir appeared again Liadain had become a nun. In response, Cuirithir became a monk. They tried some sexless friendship under the spiritual direction of a cleric, but failed and fell into each others' arms. Eventually, Cuirithir ran off in pilgrimage to avoid her and Liadain lamented:

> Hide it not.
> He was my heart's desire—
> If I loved the world beside.
>
> A surge of fire
> Has split my heart.
> Without him it will never survive.

The blame belonged to her, according to the poet, who put in her mouth another verse: "Unpleasing the deed I have done: The one I loved I have grieved." If she had kept her promise to tryst instead of taking the veil, Liadain might have avoided tragedy. She so regretted her actions that she died of heartbreak.[53]

The pseduohistorian of the *Lebor Gabála Érenn* (Book of the Invasions of Ireland) recognized a husband's sexual neglect as an excuse for a woman to look elsewhere for love:

> Honey with a woman, milk with a cat,
> food with one generous, meat with a child,
> a wright within and an edge[d tool]
> one before one, 'tis a great risk.

> The woman will taste the thick honey,
> the cat will drink the milk. . . .
> wherefore it is right
> to guard them well from the beginning.[54]

Their occasional approval of extramarital sex suggests that the literati were not using *aitheda* and *tochmarca* to make any facile Freudian point about threatening women, nor were they simply manipulating otherworldly female characters as metaphors for other conflicts in Irish society.[55] They were writing about gender, sex, and romance in order to titillate and as part of many other literary and mythological agendas, but tale-tellers were also describing extraordinary approaches of fictional women and men to union. It was not their purpose to critique the laws, but while they were spinning their tales, often nominally about other topics, the authors happened to mention an entire behavioral range that was extralegal or illegal particularly as regards the actions of women, and yet sometimes tolerable to the early Irish. In many kinds of narratives, although women may not have initiated the affair, they certainly cannot be called passive in their sexual responses to men or in their bargaining for terms of the union. Nor were they all long-suffering victims of male desire, waiting stoically to be bestowed upon either the right or the wrong man, depending on the whim of their guardians. A series of love-hungry women met with Cú Chulainn in the Ulster cycle; everyone from servant girls to his martial-arts instructor copulated with him, although not always willingly.[56] In literature, then, sex was something sought and enjoyed freely by both women and men, married or single, sometimes with no negative social repercussions. In the tenth-century *Esnada Tige Buchet* (The songs of Buchet's house), the future king of Temair, Cormac mac Airt, tried to negotiate a formal union with Eithne, foster daughter of Buchet, but she would have nothing to do with him. Nonetheless, Cormac eventually abducted, raped, and impregnated her. Although Eithne then escaped, she agreed to marry him, apparently with her guardian's blessing. She may not have initiated the encounter with Cormac, but she did not regret it either, for it brought no shame to her, no tragedy to Cormac or anyone else, but fair compensation to Buchet and a lot of feasting and general good cheer.[57]

Whatever the function of coupling in a particular tale, lovers and lovemaking, sex and romance pervaded the narratives of early Ireland. The literati enjoyed lacing their adventure tales with sexual episodes, spicing Cú Chulainn's battles with the light relief of love affairs or ascribing the otherwise uneventful births of famous kings to incestuous unions and gang rapes.[58] Adultery between Medb and the Ulster hero Fergus mac Róich made the *Táin* even more exciting than it already was. Illicit love affairs even helped to enliven the vitae of saints.[59] By and large, storytellers represented passion between men and women as mutual, often delightful, and above all, quite commonplace. The ecstatic coupling of the love tales must also have brought vicarious pleasure to audiences of the stories. Indeed, the themes of irresistible desire and illicit coupling were so prominent in the literature that we might almost begin to believe in their social reality.

But the narratives told only one of the several stories of coupling that circulated in early Ireland. The wild, lawless, bodice-ripping love in elopement and courtship stories was in complete and conscious, although not necessarily deliberate, contradiction to the rules set down in secular laws, ecclesiastical canons, and social custom. Whereas the tales themselves differed in their treatment of shifting gender roles at any given stage of the coupling process, both *tochmarca* and *aitheda* portrayed a special kind of union that overcame social hindrances or at least challenged convention.

In laws and canons, women were passive and almost invisible participants in loveless exchanges between men. The legal ideal lacked both the women and the passion so overwhelmingly present in narratives. In effect, legal writers restricted not only the involvement of women but the passion that women brought with them. According to laws and Christian mores, marriage could lead to love, but marriage contracts had nothing to do with the useless desire inspired or practiced by women. Storytellers, on the other hand, observed no similar gender-specific limits. And it is at this point of artifical dissonance in the sources—the seeming tension between the limitless erotic coupling of narratives and the legal restrictions on coupling—that we can move from text to social reality and begin to outline actual practice in early Ireland.

The Limits of Coupling

By examining the variety of restrictions imposed by writers of laws, canons, and penitentials, we can better understand not just the tension among different approaches to coupling but also the relation of representations to reality. More than just a traditional double sexual standard was at work in setting the formal limits to coupling. Community needs and religious feeling also helped set social and sexual boundaries.

To begin with, all the proscriptive texts used the limits of coupling to send messages about what was good for the society and the individual in early Ireland. If the positions of lawmakers differed or even contradicted one another, it was not because they expressed a tug-of-war between pagan and Christian moralities, as some historians have claimed.[60] Nor did the moral messages that lay behind the limits on coupling differ so much according to the gender of the intended audience as might at first appear. The simple fact is that men, whether the tellers of love tales, the makers of laws, or those who read and heard these texts had no single opinion about the effects of coupling. They could not agree whether coupling was positive or negative, just that it was necessary. They reached no consensus about how the community might control bethrothal and marriage, about the inevitability of illicit love, about the benefits of passion. They could not even determine what exactly happened to them when they came together with women.

Nonetheless, out of their confusion arose a few shared assumptions, mainly regarding the need for, and effectiveness of, rules. The love stories, as we have seen, set only a few guidelines for successful consummation. The lovers were generally of free and noble birth, wealthy, and beautiful. The couple consisted of one male and one female, although the tale-tellers offered no negative examples of failed unions between partners of the same sex or, for that matter, partners of different classes or between a good-looking and a hideously ugly partner. The most important restriction suffered by literary characters was the taboo against taking another man's wife or betrothed; yet even this restriction was violated regularly by the heroes of *tochmarca* and *aitheda*. The storytellers did not specify approved or improper methods of wedding or lovemaking or set limits on when lovers could couple. They did suggest, with *aitheda,* that adultery or abduction was most safely practiced beyond the bounds of society, in woods or caves. That was common sense more than restriction, given that the Irish lived in one- or two-room houses utterly lacking the privacy necessary for clandestine sex.[61]

Although the couples of romance were generally free to tryst when, where, how, and with whom they would, those who tried to couple according to early Irish laws, canons, and penitentials were caught in a discouraging net of restrictions. The aim of lawmakers, both religious and secular, was to promote the heterosexual procreative couple as the basis of society. Secular lawyers considered the union between a free man and his primary wife (*cétmuinter*) the most socially valuable and that between a man and his fertile secondary wife (*adaltrach*) second best. Although even canonists allowed for polygyny, both they and secular jurists (who may well have been the same men) clearly gave highest approval to the primary union between a propertied man and woman of the same noble class.[62]

The legal texts also revealed, however, that couples sometimes formed less normative unions. That the literate elite disapproved of these unions is plain from the low social value assigned them in the laws and from the legal hindrances that jurists placed in the way of non-normative couples. Lawyers, canonists, and penitentialists all sought to determine who could love whom. Although the rule makers sometimes disagreed on details, their common purpose seems to have been to prevent the clash between the desires of individuals and the needs of the larger community. Free choice of mates carried all sorts of dangerous political implications in a society where elite unions were used as tools for crafting alliances, and deeply threatened a social order based on the orderly production of heirs and distribution of family property. As a result, rule makers idealized the married procreative couple formally approved by kin groups and other authorities.

Nonetheless, even outside saga, love and sex sometimes compelled women and men to bend the rules and disregard the perceived needs of the community. For secular lawyers, the worst rule breakers were those who coupled with the wrong partners; legal writers paid little attention to the how, where, and when of coupling. For example, the laws acknowledged a variety of unions concluded between a woman and a man of whom her kin either did not approve or did not know.[63] Now, it is true that other motives besides passion might have caused a woman to run off with a man. She might, for example, have viewed him as a potentially more successful economic partner than a spouse chosen by her parents. She might have had her own political reasons for abhorring an arranged union. She might have found her own choice less personally loathsome than other approved marriage choices. She might just have wished to make her own selection among the available men, or to annoy her kinsmen by taking someone unsuitable. But surely women in early Ireland also fell in love, as the narratives claimed, and, despite the force of custom, sometimes acted rashly upon their feelings.

That men also sometimes married, for their own reasons, women legally denied them is clear from the laws, which made provisions for legitimating the abduction of nubile women.[64] In many cultures, abduction and elopement provide ways for bride, groom, and both kin groups to manipulate formal marriage customs and laws; even when such unions are labeled bad or illegal in formal laws, they can be common and generally acceptable.[65] This understanding makes the type of union between Cú Chulainn and Emer, for instance, seem more realistic than its boisterous saga setting suggests. The very fact that such illicit unions could be formalized in early Ireland shows that the actions of love-smitten Emer, who colluded in, if not masterminded, her wooing, were familiar and legitimate to the audiences of both *tochmarca* and laws; also Deirdriu's behavior was not completely inexplicable. It further suggests that individual women and men, their social strategies, and their emotions had a greater influence on social processes than lawmakers liked to admit.

If passion sometimes inspired abduction, it could well have been the same inspiration that propelled people into legitimate unions with minimal social and legal value. Legal writers determined the validity and social standing of these lesser unions according to the class or status of those involved, which kin group claimed the woman, and whether the children produced by the couple had access to family property. For example, sons produced by men and the women called variously *meirdrech, baítsech, bé táide,* and *echlach* (all of which translate roughly as "wanton" or "whore" and referred to women of inferior legal standing) were normally unable to inherit from their fathers.[66] The penitentialists, corroborating the jurists, referred to these interclass relationships as *fornicatio* between free men and unmarried women. Although the act was illicit, the light penances set for it also suggest that it was common or at least not seriously threatening to the ideal society that penitentialists as well as jurists hoped to create and maintain.[67] According to the laws, unions of equally low worth also included those between a woman of good family and a man with no social standing, such as a slave, a foreigner (*cú glas*), or an outlaw. Without the promise of property or heirs to inspire such unions, men and women must have formed these relationships for one of two reasons: profit or personal attraction. But lawyers worked hard to limit the exploitation of marriageable free men and women by promiscuous women and foreigners and to make misalliances unprofitable. They limited inheritance by children of such unions and restricted the involvement of kinfolk in helping to raise the children.[68] Considering the difficulties they risked, nothing but sexual attraction must have moved many of these couples.

However déclassé interclass relations between freemen and "whores" or between freewomen and outlaws may have seemed to the rule makers, they were at least legally tolerable. However, lawyers, canonists, and penitentialists set stern limits on coupling among other sorts of persons. All the rule makers refused to legitimate adulterous couples, incestuous unions, or couples of the same sex, although lawyers disagreed with canonists and penitentialists on some crucial details, particularly regarding adultery.[69]

For example, if a married woman formed an illicit union with another lover, the betrayed spouse could gain a legal divorce; according to the canons, however, the adulteress could be repudiated but not divorced. Canonists made no provisions for an adulterous husband, but secular lawyers allowed a woman to divorce a man who committed either adultery or homosexual acts. Canonists also ordered the cuckold to take back an adulteress if she repented, but the laws made no such moral injunctions.[70] The penitentialists sided with their fellow clerics, making frequent condemnations of adultery and urging men to take back their adulterous but penitent wives.[71]

The prominence of adultery in laws, canons, and penitentials, whether it led to divorce or penance and reconciliation, made clear that it was both taboo and yet common. No canonist could sanction a practice so contrary to Christian ideals, but the monastic annalists took it for granted that married men and women of the highest birth made, broke, and made anew marriages for the purposes of political alliance. There was, for instance, Fland, daughter of the king of Osraige and wife successively to three other kings.[72] Her granddaughter, Gormflaith, married Cormac mac Cuilennáin, king of Munster; Cerbaill mac Muirecáin, king of Leinster; and Níall Glúndub mac Aeda Findléith, king of Temair. Even better known was Gormflaith, wife to Brian Bóruma, early eleventh-century high king, after being married to his predecessor and to the Viking king of Dublin; and the twelfth-century Derbforgaill, wife of Tigernán Úa Ruairc, who let herself be abducted by Diarmait mac Murchada, king of Leinster.[73] Nonetheless, based as it was on passion with the wrong person, adultery could never lead to legitimated unions like those formed by abduction or the illicit courtship of an unmarried woman. Not even secular lawyers allowed an adulterer or adulteress to divorce simply in order to marry a lover, although in the love stories, as we have seen, it was common enough for men and women simply to abandon one spouse for another.[74] Presumably, reality lay somewhere in between.

Even worse than coupling with a married man or woman, to lawmakers, were passion and sex between blood or affinal kin.[75] This is one of the most obvious points of disagreement between rules and stories of coupling and among the rule makers themselves. Again, mythological messages had much to do with the characterization of incest in sagas and saints' lives, where women coupled with their fathers or brothers—sometimes more than one— to produce kingly heroes and holy men.[76] Although secular lawyers promoted endogamous marriage among members of the same extended kin group in order to preserve the group's property, they did not condone incest among close blood relations. One fragment of a legal text referred to the exposure of children born of incestuous unions.[77] This reference suggests that the formal Christian definition of incest, which churchmen throughout barbarian Europe spent centuries trying to promote, may have influenced secular lawmakers, although there were plenty of non-Christian reasons for disposing of problematic babies. Canonists echoed lawyers in their sanction of limited endogamy, but some Irish penitentialists forbade marriage within four degrees of consanguinity.[78] Church councils continued to condemn Irish "incest" among cousins and other more distant relations well into the Middle Ages, revealing a deeply felt ambivalence about consanguinity as well as the long-lasting custom of marriage within extended kin groups.[79]

Neither lawyers nor canonists nor penitenialists felt any ambivalence about same-sex couples, however. The laws included no homosexual or lesbian couples among legitimate *lánamnae,* and referred to homosexual acts as valid grounds for a wife to seek a divorce.[80] Canonists made no explicit references to homosexual couples, but the penitentialists spent many pages condemning what they labeled the sexual act of sodomy between two men or boys, although they did not once refer to a long-term union or couple consisting of two men or two women.[81] The legal prohibitions against a husband's homosexual acts make it plain that same-sex couples were taboo, although neither secular nor ecclesiastical legal texts frowned so heavily on sexual relationships between women. An eleventh- or twelfth-century anecdote from the *Book of Leinster* told how one woman had "playful mating" (*lánamnas rebartha*) with another women who had just had intercourse with a man, and consequently became pregnant from transferred semen. Although their sexual contact became public, the women suffered no apparent punishment.[82]

Legitimate couples, then, consisted of an unrelated man and woman joined in marriage or, less respectably, formal concubinage with the approval of both kin groups. Community needs and religious sentiment dictated these controls. Secular jurists, canonists, and penitentialists all worked to promote the legitimate monogamous procreative couple that produced the next generation under an approving public eye. Incorrect couplings jeopardized this process.

Lawmakers had no interest in promoting affective unions between any two people who desired each other. Yet both jurists and the authors of religious texts had to admit that affection and desire sometimes propelled the most proper of matches or, at least, grew from the sanctioned mating of appropriate partners. Churchmen throughout Europe promoted a Pauline marriage of companionship and affection so that ordinary Christians might satisfy their yearnings without committing *fornicatio.*[83] Saints' lives allowed that the marriages of ordinary people could be affective and that husband and wife exchanged advice, comfort, and many other kinds of support along with love.[84] Although hagiographers had a Christian ideal of marriage to uphold, the secular laws providing for the dissolution of unhappy marriages on grounds of incompatibility seem to corroborate the expectation of affection.[85] Further support comes from *Senbríathra Fíthail,* that primer of good sense and appropriate wives, which admitted a little boldly that "true love is better than hereditary right."[86]

In fact, a marriage that developed into a love match or at least a friendly partnership could prevent the calamity of rule-breaking passion. The very possibility of a happy marriage must have caused lawyers, canonists, and penitentialists to work even harder to prevent the unrestricted coupling of illicit lovers. They accomplished their aims by regulating as thoroughly as possible the social alliance they called marriage and by eliminating from the formal process the volatile elements of desire and women. Passion transformed the legitimate into the unlawful, the sane into the frenzied, the normal into the unpredictable and uncontrollable either by law or by morals. Christian theorists such as Jerome, one of the Irish canonists' favorites, had long distrusted passion as a source of sin and utter disorder, but storytellers were just as suspicious of it.[87] The character of passion was, in fact, exactly the character of women as described by writers of *tecosca:* legally of little value, impossible to categorize, define, or control, always liable to upend hierarchies, and destructive to a society engineered by men.

Hence, the key to the vast interpretative differences between formal legal coupling and the literary intepretation of coupling lies in the sources of, and blame for, passion. Although both men and women initiated sex and love in the love stories, although both participated equally, women were associated with the worst kinds of passion. Certainly Christian theologians in Ireland and elsewhere had warned of this conceptual link for centuries, and as we shall see, one vicious strain of clerical thought in early Ireland constantly equated women with sex and sin. Not only Irish theologians, however, but also both the writers of love stories and the makers of secular and ecclesiastical laws promoted this cconnection between women and wrongheaded passion. The authors of different texts simply placed different value on variables in the equation. The heroines of love stories, the passion they experienced and inspired, and the passive role of women in the legal texts on coupling all point to such a symbolic equation. Women brought passion, and passion brought the kind of ruinous social disorder that could descend upon unwary men at any moment. This feminine-inspired disorder was repeatedly enacted in narrative literature but outlawed by the texts of the religious and secular lawmakers.

The Effects of Coupling

Two things complicated the ambivalent association of women with passion and social disorder. First, as the literati admitted, women, love, sexual desire, and its consummation were often all very pleasant to experience, to write about, and to read about. In literature, *tochmarca* turned out happily for everyone, audience included, except the guardians of the rules of coupling. The rule-breaking couple gained the greatest rapture of all. Second, and more important, the affective coupling of story had transformative effects, some legally disastrous, but some both personally and socially positive. For the male and female characters who survived sexual unions, such as Cú Chulainn and Emer, or Midir and Étaín, desire and affection in conjuction with legitimate unions brought about beneficial changes in their social, economic, and emotional status. Yet even the fugitive couples of *aitheda* enjoyed brief happiness before social bonds recaptured them. Diarmaid and Gráinne may have broken all the rules and ended their story, respectively, dead or depressed, but they were unarguably the heroes of their tale. They managed to form a union, albeit temporary, despite all the other social ties of lordship, marriage, and community which worked to prevent it. What is more, their love became legendary; everyone knew their tragic story, which has outlasted even the rules formed to prevent their *aithed*. Thus, in the eyes of the early Irish, both desire and the women who brought it were potentially positive as well as potentially destructive for the men of the love tales, even when the creation of a couple came at the expense of the individual lovers as well as the community or society in general.[88]

In real life, as the literati knew well, both men and women were socially transformed by any kind of coupling, but lustful and affective coupling caused the most profound metamorphoses. Men who formed legitimate unions with women were changed from sons to husbands and fathers, from dependents or outcasts to stable householders, from those who took from society to those who created, renewed, and sustained it. Men who were enticed into eloping with women or who were unable to legitimate another kind of illicit union such as an abduction or rape were also transformed, but less happily—into criminals or outlaws or even dead men. But in stories, men who coupled lovingly, passionately, regardless of the legitimacy of their unions, were the most marvelously transformed, at least, within the confines of the literature. They lost control of themselves, and at the same time, the laws of marriage and the rules of sex also lost hold of them. Rather than anonymous followers of laws and canons, they became Cú Chulainns, Midirs, and Diarmaits, made heroic, sometimes tragically, by desire for a willful woman.

Love tales showed men that it was possible, if perilous, to escape the whole force of law, religion, and tradition and to achieve a range of social maneuvering largely unknown in the kin-dominated communities of early Ireland. Through passionate coupling with a woman, would-be heroes could achieve a dubious freedom from the community that both contained and protected them—and in early medieval Europe, freedom was by no means an unambiguous condition—to accept or reject social rules about sexual relations. The more they defied the rules, the more dangerous they became, and the more likely that society would destroy them. Even heroes of *tochmarca* had to judge just how far across the boundaries to venture. It is significant, in this respect, that the heroic wooers of courtship tales usually caused chaos not in their own communities but in the distant communities of their affections' objects.

Once men followed rule-breaking females and liberated themselves from the laws and canons of coupling, they might negotiate with their women and achieve relations more equitable and more fulfilling than written rule and custom would otherwise have allowed. At least this was the promise of story. Deirdriu, then, was both a positive and a negative figure for the audiences of *Loinges Mac nUislenn:* she misbehaved and broke the rules, but she also loosened the social bonds that constrained Noísiu to obey Conchobar, his lord, and to wait for a more suitable bride.

Coupling transformed women, too, in some ways more thoroughly. The physical changes were profound. They lost their hymens, if they had not already; one of the "three whose spirits are highest," according to the *Triads,* was the girl who had just "been made a woman."[89] They also got pregnant, gave birth, and lactated. The cultural and social changes were even more meaningful since they directly involved the entire community. Virgins became women, moving from that dubiously gendered liminal state to become fully female.[90] Daughters became mothers—an important, if not the most important role for women in early Ireland. Members of father's kin became members of husband's kin, gaining a new home, a new family, new allies, and new enemies. From propertyless dependents worth half of their fathers' honor prices, women could become wielders of dowry, *coibche,* and *tinnscra*—still worth only half a man legally but with an economic standing that allowed for wide extralegal maneuvering.

And when affection and desire guided their coupling, women were even more fundamentally transformed. From a mere absence in the legal process of coupling, they became participants in and even mistresses of their own destinies and that of their mates. The sovereignty tales of early Ireland, as we shall see in some detail, described hags made gorgeous, man-eaters made loving mothers, and impersonal female characters transformed into the very principle of lordship, all by the simple, glorious, earth-shaking process of coupling. Thus, for women, the love tales also signaled the social opportunities that existed beyond and outside the oppressive laws of coupling. None but a few fools could have believed that love and sex actually happened the way they did in traditional *tochmarca, aitheda,* or other love stories, but narrative romances intimated that, at the very least, women and men recognized possibilities for coupling and gender relations beyond the laws.

None of the possibilities for transformation escaped the notice of the law-makers. They, at least, were never duped by passion. The jurists' and canonists' very restrictions and their exclusion of women, symbolic or real, from the formal legal process indicate their awareness of the powerful effects of coupling. Their attempts to control it make clear that they, too, believed it brought deep and irresistible change to individuals, communities, and society. And they wisely feared that this change, which both they and storytellers purposely expressed in a vocabulary of unruly wooers, was so dangerous and volatile that it could destroy even as it transformed. Storytellers may have encouraged this transformation or, at least, offered it as a viable alternative; legal writers feared its consequences. Indeed, the annals of early Ireland recounted more than one feud over women.[91] But as lawmakers also plainly realized, such peril always attended the fundamental realignment of a society's members. The dangers had to be faced because men and women were going to couple, sometimes passionately, no matter what restrictions rule makers placed in their way. Legal writers tried only to limit the negative effects, never to prevent the process.

In other words, the lawyers and storytellers of love were in most meaning-ful conflict. Laws and love stories were part of the same canon of coupling, and the signals of one genre's authors were recognized by the authors of other genres. Together the text makers defined the extremes. Their stories and rules reflected the constant negotiation between women and men about the social and sexual process of coupling. Together, rule makers, tale-tellers, and the men and women who coupled worked to balance the desires of lovers with the needs of community and society. Only considered together, particularly at the points of conflict over the roles of women and the limits of coupling, did laws and literature suggest the actual practice in early Ireland. The texts betrayed a professional legal class willing both to make and break the rules, a literati happy to raise romantic ideals only to smash them with social reality, and a society flexible about its own laws for the most intimate of gender rela-tions. What is more, only taken as a complex and sophisticated canon do the texts disclose, in their tensions and dissonances, the disparity between legal and romantic ideals and the possible reality of the love hungry, the sex crazy, and the objects of their desire.

4

Procreation Tales

physical love was a wonderful thing for couples who practiced it safely and conservatively. The wedding and bedding of a nobleman with his *cétmuinter,* accomplished with the blessing of both kin groups and conducted according to canonical guidelines, normally brought no evil social consequences. Affection was a mere complement to the union, but sex was crucial. And sexual intercourse, ultimately, lay at the root of the Irish ambivalence about coupling.

For sex, often as not, produced babies. More specifically, the early Irish believed that socially and religiously tolerable sex produced babies that were legitimate and desirable additions to families. The wrong kinds of sex did not or, more important, should not produce babies. Illicit sex, especially when indulged in purely for pleasure, could bring illness and even death to a body. What we conceive of as a physiology of sex, the early Irish believed to be a pathology of sex.

The profusion of Irish stories about sex and procreation, besides expressing the rules and fears of coupling, also reveal the hopes of a people obsessed with reproducing themselves. Some of these birth myths were more solemn, some more ancient, some more religious than others; some were expressed in descriptive and some in proscriptive terms. Yet, they all rehearsed a process of sexual intercourse, conception, pregnancy, and birth—although not always in that order and not always including all four steps.

The early Irish distinguished between different kinds of sex and the relation of these to pregnancy and birth. Besides differentiating between pleasurable but sterile sex and fruitful, procreative intercourse, they could certainly tell when normal conception and pregnancy had been unnaturally prevented by contraception or abortion. They also reserved special veneration for magical pregnancies that came of no sex. Rather than confusion, these diverse kinds of birth myths brought order to the fearsome mystery of reproduction. In fact, the birthing myths fall fairly neatly into five heuristic categories, each describing a model for procreation weighted with specific social meanings.

These concurrent models were neither specifically Christian nor secular. Nor, probably, were they entirely male creations. The sheer wonder and power of birthing was too pervasive and the ideologies of reproduction were too prominent for women to have had no part in producing the stories. Yet, if women's own birth stories lie submerged within male-authored texts, they were buried so deeply that they appear to modern readers only as tensions or contradictions in the narratives. For instead of giving insight on the actual childbirth experience of women, Irish stories of birth and babies tell us how men rehearsed the birth process.[1] In fact, procreation stories celebrated and justified men's attempts to mastermind the process of reproduction.[2]

The danger in studying procreation as a man's story with cultural, social, or political morals is twofold. First, we could forget the biosocial reality of birth in a specific historical context. A famous example of this mistake is Bronislaw Malinowski's assumption that the Trobriand Islanders, because they gave little cultural importance to biological fatherhood, were ignorant of it.[3] Second, we could succumb to one particular myth, attempting to interpret the entire culture through it. The few historians of early Ireland who have treated the subjects of birth and babies have been duped in this second way, tending to attribute sexual and procreative freedom to women and to assume that women derived high social status from bearing heroes and kings.[4]

Instead of reducing birth stories to a single message about women's experience and men's interpretation of it, we must exploit the diversity of the sources. All the birth stories reflected two dominant but contradictory themes. First, they told of the conflict between, on the one hand, the terrible destructive power of sex, especially the fruitless sex of unsuitable couples, and, on the other hand, the joyfully positive power of birthing in a society that longed desperately for babies. Hence, the fundamental concepts prominent in stories of procreation—desire and despair, birth and death, sex and society—allow us an unprecedented look into both the public mind and the most intimate chambers of early Ireland.[5] Second, the sources reveal a determination to produce those babies—that is, to persuade women to produce them—no matter what the cost to, or desire of, women.

Yet, precisely because regular, regulated reproduction was so fundamental to the sociopolitical organization of early Ireland, the overwhelmingly magical, multivalent power of birthing could never be fully contained by the tidy stories of the literati. Even when they tried, women simply did not always fit the reproductive roles tailored for them by men. Women retained procreative choices, both legitimate and subversive. They had their own not-so-mysterious reasons for bearing children. They also had their own strategies with which to counter men's organization of their labor. For how could those undefinable, unpredictable female creatures, those otherworldly, lustful, eloping brides-to-be, ever be bound to a single, orderly ideology of sexless procreation?

The Physiology and Pathology of Sex

Early Irish physiologies of sex, expressed in legal tracts and narratives, provide important background for stories of birth. Early Irish writers agreed with continental medical theorists on two main medical principles. First, as we have already seen, men and women had the same bodies, except that women's were deficient and less valuable. Second, just as passionate coupling could be dangerous to society, excessive sexual activity, like too much food or exercise, was dangerous to personal health.[6]

The Irish believed that moderate appetites kept a body healthy, but gluttony, physical exertion, or too much sex could weaken an ordinary man or woman. Although professional physicians may have had a good idea of excess and insufficiency, a variety of texts betrayed anxiety about calculating a healthy sexual regimen. Further, while some believed that even men found it difficult to order their sexual behavior, most of the literati were convinced that it was almost impossible for women to do so. As *Tecosca Cormaic* put it, women were "dermatcha seirce, ítfaide toile"—"forgetful of love, thirsting for lust."[7] In fact, the sources suggest that sex and its causes, love and lust, were so difficult to control that the early Irish sometimes regarded them as illnesses. Women, those passion mongers, were both victims and carriers of the disease. Of course, plenty of harmless sex appeared in the sources, but just as significant, the tellers of procreative tales repeated a persistently disturbing theme in both religious and secular literature: men and women copulated their way into illness and even to death.

For example, according to *Bretha Crólige*, which detailed the legal responsibilities of assailants toward their wounded victims, only three men were allowed to have a woman in attendance while they recuperated from their wounds. One was the male child of a nursing mother. The other two men, like unweaned babies, could not survive without their women; these unfortunates were *fer fora llither forcraid nétraid* ("a man who is accused of excess lust") and *sesmach pecta* ("a constant sinner"). They suffered from such excessive lust that, even while wounded, they had to have sex. To protect any nearby ladies and to promote the patient's recovery, the patient's own woman had to satisfy his needs in the sickbed.[8] *Sírechtach toile,* another kind of oversexed male patient mentioned in *Bretha Crólige,* was one of three persons so chronically ill that, even when wounded, his care devolved upon his own kin rather than his assailant; this "lustful longer" was in medical company with a madman and a quadriplegic.[9]

While the laws conceded special treatment to male "lustful longers," a woman who suffered from the illness of desire got no relief. *Bretha Crólige* made no provision for an amorous wife to bring her husband along while on sick maintenance. In fact, a woman so driven by lust that she "cares not with whom she sleeps," along with a female thief and a witch, deserved no compensation at all for her injury.[10] Such laws suggest the view that women were practically incurable, and other sources confirm it. The post-800 hagiographer of Saint Ciarán, for instance, was just one of many writers who assumed that women were prone to sexual excess. He described how the saint temporarily healed the queen of Munster of her adulterous passion for the king of Osraige but could not completely cleanse her body of lust; the infection continued to inflame her soul with sin, for which she was eventually punished with death.[11]

The rare woman could, with proper direction, cure her symptoms. Among the ninth-century anecdotes about the reforming monastic community at Tamlachta, was the story of Copar, upon whom *accobar,* Augustinian concupiscence, lay heavy. After three years of increasingly severe fasting at the order of Saint Molaise, she had chased the illness from her body so that, when pricked with a needle, not a drop of desire-bearing blood came out of her. Even the early Irish knew that no blood meant no life; Copar achieved nothing short of a medical miracle by ridding herself of liquid lust.[12]

For most men and women, though, the only real cure for desire was also its symptom. A little sex, like a modern inoculation, could revive a patient consumed by the heat of love. Male characters in the secular tales took to their beds when overcome by sexual longing, languishing there until a woman brought what they needed. In *Aislinge Oenguso* (The dream of Oengus), Oengus dreamed nightly of an otherworldly temptress. When a physician diagnosed his disease as love, Oengus could not be healed until he had found and slept with his woman.[13] Women who caught the disease suffered as badly as men but betrayed different symptoms. Instead of losing their strength, women inflamed by love became aggressive, uncontrollable, even mad. The cure for Deirdriu's feverish passion was Noísiu; she was ill until his body healed her. As for Noísiu, as we know, her cure was his downfall. He was happily minding his own business on the ramparts of Emain, singing the special chant-song of the young warrior when she tricked him into eloping with her. Once she infected him, Noisiu's chant became a shriek that roused warriors and ended in his own destruction and disaster for his people and land.[14]

Women stricken with longing but unable to satisfy their desires turned ugly.[15] The well-known female symbols of sovereignty who wandered through the pseudohistorical tales of early Ireland were hideous, barren hags until they copulated with the right royal aspirant. At the moment of consummation the loathly ladies turned into beautiful young women and the men became kings. The cycle of stories surrounding Mór Muman and her sister, Suithchern (or Ruithchern), provides an excellent example.[16] When at their most nubile, both sisters became deranged and roamed the land, seeking lovers. The sisters lost what the early Irish considered one of their most womanly attributes: their natural beauty, symbolic of their fertility. Clothed in rags, caked with the mud of the roads, each arrived at a king's hall where the foolish queen challenged her husband to sleep with the hag. When he did, the king discovered that his partner was a stunning princess whose lineage was better than the queen's, whom he then cast out. Both Mór and Suithchern regained their senses and their beauty. Whatever the political morals and other symbolic messages of these stories, the vocabulary was sexual healing.[17]

Such cures often had serious side effects, however, including sterility and impotence. Just as Deirdriu's sexual aggression turned Noísiu's song of prosperity into a death shriek, so a woman suffering from chronic excessive desire could lose the ability to reproduce. In the story of Uisliu's sons, Deirdriu bore no children. As continental physicians taught, a fetus was formed of the mingling of male and female seeds; yet even the most fertile woman was unable to conceive when the uncontrollable fire of lust lit her womb and boiled the seeds. Similarly, in early Irish tales, women's aggressive sexuality could impair men's ability to inseminate them.

The Irish seem to have feared promiscuous women for these very reasons. One highly ambivalent example is that chronic nymphomaniac Medb, queen of the Connachta, wife of nine husbands, and lover of Fergus mac Róich. In the earliest legends, Medb may have been a territorial goddess responsible for nurturing the land and its people.[18] The tenth-century text *Cath Bóinde* described Medb's husbands, each of whom she chose, made into a great king simply by copulating with him, and then discarded, but not before she bore some of her husbands many children.[19] Her name means "intoxicating" or "she who intoxicates"; she offered the drink of dominion from her own fertile body.[20]

But in *Táin Bó Cuailnge,* first written down around the eighth century, Medb's drink, like too much alcohol, could also rob a man of his virility. Her last husband, Ailill, she accepted because he was neither "greedy nor jealous nor sluggish." Indeed, Ailill was a pale shadow of a man who could neither best nor control his voracious queen and who reigned as her consort on her own patrimonial land.[21] In one famous scene of the *Táin,* Medb's lover, Fergus, had his sword stolen while having sex with her; the symbolism is obvious.[22] The saga's final image of Medb was more ambiguous. The queen squatted, pissing in the dust, while her lover, Fergus, and her enemy, the hero Cú Chulainn, mocked and insulted her. Urination carries connotations of sexual prowess in many cultures; and whatever Medb was doing, whether it was sexual, female, or just disgusting, was powerful enough to stop Cú Chulainn from killing her.[23] But too much of a good thing, even sex or urine, threatened both the men and women of early Ireland.[24] Medb's stream was productive, flowing into the land as rivers, but also polluting; it was called *fúal Medba,* literally the "urine flow of Medb." According to the fourteenth-century manuscript of the saga, which may well record an earlier interpretation, Medb's filthiness was not urine, but worse; she actually got her "gush of blood" either instead of urinating or while she urinated.[25] According to the menstrual mythology of premodern Europe—transmitted by, among others, Pliny and Isidore, the Irish favorite—Medb would thus have been unable to conceive. That intoxicating symbol of fertility had become a potentially barren dominatrix. She made her men impotent and was unable herself, according to at least one interpreter, to bear fruit.[26]

Luckily for Medb's lovers, none of them died as a direct result of following her "misguiding rump," but sex could and did kill.[27] Uncontrolled lust could bring the ultimate sterility of death. The legendary king of Ulster, Conchobar mac Nesa, died of a head wound, not from desire, but during his last days, the doctors ordered him to refrain from a variety of activities that could bring the end, including gobbling his food, flying into a rage, mounting a horse, and having sex with a woman.[28] And of course, Diarmaid and Gráinne, Deirdriu and Noísiu, and all those other tragic couples who eloped, believing that they could escape restrictive social networks, died as a result.[29]

These stories gave no simple warning about the hazards of love and sex. That was neither their purpose nor their primary message. But uncontrolled desire, usually initiated by a woman, and complicated by the rules of love and coupling, lurked somewhere in the chain of sad events that composed these tales. Desire brought death to the tales' protagonists, if not from specifically physiological causes, then from the pollution and disorder that accompanied illicit sex. Excessive desire disrupted the balance of both the body and society; it always resulted in dangerous sex, illicit sex, or both. This terrible idea is an elaboration of the ideologies of coupling and yet an argument with those ideologies; in the literature, by and large, only illicit couples had illicit sex, although not all illicit couples' sex was illicit. But the connection between wrong sex and the degeneration of the body is also one of the most enduring sexual myths in Western society. In the central Middle Ages, lustful sinners caught leprosy; after the sixteenth century, immoderate sex brought Frenchman's disease and other venereal diseases; and today, of course, AIDS kills some who supposedly deviate from sexual norms.

In the early Middle Ages the alternatives to dangerous sex were two: no sex or safe sex. Complete chastity had its proponents in early Ireland, as canons, penitentials, and saints' lives show.[30] But this literature was not meant to transform all Christians into saints.[31] The penitentialists prescribed exhaustive yet relatively light penalties for most sexual sins, even those committed by supposedly celibate churchmen.[32] This leniency suggests two notions among Irish theologians: first, that no one, not even those sworn to celibacy, could completely repress sexual desires and, second, that few could help consummating their desires one way or another. The saints' lives are full of fallen monks, wayward nuns, and adulterous laics who lost status, community, and sometimes more when their bodies got the better of them. Precisely because the hot blood of desire raced through their veins, most believers were destined to love, copulate, and produce new generations of Christians.

In keeping with continental theology and praxis, strictly Christian couples were not to have sex whenever they felt like it for the sake of their own pleasure. They were to engage in intercourse only on certain days of the religious calendar; their motive was to obey Genesis and be fruitful. Such observance prevented pollution of their union and risk to the safe production of future heirs.[33] For the great theologians such as Ambrose and Augustine, who inspired this sexual schedule, unchastity lay not only in the performance of sex but in thoughtless enjoyment of sexual intercourse at any time.[34]

The rule makers of coupling echoed these sexual guidelines, the common theme of which seems to have been a care for the physical well-being of copulators. Lawyers had little to say about a couple's sex life beyond promoting procreative sex and preventing a husband from blabbing the secrets of the marriage bed.[35] They did, however, insist that sex between the couple be voluntary. Rape, which for the early Irish was not a political act but either a particularly rambunctious form of intercourse or a form of property destruction, was intolerable to lawmakers except in cases where the victim invited or sanctioned it. If a man committed forcible rape (*forcor*) or in any other way subjected a woman to intercourse without her permission (*sleith*), he was liable to pay a fine to her guardian, calculated according to her legal status. For instance, if a man seduced a drunken woman, he was committing rape rather than creating a legal union, temporary or otherwise, with her; it seems that jurists recognized limits to a woman's passivity in legitimate coupling after all. If a woman was aggressive enough to visit an alehouse alone however, and, after drinking herself into oblivion, was raped there, she had effectively consented to a temporary union with any man present and had no legal redress. Nor did a promiscuous woman or an adulteress merit any compensation for rape. Presumably, by initiating illicit unions herself, a woman legitimated any other unions forced on her. By no legal means, however, could any violent rape become a long-term union; marriage by rape was not the same thing as marriage by abduction or what German historians have called marriage by capture. Only in the narratives, such as the tale of Cormac and Buchet's foster daughter, Eithne, could a man rape a victim who then became the happy bride of her assailant.[36]

Canonists and penitentialists imposed more far-reaching limitations on the sexual methods and satisfactions of couples, which they interpreted strictly as monogamous, heterosexual couples. Theoretically, their aim was to promote the health of the couple's souls. They tried to restrict sexual positions during copulation. They also forbade sex on the nights of Monday, Tuesday, Thursday, and Saturday except during the three forty-day fasts of the Christian calendar, when they permitted no sex at all. They allowed no intercourse during menstruation, pregnancy, or a for a month or two after childbirth.[37] Of course, illegitimate pairs had no legal or canonically correct time to copulate. In short, both jurists and religious rule makers, who worked so hard to control the coupling of men and women, also tried to restrict the physical consummation of passion even once a man and woman were legally joined. And as with the rules of coupling, strictures on sex derived not necessarily from any prudishness or Christian intolerance as from a sincere concern for the moral and physical health of the couple and the community.

The early Irish, like all early medieval Christians, were caught in a catch-22: for all but a chosen few, sex was dangerous and sinful but unavoidable. Sex polluted body and soul as well as, paradoxically, the reproductive process itself. This theology simply expressed the threat of sex, so obvious in the narrative texts, with a vocabulary of sin rather than a vocabulary of disease and death. The early Irish believed that their bodies could overcome their wills at any moment; the sight, sound, or even mention of the opposite sex could send the juices racing through their systems to erupt in a feverish fit of desire and love, relieved only temporarily by the physiologically and canonically correct dose of sexual activity. The ways to prevent this awful affliction were few and difficult, especially for women, for whom it was well nigh impossible. Yet such an outbreak of desire had lethal consequences for the individual, his or her object of lust, and potentially, the whole society. If too much sex brought disease and disaster, then abstinence, impossible to achieve for ordinary laboring lay people, often simply aggravated the condition. The only workable solution was to administer regulated doses of the medicine of sex—but how to determine exactly what constituted safe sex?

Procreative Models

In the literature, only one kind of sex usually ended safely: reproductive sex. In fact, the process of reproduction functioned as the exact opposite of dangerous sex in both secular and religious texts. Dangerous sex came of excessive lust and led to sterility, illness, and death; safe sex was legitimate, orderly, and above all, fruitful. For the early Irish, the very goal of safe sex was pregnancy and birth, which conveniently provided a means of controlling the sexuality of women while it produced the next generation. Yet the link between sex and birth was more complex than this theory suggests. Birth stories did more than warn against deviations from sexual and social norms.

To begin with, the Irish were well aware that pregnancy and childbirth were physically painful and dangerous to women. None of the sagas or king tales said so directly, but incidental information from saints' lives, ecclesiastical laws, and other texts shows that the literati were conversant with the physiological process of pregnancy and birth.[38] They also knew that women and their babies could suffer and even die. The early Irish worried about the pain of childbirth and knew that complications at parturition could be fatal.[39] Saint Gerald of Mag Eó was born clutching a massive blood clot that he had torn from his mother's guts on the way down the birth canal; other women presumably appealed to Gerald to save them from the same problem.[40] Harm could come to fetus as well as mother; the vitae referred to many babies born dead and later raised by saints, and to babies born disfigured or disabled.[41]

Demographic information, particularly sex ratios and birth rates, could help us assess the perceived perils of women's reproductive roles. Yet we have no idea how many people lived in Ireland and only guesses about even the broadest population trends, let alone sex ratios or birth rates. Figuring back from the Anglo-Saxon Domesday Book, we can cast the population of Norman Ireland at around 250,000 or more, although what percentage of that was female is impossible to say.[42] On the Continent, where meticulous Carolingian and Italian officials counted the peasants on their estates, the ratio of adult men to women ranged from 102 : 100 to as high as 156 : 100.[43] The normal ratio at birth is about 105 : 100, although in the modern West a lower ratio is considered normal for adults. A higher number of males to females, in any society, hints at peril for women—at best, poor health conditions that raise mortality rates from childbirth-related deaths; at worst, the neglect and murder of girl babies and women.[44]

The medieval continental statistics suggest all these conditions. For instance, on the estates of the abbey of Saint Victor at Farfa in the eighth century, the sex ratio at birth was 102 : 100; the ratio fell to 93 : 100 for young children, but rose to 105.8 : 100 for adolescents. That is, assuming the statistics are reliable, boy children did not survive childhood as well as girls, but young women died at a terrible rate once they passed menarche and reached childbearing age.[45] Among peasants reported at Saint Germain-des-Prés in the same period, the sex ratio rose in proportion to the number of inhabitants per household dependent upon a single manse; that is to say, the larger the group dependent upon a limited amount of land, the more likely that extra female mouths would be disposed of through infanticide or neglect. When a larger amount of arable land or a smaller number of other household members allowed, sex ratios fell. Only when families had enough surplus could they afford to keep their baby girls. Comparison of children's sex ratios and adult ratios on the same estates supports this dreadful conclusion.[46]

The single positive result of such population control was that adult women gained greater worth as reproducers. At Saint Germain, women of free status became desirable matches for lower-class men with enough property to support them, because their children's status derived from the mother. Social-climbing farmers could thus ensure the advancement of their offspring, and their wives became valuable again to their own kin.[47] This was not one of women's reproductive choices; women were not choosing to thin their own ranks in order to increase the economic value of female survivors. Because there were relatively few of them, however, barbarian free women with reproductive potential became a precious resource; they won high social status and economic liberties. Some Germanic laws set extremely high wergelds for women generally, but particularly for women of childbearing years. Women were probably as scarce in early Ireland as in the Frankish kingdoms or Italy.[48] Mothers in early Ireland were treasured, as we shall see in the next chapter. Irish hagiographers also told spicy stories of the abductions of nubile women and bemoaned parents' reluctance to allow women to enter nunneries; no one but the saints wanted women to waste their reproductive years in a convent.[49] Most women themselves chose to join a man in legitimate union and have babies, seeking the assorted benefits of motherhood despite an awareness that childbirth could be deadly.

Perhaps because of their well-justified anxieties, early Irish writers also perceived an otherworldly element to the birth process which reveals even deeper fears about procreation. Although they feared losing mother or child in the very act of birth, the literati were at least as worried about control over the act itself. Sex, conception, pregnancy, and birth were dangerous to women, never completely comprehensible to men, and thus magical. Fetuses screamed, prophesied, and celebrated mass in the womb.[50] The pregnant mothers-to-be of saints, suffused with spiritual joy, received visions of fireballs, breasts brimming with light, and cloaks of rainbows.[51] The supernatural connotations of pregnancy and childbirth were neither specifically Christian nor unchristian, but were sometimes both simultaneously. Eithne, mother of Saint Máedóc, gripped the *bacan na bainfighidh* ("weaver's hook") while in hard labor; afterward, the stick became a live hazel tree, and when the soil around it had nine masses chanted over it, that blessed soil could dissolve the chains of prisoners.[52] The mundane and magical, the pagan and Christian existed side-by-side in early Irish stories of birth.

In this way, Irish writers claimed that certain aspects of procreation were mysteriously incomprehensible. Deirdriu's mother summed it up when, heavy with that ill-fated fetus, her womb shrieked disaster. "No woman knows what her womb bears," she said.[53] But if mothers themselves did not understand, who did? Although the literati knew very well where babies came from, they were compelled to express the procreative process not with simple medical theory but in birth stories informed by the fear of sex and the occasional denial of the fact that women, who were physically and morally weaker than men, had at least some sort of precarious control over the mysteries of reproduction.

The ambiguous concept of childbirth in this premodern world led to a variety of explanations for what is, in our society, a straightforward physiological process. It is useful to consider Irish stories of procreation as falling into five separate but related models, each of which includes some, but not necessarily all, of four variables: sex, conception, pregnancy, and birth. The five models are: sex that did not lead to conception and pregnancy; sex that caused conception and pregnancy but not birth; sex that led to conception, pregnancy, and birth; sex performed specifically for the purpose of conception, pregnancy, and birth; and conception, pregnancy, and birth that occurred without sex.

The five models are neither random nor equally represented in the sources. The literati and their audiences clearly negotiated these models and the procreative ideologies that they represented; that is, everyone had different ideas about where babies came from, but it was left to the literati to create different types of birth stories and—because the Irish thought of procreation, like everything else, in terms of hierarchy—to choose only one type, the sexless model of the Virgin Mary, as the best.

The first model consisted of one variable only: sexual intercourse. It was a negative model, the disastrous model of Deirdriu and the *Táin*'s Medb (although not the fertile Medb of other texts), and of the sterile women and impotent men who appear in the vitae, canons, penitentials, and secular laws. In the laws, for instance, the word for "barren" (*sesc*) was a metaphor for someone or something worthless.[54] Laws and canons alike allowed the spouse of a barren woman or sterile man to divorce him or her.[55] In fact, the laws allowed the husband of an infertile woman to leave her temporarily and impregnate another woman in order to produce heirs; this may be a more orthodox version of other laws that allowed polygamy for the same purpose.[56] Theoretically, a woman whose husband was impotent could also leave him temporarily in order to conceive by another man.[57] In the context of canons that forbade adultery and laws that permitted an unfaithful wife to be repudiated, this formal emphasis on the value of reproductive sex is significant indeed.[58]

In the second procreative model, sex led to conception and pregnancy but not birth. This, too, was a partially negative model. Laws, canons, and penitentials all condemned contraception and abortion. The canonists spoke darkly of *potationes diabolicae* that prevented women from conceiving or that induced abortion.[59] These canons were completely consistent with the Christian theology of the early Middle Ages, as James Brundage and John T. Noonan have shown, and with the desperate need to produce legitimate heirs which, David Herlihy has demonstrated, was felt so keenly in barbarian societies.[60]

Yet this second procreative model was not completely negative. Abortion took place, if not commonly, then at least often enough to appear without comment in both secular and ecclesiastical sources. The life of Saint Ciarán, probably written not long after 800, told the story of a young virgin, Bruinech, kidnapped and rapped by Dímma, king of Cenél Fiachach. She became pregnant and appealed to Saint Ciarán, who miraculously aborted the fetus ("impresso ventri eius signo crucis, fecit illud exinaniri").[61] Later and less candid versions of this vita showed Ciarán simply making the fetus disappear rather than aborting it.[62]

The birth story of the hero Cú Chulainn displayed a similarly blasé attitude toward abortion. The hero's mother Deichtine at first conceived a child by swallowing a tiny symbolic creature and then dreaming of the god Lug. When rumors flew about the possibility of incest between the pregnant unmarried Deichtine and her brother Conchobar, she agreed to wed one of Conchobar's men, Sualdam. Ashamed at climbing into the marriage bed pregnant, Deichtine somehow ended the pregnancy, either vomiting up the fetus or rolling onto her stomach and crushing it.[63] These tales suggest that the early Irish were aware of and, in some cases, may sometimes even have approved of consciously controlled fertility. Irish clerics took an ambivalent stance on fertility control, condemning infanticide and abortion but assigning lighter penalties for fornication that did not lead to pregnancy and childbirth.[64]

The third procreative model was the one we take as the sociobiological norm: sexual intercourse that led to conception, pregnancy, and birth. This is the model implicit in the scores of folios of early Irish genealogical manuscripts, and in the unremarkable depiction of families that occured in narratives of all kinds. The laws and canons, with their insistence on the orderly distribution of property to legitimate heirs, also embodied this model. Indeed, D. A. Binchy, among other historians, has declared the entire society to be "familiar" in the sense that it employed a kinship vocabulary of patrilineal descent for its political organization.[65] Most married couples in early Ireland wanted male children for heirs; those Christians who could not produce them and who rejected divorce or polygamy begged the help of the saints. The parents of Saint Máedóc, like many other childless couples, gave abundant alms to various monasteries in hopes that the monks would intercede with the saints who, in turn, would demand that God grant them a son.[66]

Yet this procreative model was not wholly positive either. Not everyone could engage without censure in sex that led to conception, pregnancy, and childbirth. As we have seen, social class, kinship ties, and religious vocation determined who could sleep with whom, if with anyone. Ultimately, only sane, monogamous, married laywomen could legitimately indulge in sex—and only with their husbands—that led to conception, pregnancy, and birth. On the other hand, cleric or layman could sleep with his own wife, as well as with an unmarried laywoman, so long as she was not related to him by blood, and produce an acceptable heir.[67]

Yet the sources show that the early Irish found it difficult to procreate within these restrictions. Illicit couples produced babies. When they did, they had to choose whether to raise a child who brought shame to themselves and who may have faced a future without status or property, or to destroy the child. The ambivalence of the texts concerning sex thus carried over to attitudes toward pregnancy and birth and their products. Sex could be dangerous or sinful, but even relatively safe sex led to unacceptable pregnancies. Some babies were welcomed, others disposed of, not always because of some defect in the children themselves, but because of the circumstances that created them. It seems that sex could be fatal not only for those who enjoyed it but also for those born of it.

The fourth model contained little ambiguity, sexual or moral. In this model, a man and a woman had sexual intercourse for the sole purpose of creating a child. As we have seen, this was the Christian ideal for devout laics. But this model, in which sex had a reproductive purpose, was not exclusively a theological notion. It also found expression in the secular literature, which held that some days and certain partners were propitious for conception.[68] In the story of Conchobar mac Nesa's birth, the princess Nes was sitting outside her father's hall one day when the druid Cathbad strolled by. What was the day lucky for, Nes asked him. Begetting a king on a queen, he told her. The day was also lucky for Cathbad, since he was the only man around. Together, Nes and Cathbad produced Conchobar, future king of Ulster.[69] The story of Liadain and Cuirithir represented a variation on this theme, showing what happened when people missed their chance to engage in reproductive sex on the right day.[70] As the unhappy couple discovered, failure to engage in safe sex and produce a much-needed heir could prove as dangerous as indulging in the wrong kind of sex.

Liadain and Cuirithir were exceptions, however, for the only real shadow over this fourth procreative model was the one that hovered over all sexual activity. According to canonists and penitentialists, any conception and any pregnancy were by nature polluting. Pregnant and recently delivered women, bearing evidence of their sins, were excluded from holy places, in keeping with Leviticus.[71] Even women who were neither pregnant nor nursing—that is, all other women—could corrupt holy places by their very history of, or potential for, sex and childbearing. Again, drawing on the Old Testament, canonists barred all women from the *sanctum sanctorum*.[72] Women in the vitae of Máedóc and Aed were punished for washing their clothes, their hair, or their bodies in the vicinity of monasteries.[73] In practical terms, bathing women were a temptation to monks because they were naked, but in symbolic terms, the women represented the defilement of things sacred and the disorder of the otherwise neatly arranged, male-focused cosmos. Sin could flow down the polysemic stream from the women to the clerics.[74]

The fifth and last procreative model resolved all tensions between the dangers of sex and the urge to reproduce. This model depicted conception, pregnancy, and birth accomplished without sex. This was the achievement of the Blessed Virgin, whose image was manipulated by theologians from early in the spread of Christianity, and whose "strong fortress" of chastity the ninth-century *Félire Oenguso* (Martyrology of Oengus) praised.[75] But the holy mother was not the only woman to conceive without sex. Both Deichtine, Cú Chulainn's mother, and a character in the mythological *Tochmarc Étaíne* (Wooing of Étaín) became pregnant by acts symbolic of sex: they drank liquids in which tiny creatures floated, swallowing the creatures and thus conceiving.[76] *Félire Oenguso,* copied from continental models, described several similar examples of divinely inspired conception without physical intercourse, but through acts symbolic of sex: a woman swallowed a star, golden light, a salmon, or cress covered with semen.[77]

A pseudohistorical tale of the birth of a late sixth-century king, Aed Sláine, showed the same sexless procreative model in the capable hands of Christian clerics. In this story, Mugain, a secondary wife of Diarmait mac Cerbaill, sought the help of two saints when she was cursed and made unable to conceive. Mugain was afraid that Diarmait would abandon her if she could not bear him heirs. The saints, Aed and Finnian, gave her blessed water to drink, promising that she would become pregnant; nowhere did the text mention sexual intercourse. Mugain drank the water, became pregnant, and gave birth, but to a lamb. Understandably annoyed, she returned to the saints, who explained that the lamb symbolized Christ, and gave her another drink. Mugain again conceived and gave birth, this time to a salmon. Aed and Finnian took the fish away and gave the skeptical Mugain another drink of holy water, which she also bathed in. The result was Aed Sláine, one of the legendary kings of early Irish history.[78] Rather than polluting a pure river, Mugain, under clerical guidance, was herself made pure by her bath; the saints washed her clean of any sexual stains and thus facilitated her exceptional pregnancy.

This last procreative model was the complete opposite of the first barren but sexual model. That model, ruled by lust and women, produced nothing but danger and sins. This fruitful model, guided by gods or male saints, led to the births of heroes, kings, and Jesus Christ. Between these two extremes were most types of procreation: sex, conception, and pregnancy that usually and ideally, but not always, brought ordinary babies into the world.

Ideologies and the Control of Reproduction

All five models—positive or negative, secular or religious—allowed their composers to make statements about reproduction, gender constructs, social relationships, fundamental social values, political organization, and themselves, the male tellers of females' birthing experiences. Together, the models reveal three coherent agendas. First, and most obvious, is the urgent need to reproduce felt by the early Irish. The sheer volume of birth stories shows how intensely the society was permeated by the desire for survival of the species. Second and equally clear is the need for cooperative childbearers. All early Irish texts identified women according to their sexuality and fertility. Women were never primarily political or economic actors, but beings who produced, or were unable to produce, or refused to produce babies. The ability to bear children brought them prestige as well as all sorts of restraints on their economic and social opportunities. There was nothing naturally empowering about the fertility of women or their ability to give birth; as the paradigmatic stories of procreation demonstrated, copulation, pregnancy, and childbirth represented a series of social choices in which women were influenced, guided, or even coerced by the actions and ideas of their men.[79] This pattern is clear from the third and most important agenda of the early Irish literati: the need for men to order and control the reproductive process as well as its ideologies.

The literati expressed the desire for children and the concept of reproductive womanhood quite neatly in their birth stories. However, they realized that conceptual categories did not always reflect real life around them, for the texts also reveal an awareness that procreation was impossible to control completely. With the right partner at the right moment—even with a lustless woman in the cleanest of circumstances—sexual intercourse might not produce a baby. Something might go wrong at any step. The woman might not be fertile; the pregnancy might miscarry; the fetus might be malformed; childbirth might cause the death of mother or child; the infant might not survive. Women, despite their knowledge derived from the collective experience of repeated pregnancies and despite the wishes and efforts of men, could not always ensure the successful generation of heirs for their men. Men had even less control over the process.

What was worse, women might refuse to reproduce. As anthropologists long ago pointed out, in societies where women are objects of marital exchange, women must agree to be both object and participant in the exchange. Not only must they go willingly from father's family to husband, but they must preserve their virginity and thus their family's honor until they do so.[80] Despite laws and rules that organized their labor, every moment of the process of reproduction was a moment of choice for women. From coitus—whom to choose as partner, whether or not to become pregnant, when, how, and where to do it—to pregnancy, birth, and nurturing, women had to decide on the circumstances, the method, the milieu, and even whether or not to carry on. Just as women chose to prevent or end pregnancy in some cases, so they chose to become pregnant, have a child, and keep and protect it.

Sometimes, granted, their options seemed circumscribed. Women were, without doubt, oppressed and restricted throughout early medieval Europe, Ireland included, just as were slaves, non-Christians, non-elites, and many other social groups. Women, like the others, colluded in their own oppression. Yet, Irish sources show that some women resisted their reproductive identity and, as a result, endangered their value as objects of exchange as well as their family's honor. Laws that legalized marriage by abduction and prohibited inheritance by bastards suggest that women did not always agree to sleep and reproduce only with men chosen by their fathers, which was one reason for the ambivalence in the procreative models. Just as the literati challenged the fertility of highly sexual figures such as Medb, they often also represented women's role in procreation, as in the choice of reproductive partners, as less active and responsible than it actually was.

The written sources thus proclaimed another paradox. Through the vagina, that small bodily aperture that was not even deemed a legitimate "door of the soul" by the medical authorities, crept the fate of all. Yet the reproductive process could not safely be left in the hands or loins of women, who found it impossible to control their own desires and bodies. Sex initiated or controlled by a virago such as Deirdriu produced no heirs; pregnancy was safest when sex, passion, and women had no part in it. When male saints could pour the fluid of fertility directly into a woman's mouth, the product might be a saint or heroic king. The fifth, sexless procreative model created by the literati did not empower women but reflected the fears of the larger society (which was run by men) and its desire to seize control of procreation.

The tellers of procreative tales worked in many ways to eliminate that terrifying contradiction between ideals and the biosocial reality of pregnancy and birth. They ignored or buried stories of procreation in which women took positive and dominant roles, leaving only faint tensions and minor contradictions in the literature. Jurists generated a system of marriage laws designed to maximize the potential of childbearers by directing women into reproductive functions above all other roles. Men also became the scholarly, religious, and medical professionals who led women through the process of pregnancy and childbirth. Male saints saved mother and child when pregnancy went wrong or birth became endangered.[81] Male physicians tended women's bodies, although midwives certainly existed in early Ireland.[82] Lawyers judged the social value of childbearers. Learned men rehearsed and explicated the procreative process for women, interpreting the visions of prospective mothers, developing a vocabulary of symbols for childbirth, and deciding what days were best for conception, who should procreate with whom, and even whether or not sexual partners should enjoy themselves during fruitful coitus.[83] Men, in short, saw themselves as the managers and interpreters of women's most important labor.

While they were trying to seize control of the process itself (or maybe because they were unable to do so), the literati also co-opted procreative ideology in their tales of pregnancy, most subtly with the manipulation of fertility symbols, as in the story of the Ulstermen's pangs (*cess noínden*). This famous tale in the Ulster cycle relates how the woman Macha wandered one day into the house of Crunniuc mac Agnomain, an Ulsterman, and took up housekeeping. Soon she became pregnant. Crunniuc went alone to the yearly fair (*oenach*) where everyone in Ulster gathered for politicking, feasting, and games. Although Macha had warned him not to speak of her, when the chariot races began, Crunniuc boasted of her swiftness. When Conchobar heard of this, he forced Crunniuc to bring her to race, like an animal with the animals, even though she was on the point of delivery. Macha appealed to the crowd, who were unmoved by her distress. She cursed them while she ran; first at the finish line, she gave birth to twins and screamed that all who heard her suffer would, in their times of greatest difficulty, endure the same pangs for five days and four nights, and have only the strength of a woman in childbed ("Nert mna siúil ba hed no bíd la cech fer di Ultaib fri saegul nonbair").[84]

Scholars dispute the meaning of the Ulstermen's pangs in this and other texts, but the author of the story clearly relates them to Macha's own travail and to the pain of childbearers generally, and he was probably not the only man in early Ireland to do so.[85] We need not posit any historical ritual or couvade to see that, whatever the precise meaning of *cess noínden* and whatever the symbolic importance of Macha, in this tale Macha cursed the Ulstermen with the ability to participate in women's only unique biosocial function: childbearing.[86] Although the Ulstermen suffered for wronging Macha, the storyteller almost succeeded in seizing control of reproduction. The Ulstermen could not bring forth babies, but their labor produced something even more valuable to Irish society: warriors reborn with extraordinary prowess. And the tale-teller himself, by his labors, recreated the very process of reproduction, reducing it to the prologue to a cycle of Ulster war stories.[87]

By assuming ideological control of procreation, men crossed the boundary between genders. They raided the concept of woman for potent attributes of femaleness. With few exceptions in early Irish literature, women who tried to take male attributes became less womanly. For better or worse, they became androgynous or lost their definitive fertile and maternal characteristics. But according to the same texts, men lost their maleness only temporarily when they acquired the symbolic ability to give birth. In the long term, they became stronger because they gained some of the mysterious, otherworldly power to reproduce without losing any specifically male attributes. After their pangs ended, the Ulster warriors were able to leap up, ready once more for the man's game of battle.

The texts of the male elite sought to remove reproduction from women's control and take it for men. The male literati reduced the biosocial process of procreation to a series of fertile, potent, multivalent political symbols of an orderly world under male dominance. God the Father gave birth to Adam; Adam and his rib gave birth to Eve. After the Fall, the formal interpretation of birthing, as of all social, cultural, and political processes, became men's prerogative. Women negotiated with their men and participated in these formal birthing ideologies. Women, too, wanted babies, and they, too, valued most highly childbearers who produced the most and best babies.

5

Mothers, Mothering, and Motherhood

According to the ninth-century narrative of the *Cáin Adom-náin* (Law of Adomnán), it was Adomnán himself, the saintly seventh-century abbot of Í, who pioneered the concept of motherhood in early Ireland. Before Adomnán took action, Irish women were slaves to men. "*Cumalach* was the name for women until Adomnán came to emancipate them," explained the composer of *Cáin Adomnáin*, "and this was the *cumalach:* the woman for whom a pit was dug at the head of the sluice-gate so that it hid her nakedness. One end of the crossbar was supported by her until the grinding of the load was done."[1] Worse, women in that barbarous past had to raise burning candles aloft in their bare hands while men feasted. They had no property and dwelled in huts outside their men's forts. The luckiest women went to war, babes on one arm, provisions and pikes on the other, their husbands flogging them on to battle.[2]

Adomnán liberated women from their suffering, according to the *cáin's* prologue, but only because his mother made him. Together, the saint and his mother, Rónnat, stumbled upon a battlefield strewn with the female dead: "They did not see anything which they thought more pitiful than a woman's head on one bank and her body on the opposite bank, with a child asleep at the breast, a stream of milk on one cheek and a stream of blood on the other."[3] At first, neither this nightmarish scene nor his mother's nagging could move Adomnán to work his saintly magic on women's behalf. So Rónnat had to act in the most unmotherly way to force him to obey her. First, in a kind of antipregnancy, she denied him food and drink for eight whole months. When, hollow and wasted, he still refused to intervene on women's behalf, Rónnat buried her boy alive, "so that worms devoured the root of his tongue, so that the slime broke forth through his ears." Finally, after four years in the cold

84

ground Adomnán learned his lesson and bargained with an angel for the liberation of women.[4] Adomnán was able to promulgate a divinely sanctioned decree that gave all women safety, status, and property forever.

Adomnán decided to save women for the sake of his mother and because women, all women, are mothers. "For," wrote the *cáin*'s author, "a mother is a venerable treasure, a mother is a goodly treasure, mother of saints and bishops and righteous folk, an increase of the kingdom of heaven, a creator."[5] Yet the fantastical narrative of Adomnán's torture and women's transformation from warriors and slaves to mothers was a departure from the other earlier versions of *Cáin Adomnáin*. Only the ninth-century narrative promoted affective motherhood as women's identifying mission in life. The seventh-century stratum of the *cáin*, the law that the saint may actually have proclaimed, was a simple *lex innocentium*, a law against harming women, children, and clerics, with no mention of the specific importance of mothers.[6] Another early section of the law listed extensive fees and penances for those who assaulted or murdered women, although not necessarily mothers.[7]

Elsewhere in the canon of early Irish texts, particularly in the secular legal material, references to mothering bore little resemblance to the ideal represented in Adomnán's story. Secular jurists treated mothers as procreators who brought children into the family and secured children's place among both horizontal and vertical kin, but not as the preferred nurturers and educators of their own babies. In laws and narrative literature alike, foster parents appeared primarily responsible for bringing up children and for loving them.

Yet the message of *Cáin Adomnáin* was not unique; it simply emphasized one in a range of opinions of mothers and motherhood which appeared in different genres of texts and sometimes even within the same documents. The earliest stratum of Adomnán's law confirmed what lawyers themselves demonstrated in laws regarding inheritance and status: that as early as 697 the entire society felt a need to protect its procreators in order to promote reproduction. The sentimental ninth-century narrative resonated with incidental evidence in hagiography and related texts, which presented an ambivalent picture of mothers, suggesting an unsystematic arrangement in which sometimes birth givers, sometimes fosterers, mothered children. This kind of information contradicted the severe legal paradigm of an otherwise loveless culture where mothers brought forth babies only to give them away to other women.

Above all, *Cáin Adomnáin*'s melodramatic ninth-century narrative, in the context of this intertextual conversation about motherhood, suggested that real mothers not only cared for their babies but worked around the laws of early Ireland to ensure a place for their children among both paternal and maternal kin and, further, that society expected them to do so. Women's manipulation—legal and extralegal—of their relations with their blood and affinal kinsmen were as crucial as the rules of patrilineage in determining a child's place in the early Irish world. Thus, peculiar and complex as it is, *Cáin Adomnáin* is actually the key to the cipher of motherhood in early medieval Ireland.

The Social Functions of Máithir

Jurists, who created and kept the secular laws of early Ireland, defined the initial relation of mother to child as one of rights and responsibilities rather than natural affection. On this principle, lawmakers theorized about the fitness and functions of mothers, and kin groups were to shape the relationship of mother and child according to these theories. It is important to remember that jurists paid most attention to people with property and high status; hence laws of fosterage and legal theories regarding mothers pertained primarily to the social elite.

In early Ireland, the woman who gave birth to a child was his or her mother (*máthair,* pl. *máithir*) but not the child's mommy. *Muimme,* the intimate and affective form, is the Old Irish word for foster mother; no such term exists in the language for birth mothers.[8] Lawyers helped determine who a child's mommy was to be. Among the sociopolitical elite at least, parents were to send both boy and girl children to cultivate affective relationships with foster parents from as early as age seven until young adulthood, officially so they could be educated and provided with additional allies unrelated by blood. Hence, according to jurists, mothers gave birth to babies, endowing them with name, family, and eventually, inheritance; but foster mothers were the mommies who supposedly instructed and loved children. Mothering and fostering were thus complementary forms of nurturing which together reinforced social networks and assured the high status of birth givers, particularly those of the elite, but considerably limited mothers' relations with the products of their labor.

The jurists who organized marriage and procreation for women also decreed that they should send their children away. Written into the laws for marriage contracts, along with guidelines for buying breeding cattle and disposing of old plough animals, was the suggestion that "the entrusting of children to gratuitous fosterage" was an arrangment that "brings well-being to the community of [a couple's] joint household."[9] Part of the marriage bargain itself was the provision for placing offspring of the union in other homes, a practice that contributed, according to the laws, to the stability of the marriage. Not just noble parents but those of all free ranks supposedly participated in the system whereby a couple usually of lower status than the parents raised, either for money or love, their social superiors' sons and daughters.[10] Women acknowledged the propriety of fosterage simply by accepting marriage laws; they knew what awaited their children and agreed in their marriage contracts to pay up to half of the fees for fosterage.[11]

No laws set an age at which mothers bade farewell to their babes, but jurists hinted that the age of seven, when sexless infants became educable little boys and girls, was the appropriate time to begin a child's training.[12] Until then at least, a child usually remained at home. Some, if not all, mothers must have nursed their babies during those early years, providing the crucial emotional and physiological basis for their children's later well-being. None of the laws or any other sources explicitly mentioned wet nurses; they may have existed, but were not common enough to merit comment. On the contrary, according to one legal tract, breast-feeding by birth mothers was so much the norm that even the infant of a dead woman had to be forcibly and legally removed from her breast for its own good, although whether to the breasts of another or to cow's milk is unclear.[13]

Jurists assumed that every mother, along with the child's father, was initially responsible for her own child, but lawyers also helped kin groups make custody decisions when a parent was so morally, physically, or socially unfit that a child had to be removed from his or her care at an unusually early age. The definition of fit mothers must have been of special concern to lawyers and those they represented, for lists of bad mothers appeared in at least four separate law tracts.[14] Lawyers based their decisions on questions of the right and responsibility to raise a child without referring to biological ties, as lawyers do today. Women who were chronically or mortally ill or physically or mentally disabled were released from the legal responsibility of raising their children. Also, women who bore children without the permission of their guardians—father, owner, or legal husband in the case of adultery—or after being raped were not bound by law to keep their babies, but the responsiblity and cost of nursing fell upon fathers. A woman who had a child by an ill or demented man, a foreigner, a criminal, certain professional men such as clerics or jurists, or an underage boy was herself responsible for parenting and paying for the child's fosterage. What is more, a woman who was too free with either thighs or evil words—a whore or a satirist—lost the right to raise her baby.

Thus, a woman had the right, if she was neither leper nor lunatic, neither promiscuous nor partner in an illicit union, to care for her baby and the responsiblity to do so if the father was unfit or unwilling. But lawyers also took it upon themselves to determine the fitness of the mother and the disposition of her child. A mother had very little choice about it all.[15] If she were fit, she had to raise her child, unlike a jurist or cleric who denied his offspring. If she were raped, she was not always legally allowed to raise the baby even if she wanted it; theoretically, a man could forcibly impregnate a woman and then, if she formally accused him of rape and her own family rejected the baby, he could claim her child for himself and his kin group. Even if she were legally married to her baby's father, if she were deaf, blind, or wasting away, the father's kin could legally and formally remove the child from her care.[16] A woman's only choices regarding custody were extralegal or illicit, such as the negative choices of infanticide and neglect. If the law and the child's father made a custody decision contrary to her wishes, she was helpless unless her kin were sympathetic and powerful enough to enforce her desires.

The lawyers' assumption, however, was that not only both parents but other blood relations also normally wished to share a child's first years. Further, they saw fathers as responsible for its material support, mothers for its nurturing, and both for affiliating it to their own families. Though the laws regarding child raising referred specifically to the duties of mothers and fathers, they actually represented the reponsibilities of larger blood-related groups of which parents were members. No one envisioned a single mother struggling, in twentieth-century fashion, to care for her children while holding down a steady job to support them. Nor was a father who lost his wife to leprosy or lunacy ready to rise for night feedings and diaper changes and then, next morning, march off to labor in fields of corn or fields of battle. The contest over rights and responsibilities to nurse probably took place between families, not individuals, and was based less on issues of personal fitness to parent than on fundamental matters of inheritance, lineage, and collective survival.

The laws articulated their ideology of mothering less explicitly than they stated custody decrees. The texts implied, rather than declared, that a mother, even more than a father, had the duty of giving her baby a family. In the eyes of the early Irish, a mother proved her devotion to her child as much by swaddling it in a network of kin and foster relations as by wrapping it in warm blankets. Bad mothers were not women who abused or neglected their children but those who refused or were unable to affiliate them with all their grandparents, cousins, uncles, and aunts. Similarly, bad daughters produced children unacceptable to their families, children of unfit fathers or illegitimate children. Daughters who were even more impious and undutiful brought no children at all to their kin or even broke the laws of clerics and jurists to kill the fruit of their wombs, thus depriving their kin groups of a next generation.[17] A woman's greatest social purpose was not simply to bear a child but to give it an identity by securing its place among both horizontal and vertical kin in both maternal and paternal lines.

A mother's ability to affiliate her child depended on her own personal circumstances, who had helped her produce the child, her relationship with him,

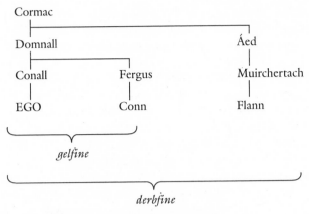

Kin groups: *gelfine* and *derbfine*.

and her ties to both his and her families. An adult woman's first responsibility, should she plan to bear children—and every free lay woman was expected to do so—was to get herself a legitimate mate and make herself acceptable to his family. If she engaged in a recognized legal union with her baby's father— whether formal marriage, secondary marriage, concubinage, or a legal but temporary union—then her second responsibility was made easier: to endow the child with official membership in its father's *fine,* or corporate agnatic kin group.[18] This patrilineal group included the sons of its sons and their wives, but not its married daughters, who had joined other families and transferred their affiliation and offspring there.[19]

Within the larger *fine,* which was more a theoretical concept than a viable social unit, the operative group was a smaller family. This was the basic landholding and legal unit in Irish society. Lawyers theorized about this smaller family as normally consisting of all the descendants of a single great-grandfather (*derbfine*) or grandfather (*gelfine*).[20] From the *derbfine* or *gelfine* or from his father, a boy expected to inherit his share of the family land (*fintiu*); a girl expected her premortem inheritance or, when no male heirs existed, her life interest in family land. This family also paid fees for its children's crimes and debts and claimed payments for the injury or murder of its members or, when the legal system failed in such cases, used force to settle offenses and suits.[21]

Hence, in addition to being a socially and physically fit woman joined in legal union to her man, a good mother was also a woman whom her in-laws liked or at least considered part of the family. She was easily able to integrate her child into the *fine* and *derbfine* when she herself was a member by marriage.

As Binchy and others have shown, the women of highest legal status were those who had made the transition from their own kin to that of their husbands and more fully established their place in a foreign household by having children.[22]

Yet, on some levels, the transfer to husband's guardianship and affinal kin was never thorough, and the wife always remained an intruder. What was worse than marrying a harlot, asked *Senbríathra Fíthail;* taking her home to meet the family, the text answered itself.[23] What is more, if a woman's union with her child's father was illegitimate or legally dubious, or if her own sexual conduct was suspect, then her affiliation with his kin became even more tenuous, her own status decreased, and she found it harder to place her baby among its father's kin. If, for instance, her partner's family took no part in arranging their union because it was somehow illicit—for example, an abduction or a rape—the paternal *derbfine* might well reject both union and its offspring. Similarly, if the father's family had already abjured him as a criminal, or if they did not approve of the union on account of his ill health or tender age, or if the union took place outside paternal territory, then they might well refuse to accept his child.[24] Finally, if the paternal kin objected to the bride on grounds of her health, her family, her status, or her sexual behavior, then she might find it legally difficult to affiliate her child with her mate's family. It was entirely up to the paternal *fine* whether or not to take a child of dubious legitimacy.[25]

In such a situation, a mother could sue. Her success depended not so much on the strength of her case as on the willingness of her own family and her child's *máithre,* or maternal kin, to support her in legal negotiations. No woman ever left her family completely, although historians have maintained that the more legitimate the marriage, the more fully a woman transferred her affiliation to her husband's kin.[26] Jurists calculated affiliation in terms of financial responsibility. In the case of a *cétmuinter* who offered her husband the treasure of sons, for instance, two-thirds of her inheritance and her honor price went to her new family, and only a third was left to her own blood kin. For a woman whose marriage was not arranged by her family but was eventually legitimated, the equation was reversed. Her family got two-thirds of the inheritance and was responsible for two-thirds of any debts or fees she might incur, while her husband's kin got only a third.[27] Thus, a woman whose marriage was not completely legitimate might face not only rejection by her husband's kin but also alienation from her own. As a result, her child's *máithre* might not be ready to take up its paternity case. Everything depended not only on the legal complexities but on matters of personal judgment, goodwill, and affection among all parties involved.[28]

That mothers did struggle to establish paternity shows how important it was to connect a child to its paternal kin. They occasionally did so without the jurists' support or the legal oaths and physical force of their own families to back them, for when mothers suffered any imputation of promiscuity, the laws protected her impregnator.[29] The author of the ninth-century *Cath Maige Mucrama* described the difficult judgment put before the legendary king of Temair, Lugaid Laígde, "how a son may be brought into his father's hereditary property" ("co tabairdar mac morbe nathar"). Lugaid ruled that if the mother raised the child, knew who the father's family was, maintained an otherwise chaste life, and did not associate with other unmarried mothers (called by the text *báeth*, whore) or let her child mingle with theirs, she might swear with some credibility as to the father. Her son might then be accepted by his paternal kinsmen.[30] But the burden of proof clearly lay upon the mother's shoulders. Commentators on the laws decreed that if the mother could not prove that the baby had the familiar voice, looks, and behavior of the putative father's *fine*, she and her child were out of luck. Even if she could demonstrate one of the physical similarities between her baby and its father, as the jurist put it, "every time that the man swears by his member [*a meamar*], the proof is with him" rather than her.[31] On the other hand, another commentator suggested that a married woman who duped her husband into formally accepting her child by another man required no further evidence.[32]

According to hagiographers, it took a miracle to decide paternity cases. They recorded several instances in which a mother appeared before an assembly of clerics in order to name the father and demand her child's affiliation with his family. These were women, often fallen nuns, whom secular laws and family had failed and who were forced to appeal to the extralegal authority of ecclesiastics for justice. The hagiographers made it clear just how difficult it was for a woman abandoned by her own kin to prosecute a paternity case. In most of the episodes, a saint caused the infant itself to name its father, thus establishing paternity, or not, as the case might be. The infant most often denied the paternity of the accused man, which shows how little the hagiographers thought of women who were reduced to such extraordinary measures as ecclesiastical assemblies.[33] Clearly, even in churchmen's eyes, a child's social status and that of its mother were intimately linked; a fallen woman could only bring forth a fatherless child.

A mother sought affiliation for her child not only in order to create and maintain a social identity for them both and to provide all the legal security and emotional support that family could bring but also in order to provide for the child materially. Only a legitimate child could inherit property from his or her *derbfine*, although legitimacy was defined quite differently than our own society defines it. According to a tract on the inheritance rights of sons, only three types of boy children were legitimate heirs: *mac aititen*, "recognized son," *mac óige*, "son of a pure woman," and *mac adaltraig[e] urnadma*, "son of a betrothed concubine"—all of whom were boys formally recognized by their kin.[34] They were the products of the most formal and valued legal unions. Any doubt as to a boy's paternity excluded him from his share of the *derbfine*'s property.[35] The lawyers did not specify the same conditions for girl children, but given the laws already limiting female inheritance to movable goods, gifts of property, or life interest in family land, it seems likely that the same rules of legitimacy applied to female heirs.[36]

Further, the less formal a mother's union with her mate, the less able she would have been to assist her child materially unless she secured support from the child's *máithre*. But maternal kin would be unwilling to cheat their own male heirs of property, especially land, by giving it away to someone fathered by an outsider in a dubious union. Although sisters' sons sometimes returned to their maternal kin for fosterage or other temporary residence, as we shall see, the early Irish harbored profound doubts about the wisdom of incorporating another man's son into the family.[37] So a woman had to look chiefly to her partner's family or to her own resources in order to supply her child. Yet only primary wives had extensive rights over their own property, which was assumed by lawyers to be considerable, as well as rights to help manage the property of their husbands.[38] If mothers were wealthy noblewomen—the sort of women who normally made prestigious and legal marriages—and had been given dowries or gifts of land from their own relatives, then they could transmit such gifts of property to their children. In such circumstances, these women would not normally need to do so, since their children would most likely be acknowledged legitimate heirs to their father's property.[39] Far greater burdens fell upon a mother who had already failed to protect her child by placing it among the paternal *fine*. She would also be less able to find property for it either on the father's lands or on lands of her own.[40]

Ultimately, a child's chances for full affiliation and inheritance depended mainly on the status of its parents' relationship to each other. Lawyers seem to have held women to be as responsible as men for establishing an appropriate and amicable union. If a mother could not find a home and family for herself, she could do no more for her baby. This must have been a common enough problem. Polygyny, historians agree, was normal among the elite of early Ireland; both secular and religious narratives abounded with references to illicit affairs, temporary liaisons, and children of secret or adulterous unions. All those eloping heroines and the brides by abduction who appeared in the legal tracts faced serious burdens of motherhood once the romance had faded and the reality of child rearing took over. If a woman's family and that of her husband remained unfriendly to children of less than legitimate unions, then a good mother had to search elsewhere for the support her babies needed. Even competent, well-married mothers and their offspring could always benefit from some outside assistance.

Fosterage

It was in the context of just such social ambiguities that fosterage became so important in early Ireland.[41] One solution to the problem of conflicting and insufficient kinship bonds, for both successful and unsuccessful mothers, was to shelter and comfort their children with a blanket of fosterage ties. For the sons and daughters of elite women, the removal at age seven to another friendly household was supposed to be customary and predictable; however, for the children of women with less wealth and social legitimacy, who might have needed even more sorely the extra support of surrogate kin, fosterage was less certain. A woman whose status was already insecure and who lacked support from husband, his *derbfine,* and her own kin, was not as likely to find a willing fosterer for her child.

For one thing, even when a child went to very close relations or friends, there were usually costs.[42] According to the jurists, a father, sometimes legally and financially assisted by a mother, made a deal with another man to be the *aite,* fosterer and teacher, of his child. Money or goods changed hands along with the child. If the deal went bad, provisions existed for ending the contract. Fosterers had excellent incentives to take good care of the children entrusted to them. Unless he agreed to accept a child out of "love" (*serc*), which probably referred to the loyalty between kinfolk or patrons and clients, rather than fondness, an *aite* was well paid for his services.[43] Presumably he shared his rewards with his wife, the *muimme,* or foster mother, according to the laws of property division within marriage. He was entitled to collect from three *séts* (a *sét* being a unit of value equal to one-half a milch cow) for the son of a small farmer, up to thirty *séts* for a king's son, or even more for a daughter, who purportedly cost more to raise.[44] A foster father could also receive a portion of the regular fines when his fosterling was injured or killed, and he might also be liable to avenge the crime.[45]

Fosterers had to provide for the child as they would for, and along with, their own. The jurists set out exact requirements for the clothing and equipment of fosterlings, regulating everything from the color of the clothes to the quality of underclothing, as well as the child's food, jewelry, and even horses for a prince.[46] In addition, fosterers taught their fosterlings everything they needed to become successful adults. The recommended curriculum for a king's son included riding, swimming, and fighting as well as playing board games in polite company.[47] A farm boy was taught to herd, raise and harvest his crops, find fuel, and generally handle his land.[48] A girl learned wifely skills: sewing, embroidery, or if she were of lower status, how to use kitchen equipment.[49] Presumably, an *aite* taught his foster son, and a *muimme* passed her womanly skills to her girl fosterling; in exchange, the children were expected to put those skills to use in the service of their fosterers.[50]

Some laws suggested that parents often tried to foster down (although this practice may have differed according to the gender of the child, as we shall see in a later chapter.)[51] That is, a child was given to fosterers of lower status than the parents, unlike, say, the page boys of courtly France or the adolescent children who entered domestic service in seventeenth-century America.[52] The function of Irish fosterage was not to educate a child in skills that would allow him or her to scale the social hierarchy, as in these other societies but to inculcate the social and vocational skills necessary for survival in the child's assigned station.

In addition, Irish fosterers provided their charges with two things that their higher-class parents could not. They offered both the fosterling and his or her parents all sorts of social and political support that was free of the competition for resources characteristic of the *derbfine*. They also offered fosterlings affective ties both to themselves and to their own children, foster siblings of their charges. Sagas and saints' lives depicted fosterage as generating ties based on deep affection, derived often from blood kinship with the mother's family.

Thus, if parents could secure a capable fosterer for their child, the potential benefits were great. The child ideally formed a close relationship with its foster parents and also with their natural children and other foster children. What is more, the child's parents created or reinforced a contractual tie with the fosterers.[53] Given the inheritance customs governing both property and political leadership, a dynamic of competition among heirs was inevitable in early Ireland. The monastic annals chronicled endless feuds among brothers for kingship and political clients. Judging by the extensive laws of property distribution and the resolution of disputes, jurists were constantly busy sorting out who deserved what portion of the family estates.[54] In the secular narratives, *fingal*—the slaying of close blood kin—ranked with regicide and incest as the most hideous of crimes, but it happened, and usually the cause was contested power or property.

Exacerbating an already tense relationship among siblings of the elite was the likelihood that they might not share the same mother and that their ties to each other were dependent upon a father whom none of them may have seen very often. Both serial and contemporary polygyny were likely to set a woman against her husband's other children, particularly sons; even the sons of women in informal but legal liaisons were liable to inherit from their fathers at the expense of the children of a legal wife.[55] In saga and vita, stepmothers tried to harm or seduce other women's sons who might oust their own children from inheritances. In a vita from the end of the period, Saint Cóemgen battled a *malifica* [*sic*], a witch, who was the discarded wife of Colmán mac Cairpri, king of Uí Muiredaig; she snatched her ex-husband's new baby and tried to dispose of it through her wizardry. The saint triumphed over this antimother, but it never entered Colmán's mind that his own polygyny caused the problem in the first place.[56] Women in the narratives also persecuted their stepchildren and tried to manipulate their husbands to favor their own children, but they rarely appealed directly for support against their man's other women and other children.[57] Wives and mothers knew well that a nobleman whose status and allies increased with each woman he acquired would not normally be open to suggestion—either from one of his women or from monogamy-minded hagiographers and canonists—that he limit his liaisons or his progeny.[58] Since his reproductive agenda traditionally aimed at producing as many sons as possible, a man might actually have promoted competition among his women and their sons.[59]

A woman probably worried no less about her daughters since girls faced equally serious competition for resources. Even the wealthiest father might have trouble providing several daughters with the goods they needed to contribute to a marriage. The laws suggested that women brought some share of animals, household goods and equipment, and clothing, if not land given as gifts, to marriage as a *cétmuinter*. Women of lower status or involved in informal unions might have brought less, but it was probably rare that a woman entered a union with nothing of her own. Although mothers were also expected to ante up, the burden of supplying a daughter with her premortem inheritance no doubt normally fell to the father.[60] The result was that girls competed with their siblings too. Indirect evidence comes from the ninth-century life of Saint Brigit. When Brigit refused an advantageous marriage to a nice young man of quality, her half brothers "grieved at her depriving them of her bride-price."[61] Luckily for her siblings, Brigit never demanded the premortem inheritance that would set her up in marriage, but neither did she bring her family a bride-price or alliances with affinal kin. Her half brothers took her refusal personally as a sign of animosity.

If a mother could not appeal to her children's father in the race to inherit, as well as for other sorts of support, she could turn to those whose loyalties were less dispersed. Her own kin might favor her children if they had property or affection to spare and if she had not alienated them with an improper union. The tie between a boy and his mother's kinsmen, particularly her brothers, could be strong if it were reinforced by other sorts of alliances, such as clientage or adoption. This relationship, called the avunculate by anthropologists and Indo-Europeanists, was apparently important throughout ancient Europe; one of the Irish words for a sister's son, *nia,* derived directly from Proto-Indo-European *nepots,* which supplied many other societies with similar terms for the same social bond.[62] According to the secular narratives, the *nia* was the boy rejected by his father's family and brought up by his mother's kin from birth; he caused trouble by demanding the property he would normally expect from his paternal *fine.* A *gormac,* literally "dutiful son," was a sister's son who was voluntarily adopted by his maternal kinsmen and who temporarily resided with them. He bided time with them, fighting their battles and helping in their fields, but did not lay claim to the maternal *fine*'s lands and returned to his father's family when it had property to spare for him. Cú Chulainn was the *gormac* extraordinaire. The son of the god Lug and an Ulster princess, Deichtine, he was sent off to his mother's brother Conchobar at age seven—the age of fosterage—and spent his superheroic adolescence defending his *máithre* from their enemies. He never demanded even the puniest field for his trouble.[63]

As with Conchobar, the fosterer could be a blood relation of the child's mother or, occasionally, of its father. Many of the saints were sent to either maternal uncles or maternal aunts to be fostered.[64] Maternal aunts might feel less encumbered by loyalties to their *fine*s, since they had less formal affiliations than their brothers; as we have seen, a maternal uncle had to calculate just how great an entree into his *fine* to offer his sister's boy, who belonged, legally, to another man's lineage.

Formal fosterage made the calculation easier. Officially, the child returned to his or her *fine* (or, if a girl, to a husband) at the "age of unfosterage," somewhere around puberty.[65] After that the fosterer and fosterling retained an affective tie, but the economic responsibilities of the fosterer ceased with his parting gifts.[66] In general, despite their bias in favor of patrilineages, the laws were a help, not a hindrance, to a woman seeking extra support in this way for her child. In the rules of fosterage, jurists set limits to the claims of a sister's son on his maternal kin and at the same time provided for the child's upbringing by surrogate parents who felt no direct competition with the child for paternal resources.

The laws did not equate fosterers and *máithre,* except in a few instances, but hagiographers often assumed that the two were one and the same.[67] If so, fosterage among *máithre* provided a child and its mother with the best of both worlds: affectionate relations with blood kin and nurturing from the theoretically disinterested parties who were paid to take good care of the child, along with a reinforced alliance between a woman and her kin. Her husband, the child's father, could benefit from such a strong relationship, too, for he gained allies devoted to his child and his wife, which must in turn have helped his wife and child in the polygamous competition for his loyalty. Indeed, when it worked, fosterage among *máithre* worked well, and all because of the pivotal figure of the mother.

Scholars who have studied the avunculate tend to forget the most crucial person in the relationship: the boy's mother, the uncle's sister. Yet the tie between *gormac* or *nia* and *amnair*, mother's brother, could have worked only when the mother got along with her brother, especially in cases where her man and his family wanted no part in her children. Deichtine and Conchobar were certainly close—close enough so that when she became mysteriously pregnant by Lug, the Ulstermen suspected that Conchobar had fathered the baby after having drunk himself into bed with his sister one night.[68] The hagiographers also described less intense but amicable relations between siblings as the context for the avunculate. Saint Berach's mother gave birth to her son in the house of her brother, the presbyter Fráech; her boy was raised there and became "the one person in all the world who was dearest to Presbyter Fráech of all who ever received human nature save Christ alone."[69] What is more, in the vitae this happy compatibility of siblings and nephews extended to sisters, as well, although not apparently to nieces. Because Íte and her sister were close, the sister's child became Íte's fosterling and, under his aunt's tutelage, grew to be a saint himself.[70]

When a mother was on good terms with them, her siblings took interest in her children, or at least in her sons. A woman could benefit from bringing a useful *gormac* to her folk; her credit with her kin could only rise when they took on her boy as a fosterling and he, in return, worked and fought without asking for a piece of the maternal *fine*'s property. But when a woman could not maintain her place in her own *fine* or brought them a *nia* with no other resources and nowhere else to go, neither her sons nor her daughters could expect to find a haven among their mother's people. She herself must then have felt her tenuous ties to her blood kin stretching to the breaking point. And what could she do if her husband and her family both refused her and her children? A woman had to judge very carefully just how much to demand of her kin for her babies.

A vicious circle entrapped mothers who needed, and whose children needed, social, material, and emotional support that they could not gain from blood kin. Only a woman who had already established a network based on kinship could afford to seek extra help from others who had unambivalent feelings about her child. Such a woman could seek affiliation with those who had no biological ties to her children, such as neighbors or clients, or she could try to reinforce existing kinship ties with other sorts of relationships, such as godparentage.[71] But even more reliable than any of these ties was the relationship of fosterage. Ideally more trusty and loving than otherwise unaffiliated kin were the couple whom a woman and her husband paid to raise and educate their son or daughter: the fosterers, *aite* and *muimme*. Occasionally, maybe even frequently, fosterers and mother's kin were one and the same.

Muimmi *and the Bonds of Affection*

Fosterage cleverly filled all sorts of holes in the social fabric. For boys and girls in competition with kinsmen over inheritance, fosterage provided sustaining allies. For mothers seeking to fortify ties to their own kin and maintain partial control over the raising of their children, fosterage supplied the means. Yet for these same reasons, fosterage created some disturbing tensions in Irish society. To promote competition between heirs to the *fintiu* was to threaten the *fine,* the basis of all formal sociopolitical organization; and to establish a strong bond between fosterers and fosterlings was to undermine a mother's potentially affective relations with her babies. As the author of *Tecosca Cormaic* wrote, with far more relevance than he intended, "Everyone is tranquil until fosterage."[72] This aphorism must have been particularly true for a mother battling to find a haven for her children from the harshly patriarchal world—but not so attractive a haven that her sons and daughters forsook her.

Predictably, Irish laws stressed the contractual nature of fosterage ties, hardly mentioning that the bond could include kinship and affection as well. Nor did the laws emphasize the vital role of the *máthair* and the *muimme* in negotiating fosterage. The laws occasionally included the *muimme* in the fosterage contract—she, for example, was in charge of the underclothing— although normally the assumption, as in all legal dealings, was that the man of the house was chiefly responsible; the laws used mostly the masculine singular when referring to the fosterer. Lawyers never considered the possibility that a *muimme* or *aite* might take on fosterage alone, however. They clearly believed, as did the storytellers, that a child needed surrogate parents of both sexes for different functions, and they assumed that the fosterers would be a married couple.[73]

If a *muimme's* relationship with her fosterling was less regulated by laws, it was supposedly more affective than that of *aite* to *daltae* (fosterling).[74] According to the spurious philology of legal commentators, the very name of *muimme* proved her greater love: "'Mo ime,' she more (*mo*) folds his clothes about him (*ime*) to warm him and nourish him than the fosterfather."[75] The secular narratives demonstrated that foster fathers and their foster sons were loyal to each other, as were foster brothers, but in the literature *aite* rarely displayed outright affection for his young charge.[76] An often-cited example was the relationship between the hero Cú Chulainn and one of his fosterers, Fergus mac Róich. Although on different sides of a major war between Ulster and

Connacht, the two managed to protect and do favors for each other throughout the conflict.[77] But no touching scenes of Cú Chulainn being cuddled by or playing with Fergus leap from the saga, or from other stories. To be fair, few of the secular narratives mention children, except abnormally heroic boys such as Cú Chulainn; so happy scenes of a *muimme* and her charge did not appear either.

The saints' lives, however, told another story.[78] In the vitae, *muimmi* loved their little fosterlings unless they were very poor foster mothers indeed. Pátraic and his foster mother were the exemplary couple, according to the ninth-century tripartite life of the saint. Although Pátraic was a Briton, his hagiographer conceived of his upbringing as typically Irish. A patrician child, Pátraic was sent to fosterers. His *muimme* was, according to some traditions, his maternal aunt; the hagiographer mentioned an *aite* only when he died.[79] Many miracles and marvels of the boy saint occurred while he was "i toig a muimme," in his foster mother's house, but at first his *muimme* did not much appreciate her charge. Once, for example, during a rough winter, their house was flooded, so that pots and pans floated around the place and the hearth fire was doused. When Pátraic whined for food, his foster mother scolded him because she had more important emergencies to attend to. Pátraic crept into a dry corner to sulk and dipped his little hand in the water, whereupon the five drops off his fingers became five sparks that blazed into a cozy fire, and the waters receded.[80] He got no thanks from his *muimme*, though. To be fair, Pátraic was not much help about the house, except when he resorted to miracles. When they needed firewood, Pátraic brought home icicles. When he minded the sheep, he let wolves ravage the flock. Other boys brought their mothers honey from the combs of wild bees, but Pátraic's *muimme* complained, "You bring none to me."[81] Clearly, if a *muimme* were to care for a *daltae*, he was supposed to perform little-boy chores, and these were not Pátraic's forte; his character in these boyhood episodes derived from a strong Irish tradition of unworldly, tuned-out saints.[82]

Yet, despite his inadequacies and her scoldings, the relationship between Pátraic and his foster mother was clearly meant to be affectionate. The hagiographer reported that when Pátraic's *muimme* "saw that God's grace was growing in him . . . she loved him greatly and did not like to go anywhere without him."[83] When she went to do the milking, for example, she brought him along for a drink of the warm, frothy stuff straight from the cow—which was handy, as it turns out, because when the cow became demoniacally deranged and killed five other cattle, Pátraic was able to cure the mad one and revive the others.[84]

A child and his or her *muimme* were meant to love each other. Other saints were just as attached to their foster mothers as Pátraic to his, whether they lived on the farms of the laity or in monastic enclosures. Saint Íte had a lifelong relationship marked by affection, loyalty, and intellectual exchange with her *daltae* Brénainn. She taught him letters and first prayers. Later, when he needed advice about his pilgrimages on the sea, he sought out Íte.[85] Máedóc, who had many different fosterers as befitted a boy of superior status, was adored by his foster mothers and nurses, "as was the way of loving and affectionate fostermothers." According to a twelfth-century vita, because of the love and affection (*serc, grádh*) these women felt for the boy, whose real name was Aed, they gave him his nickname: "mo Aodh óg" or Máedóc, my little Aed.[86]

Whereas the hagiographers depicted affective relations between abbots and their foster-child novices, male-to-male bonds were usually more restrained than *muimme-daltae* ties. Comgall, for example, was a benign but distant authority figure to the little boys he raised at Bennchor; Colmán Ela was a sensitive but not demonstrative tutor to his charges, the two illegitimate nephews of Saint Columcille.[87] Even though Colmán Ela was the most affectionate foster father to appear in the vitae, the hagiographer's image of him was entirely feminine: like a wet nurse, he offered his boys breasts full of milk and honey.[88] Rather than play the loving father, he could express his feelings only with female gestures and metaphors; the hagiographer had no common foster fatherly attributes with which to endow Colmán in order to illustrate the love he felt for his *daltai*.

In fact, foster mothers became for religious writers the symbol of all that was best about women. They devoted themselves to their babies fully, selflessly, and demonstrably. Joseph may have been the *aite álainn*, "beautiful fosterer," to Jesus, but he was no doting papa; Saint Brigit, on the other hand, was *muimme Goídel*, foster mother to all the Irish.[89] Saint Íte, the virgin seer, however, was the fondest nurse on earth, snuggling the baby savior to her maidenly breast and singing her well-known poem to him:

> Ísucán
> who is in fosterage with me in my hermitage—
> though a cleric have many *sét*s
> all is false save Ísucán. . . .
> . . . Sing a fitting harmony, maidens
> to the legal recipient of your tribute.
> Ísucán is at home on high
> even though he be in my bosom.[90]

When Íte held her fosterling, she had no other men competing for her affection, no husband, no other sons or daughters. Unlike a birth mother, Íte had no kin ties against which to balance her devotion to Ísucán.[91]

Indeed, it was because of this ideal of romantic, single-minded love—as well as all the other benefits—that mothers and fathers sent their children into fosterage. While the laws allowed for cases in which parents did not send their children away, as we have seen, and the vitae mentioned the occasional child kept at home, most mothers of the elite were probably bound to see some, if not all of their babies, leave home at age seven.[92] Even when pleased at the affection tendered by foster parents, mothers who sent their offspring away must have missed their young children, for *pace* Philippe Ariès, Irish mothers loved their children, as did mothers and fathers throughout the early medieval world.[93] They wanted babies desperately, and when they got them, they cared for them during childhood and beyond. A charming episode from the vita of Molua describes how the boy saint was playing while his mother was busy elsewhere. Caught up in a game with three mysterious and suspiciously angelic *pueri*, Molua unthinkingly levitated. His mother became distraught when she could not find the boy, crying and searching frantically until Molua landed.[94]

In a way, the ability to select or help select her child's fosterers may have compensated a mother for the temporary loss of her child, especially when fosterers came of her own kin. It was probably easier for her to maintain contact with her sons or daughters if they were living with her own kinfolk, especially if she herself lived on or visited her own dowered property among them. If the fosterers lived in an accessible place—nearby, or in maternal territory where a woman could visit or might even live part of the time—then a devoted mother could continue her affective relations with her child more effectively.[95]

In return for this continuing affection from their mothers and for early material support, children fostered elsewhere were supposed to reciprocate later in life with both love and goods. The laws made all sorts of exceptions for the continuing close relationship (*lánamnas*) between mothers and sons and fathers and daughters, just as they did for spouses, which proves the extraordinary affection that supposedly informed these ties. For example, three gifts between parents and children were immune to claims by others (presumably kinsmen): the gift given a child in exchange for support in a parent's old age, a gift given to a cheer a child up, and a gift purely out of love between the two.[96] In addition, in exchange for a mother's nurture, the son or daughter was to "aid her in poverty and support her in old age."[97] Jurists castigated the son who left his mother "in a ditch" and declared a child who failed to support his or her elderly parents to be *elúdach,* an "evader of the law," who deserved no legal protection or inheritance.[98] While such laws suggested a lifelong bond between biological parents and children, the vitae gave illustrations: Ciarán, for example, whose mother and kinswomen took the veil and built a nunnery next door to his monastery, in order to enjoy his affection and guidance; and

Munnu, whose mother so pestered him for companionship that he threatened to leave the country.[99]

Both *máthair* and *muimme,* then, were to cherish their child, who was to love and support both mothers in return, as well as—but not as much as—his or her father and foster father. For the child, such an arrangement meant double the affection and help that one mother could give, along with the creation or reinforcement of a network of alliances with foster relations and possibly his or her *máithre.* Both *muimme* and *máthair* stood to gain from the social solidarities that resulted from fosterage.

Although the *máthair* theoretically had to yield her child to the *muimme* for seven or more years, remarkably, the sources showed no trace of competition between the women. No saga described the machinations of one mother figure against the other; no laws regulated feuds between them, as laws dealt with the assaults of primary and secondary wives upon each other. Fosterer and birth giver were theoretically united in devotion to their mutual child, as well as to each other—or else the sources lied, and women squabbled jealously over their precious children. But the functions of a *muimme* and *máthair* were distinct enough and yet closely enough related to discourage competition. Class may have distinguished the noble *máthair* from the less aristocratic foster mother and prevented tension between them if, indeed, the Irish fostered their daughters and sons down. Also, their roles may have been differentiated by age. It may be that a mother was relieved to yield her child to a woman who was herself past childbearing age, while she coped with another pregnancy. It is also likely that many mothers were themselves fosterers at some point in their careers, perhaps after their childbearing years.

On the other hand, given the emphasis on ties between foster children and natural children, some fosterers must have been mothers and *muimmi* to both kinds of young children simultaneously.[100] Of course, mothers and foster mothers need not have been distinct social groups, but were simply roles made discrete by laws and practice; a woman could be either or both at any point in her adulthood. Perhaps this very fluidity of roles prevented friction among the co-nurturers of a child. A child's maintenance of affective ties with its birth mother during and after fosterage, and the lifelong loyalty he or she owed to the *muimme* also helped prevent conflict. Finally, if a mother had a hand in selecting the *muimme* for her child, possibly from among her own kin, she could forestall any possible competition for her baby from the start. A carefully constructed fosterage relationship helped everyone and hurt no one, not even the most doting mother.

Yet an early Irish mother still had reason to suspect the ideological effects of fosterage because, theoretically, Irish fosterage worked to decrease the cultural importance of birth givers. According to jurists, a child owed equal allegiance to the *muimme* who nurtured him or her and to the *máthair* who did more, who risked death to carry and deliver the child, who nursed and gave earliest care to him or her, who did her best to secure the child's recognition by father, paternal kin, and *máithre*. The greater efforts and responsibilities of the birth mother, however, received proportionately less reward.

A biological father was compensated for his procreative role, when the child was a legitimate heir, by gaining another member for his patrilineage. True, lawyers worked hard to balance this inequity by allowing a mother to attach her child to her own kin through fosterage, thus forming a countersolidarity to the patrilineage and keeping affectionate hold of her child. But even this security was not assured a woman and her child, and her own benefits from the tie remained more doubtful than those of her child. Jurists and the patrilineage they represented simply could not afford to let women intrude too far upon their own *fines* by forcing other men's children on them; nor could they let the solidarity of mother, child, and maternal kin compete too closely with the paternal *fine*.

With fosterage and the removal of a child at an early age from a mother's care, the Irish elite imbued the roles of *máthair* and *muimme* with similar, if not equal, importance. Any woman, they proclaimed, could care for a child, not just the woman who brought it into the world. As a result, birth mothers lost what might have been their natural and unique status in a procreation-obsessed culture. By first attempting to comandeer the reproductive process and then by alienating from women the product, as well as the means, of their own labor (at least for the term of fosterage), the rule makers and rulers of Ireland proclaimed mothers to be mere birth givers. Women may have maneuvered around the system, but to men what mattered was not the woman; it was the child and the strength of its blood connection to the paternal *fine*. Women alone could not protect and provide for their babies. This, at least, was the ideological message lurking behind the laws and the formal practice of fosterage, which mothers subverted by using fosterage to their own advantage and that of their children. The ideology indicated an enormous juridical rift between fosterers and birth mothers, which women, with their manipulations of the legal system of fosterage, did their best to mitigate.

Adomnán and the Creation of Motherhood

According to jurists and the later interpreters of his *cáin*, Adomnán decreed that all women were mothers of equal, and supreme, cultural importance. Unlike the laws, however, *Cáin Adomnáin*'s prologue promoted the combined position of birth giver and nurturer as a positive and even preeminent one for women. Moreover, the *cáin* professed responsibility for transforming women from slaves forced to perform the lethal opposite of nuturing, the act of war, to mothers. The *cáin* also claimed credit for creating the very concept of natural, God-given motherhood. The author(s) of the ninth-century *cáin* drew on both the Christian tradition of sacred motherhood, exemplified by the Virgin Mary and motherly saints, and on legal ideals of good mothers.[101] *Cáin Adomnáin* echoed the voices of those who did not believe, as formal laws told them, that birth givers were no more distinguished than the sheep who increased the flocks and that just any woman could mother just any child. Adomnán's law added yet another voice to the confusion over mothers and motherhood. It limited women's social roles to the single role of mother, but at the same time imbued motherhood with a unique status and emotional importance lacking in other texts.

Unlike most texts produced in early Ireland, *Cáin Adomnáin* is datable and linked to an authenticated historical figure. We know who Adomnán was, when he lived, and what he did, and we have several texts, including a tract on relics and a life of Saint Columcille, written by him.[102] Adomnán may or may not have composed the seventh-century stratum of the law that bears his name—the *lex innocentium* prohibiting the murder of all noncombatants, including women, children, and clerics—but the text can reliably be assigned to a decade of the saint's life, 690 to 700, and to his communities of Cenannas (Kells) and Rath mBoth (Raphoe).[103] The annals claimed that Adomnán himself returned to Ireland from his monastery off the coast of Scotland, Í (Iona), to promulgate the legal concept that anyone who could not fight should not be made to suffer battle.[104] Not just women were to be protected by his law, but anyone who could not or should not wield a sword. Mothers, per se, had nothing much to do with the earliest version of the *cáin*.

By 900, *Cáin Adomnáin* had become another text with a very different purpose. The entertaining story of Adomnán and his tough mother, Rónnat, which formed the preamble to the *cáin*, had become part of an ongoing discussion among the literati over the function and importance of mothers and of Christian women generally. The narrator must have been well aware of the tension between the roles of mother and fosterer, and the larger conflicts over women's position vis-à-vis patrilineage, property, and kinship networks to which this discussion referred. He also knew of the ideological effects on mothers of laws upholding patrilineage and fosterage. The storyteller took a well-defined stand on the issue. He had an ideal of motherhood, borrowed from Christian writers elsewhere, which he used to fashion his appeal for the preservation and eminence of mothers in Ireland. His was not a normative position, especially given his rejection (by silence) of the nun's life, but one that negotiated among the many views of mothers held by the early Irish.[105]

The writer of the *cáin* was well aware that his was a newly articulated position in several respects. First, he acknowledged, the *cáin* proclaimed in 697 had been a legal innovation: "The law of Adomnán is the first law made (for women) in Heaven and upon earth," he wrote.[106] The form of Adomnán's *cáin* was an extratribal, noncustomary, proclaimed and written law quite distinct from the larger body of traditional law maintained and guarded by jurists.[107] So unusual was it that the author imagined intense opposition to Adomnán's efforts from those bound by the formal legal ideals of the *senchas,* or "learned tradition", of secular texts. In the narrative, once Adomnán was finally persuaded to take up the cause of mothers, the tribal kings of Ireland protested. "An evil time when a man's sleep shall be murdered for women, that women should live, men should be slain," complained one; "women should be in everlasting bondage to the brink of Doom."[108] Adomnán brought out all his saintly paraphernalia and employed supernatural tricks to force the compliance of secular authorities. He rang his holy bell against those who would not accept his *cáin,* cursing them appropriately with a lack of "seed and issue."[109] The refusal to protect women, Adomnán's curse instructed the recalcitrant kings, meant the loss of mothers and the children they could produce.

But the author of the ninth-century narrative used his story of disobedient kings to urge his own contemporaries to resolve the tension between the roles of birth mother and foster mother. He wanted to force his readers to acknowledge the conflict between the laws, which declared women to be mere passive links in kinship alliances, and the actual, aggressive participation of some women in creating fosterage as well as other kinds of support relationships for their children. The *cáin* posited a completely different social hierarchy from that of the secular laws; in Adomnán's scheme, women were of much greater worth than in the old legal schedules.[110] In the laws, a woman's social value, determined by her honor price, was never more than half that of her male guardian, be he father, husband, or another kinsman or surrogate. *Cáin Adomnáin,* which prohibited any kind of injury to women, assigned astonishingly severe penalties and high fees for harming women: "Whoever slays a woman shall be condemned to a twofold punishment, that is, his right hand and his left foot shall be cut off before death, and then he shall die, and his kindred shall pay seven full *cumals*."[111]

The *brithemoin* and the elite they served did not take kindly to obvious change; so, to validate his legal innovation, the prologue's narrator posited the God-givenness of Adomnán's law. First of all, Adomnán extorted approval for his law (at his mother's urging) from an angelic representative of God himself. Further, the saint did not rest satisfied, according to the narrator, until he secured sureties representative of the highest clerical and secular powers in Ireland and symbolic of the greater cosmos for the emancipation of women.

Not only did he call upon sympathetic clerics and kings to support him, but the holiest saints and the very elements of the universe itself, the sun and moon, attested to Adomnán's innovation, so natural a law was his *cáin*. The strength of Adomnán's conviction on this matter of mothers inspired a second conversion for those who supported him. His *cáin* brought unbelieving kings to a new faith. The author used the words "oc a tabairt dochum creitme," *creitem* being the normal term for faith in Christianity. To protect mothers was as natural as being a Christian.[112]

Finally, it was the will of the Virgin Mother that Adomnán and his supporters promote the *cáin* protecting women—or rather, protecting mothers, for all women, according to *Cáin Adomnáin,* were mothers like the Virgin herself. As the angel told Adomnán,

> You shall establish a law in Ireland and Britain for the sake of the mother of each one, because a mother has borne each one, and for the sake of Mary mother of Jesus Christ, through whom all are. Mary besought her Son on behalf of Adomnán about this Law. . . . For the sin is great when anyone slays the mother and the sister of Christ's mother and the mother of Christ, and her who carries the spindle and who clothes everyone.[113]

Mary was the mother of all Christians, and every mother was a mother to Mary, a sister to Mary, and a mother to Christ himself; and what is more, every woman was a mother. Adomnán's *cáin* transformed all women from androgynous slaves with no social identity to human beings with the single highly valued social role of motherhood. Once women had labored, like inanimate objects, to hold up sluice bars and burning candles; they had lived outside the humanized space of men's farms and forts, in the dirt beyond the gates. Once they had been forced into the filthiest gender-transgressing deeds, the acts of war. This is why the most eloquent episode of the *cáin* juxtaposed the image of slain warrior woman with that of dead mother, her suffering babe at her bloody breast. Adomnán's law changed all that, turning nonwomen into the most womanly of women: mothers. Thus, whereas the earlier *lex innocentium* sought to protect all nonmales, the ninth-century *cáin* set out specifically to guard mothers from harm. It did so not because mothers bore babies to patrilineages, but because everyone owed a debt of affection to mothers for the pregnancy, labor, and nurturing they performed and a debt of worship for embodying all the same sacral principles as the Virgin Mary herself.[114]

Cáin Adomnáin's author was no lunatic voice in the emotional wilderness of early Ireland. To begin with, other religious texts promoted the Marian exemplar of motherhood held up in the *cáin*. As early as the seventh century, Irish monks were calling Saint Brigit another Mary, in the sense of sharing

Virgin and child from the *Book of Kells* (ca. 800 C.E.). Reproduced by permission of the Board of Trinity College Dublin.

the Virgin's motherhood of Jesus; in the same tradition, Íte nursed her little Ísucán.[115] Just as Mary, the *mater intacta,* tended her divine son, so these virginal abbess saints lavished affection on their fosterlings, real and imagined, through ecstatic vision.[116]

The image of virgin mother was an attractive one to the same literati who promoted sexless conception and clerically controlled childbirth. But the virginal mothers of saints' lives and Marian poems also appealed because, as with foster mothers, no other kinsmen or kinswomen competed with their babies for their attention. Mary, Brigit, Íte, and their like were perfect mothers because that is *all* that they were, in early Irish eyes. They sheltered, protected, and loved their children, nothing else. Monastic poets addressed devotional poems to Mary in the hope that she, like a good mother, would intervene with the higher male powers to protect her poor babies from all sorts of worldly evils.[117]

The storyteller of *Cáin Adomnáin* wrote, "Mary besought her son on behalf of Adomnán about this Law." Similarly, Rónnat besought her son Adomnán, although she also tortured him, to proclaim his *cáin* in order to preserve her other charges, the women and clerics and children of Ireland. Rónnat did "what not many women would do to their sons" in order to save her sisters and daughters. And although Adomnán suffered hunger, thirst, and eventually even death before he was persuaded, the aggressive persistence of Rónnat and the supplications of Mary paid off. Like mother and foster mother, the women worked together within the traditional structures of kinship and law to modify existing social relationships, thus making the world a little safer for their children.

In this sense, *Cáin Adomnáin* helped explain the tensions between the roles of fosterer and mother, revealed by juxtaposing secular laws and narratives. For men concerned to maintain their patrilineages, the complementary nurturing systems of motherhood and fosterage worked perfectly. A boy (and, less important, a girl) born of a legitimate union was nursed first by his mother, then by a foster mother and foster father chosen for reasons of social and political utility. A man might have several children of several wives so disposed. A mother's job, however, was far more difficult and fraught with ideological ambiguity. According to law, she was to cherish her child and maintain a bond of affection throughout both of their lives. Yet she was also to yield her child when it reached the tender age of seven to another mother who, according to one tradition, loved, and was loved by, the child as much as or more than the birth mother herself. The laws suggested, and the saints' lives confirmed, that a birth mother resolved this intolerable situation by helping to choose the fosterer, trying to place her child among her own blood kin where her baby would be accessible and continue to receive, indirectly through her brother or sister, her own support and love. She may also have coped by becoming a fosterer herself. A good mother used law and custom to her advantage and that of her child, just as Rónnat and Mary did. She intervened with powerful husband and kinsmen, persuading them to do what was best for her baby and for herself.

Cáin Adomnáin at once validated the role of mothers as intercessors among their blood and affinal kin on behalf of their children, and raised that role to a new, affective, sacral height. The text revealed that some, at least, of the early Irish literati recognized the obligation of mothers to secure kinship affiliation of both kinds for their children and to supplement those blood ties with the love and support of a specially selected foster mother. In fact, the *cáin* suggested that the early Irish expected as much of their mothers, despite laws that relegated mothers to the passive position of childbearer and persuaded them to give up their young children to other, supposedly equally qualified nurturers.

Cáin Adomnáin's picture of mothers differed from that of other sources in one important respect: the author of the *cáin* demanded that mothers be rewarded for their efforts with high honor prices and the same kind of protection that mothers wished to extend to their children. It was a practical but severe law. It set out specific penalties for any sort of injury to the women who brought, or would some day bring, babies into the world. It allowed for no striking, no' blemishing, no raping or fondling of women, not even the imputation of unchastity or the unjust denial of the legitimacy of their offspring. And unlike other laws of assault and murder, the *cáin* allowed for no plea bargaining or paying off the injured party: "There shall be no cross-case or balancing of guilt in Adomnán's Law, but each one pays for his crimes from his own hand."[118] Not even women were allowed to harm women, so precious were mothers to Irish society.[119] Adomnán's mother could kill her only boy, but no one could touch a mother.

For the jurists, a bad mother was a woman who failed to bear legitimate children or to secure a place for her children among her kin and that of her husband or to find another couple to foster her children. For hagiographers, bad mothers were like bad foster mothers, women who failed to love or tend their babies. For the teller of Adomnán's story, however, all mothers were good mothers. The only villains in Adomnán's scheme were the Christians who failed to recognize that all women were mothers whose aim in life was to intervene on behalf of their children with the powerful patriarchs of this world and the next. For God himself, like an Irish nobleman, had many wives, who had many sons and daughters, all of whom needed to be brought to his attention in order to secure his protection. It was the business of mothers to arrange this protection for their children against sometimes cruel society and the obligation of their children to offer thankful love, support, and worship in return. For the one thing revealed by all these divergent sources is that, despite laws, despite formal ideologies, mothers of the early Irish were no passive bearers of babies. They were active participants in the social networks that bound them to their families, husbands, children, and other allies.

6

The Domestic Economy

I f courtship in early Ireland consisted of contractual negotiations spiced with sex, marriage represented the done deal and the production of children. Man and woman could love or make love without ever forming a legal union, but there could be no marriage or similarly formal arrangement without a contract. *Lánamnasa cumtusa comperta,* the jurists called them: contracts or unions for the purpose of reproduction.[1] But such contracts also implied a wide variety of other kinds of production that, together with the production of children, formed the domestic economy (a term used here to include the household economies of all formal and legitimate couples, just as "marriage" here is shorthand for many different legal unions). Although contractual unions between men and women betrayed juridical, social, and ideological functions, they also had a fundamental economic purpose. For most women this domestic economy defined normal economic experience. A couple joined contractually usually set up house together, pooling their resources, although the laws allowed for other kinds of arrangements too. For instance, one or the other partner might bring all the goods, or the two might not actually form a household.

A man and woman united in economic union practiced many kinds of production, with most of the labor divided by sex. He farmed or herded; she minded the children, house, and farmyard. If they were wealthy, he managed the male clients and slaves, and she oversaw the female laborers. He traded gifts with his lord and took the family surplus to trade; she carded, spun, wove, and sewed. Sometimes they helped each other, but generally they kept to their own gender-specific tasks.

Similarly, when each brought his or her own property to the union, both had some use of the common capital but the property itself belonged to the original owner. The pair decided between them, guided by their vocational training, community opinion, and traditional expectations of gender roles, how to assign labor and profits within the union. And if they should decide to divorce—the laws show that there were plenty of reasons—lawyers ordered the redistribution of capital and profits between the two. Despite their often low opinion of women, jurists came up with a remarkably fair formula for settlement.

Not only was marriage, or a marriage-style relationship, the normative economic experience for free women in early Ireland, but it could also be a relatively equitable one, despite the legal restrictions on women as economic actors and the gendered division of labor. At work within the walls of their houses and the hedges of their fields, men and women most closely approached similar status. When Cormac delved and Derbforgaill span—or when both were hauling the harvest to the barn, or slopping the pigs in a pelting rain, or anxiously tending a sick child—their labor became equally valuable to their shared household. One economic partner could not maintain a house and farm without the other, and one alone could certainly not produce the children so necessary and precious to their little economic island, as well as to their families and society. Neither production nor reproduction could occur within the domestic economy without the resources and labor of both husband and wife. Further, this mutually dependent arrangement gave each of them the status of participant in the larger economy, permitting them to labor outside the household if time and profits allowed.[2]

Women had choices within the conjugal economy, just as they had choices to make about courtship, sexual unions, and procreation. The sources insisted that reproduction was women's foremost economic, as well as social and political, function. Lawyers, literati, and the political elite believed that women's duty and aim was to bear children, and that women's other tasks were to be adapted to this, their metier. But the assignment of childbearing is a social and economic choice made both by the childbearers themselves and those who nominally control them. In fact, women were exposed to a variety of economic experiences out of, as well as in, bed; whereas most chose to reproduce, they also pursued many other economically profitable labors besides fornication, pregnancy, and childbirth. In particular, women were responsible for dairying and for every stage of cloth production in early Ireland. Women adapted childbearing and rearing to these other jobs.

Men and women agreed upon—and text and reality coincided in representing—a balance of production and reproduction in women's lives. They disagreed over the extent to which women themselves controlled the balance. It is exactly at this point of dissension over the limits to, and nature of, women's

economic choices that the sources reveal the actual economic experience and
strategies of women.

The Creation of Domestic Capital

An exchange of property made a marriage or another sexual union in
early Ireland, and such a union turned a woman into an economic actor. Before marriage, a woman was completely dependent upon her father or male
guardian, with no resources of her own. At marriage, she became able to make
economic decisions for her good and the good of others. Of course, from
birth women had economic value. As babies their worth lay in their potential
as laborers and wives; as children, they helped about house or farm; as adolescents, they trained for the more complicated labors that they would later
take up. But only at the point of forming the most important contract of her
life did a woman gain the property and the right to use it that made her a full
partner in the microeconomy of whatever family she became, or remained,
affiliated with. The economic changes that accompanied her marriage were
the most momentous in a woman's life. She achieved adult status, signified by
both her sexual union with a man and her new economic role. To a varying
extent, she gained affiliation with her husband and his family and thus secured
their physical and legal protection of herself, her children, and her property.
She was transformed from a penniless dependent on her father or other guardian to a partner with her husband. Finally, she began the process, unique to
her kind, of producing that most precious of commodities, legitimate heirs.

The contract that initiated all these profound changes signified little of their
eventual impact. No written contracts remain; families, as we have seen, exchanged promises, guaranteed by others in the community, that boy would
marry girl and that each would contribute something material, together forming the *comthinchor,* the common capital of the union. The bride's family took
a *coibche* or *tinnscra* from her husband, or the bride took it from her father,
who got it from the groom. This may or may not have been different from
her unofficial dowry, a kind of premortem inheritance from her parents. In
other words, bridewealth and dowry seem to have coexisted in early Ireland,
although dowry may have been more popular among the nobility.[3] A man
brought to marriage his inheritance, or the expectation of it, and whatever
other property he might have accumulated by gift or purchase.

Perhaps a range of other gifts and trades accompanied the union, depending
on social class and other circumstances, for although the laws made a formula
of marriage, we have seen that personal interpretation of the process could

vary widely. Certainly, no *morgengabe* ever changed hands in early Ireland; no source records the exchange of this typical Germanic payment made by groom to bride on the morning after the wedding in thanks for her coming chaste to the marriage bed.[4] Marriage was never a matter of sexual consummation for the early medieval Irish, as continental canonists urged, but of alliance, affective or other, exchange, and the pooling of capital. Nor was marriage an exchange of bride for other goods. The Irish distinguished between free women and livestock or other kinds of property, although the female slave (*cumal*), like the cow (*sét,* half a milch cow), was once used as a unit of value.[5]

Theoretically, according to lawyers, the ideal contract between man and woman was a "union of equal property" (*lánamnas comthinchuir*) in which they pooled equivalent amounts of land, cattle, and household goods into their marriage.[6] This was, of course, a marriage of the noble and wealthy; among the commoners who married, the more normal union was probably a *lánamnas mná for fertinchur,* to which a woman brought household goods and a man a rented fief.[7] The original law was ambiguous, however, as to whether a wife would have brought as much (of each) of land, stock, and goods as her husband, or just the equivalent value of his contribution, not necessarily including land. Presumably the value of each partner's contribution, like all other points of the contract, was haggled over by his and her families.[8] In Ireland, as elsewhere in the early medieval world, women were legally prohibited from inheriting family land and taking it with them when they left home for another man's kin group.[9] Only a woman who competed with no male heirs could legally inherit the usufruct, not the absolute ownership, of patrilineal lands. She might acquire as much as seven *cumals*' worth, or even fourteen according to commentators—possibly as many as 480 acres.[10] Before she could take control of it, her close male relatives had to provide guaranties that she would not try to alienate the property by handing it over to her in-laws, leaving it to her children, or selling or donating it.[11] Indeed, both canonists and lawyers urged that an heiress marry a responsible man from within her extended kin group, just to reassure her *fine.*[12] If she insisted on marrying someone else, bringing all the land into a conjugal economy and creating a *lánamnas fir for bantinchur* (union of a man on a woman's property), her husband was legally out of luck and land at her death; the property passed neither to him nor to their children but back to her natal kin.[13] Daughters could also inherit what lawyers called *orba cruib ocus slíasta,* "land of hand and thigh," which probably meant land their mothers had gained by their own labor (*orba cruib*) and land that their mothers had received as part of a *coibche.*[14] Such property could have been passed down from their mothers' families but could only come to a daughter who had no brothers. This land women held absolutely.[15]

However, women and their families in Ireland and elsewhere also ignored the laws, devising other ways to endow new wives with land and other property. The women and men of Merovingian Gaul and Anglo-Saxon England left charters and wills to prove the point. Frankish fathers deeded farms to their daughters, complaining about the stupid legal restrictions that they had to circumvent, and English mothers fought with their children over their right to bestow fields upon distant kinswomen.[16] In Ireland, too, women gained land as gifts from their parents, in loving recognition of the injustice that decreed the *fintiu* to their brothers.[17] Hagiographers gave indirect evidence when they wrote of brides who opted for Jesus, rather than more tangible spouses, and against their parents' wills took the land they had been given in premortem inheritance to the nunnery.[18] This land seems to have been granted prior to any specific decisions about marriage, as the daughter's just due and her support in her adult life. The practice of giving daughters premortem inheritance in defiance of formal law proved remarkably durable. Evidence from as late as the 1960s shows that in the isolated rural settlements of northern Ireland, which were organized on the medieval rundale system with partible inheritance, families often doled out their land according to informal notions of fairness rather than formal laws. By this system, women who needed it received bits of land at marriage.[19] Likewise, in an earlier Ireland, lawyers parceling out theoretical property may have forgotten daughters, but parents did not.

How much land women finally acquired is unclear, varying by class, region, and family situation. Theoretically, all good land was somebody's *fintiu*. Farmers had developed and enclosed most of the arable of Ireland by the time jurists managed to record the laws.[20] Legally, not much land could have changed either female or male hands, since jurists restricted any alienation of the *fine*'s property without the entire kin group's consent.[21] Among families that obeyed these rigid laws, partible inheritance must have played havoc, as the laws themselves suggested; generational expansion and contraction aside, any demographic growth would have compelled men and women to break the laws, some selling and some buying in order to create workable properties. What is more, the sources are full of incidental references to men and women purchasing and alienating land, especially to the church. Although the laws emphasized the authority of larger families in these matters, it seems clear that nuclear groups and even individuals made their own decisions about their properties.[22]

As with other family business, what to do with the land—including the problem of endowing a daughter with a marriage portion—must have occasioned discussion, negotiation, and anxious argument for parents and children in early Ireland. Which of the fields scattered about the countryside should be given to one of several daughters, when there were also sons to provide for? The opinions of uncles and cousins about keeping some sort of coherent estate must have been considered, accepted or rejected. Parents must also have faced community pressure to marry off a troublesome daughter, whatever the cost in property, or instead, to keep a good worker at home and conserve the family fields, or maybe to send her off to a house of religious women with a small farm as a gift of entry. Whatever the neighbors, local lord, and local clergy might have thought about the distribution of fields, the balance of nubile men and women in the area, the character and standing of any given candidates for marriage, and the effects of the proposed merger of properties also influenced the bargaining. The complex associations of family land, genealogy, and patrilineage, so beloved of lawyers, were less compelling in the real world of needs, wants, and negotiations.

What is more, land was not the primary basis of a person's status or wealth in early Ireland. Instead, the humans and animals that moved across the land, and the goods that could be accumulated upon it, established the worth of a man and, indirectly, a woman. Legal tracts on social rank measured freemen and nobles in terms of their movable goods and their relations to clients lower on the social scale and to lords higher up. For instance, an *ócaire*, the lowest legal class of freeman, was to be estimated by his "sevens" according to the eighth-century *Críth Gablach:* seven cows with a bull, seven pigs, seven sheep, and a horse; land did not make the *ócaire,* since he rented the pasture to support his stock.[23] Kings, on the other end of the scale, derived status from oath helpers and fighters bound to them by grants of stock and more prestigious gifts, such as weapons or jewelry.[24] As for women, according to the lawyers' schemes, they got their status from their men. In theory, it did not matter whether men thought in terms of fields or cattle when judging the worth of a female.

Land and lineage may have given a man his name, but goods and dynamic social processes such as clientage gave both men and women their status. People with important names constantly slid down the social hierarchy, their genealogies lost and forgotten, while those with cattle and clients prospered and propagated.[25] This mobility caused a small fissure in the formal social structure through which all sorts of economic opportunities for women slipped. For if patrilineal groups did actually guard their lands as jealously as lawyers imagined, if land meant mostly membership in a family rather than economic worth, and if men measured men by movable goods and clients, then women, whose changeable, tenuous family ties were a matter of constant negotiation anyway, could participate in the economy as almost equal partners with men. This is not to say that women had as many economic opportunities as men or were able to become as wealthy on their own account, for women's limited ability to act as landlords, sureties, and military leaders restricted their relations with tenants and clients. Nevertheless, everyone agreed that women could own as much movable property as they could get their hands on, and livestock, handicrafts, and the goods and services that could be traded for them were the real basis of wealth in the early Irish economy.

Only in the heathen past imagined by *Cáin Adomnáin* did women have "no share in bag or basket"; in the Christianizing early Middle Ages, women had clothing, flocks of sheep, and even gold with which to thank Adomnán's churches for his *cáin*.[26] Lawyers and canonists agreed that women had a right to clothing, jewelry, household goods, and farm animals and their products, and that these were the proper items for a marriage portion. In fact, wives were expected to bring their personal effects and the equipment needed for work to their new households, just as husbands contributed traditionally manly tools such as oxgoads and ploughshares.[27] *Lanna, ranna, ocus bregda,* the lawyers called them, literally, "cloth, portions [of livestock], and [household] implements"; canonists rephrased it in Latin: *vaccas, vesta, et vasa,* "cattle, clothing, and pots and pans."[28] Another tract got down to the details of household equipment, which ideally included a griddle, beetle, scale, bucket, kneading trough, sieve, dishes, cups, hides, pillows, and cookpots.[29] No doubt these movable goods formed the basis of the property of women from less wealthy families, whereas aristocratic ladies may also have added more precious movables, such as jewelry or fine clothing, to their landed inheritance.[30] If, in the ideal union, each partner actually made a contribution of equal value, then some land-poor but wealthy women must have brought considerable trousseaux to match their grooms' farmlands. Gregory of Tours described fantastic amounts of gold, jewels, and fancy clothing that Frankish princesses carted off to their new lives.[31] In the Irish narratives, princesses and *mná síde* arrayed themselves with whole treasuries of ornaments on costly tunics and cloaks — perhaps a literary reflection of the gold and silver that noblewomen took to marriage in the real world.[32]

It was easy enough, after the marriage negotiations ended, to reckon up the property each partner brought to the union. Man and wife — or, more likely, their kin — probably counted the cows and kept track of the rest of their respective contributions to the common capital of their household. Although both made use of the conjugal fund, what was his remained legally his, and hers remained mostly hers, ostensibly in case of divorce and for inheritance purposes. But spouses also made personal gifts to each other, such as rings, that never appeared in formal legal documents.[33] Further, they made less tangible contributions to the partnership itself, designed to cement the personal bond between the partners and thus ensure the durability and profitability of the economic union. Like modern business partnerships, early Irish *lánamnasa* needed more than money to make them work.

For instance, spouses provided support and advice for each other. When a man could bring no other contribution to his union with a *banchomarbae*, the least he could offer was *comairle comnart*, strong advice. Since this particular union was ideologically fraught with gender reversals—"the man takes the woman's place and the woman takes the man's place," according to *Cáin Lánamnae*—lawyers must have assumed that a wife normally owed her husband such good counsel.[34] This is exactly the sort of service Mac Dathó's wife provided when he fell sulking over his famous dog; and it is the same advice that could, according to the sour author of *Tecosca Cormaic,* ruin a man with a vicious, ill-meaning wife.[35]

Spouses relied on each other's family connections as a kind of common capital, too. In times of need, a husband or wife expected help from the in-laws. The sources revealed this attitude mostly at elite levels, but it is easy enough to imagine a young wife begging a loan from her father when her own farm, shared with her mate, fell on hard times or a man calling on his brothers to act as oath helpers when his in-laws got into legal trouble, especially if he liked his affines and if they were all neighbors. (However, it is important to bear in mind that any woman's ability to summon help from natal or affinal kin rested mainly on informal obligations, rather than formal legal powers, as we shall see in the next chapter.) The annals revealed that noble spouses lent exactly this sort of assistance to each other. Some marriages were even designed to provide political assistance to the bride or groom and her or his family. The Uí Sínaig, who ruled Ard Macha for generations as its abbots and officers, married their sons and daughters into political alliances in order to secure their own grasp on the abbacy. Their expectation was that a woman from, say, a family competing for ecclesiastical office at Ard Macha could persuade her relatives to support her husband's kin instead. Likewise, when the wife's family needed help in freeing a political hostage or fighting a small war, she could call on her Ard Macha in-laws to wield swords or holy relics on her behalf.[36] The Uí Sínaig offer only one of many such examples that might be traced through years of annal entries and genealogies. Such manipulation of kinfolk on behalf of a spouse was among the predictable contributions to the conjugal economy. When a man legally took a woman or a woman accepted a man, each also gained a potential wealth of political, social, and economic support from affines, which helped keep their household intact, their economy afloat, and their union amicable.[37]

Finally, the couple exchanged sexual services, which were not capital but ideally resulted in precious products: babies. In a society where adults sought to control the marriage and reproduction of their young, the most intimate mutual contributions of spouses could hardly be simple acts of love or desire. The canonists described sex in Pauline terms of conjugal duty, and lawyers were even more matter-of-fact about the responsibilities of partners in a *lánamnas*. They set down, in commentary on the law of legitimate procreative unions, exactly who owed what to whom. Woman contributed "sex and fertility and her womanly function" (*toil ocus genus ocus bangním*), and man supplied his "male function" (*fergním*).[38] The man owed not just sex but the reproductive function; likewise, his spouse had to give him not just carnal pleasure but exclusive rights to her body and its offspring. For when a man took a wife, he also acquired every child that she produced for his lineage. That was part, even the most important part, of the bargain.

Thus a legitimately joined couple together created both conjugal capital and, from the capital, profits. They each brought their cows or pots or fields, their more intimate possessions, their support and counsel, the help and advice—wanted or not—of their kin, and their bodies. And one more thing became part of the household economy to be hoarded and prized and, should it ever come to a rough divorce, seized by the father and his kin: the children. This wealth that neither partner brought along to their new household but that a woman, with some help from her man, could produce became the very basis of the conjugal economy and the source of a wife's economic opportunities.

Domestic Labor: Reproduction

The author of *Cáin Adomnáin* claimed that women were the producers of saints and bishops and righteous men; they were creators, even as Jehovah himself.[39] Inevitably, given the elite's desire for legitimate heirs and the whole focus of patrilineal ideology on orderly procreation, women's most important domestic labor, in the eyes of the literati and their patrons, was the bearing of children. A man could not discard his bride for shoddy housekeeping or lousy needlework, but a marriage contract could be broken if a woman failed to produce babies or if her spouse proved unable to impregnate her.[40]

Ireland was no exception to the rule in traditional agrarian societies, particularly those practicing intensive plough agriculture, that women get left at home. Historians and anthropologists long ago decided that when women were happy foragers of the paleolithic, they were the primary food producers for their groups and, as far as anyone can determine, enjoyed gender symmetry. According to this scheme, women lost their economic value as producers when humans turned to settled agriculture; foragers were no longer needed and, what is more, fieldwork was supposedly incompatible with having and raising babies. Pushing a scratch plough or forcing animals to pull a heavy plough was hard work, completed at a distance from the house and yard, and dangerous to both pregnant women and small children. As a result, women's work became both circumscribed and invisible. Friedrich Engels claimed that the economic surplus that came with agriculture allowed men to invent private property, which in turn led to the creation of families, which became patrilineages. Women were forced to produce heirs to the private property of patrilineal groups and all women's labor henceforth depended on its adaptability to their reproductive priorities.[41]

The economic experience of women in early Ireland fits this deceptively neat developmental paradigm perfectly in some ways, although not in others. Irish jurists recorded ideal evidence for Ester Boserup's classic association of a growing population with limited polygyny at elite levels, a dowry system, plough cultivation, and devaluation and restriction of women's labor.[42] What all the classic studies of the sexual division of labor—from Emile Durkheim's theory of small-brained women and the ideas of Engels, Malinowski, Margaret Mead, and Claude Lévi-Strauss to those of Judith Brown—miss is the imposition of their own nineteenth- and twentieth-century values on an economy long gone and on barbarian women and men who would have found the anthropologists' deprecation of reproductive functions truly appalling.[43] For while most theories regarding the sexual division of labor and the economic oppression of women focus on motherhood, holding it accountable for women's low status and restricted economic roles, they also assume that reproduction limited the value of women and that reproduction was forced on women who would have preferred other economic tasks.[44]

It is true that Irish men and women, too, put pressures both crude and subtle on women to reproduce. *Cáin Adomnáin*'s effusive hymn to motherhood was just one of the subtler examples; calling contractual sexual relations between women and men *lánamnasa cumtusa comperta* and constructing an entire political ideology based on patrilineages were other, less subtle instances. Some men tried to direct women to reproduction above all other economic activities, and they tried to manage that particular labor of women, as we have seen.

Yet whether or not their alternatives were limited, women retained economically meaningful reproductive choices.[45] The importance of women as childbearers did not necessarily lend them higher legal status or political power, nor did it enable them to control the entire process of reproduction or its products. Motherhood did, however, bring women opportunities as economic actors and, as a result, informal influence among families and neighbors. What is more, women surely knew enough to exploit this status, manipulate their choices about childbearing, and use motherhood as a resource. Some men believed so. That they did is clear, for example, in the tale of Mugain, wife of Diarmait mac Cerbaill, and eventually mother of a lamb, a fish, and Aed Sláine. She was so desperate to reproduce and thus maintain her position as queen, with all its resources, that she sought the aid of holy men. Her aim was to bear a son, keep her husband, and remain the rich and powerful woman she had become at marriage. Mugain's storyteller made clear that women's reproductive choices, like their other productive choices, allowed them to increase their economic participation. By such a strategy, women could endure and even counter the formal misogyny of their society.[46]

Still, more besides a woman's choice to reproduce, which was itself enmeshed in all sorts of related decisions, shaped her childbearing career. If women turned themselves into economic actors by producing babies, then it seems logical that they would have sought maximum fertility, because the more babies they had, the more valuable they became to their husbands and kin and thus the more economic opportunities they won. In fact, European women in the early Middle Ages averaged about twenty years of childbearing potential, but all sorts of physiological and cultural factors could alter this span. Age at menarche, for example, could be considerably delayed if a girl did not get enough to eat.[47] In hungry years and at other bad times, social pressures as much as age at puberty set the age of sexual union and legitimate childbearing. A girl might choose to wait, garnering her resources and wasting her reproductive years, before beginning a family of her own. Throughout Europe, women, sometimes together with their men, also chose purposely to control their fertility for economic or religious reasons. Some couples may have strictly observed Christian sexual prohibitions and thus limited their moments of possible conception, or else they decided to limit the number of mouths they had to feed.[48]

Given all these conditions, if a woman chose to form a legitimate union with a man and begin her childbearing years when she was in her early to midtwenties, as seems normally to have been the case, she could expect to continue reproducing regularly until well into her forties. Further, given the effects of nursing on conception, a woman might ordinarily expect to conceive about every thirty-two months. Add factors of diet and culture—whether a woman was healthy enough to carry successive fetuses to term, for instance, or notions about the proper seasons for conception and birth—and the usual cycle of births during the Middle Ages seems to have lasted about three years.[49] As sex ratios suggest, not every woman was such an efficient reproducer. Some died before their twenty years were up. But many of those who survived the hazards of childbearing could expect to remarry and continue reproducing after their spouses died, for many women and men outlived their mates to remarry.

Hence the fecundity of women in the early Middle Ages may have been between five and six children, the highest of the entire premodern period in Europe. The average of births necessary to maintain the early medieval European population was about 3.5 per woman, except during plague years. Archaeological remains from cemeteries outside of Ireland have yielded women's pubic bones, the parturition scars of which give slightly higher figures of about 4.2 births per woman, which is in accordance with an expanding population, although not an entirely trustworthy statistic.[50]

Fecundity was only one factor affecting women's reproductive choices, however. A woman determined to produce the maximum possible babies, who successfully brought forth infant after infant, would still be lucky to see half of them survive childhood. Evidence from late medieval England suggests that in households consisting of two parents and five children, which is just about the maximum a woman could deliver, only 3.2–3.5 members were alive at any moment; accident or illness carried off the others.[51] The stark numbers make the anxiety of early Irish mothers to find kind fosterers and adequate inheritances for their children all the more comprehensible. The figures also suggest why a woman who successfully bore and raised a child, particularly a boy child, was so prized by her kin and the society in general.

The Irish kept no statistics, and their graveyards yield no scarred bones to parallel the continental evidence, but the sources do confirm that women who were trained to reproduce did so with varying success. The hagiographers told sad tales of desperate parents who begged the saints for babies when all other methods had failed. The jurists described in their divorce laws what could happen to a woman who did not live up to her reproductive potential: her value as an economic partner in a sexual union fell to nothing.

Yet, as the literati made clear, a woman who bore a whole flock of babies was not necessarily the most valuable reproducer, either. If she produced quantity rather than quality, she was a bad wife and an expensive partner in *lánamnas*. *Senbríathra Fíthail*'s author declared that "being heirless is better than great fertility."[52] A family needed only enough children so that one or two males survived to adulthood. Overproduction decreased the value of both reproducer and products, as both women and men realized. Saint Berach's hagiographer wrote how, during a famine, a well-to-do farmer went hunting, leaving his pregnant wife at home to deliver. His instructions to her were to kill the child as soon as it was born. After delivery, when her attendant asked the new mother what to do with the infant, she replied simply, "A mharbadh": "Kill him."[53] Both parents made an economically informed decision for the good of their household. Yet the hagiographer believed it a bad decision, as is clear from the story's resolution: the baby's rescue. Nor was this an isolated instance, as the penitentialists attested with their laments about contraception, abortion, and infanticide.

The Irish considered a mother's product to be of better quality when it was both legitimate and male. Jurists specified more extensive rights of contract for the *adaltrach* (secondary wife) who gave birth to sons.[54] Mugain's story would not have had a moral if she had stopped giving birth after the fish and the lamb or had produced a daughter instead of the great king Aed Sláine. And it may be no coincidence that the mother in Berach's vita ultimately chose not to kill her child because it was *mac,* a boy. As we have seen, no evidence exists for gender-specific infanticide in early Ireland, as elsewhere in Europe, but we have also seen how men valued men more than women, legally, politically, socially, and in all ways. Women, too, were persuaded to apply this scale of values to the products of their childbearing labors.

Women's reproductive labors began with conception and ended, often, with their babies' early childhood. Just as men seized the role of managers of reproduction, they also participated in parenting; for although women produced the raw stuff that became farmers, warriors, and monks, male fosterers helped finish the product, at least among the elite. In a sense, then, men helped with the reproduction of the work force by taking the most precious products of women's labor, their male babies, and placing them in training with men.[55] But women participated in the decision to foster out their children, and some took in fosterlings of their own. And if men reproduced male laborers, then women reproduced the reproducers, training girls to become full partners in households of their own.

A *cétmuinter* who produced the desirable quantity and quality of babies gained economic opportunities that childless women, with the possible exception of some nuns, always lacked. An *adaltrach* could enhance her status and expand her economic experience by having sons. But a wife who produced inadequately or who failed to produce could lose not only economic opportunities but husband, household, and status.

Dairying and Cloth Production

Reproduction was not by any means women's only economic function, although they learned that it was their most important. While they grew fat with pregnancy, while they nursed their babies and chased after their toddlers, women continued to do other jobs. When finally their babies had gone to fosterers or grown up enough to take care of themselves, women were free to devote themselves to other kinds of production, unless they took in other women's children as fosterlings. What women did mostly was hard farmyard and household work, especially dairying.[56] If they were among the elite, they did farm and household-related managerial work. Slaves and semifree women may have hauled water, cooked, ground grain in a quern, or worked in a mill.[57] What they were most valued for, after reproduction, was cloth production, particularly the thoroughly feminine needlework that the lucky noble few had the opportunity to practice. Only seasonally did women participate in men's work away from the farmyard, and only the odd woman seems to have pursued prestigious, traditionally male callings, such as poetry or healing.

Every wife in the cattle-based economy of early Ireland was a milker, churner, and cheese maker, or a manager of her dairymaids.[58] Divorce laws drew the most vivid, if incidental, picture of women's work in the dairy. Lawyers estimated the relative worth of the conjugal capital, the investment of labor in increasing it, and its profits, in order to decree the percentage of the property that each partner took away from the broken union. When it came to counting and dividing up the cattle of a couple bound in *lánamnas comthinchuir,* for instance, some of the profits, the calves of the original herd, fell in equal parts to the owner of the land on which they grazed, the original owner of the cattle, and the person or persons who attended the animals (assumed in the laws to be cowherds hired for the purpose).[59] Theoretically, the owner of land or cattle could be either husband or wife, as could the party who hired the herders; the jurists' formula would have been applied to each distinct field and herd held by the couple. Similarly, of milk products derived from the cattle, a third went to the owner of the grazing land, a third to the cattle owner, and a third to those who performed the labor that produced the milk, butter, and cheese.[60]

Jurists routinely assigned at least half of the laborer's third of the dairy profits to the woman of the house on the principle that "every woman is a great worker in regard of milk."[61] The saints' lives depicted plenty of such great workers, adding more incidental evidence to the legal paradigm; Saint Pátraic's foster mother, for instance, who encountered the demonic cow, included milking among her daily chores.[62] Even Ireland's premier female saint, Brigit, churned "as other women do," according to Cogitosus. Another hagiographer associated soft, rich cheeses with the women who made them, and women with the temptation that would lure a monk from his ascetic regimen.[63]

Jurists and hagiographers agreed that dairy production was important both to the conjugal economy and to a wife's working identity, so that one commentator demanded nothing more of a good wife than that she be home in time to milk the cows.[64] Certainly, dairy products formed a large part of any family's diet.[65] *Críth Gablach,* which detailed the rents owed by farmers to their landlords, routinely listed the "summer-food" of dairy products as half a tenant's food rents, the other half consisting of grain and meat, the products of men's labor.[66] Women's dominion over the cattle did not extend to herding them or killing them to dress their flesh, nor was it primarily women's responsibility to drive cattle or oxen before a plough, although they sometimes helped.[67] Women did not normally produce milk or butter for external markets either, at least not until the nineteenth century.[68] A wife and mother produced or oversaw the production of what her family needed for themselves and their rent. Her dairying dovetailed perfectly with child care, for she could tote her babies with her when she went out at dawn to milk the cows, whereas she could not carry them off to the fields at any distance from the house or watch them while guiding the plough.

In addition to milking, churning, and cheese making, women practiced what lawyers called "crud ocus biathad ocus méthad": penning the young pigs and calves, feeding them and their herders, and fattening up the beasts.[69] Even when women cared for the pigs, they tended only the special swine kept close by the farm, not the semiwild herds let loose to eat mast in the woods. Male swineherds, who achieved the dubious reputation of shapeshifters and seers, took care of the herds beyond the civilized bounds of the farm.[70] But ordinary farmwives slopped the *mucca crai,* sty pigs, and fed them grain or the milk products, such as whey, which women themselves produced.[71] Pigs rooted around every farmyard, providing the bacon that helped feed the family and pay the rent but also worrying the mother who could never quite keep track of all her small children. At least one saint was summoned to reconstruct a little one attacked and chewed by hungry swine, and jurists also worried about culpability in cases where pigs devoured children.[72]

But the animal that figured most importantly in women's half of the conjugal economy was the sheep, even though sheep were not animals of the yard and barn but small-brained roamers of scrubby fields and stony hills. The saints and their hagiographers associated women with sheep, as well as cows and pigs, but not necessarily with their herding. It may be the case, as has been argued, that women were left to care for the sheep because they were dirty, low-status, feminine animals in the minds of the early Irish.[73] Certainly male saints were known to flee when they heard sheep bleating, fearing that seductive women were not far behind.[74] Nevertheless, women were not so closely identified with sheep that they always took care of them. The vitae also showed boys, including young saints, as well as women herding sheep. Mothers could not always traipse after the animals wandering the hills, and it may not have been safe to send a young girl after them.[75]

Furthermore, the few legal references to women herding sheep appeared only in the special context of cases of legal entry, a process by which the putative owner of a piece of property formally entered the land to claim it. The female claimant described in the laws drove sheep onto the land to signal her occupation and use of it, whereas men making formal entry normally drove cattle.[76] But nothing in the episode suggested that the woman herself ordinarily chased the sheep around the countryside. The other equipment she was supposed to have brought along at legal entry, a kneading trough and sieve, were clearly symbolic of her economic functions on the disputed land, just as were the sheep, and not implements she ordinarily carried with her. The trough and sieve were her means to bread, just as the sheep were her source of cloth.[77] Men could and, according to *Críth Gablach,* were supposed to own sheep; sheep were one sign of a farmer's status.[78] So, it was not so much sheep that belonged to women as what sheep produced, for if babies bought a woman's place in the domestic economy, cloth was most likely the one object she offered for exchange.[79]

It was the sheep's wool, like flax, that was women's to work and finish. Women greased the wool, combed and spun it, and dyed the yarn; they also rippled, retted, washed, and hung flax to dry before scutching it to extract the fiber from its casing, hackling or combing it and, eventually, dyeing it before turning it into thread. Then they made the thread or yarn into cloth and the cloth into clothes.[80] The writer of *Cáin Adomnáin* claimed that women carried the spindle and clothed the world; if he meant that women were the managers as well as laborers at all stages of cloth production, he seems to have been right.[81] At divorce, their labor with wool and flax earned them half the finished product no matter whose sheep produced the wool or whose land fed the sheep. The less labor women put into the product, the fewer profits they gained when dividing the communal property. Similarly, women deserved more of the dyestuff derived from plants called *róid* and *glaisen* (woad) and beans called *seip.*[82] They also took more of the linen and flax when they had worked to prepare the dye and finish the linen.[83]

Clearly, a good housewife was expected to take raw wool and flax and turn them into fabric and then to make clothes from it. Just as clearly, the value of her labors was acknowledged by the men who made the laws. Another eighth-century legal tract, *Di Chetharślicht Athgabála,* described the equipment of cloth production in detail that overwhelms the reader untrained in the weaver's craft. The tract concerned distraint, the process by which a plaintiff legally seized the property of a defendant who owed a debt to him or her; the Irish word for the procedure is *athgabál,* "taking back."[84] The plaintiff gave formal notice of intention to impound the defendant's property in one to five days (always two days if the plaintiff was a woman); if the defendant did not begin to pay up or negotiate, the plaintiff legally entered the other's property and took cattle or other livestock in the amount due.[85] The plaintiff kept the animals separate from his or her own herd until the debtor settled, or after a proper amount of time, the plaintiff kept the impounded herd.[86]

The tract's author assumed that women distrained the property of other women for cloth-making equipment borrowed and never returned or bought and not paid for. The lender could seize the animals of someone who borrowed her wool bag, her weaving rod, the pattern for her cloth which she had set out on a bit of leather, or a variety of other essential tools or raw materials. A woman could also sue over the price or wages she expected for finished cloth or even for the blessing (*apartain*) she needed upon her work from another woman.[87] Every bit of wool or flax, every tool, every step in the process was valuable enough to sue over, according to the laws constructed and enforced by the men of Ireland. What is more, the tract implied a community of weaving, spinning, and sewing women. Some were better equipped than others and lent their tools. Some exchanged their labor and its products for other goods, and generally treated cloth making if not as a business then at least as a basic sector of the domestic economy, its products important items of exchange. Although women may or may not have actually sat and worked together, cloth makers seem at least to have formed laboring networks similar to groups of men who shared ploughing equipment.[88]

Cloth making took place in the house, the seat of a woman's many social and economic functions and the site of her mothering. Nothing remains of looms or cloth, as at Scandinavian sites, to place cloth making in early Irish homes rather than specialized outbuildings. Although spindle whorls are ubiquitous at domestic sites, the laws did not list dyehouses, spinningrooms, or weaving sheds among other outbuildings and barns.[89] The looms that Irish women used were probably small and portable enough to fit into the tiny one- or two-room houses they inhabited, and no doubt they boiled the smelly cauldrons of dyestuff in the house or just outside, where the occasional large-scale cooking took place safely out-of-doors.[90] One of Ciarán's later hagiographers suggested that at least one stage of linen production happened at home when he mentioned the unfortunate mother of the saint, who dried flax on the walls of her house; the stuff was a fire hazard, as she soon found out.[91]

Despite its acknowledged importance to the household economy, as well as the larger economy of the community, cloth making and sewing remained the *lámthorad,* handwork or craft, of women.[92] Men did not seize or manage it as part of their own labor, heavy or skilled, until the Norman period.[93] The Irish words for work are themselves neutral, but their connotations were made profoundly gender-specific. For instance, in the tenth- or eleventh-century tale *Airec Menman Uraird Maic Coisse* (The plan of Urard mac Coisse), a humorous list of women includes Lenn ingen Lámthora, "Cloak daughter of Handiwork," along with Léne ingen Línghuirt, "Shift daughter of Flaxfield," and Certle ingen tSnímaire, "Kirtle daughter of Spindle," among others.[94] Nothing more securely identified these figures as working women than clothwork, most of which was the light work of the hands which women could take up during a break from their other tasks. The wool would never spoil while a woman milked or cooked, and the thread could wait while a mother busied herself elsewhere. Having babies and clothing babies were all part of the nurturer's duty, as *Cáin Adomnáin*'s author acknowledged. Similarly, when Adomnán himself wrote his life of Columcille and searched for the perfect metaphor for an exceptional pregnancy, he chose cloth making. Saint Columcille's mother, about to give birth, had a vision of herself weaving a marvelous cloak colored like the rainbow. The dazzling garment was her baby saint-to-be, Columcille.[95]

If cloth making was women's work, then its ultimate product was the fine embroidery of a few highly skilled workers. The embroideress, *druinech,* did not find a place in any of the conventional status hierarchies articulated in the laws; like every other woman, her honor price depended on that of her male guardian. But lawyers listed the *druinech* among the people "difficult to maintain," by which they meant prohibitively expensive to support when sick or injured.[96] When a *druinech* was temporarily lost to the work force, lawyers declared, "there is needed someone who should perform [her] work"; yet, like a king, hospitaller, smith, carpenter, or wise man, a well-trained embroideress was so skilled, her talents so rare, and her product so richly valuable, that she was irreplaceable. Her artistry earned her more prestige than any queen had, according to one law.[97] The ability to create the decorative cloth that adorned the shoulders of warriors and the shrines of the saints could even raise a woman to sainthood; such skills earned a few women the companionship of Pátraic himself, and Saint Ercnat's chief claim to sanctity seems to have been her abilities as embroideress, cloth cutter, and seamstress for Columcille.[98] Measured by the value of her labor, then, rather than her relation to men, a *druinech* ranked near the top of the social and spiritual hierarchies.

Still, embroidery was never necessary for the survival of the Irish, as was the production of workaday cloth. A needleworker stitched her fine designs in precious metals and colored threads primarily for the secular and clerical elite, with their uniforms of gorgeously patterned cloaks and bordered tunics. As a result, the work carried such connotations of prestige that it is never quite clear in the sources whether skill with a needle added to, or derived from, a woman's social cachet. According to fosterage laws, every daughter of a chieftain was to learn embroidery along with sewing and cutting out cloth. By implication, in order to teach her, her foster mother had to know the crafts, too.[99] Certainly, only women with a certain amount of wealth and leisure could be spared for such artistic training in the production of luxury goods.

Yet, according to the narratives, embroidery was as much a natural attribute as a learned skill of the noblewomen of early Ireland as well as the princesses of the *síd*. Fíthal's *senbríathra* advised that the best kind of wife was an attractive woman with "good needlework."[100] In the narratives, too, embroidery marked a woman of noble blood as surely as her golden hair or slim ankle. When Cú Chulainn tried to persuade his wife, Emer, to allow him to continue his wild affair with the otherworldly Fand, he cited Fand's "shape and appearance and ability, needlework [*druine*] and handicraft and products of handicraft, good sense and prudence and fortitude" as reasons for his infidelity.[101] But not every well-bred girl could have mastered the needle well enough to make her embroidery priceless in legal terms and terms of trade. Like the Victorian ladies who dabbled in piano and watercolors, some of the noble daughters of Ériu were mere dilettantes. By and large, they were expected to mark their status with just two kinds of labor: the reproduction of their husbands' lineages and the stitching of pretty patterns.

Clearly needlework, like reproduction, became one focus of gender ideology. Enmeshed in myths and in laws of status, the capacity for wielding an embroidery needle—the actual ability to take the time to learn and practice the luxury craft—was a symbol of status as much as, or more than, production for material rewards. Further, like reproduction, embroidery came to represent more than the labor involved, more even than the identity of the class that practiced it or took its products. As the greater process of cloth making signified women and their work generally, embroidery represented the crème de la crème of womanhood.

In some mysterious way, putting needle and thread to cloth could steer the fortunes of the entire society. The author of *Imacallam in Dá Thúarad* (Colloquy of the two sages) best expressed the deep meaning of embroidery. He described two views of the world, one voiced by a chipper young poet and another by a dour old cynic. Néde, the upstart, considered the embroidery of women to be one fundamental sign that things were going well. Ferchertne, the elder, knew that things were going to hell and predicted that "great skill in embroidery will pass to fools and harlots so that garments will be expected without colors."[102] War, bad weather, failed crops, moral degeneracy, and dull clothes were all knotted together and dependent, somehow, on women's needles.

In the formal ideology of the culture, recorded by men, women's production, particularly of babies and clothing, carried mythic connotations. Reproduction and cloth making signified much more than their basic economic value. We have seen that procreation figured in the sovereignty myths of early Ireland. A few other labors of women also connoted myth. Milking, for example, suggested prosperity, fertility, and reproductive ideals for those attuned to such notions.[103] However, the ladies who managed noble households, ordinary farmwives, and unfree female laborers also produced a great many other goods and services less subject to mythmaking. Slopping pigs or wiping a toddler's nose held little romance for the scribes of early Ireland; tale-tellers and lawyers recorded little, besides, of housekeeping, laundry, or the grinding of grain and making of bread.[104] The source makers never wrote about men's labor, either, except the glamorous work of warriors and the pious work of monks.[105]

We know that women must have filled their days with hard, dull labor and distinctly unglamorous kinds of production. They must also have trudged through the fields with men, helping to plant, weed, and reap when the season demanded. Some laws listed sowing and harvesting among women's duties, despite the gendered division of labor that otherwise prevailed in the texts.[106] Other texts hinted further that a few women participated in the most elite of male labors. The eighth-century *Bretha Crólige* referred to female professionals, including a wright and a physician; the genealogies contain a *banféinnid* (woman varrior), and a single annals entry mentioned a *banfile* (woman poet).[107] There are even the odd references to illicit vocations, such as sorcery, which carried their own mythic meanings, as we shall see in a later chapter.[108] But none of these labors and none of this production merited the cultural meditation called forth by reproduction and clothwork.

Perhaps women had their own ideologies of production, separate from those of men. What could baby making and cloth making have meant to them? Were the two activities linked in women's minds as in the ideology formally articulated in texts? Were other modes of production more important to women? We have no *chansons de toile* from early Ireland, no early Irish Christine de Pisan to detail women's ideologies of labor. Irishwomen have left only their prayers and spells: the blessing upon weaving that one woman could expect from another or the curse she might sue another over; the prayers women sent to the saints when in hard travail; the churning charms that have come down to us orally, from one woman's mouth to another's ear, thence to men's texts.[109] One late vita of Ciarán suggested that cloth making did have its own exclusively feminine subculture. When the saint's foster mother set about dyeing her wool, she shooed the boy out of the house. No males were allowed to observe the secret art or to contaminate the house where it occurred. Ciarán, ever the man, responded angrily by cursing the vats of dye so that the cloth would not take the color until his *muimme* begged forgiveness.[110]

Women's own interpretation of their production may well have conflicted with the formal ideology of women's labor constructed by men and shared by women. Ciarán's hagiographer, at least, believed that the social meaning of women's work was different for the sexes. For as Ciarán's fosterer tried to go about her business—and it was *her* business—of cloth making, so women sought to control their own production and services. And just as the boy saint was bound to interfere in the name of excluded manhood, so husbands, fathers, and other male managers tried to restrict women's access to the products of their own labors and the profits of their own services. According to the literati, women's jobs of creator and clothier were basic and ultimate. For women who successfully collaborated with their male partners, or who avoided or subverted male management, however, these roles were just the hard-won route to more diverse economic opportunities.[111]

The Profits of Union

A formal *lánamnas* brought a woman economic status and the chance to produce and reproduce. Successful reproduction and production promoted a woman to a higher level of economic involvement outside the farmyard. If she submitted to the ideology of reproduction, a woman could gain material rewards and some measure of economic autonomy. Historians who have looked to the divorce laws of early Ireland for proof of women's high status have got it backward. Ironically, the more formally married a woman was and the more socially dependent on a man, the more extensive rights she gained to the products of her labor and the more access to others sorts of economic opportunities.[112] Adult women without husbands or their surrogates (for want of a more inclusive word, for no male equivalent to *concubine* exists in English and no equivalent to *adaltrach* in Old Irish) were without a secure place in the conjugal or external economies of early Ireland, at least according to the makers of laws and tellers of women's tales. Only women of dubious femininity, such as nuns, provided any sort of exception to this economic rule.

A *cétmuinter* involved in a union of equal property had the greatest control over her own property and the communal property as well as its profits.[113] She and her husband had practically equal rights to manipulate their common capital. According to lawyers, either could negotiate contracts to their mutual benefit, which is to say, either could engage in much of the managerial work of their farm without first consulting the other. As long as a woman alerted her partner to her dealings, they were legitimate; she could do nothing in secret, nor was he to conclude any farm business without informing her.[114] Just as fairly, neither partner could make certain other contracts without the spouse's permission. Formal fosterage arrangements had to be agreed upon, although we have seen the informal negotiation that might accompany these proceedings.[115] All major purchases, sales, or other business transactions were the concern of both spouses, and if one made a bad contract the other could dissolve it. But if a wife or her husband made a valid and beneficial contract in good faith, her or his partner could do nothing about it.[116] Neither whimsy nor misogyny could disturb a transaction made for the welfare of the domestic economy.

Elsewhere in the laws, jurists warned against contracts concluded by women. A man might as well do business with a lunatic or child as with a woman, they cautioned. Some laws forbade women from making any formal contracts without the presence and counsel of a male guardian; that is, any sales or purchases, the hiring of any clients, gift giving, oath making, or legal suits.[117] But the writers of *Cáin Lánamnae* contradicted this prohibition by allowing a primary wife to make partnership decisions. A wife, as well as a husband, could bargain with neighbors to pool their ploughing equipment and till their lands together. She could order the renting out (*fochraic*) of untilled land, collect food rents, and provide feasts for her husband's lord or for their clients and tenants (*fothad* and *fuiririud*)—all basic duties of a land-lord. She could also have animals transferred from field and forest to farmyard pens and buy breeding cattle, furniture, or other necessities for their domestic economy.[118] Further, *Cáin Lánamnae* granted a wife full authority over her own property and suggested that women of means bought, sold, and lent at interest entirely on their own.[119] What is more, these jurists permitted women, like men, to ransom hostages and offer legal guaranties in the amount of their honor prices, which allowed them to act as oath helpers in legal disputes.[120] Formal hospitality and guaranty were the duties and privileges of a noble client in relation to his—or sometimes her, it appears—lord.

Although general juridical principles excluded a woman from any of these legal activities, a properly married *cétmuinter* with property slipped out of her legal niche and acquired both economic opportunities and social privileges ordinarily due only to free men. In fact, the more she invested in the *comthin-chor,* the common capital of their union, the more a woman could manipulate both common property and her own private property, participate in the larger economy, and intrude upon other masculine preserves such as clientage. A *banchomarbae,* an heiress who entirely supported her husband, also acquired his duties in the partnership. She, not her husband, was the one responsible for family legal matters.[121]

Two things entitled a woman to this economic partnership with all its social and political ramifications: the contributions she made to the communal prop-erty and her efficient production of babies. Commentators on the laws allowed only four kinds of women full economic maneuverability: a *bé cuitchernsa* ("woman of equal rank"), a *cétmuinter* with sons, a *cétmuinter* without, and an *adaltrach* with sons.[122] A woman of equal social standing or with prop-erty equal to that of her partner (*bé cuitchernsa* or *cétmuinter*) gained prestige whether or not she reproduced, although her wifely status remained precari-ous until she did. But if a woman could not claim either property or status, she had to be a first-rate reproducer to earn her economic opportunities.

Women whose unions were more tenuous had lower status and less room to maneuver within their domestic economies if, indeed, they even participated in one with their mates. As a result, they had less access to the domestic capital and its profits, and they participated less actively in the economy beyond their farms. The woman who lived apart from her partner, whether with her own family, on her own homestead, or set up on a farm by her mate, never gained the entree to contract making that a *cétmuinter* had.[123] Such a woman could conduct only limited business on her own, and she had little ability to manipulate any common property, nor could she impugn her partner's contracts, good or bad, since she originally invested less in the union.[124] She who brought just herself and perhaps some personal effects could expect only material support, and maybe a little sex or love, in return. But even this less equitable sort of union endowed a woman with the potential for more economic options than she had as a daughter in her father's home, where she awaited the magic touch of a man or the hand of God leading her to a religious vocation, which transformed her from laborer-in-training to economic actor.

The confusion and outright contradiction in the laws over what women could and could not do with property, whether theirs alone or theirs with a mate, suggests that women were making the most of their opportunities. Why would jurists haggle over a wife's ability to form a contract if she never tried to make one? Jurists were also at odds with canonists over the specific issue of land and its alienation. One particularly telling point of disagreement was whether an heiress could give away land held in usufruct to a religious settlement.[125] Hagiographers, to their own advantage and that of their saints, told of noblewomen who gave hereditary land to monasteries, sold the profits of their cloth making in order to purchase land for donations, and brought premortem inheritances along to nunneries.[126] Jurists were not willing to allow so much, but some did consider religious donation to be one of the inviolable gifts (*tabarta*) of any woman; stingy as they were about calling it an official contract (*cór*), lawyers allowed that a woman's donation was her own business, be she *adaltrach, cétmuinter,* or anyone else.[127] This very act of donation became far more common across the European continent around 800 C.E., signaling the rising status of free women throughout Christendom. More important, the religious donation of lands further indicates at least limited economic autonomy for some wives and mothers.[128]

At home, women took care of house, children, and farmyard. Women also went down the road to buy, sell, lend, and hire. They worked with their hands and sold the product for wages or goods or a decent price, when they could get it. What exactly they bought and sold, who they traded with, and where remain unclear. Before the Vikings came to establish trading towns, men and women with an economic surplus probably met at monasteries, mills (often owned by monastic communities), or other public places to conduct their business, as we shall see in the next chapter. After Dublin and other Viking settlements were integrated into local economies, women may well have gone there, too.[129] Incidental evidence in saints' lives hinted that sometimes women went to these places, gathering where men also gathered, and transported their goods wherever they might sell them. The unwelcome women who brought cheeses to Saint Cóemgen's community, or the occasional wife who traveled the road of the vitae with her cow had to have some reason to be away from home. Similarly, the professional embroideress had to reach her customers; maybe they came to her, maybe she went to them, or maybe she lived with them. Opportunities to buy and sell the products of her labor may have appeared at the gate, but only for the woman who had the marital or motherly status that allowed her to seize them.

Women who were without men could not go out to trade. The source makers refused to mention women who never married, and women who lost their spouses to divorce or death either remarried, according to secular laws, or—even better, according to the canonists—became religious women.[130] Divorcées took away their property and, if they had not sullied themselves by adultery, some profits of the common capital with which to start a conjugal economy with a new man, but they did not set up on their own, at least according to jurists. Unfree women participated in the conjugal economies of others, not in order to win any economic opportunities for themselves but to help their mistresses become full economic actors. Slave women, like their male counterparts, rarely appeared in the sources.[131]

And bad women, recidivists who routinely broke the rules about extramarital chastity and orderly procreation, paid for their transgressions with poverty. No happy adulteresses or prostitutes passed through the early Irish sources, living off divorce proceedings or grown rich from their earnings as fallen women. The laws mentioned whores not as profiteers but as promiscuous and degenerate women who lurked on the edges of the community, with only one thing on their minds—not money.[132] Indeed, harlots symbolized a poverty of both morals and material goods for Adomnán, who depicted Saint Columcille as cursing evil clerics with harlots for companions.[133] A well-known eighth-century poem described such a woman, called the nun or hag (*caillech*) of Béirre: a childless former concubine, once seductive, now broken, her beauty lost, her hair thin and dulled, her eyes gone, her body wasted, and her embroidered robes yellowed and shredded to rags. She had enjoyed the sexual favors of warriors and kings, but not necessarily as wife. "No wethers are killed for my wedding," she sighed. She was left alone in the poem to lament a cold and hungry fate. The nun of Béirre may have symbolized sovereignty, prosperity, fertility, time, space, the otherworld, and other highbrow concepts, but her poet also painted her as an unloved (not necessarily repentant) penitent with nowhere to go, nothing of her own, and no one to care for her.[134]

The only exceptions to the rule that marriage and motherhood made economic actors were religious professionals, but they were not so exceptional after all. The *sponsa dei* was, after all, a wife; she came to her union with Jesus complete with dowry, as the hagiographers hopefully showed, and became a partner in a conjugal economy of sorts. Every nunnery had its surrogate husband, either a clerical official or a kinsman of the nuns who advised the women in return for their gifts and hospitality, as we shall see in a later chapter. Every successful settlement of religious women was also a farm with fields to be ploughed by tenants, animals in the barn, gardens to tend, and cloth to be made. Professional religious women practiced many of the same household and farmyard chores as secular wives. They fattened animals, milked and churned, cooked and sewed, or at least managed the laborers who did so. The richest and noblest among them also bought and sold property. Of course, religious women performed some distinctly unwifely tasks, too, such as formal prayer, reading, writing, and teaching.[135] But according to hagiographers, even the miracles of nuns were the wifely wonders of filling butter jars and providing ale for a feast when none could be found in the storeroom, or maternal miracles, such as Saint Íte's miraculous freeing of a political hostage to stop his mother's tears, or her nursing of the baby Ísucán.[136]

All women had to labor as wives and mothers in the subsistence economy that was early Ireland if they wished to become full participants. The procreative ideology that informed politics and the hierarchical social structure permitted them few other roles. Women who could not achieve a stable formal union or who failed to produce babies had fewer opportunities for material gain and the relative autonomy brought by wheeling and dealing. Women who were prevented from assuming these roles, such as slaves, or who resisted them, such as adulteresses or promiscuous women, remained marginal to the economy.

Formal ideology further intruded upon women's lives when men emphasized two labors above all others, urging women to reproduce and to produce cloth, to have babies and to clothe them, complementary activities that placed women securely inside their houses. "Productive work is increase and clothes," announced one legal commentator, by which he meant that these labors of women actually brought forth tangible fruits; "nonproductive work is quernwork and kneading and nursing," for grain, bread, and mother's milk disappeared with their consumption, leaving no trace in the ideologies of women's work.[137] But this emphasis on childbearing and cloth production also proved beneficial to women who could use their status as reproducers to win control of conjugal resources and their profits from cloth making to enter other economic arenas. And the ideology of reproduction and cloth production was, after all, only ideology. It influenced attitudes toward women's economic activities and enhanced the status of fertile married women, but it remained an expression of ideals and attitudes. The laws showed that women pursued many other economic activities in addition to their work in bed and with a spindle, and that this work was both expected and valued by their men.

The benefits of marriage and motherhood were indisputable, and it would be foolish to think that the women of early Ireland did not realize as much. If male peasants in eighth-century Francia could consciously aim to marry up the social scale in order to raise the status of their offspring, then early Irish women could marry for profit, or the chance at it.[138] Lawyers implied that unscrupulous men wedded *banchomarbai* for their property; presumably some women in *lánamnasa mná for fertinchur,* in which the husband contributed the capital, also married for the same reason. Further, women must have known that they had to produce babies to keep their husbands, their houses, and their social status. Mugain knew it when she desperately sought the aid of the saints in conceiving; her husband's other wife, Mairend Máel, was aware of it, too, when she cursed Mugain with barrenness.[139] And even women must have understood the decree of lawyers that the more formally married a woman was and the better a reproducer, the higher her status and the greater her chance for satisfying labor.

The possibilities for successfully avoiding or subverting legitimate economic roles were few. There were no towns to which women could run to lose themselves, no boats to hop to faraway places, no refuges for dissident female workers. But the possibilities for exploiting the conjugal economy and its legal framework were diverse. Fortunately for hardworking women, lawyers always disagreed about the most important issues: whether women could inherit or alienate land, whether they could keep or act as clients, what exactly they were expected to do about the house and farm. The legal confusion betrays what must have been constant negotiation, for the early Irish, like their cousins all over the Continent, were a society of negotiators, squabbling about everything from the authority of kings to the daily business of an ordinary housewife. And where lawmakers and ideology mongers disagreed, the disenfranchised always had a chance to improve their fortunes. Whenever a woman gave family land to a local church or lent some of the family property to her own client, she turned lawyers against each other and set supporters of the patrilineage at odds.

Nonetheless, the ability to sell some embroidery did not necessarily empower women, nor did economic involvement automatically imply status. The early medieval period was no golden age of economic opportunities for women in Ireland or elsewhere; nor did Irish women progressively gain rights and economic opportunities between the Iron Age and the Norman invasions.[140] In the first place, the misogyny of Irish culture manifested itself in too many other restrictions upon the lives of women. Second, the economic opportunities available to a well-to-do *cétmuinter* with sons were denied to the majority of her sisters. The *cétmuinter* in *lánamnas comthinchuir* with all her rights and properties was the ideal of *Cáin Lánamnae* but not necessarily the norm in real life. The success of some lucky women within the economic system helped perpetuate it and its attendant social structures, which also frankly oppressed women. It would be anachronistic to suggest that women could see beyond the system in which they lived.

In fact, women who flourished despite the net of economic restrictions upon them helped men catch other, less fortunate women in the same net. Noblewomen helped enslave and exploit other women. Nor could women conceive of economic solidarity as a means of escaping or changing the laws that made them dependent upon marriage and motherhood. By and large, women did not labor together in large groups, did not strike or riot or assault the halls of the noble and rich. Women practiced a certain amount of social solidarity, as we shall see in the next chapter, but nothing so modern as the economic or class solidarity that could truly empower them.

Economic opportunities may have brought an illusion of power to some individually prosperous women, and domestic labor may have endowed them with temporary equality, but power and equality are historians' concepts, not something that mattered much to the women of early Ireland.[141] The chance to work with their partners to make a little surplus, to raise a few fat hogs and get ahead of the rent, to get out of the house and trade a nice piece of stitchery at the local gathering place, and to gain recognition and returns for their labors—these things mattered to women. If they had to keep themselves chaste until marriage and monogamous afterward, if they had to risk illness and even death to have babies, if they had to invest in child rearing in order to win the chance to do other interesting and profitable things, then they did. And for their efforts, women won rewards. They never fully controlled the balance of reproduction and production in their economic lives, but they could often tip the scales one way or the other.

What is more, their economic partnership with men both at home and beyond their farms contradicted the formal misogyny hurled at them from the texts of the literati. The men who sweated in the fields beside them, who together with women created and loved and played with their babies, who wore the tunics woven by women and accompanied them to trade, sued and were sued by them, and engaged in countless other economic interactions with women, these men knew that the women of early Ireland were not all the harlots and hags of woman-hating rhetoric but respectable companions in the struggle for subsistence.

7

The Land of Women

hen properly nurtured, the partnership of man and woman flourished within the dark, enclosing walls of an isolated farmhouse, but once the couple emerged into daylight outside their domestic fortress, they parted. Each of them tended to cling to others of the same sex. The social networks of the two sexes touched, grew parallel, and occasionally even intertwined, but their roots remained distinct. Everything outside worked to separate them: the culture's suspicion of women, the gendered division of labor, political structures that granted power to men but not women, and legal arenas that reinforced those politics. Only at the point of one *lánamain,* the legal domestic couple, did they graft together, and then not always successfully or permanently.

Laws, stories, and genealogies charted the relationships between men and women, as well as relationships among men themselves. *Tochmarca* and *aitheda,* marriages, and mother-child ties filled the pages of manuscripts beside tales of fond foster brothers, loyal clients, and devoted disciples. But missing or at least less obvious were accounts of women's associations with women. Men wrote the stories, perhaps taking the voice of a heroine who mourned the loss of her male lover or a saintly lady advising and comforting men, but never telling a simple tale of women's friendships. None of the literati approached social ties from a female perspective or defined a woman in relation to other women; they never alluded to any kind of erotic bond among women. Why should they have? The composers of sagas, canons, penitentials, and laws were preoccupied with women as lovers, wives, and mothers to men. But they were even more interested in the ties of man to man.

Jurists, for instance, in the business of legal arbitration, constructed elaborate hierarchies of men which operated publicly according to formal rules.

Laws provided a blueprint by which kings related to *túatha* (tribal kingdoms), lords to clients, and generations of fathers to sons. Men organized themselves in solidarities based on the institutions of kinship, fosterage, and clientage, to none of which they fully admitted women, who had to find other sources of support and friendship.

Similarly, in the gnomic texts, women's own goals in constructing kinship ties, friendships, and other kinds of alliances with men or with other women were inconsequential unless, of course, women's purposes were at odds with those of men. Both gnomic writers and jurists endowed social intercourse among men with the higher purpose of creating good morals and an orderly society. Women, the literati believed, sometimes joined men in this noble endeavor, but more often hindered it. Women instigated male misbehavior, especially when they lured men out of their solidarities, or assembled in troublesome groups of their own. Thus writers of *tecosca,* like lawyers, storytellers, and hagiographers, described only superficial contact among women without revealing any depth of connection.

If women created hierarchies for themselves, they did so according to different criteria from men's. Philip O'Leary has suggested that women in the narratives competed in their own game of chastity, ranking each other on a scale of virgin to harlot. According to O'Leary, some sacrificed themselves according to the feminine code of honor, and others, such as Deirdriu, used it to challenge men's separate code of warrior ethics.[1] This construct, however, seems suspiciously like part of the whole narrative package of courtship, marriage, and procreation ideologies which helped tie women to men's social networks and placed them neatly in the roles of wife and mother, rather than a genuine basis for behavior or social ties that were meaningful to women. Women had plenty of other things to compete for besides "spiritual integrity," and neither their social goals nor their social ties necessarily fit men's literary constructs of them.[2]

Without women's own accounts of their friendships and alliances we must dig for evidence of their social experience. Three excavation spots are promising. First, men's talk of men cast reflective light on women's ties to women, mostly by reminding women that their links to men were stronger than any they might make with other women. This is not to suggest that men's networks were the norm against which women's must be measured, along the lines of the old male-female, public-private dichotomy so often applied in feminist analyses.[3] But we must remember that men and women expected women to participate, although marginally, in formal social structures defined by men. Even if women were not part of the public legal world of enfranchised men, they were certainly party to it. A wife knew her husband's cronies and enemies, and might offer advice, as Mac Dathó's wife did, when he got into political or legal trouble. She might accompany him, as silent witness, when he negotiated a contract or swore an oath. She was certainly privy to some of his family's affairs; otherwise she would have been useless as an intercessor with her blood kin. What is more, women and men lived, loved, and worked together on the same farms. People may even have made casual friendships and alliances with those of the opposite sex. Nonetheless, women were never full participants in men's three major social institutions of kinship, fosterage, and clientage.

Second, we can define the opportunities women found for making social contacts and locate the sites where they met other women. Women spent most of their time working near home, whereas men frequently ventured out into the community and the larger society beyond the family enclosure. Women made good use of this plain fact of their lives by creating important relationships that operated best in the private spaces of house and farmyard. They still went out to meet friends and strangers who, because of the nature and venues of these encounters, were probably mostly women. The kinds of ties they formed were probably different from those of men, and the networks they created may have been organized according to principles other than kinship, fosterage, and clientage.

Finally, we can eavesdrop on men's reactions to women's social ties with other women. For, after all, our best evidence for women's maneuvers is the literati's fear that women disagreed with, undermined, and opposed men. When storytellers and jurists observed pairs and groups of women, they sensed a certain feminine consciousness that occasionally supported male solidarities but more often proved distinct from, or even hostile toward, groups of men. Men thought they spoke the same social language as women but then found, in dismay, that women had a babble of their own; try as they might to reduce and stereotype it, the literati could not fully comprehend women's language of friendship. Hence, instead of describing the meaning of women's alliances with women, the literati saw trouble in any social ties that decreased women's dependence upon, and loyalty to, men. Women were enough of a problem on their fickle, unreliable own, but when they congregated in pairs, groups, troops, and even entire lands of women, they perpetrated the hideous crime of sabotaging men's ties to men. Ultimately, it is to the shores of Tír inna mBan, that enticing, confounding, fictional Land of Women, that we must sail in order to find women bound by friendship and love to other women.

Women's Part in Men's Networks

Women's exclusion from the legal rights and obligations of men's formal associations meant that from a legal point of view, women were nominally unimportant to men's networks. Moreoever, the laws' focus on kinship, fosterage, and clientage meant that jurists privileged these ties between men and women rather than marriage alliances or other kinds of relations which might have been equally important to women. Nonetheless, a community or a kindred was most stable when women helped men make and keep customary alliances with other men. Indeed, many women may well have considered their roles as lovers, wives, mothers, and kinswomen of men to be their most important, if not their most rewarding, or at least the status they derived from these supportive roles may have been greater than what they got from relationships with other women.

In the jurists' eyes, kinship was the hedge that kept individuals from falling out of the community and into the wilderness. It was also the most important organizing principle of early Irish society. Jurists could imagine a calamitous moment when, according to the introduction to the *Senchus Mór* legal code, clientage and other contractual ties would disintegrate, but kinship, clearly, could survive the apocalypse.[4] The concept of blood ties was so fundamental to political and social stability that the early Irish imagined them even where they did not exist. Families unrelated to one another claimed mutual ancestors when they formed tribal confederations for political motives.[5] Likewise, when a successful group seized power from a less fortunate branch of the kindred, it had them rubbed out of the recorded genealogies. Losers disappeared from the fictive family picture.[6]

Everyone in early medieval Europe, male and female, was born into a ready-made set of alliances, as Marc Bloch long ago pointed out.[7] Babies were welcomed by both close kin and larger kin groups. They grew up in villages or on farmsteads or estates surrounded by kinfolk, neighbors, coworkers, lords, clients, tenants, and spiritual advisers. From first breath, a person's place in overlapping social circles was assured, as we have seen in the battles of paternal and maternal kinsmen over custody. A kinless, lordless, friendless man or woman was as good as dead or worse, for even the dead had family and friends who remembered and prayed for them. Severance of social ties was so drastic that only the worst criminals suffered it and only the craziest ascetics accomplished it.[8]

Every man and woman existed at the center of concentric circles of kin, beginning with the largest group, called the kindred or, variously in Irish, *cenél, comocus, ciniud, clann, maicne, slondud,* and *fine,* and in Latin, *genus.*[9] Known best by its most common name, *fine,* it was a flexible corporate agnatic group consisting of a large pool of potential supporters and allies related by blood. The *fine* contained smaller, more functional patrilineal groups such as the *derbfine* (a four-generation descent group) or (after the eighth century) the *gelfine* (a three-generation descent group).[10] These smaller groups formed households or groups of households, as well as property-owning units and agricultural teams.[11]

In addition, individuals were also members of the bilateral kin group that resulted from a marriage or another *lánamnas*. Ego joined paternal kin to the mother's kin, which, as we have seen, retained some legal rights over its women and their children. The participants in the union, children of the union, and members of both families could, theoretically, be relied upon for various kinds of mutual legal and political support. Inheritance, legal suit, and the fulfilling of obligations of vengeance (none of which women, of course, could fully participate in) were by far the most important functions performed by both paternal and maternal kinsmen in barbarian Europe, and such legal responsibilities involved relatives from both mother's and father's families.[12]

No individual could honor or use all the opportunities for making social ties offered by kin groups. A practical man or woman had to select special allies from the array of candidates connected to him or her by blood and other sorts of ties. The selection process, however, differed by sex. For both men and women, the creation of personal networks was made easier by the fluid bounds of formally defined kin groups and the fact that various jurists expressed the family, its rights and responsibilities in different terms, often assigning conflicting functions to overlapping groups.[13] The process by which a daughter became a wife was one point of legal tension where people had to negotiate social ties and responsibilities. The schedule of rights to a woman's honor price, property, and children so elaborately laid out in *Cáin Lánamnae* gives only a hint of the squabbling that must have occurred among men who believed that they had a right to the woman. The two legal terms applied to sister's son (*nia* and *gormac*) suggested another set of choices and negotiations by which ego defined his or her reliable kin.

The modern adage did not apply in early Ireland: a person *could* choose his or her family but *not* neighbors. At least, a person could select which kins-people to form alliances with, although, since alliance is reciprocal, creation of these ties was not always straightforward. The chosen ally also had to select the selector—or not, as the case may have been. Canonists urged elders of the family to prune its degenerate and neglectful younger branches; churchmen aimed to carve the kin group down to its nuclear core by their praise of primogeniture and condemnation of bastardy.[14] But canonists and jurists only laid the guidelines by which a group determined its membership, deciding whom to keep and whom to cast out, whom to allow inheritance, to protect by oath, and to avenge. The entity called a *fine* by the laws was in reality a complex of shifting networks and, as Bloch wrote of Germanic septs, no fixed principle could ever limit its size or composition. The aim for every individual, according to Bloch and the French cartulary he quoted, was to obtain "the favorable opinion of 'as many kinsmen and relatives as possible.'"[15]

For all these reasons, no one had exactly the same kindred, and any two people in similar situations might make different choices about where to place their loyalty. Like the mothers who manipulated blood and affinal kin to favor their children, many must have resolved the clash of kin ties by personal preference and affection.[16] Choosing one relative as an ally meant *not* choosing another, who might even become an enemy. Annalists recorded the resulting failures of the system, as when a man hungry for power slew his brother, or a noble united with outsiders to bring down his uncle, cousin, or even father. The *Annals of Ulster* recounted how in 865 Tadc mac Diarmata, king of the Uí Cheinnselaig, was killed by his own kinsmen and his people ("a fratribus suis ocus a plebe sua").[17] Eleven years later the perpetrator, Tadc's brother Cairpre, received the same treatment "a fratribus suis."[18] Kin slaying (*fingal*) denied the whole social structure; when blood struck blood, no atonement was possible. The victim's kinsmen could never avenge the murder because they themselves would be guilty of a second *fingal*.[19] Yet such vengeance must have occurred, as the sad case of Tadc and Cairpre shows, unless the family could come to some informal resolution, such as the redistribution of its property from the killer to those more intimate with the dead man.

Such a dilemma illustrates both the stranglehold and the potential solidarity of kin ties. No one was driven to *fingal* by distance from his kin. Only the stress of choosing among allies by blood could make a man betray and murder his brother. He made his selection and, at the same time, decreased the bewildering number of available kinship bonds in a most efficient manner. And as the annals showed, many a man made a similar choice.[20]

A woman had the same pool of blood relations from which to choose her allies, but the conditions of her membership in the kindred were different from those of her brothers.[21] Since she normally gained no family land, she had no formal voice in the family, but neither did she earn the enmity of co-heirs to the *fintiu*. Even when a woman did inherit from the *fintiu,* the land returned to its proper owners at her death; she went "in place of a man" while she held it, like the wives of World War II soldiers who took men's jobs until the rightful claimants returned.[22] An heiress did theoretically gain the right of limited participation in the kin group, and her wealth and status might have made her a potential ally to her kinsmen. As we have seen, she alone of all women could take on clients, make contracts entirely on her own, and carry out other legal functions. But not many women were in such a position, and they had to be aggressive and tough to make the system work to their advantage. This is not to say that women never participated in legal procedures, but they did so extraordinarily, with their guardians' consent, and mostly in cases dealing with other women or women's matters, such as suits related to cloth making or over marital relations.[23] Even heiresses were subject to their husbands' "service and counsel," which they legally acknowledged by supporting their men financially, paying for the privilege of guidance.[24]

Most women, though, were not heiresses and, hence, simply could not fulfill most of the legal functions demanded by men of their allies by blood. They could produce and nurture new members of the kindred and could provide temporary peace by uniting its branches, but were rarely active players in its legal games. This is why the *banšenchas,* the Middle Irish genealogical tracts about women, contained mostly the mothers of men, rather than the daughters and sisters of women, and why, for most historians of women's experience (with some notable exceptions), the *banšenchas* have so far proven to be sterile ground for any meaningful history of women.[25]

Although daughters might compete with sons for shares of their parents' goods, they did not seem likely to kill their kinsmen for land, power, or vengeance. No references directly implicated any women in *fingal.* Unlike Norse sagas, in which women caused their brothers' deaths as well as their husbands', Irish texts suspected women only of murdering their spouses or driving other men to do them in.[26] On the contrary, we have seen that women needed to maintain amicable relations with their kinsmen for their own good and that of their babies, so that, in desperate circumstances, they could call upon family and the wider kin group to save them from affines.[27]

But the relation between a woman and her kinsmen was lopsided. In practical terms, in the daily business of survival, a woman's ties to her kinsmen were of only secondary importance to the men involved. The benefits of alliance with her were indirect. She brought her men potential aid from other men, whether blood kin, affines, or her children. Yet these ties between men and women were not significant unless reinforced by other relationships such as fosterage or coresidence, as we have seen. Even the tie between an adult daughter and her father had few legal ramifications if she were a *cétmuinter* under her husband's guardianship. The jurists assumed that she got nothing from him after marriage, and he deserved only a portion of her bride gift; in less formal unions, her father might receive some fraction of fines paid for harming her. Brother and sister had no legal obligations to one another at all, except one commentator's suggestion that a sister could call on her brother when "in distress."[28] As for in-laws, they owed a woman nothing.[29]

Further, when kinship and affinal ties failed a woman, she lacked the options that men had. The fosterage and clientage ties that aided men, or even supported a woman's children, were not as useful for women themselves, whose extra-kin relationships worked differently simply because they were women. Foster sibling relationships, for example, seem to have had different uses and meanings for women and men. To begin with, boys and girls did not form significant fosterage ties with each other. They seem not to have played together. The boys of saga included no girls in their hurling games or other rough play, and the saints' lives rarely showed children of both sexes at games together. Hagiographers and their saints seem to have believed that integrated frolics could lead to preadolescent sexual crises; when a girl asked Saint Brénainn to play, for example, he panicked and attacked her, for fear that she would seduce or contaminate him.[30] Nothing in the laws suggested that fosterers allowed boys and girls to mingle, and jurists described discrete duties of boy and girl fosterlings: boys hunted or ploughed or played *fidchell,* a board game, while girls cooked or sewed. Canonists also insisted that nubile boys and girls be kept apart.

Significant ties grew up between foster brothers and, to a lesser extent, between foster sisters. Foster brothers formed a lifelong bond, one of the most important in their lives. As we have seen, a tie of fosterage could supplement or even replace the potentially tense relationship between blood brothers. But foster sisters seem not to have been nearly so close. In fact, already in the early Middle Ages, the word for foster sister—*inailt*—came to mean an attendant or even a servant. Whereas jurists assumed that boys, ideally, were fostered down the social scale, that is, given to a couple of inferior status to be raised, girls often seem to have been fostered up. In practical terms, cofosterage for many girls meant nothing so romantic as the undying devotion between foster brothers. It was more like apprenticeship or like being poor cousin or hired companion to a young lady of better birth, except that the *inailt* got no pay for her hire. Her parents benefitted from the relationship they formed with their social betters, who may also have been kin or clientage partners, and their daughter received vocational training.[31]

Foster sisterhood did not, in itself, condition women to rely upon each other in the way that foster brothers supposedly did. They never tested their bond in combat, nor could they prove their loyalty later in life with legal support or other public displays. In saga, a man might be devastated to lose a foster brother. In *Tochmarc Becfola,* when Becfola's *inailt* was killed by wolves, the otherworldly heroine continued on her tryst without comment from herself or the author. In *Fingal Rónáin* (The kin slaying of Rónán), the young queen competed with her *inailt* for the affection of her stepson and several times threatened to kill her companion for disobedience.[32] In other tales, foster sisters were mere window dressing for the heroine. Emer, for example, sat sewing with fifty foster sisters or attendants, whose presence discreetly suggested Emer's status, but no scene in her tale showed Emer interacting with these women in any way. More important, the writer of her tale found no significance in the tie between Emer and her foster sisters, except that the women betrayed Emer's tryst with Cú Chulainn.[33] The fifty women displayed no obvious affection for Emer, nor she for them; she abandonned them for a man as soon as she got the chance, and given the tone of the tale, the author deemed her behavior appropriate. By comparison, the tie between Cú Chulainn and his cofosterlings offered love, companionship, and ideally, lifelong legal and military support (Cú Chulainn, however, was exceptional; he actually dueled with and killed several of his foster brothers, although he also felt terrible about it.) Predictably, neither the jurists nor the storytellers saw—or cared to see—great devotion among foster sisters.

The other major source of allies for a man, besides kin and foster kin, was the bond of clientship, which was also largely denied women. In early Ireland, a client was *céile* to his lord, a companion, the same word used for friend or spouse.[34] For a man beset or abandoned by contrary kin, his clientage partners—his lord or his free or base clients—could provide camaraderie, protection, and support. Some men deserted their inheritances and kin and sold themselves into clientage with lords who could supply all that family should but would not.[35] In return for a fief of land or stock, *céili* gave their lords rents, hospitality, manual labor, or military service and oath helping, depending on their status as clients. Free clients had additional duties similar to those of Frankish household warriors; according to *Críth Gablach,* they were in "coímthecht do flaith," attendance on a lord.[36] They were their lords' companions in the truest sense of brotherhood, socializing with them, accompanying them on missions both peaceful and violent, and forming part of their permanent retinue.[37] "Let everyone cling to his lord," advised the jurists.[38]

By his submission, the client earned more than the loan of cows or fields. He got what his kinfolk sometimes failed to give him. His lord acted as surety for his contracts, bailed him out when he could not pay debts, helped to collect what someone else owed him, witnessed and swore oaths when he was accused of crimes. Clients and lords could also assume one of the kin group's primary functions: they could prosecute blood feuds on each other's behalf.[39]

Predictably, clientage and kinship overlapped, making both kinds of relations more useful to men but less hospitable to women. According to *Cáin Aicillne,* a man was better off taking a kinsman for his lord, presumably because the already existing blood tie reinforced the bond between lord and client.[40] Likewise, the commitment to clientage helped a man choose which of his relatives to seek out as allies. Women did something similar when they used fosterage ties to strengthen relations between their children and their blood kin. The more links between two people, the more likely they were to become and remain allies and even intimates.

Overlapping social ties were the only kind likely to lead to affection. Friends were not so easy to come by if the narratives are to be believed; a man or woman did not casually invest affection in a stranger but caught a person in a net of social ties before offering sweet friendship. Comrades of saga were also bound by the hierarchical ties of clientage or servitude, as were warriors with their charioteers; or by fosterage, as with Cú Chulainn and Fergus; or by kinship; or by all three. And even these many ties were not always sufficient to bring about lasting friendship. Too often client betrayed lord, foster brothers found themselves on opposite sides of a feud, and kinsman ran afoul of kinsman. True and lasting friendship was rare and even better, as *Senbríathra Fíthail* pointed out, than beer; like love in marriage, it was a felicitous side effect of a more important alliance.[41] Most men constructed their social networks for reliability rather than affection: whether their comrades could be counted upon to swear for them, make a loan in hard times, or fight for them, not whether they were fun to be with.

Women could be amusing or affectionate companions, but they could not fit easily into men's networks. They could not do the things that men demanded of kinsmen, clientage partners, or foster brothers, although they participated in men's networks as mothers, wives, daughters, and lovers. How could men invest in those who could not help them in public as well as private? Beyond practical questions of reliability and legal restrictions lay the vexing problem of the indefinable nature of women, for women's unreliability supposedly came of their fickleness as well as their legal incompetence and political marginality. Even if she could have wielded sword and shield for her man, a wife always retained her legal ties to her blood kin; even when officially bound to affines, she might retain sneaking affection for her brothers or uncles, or for a lover from another kindred altogether. Enough sagas and folktales existed to show what happened when men made friends, or even friends of friends, with women. They got killed, like the Ulstermen tangentially involved in Noísiu's entanglement with Deirdriu or like all those foolhardy warriors who agreed to follow Medb into her *táin*. Plenty of men had also heard the story of Suithchern, daughter of Aed Bennán. When Suithchern was carried off from her husband by another lover, her brothers attacked her husband's allies for failing to protect her.[42] But according to the storyteller, Suithchern herself was not much exercised about the strife.

This is not to say that women never participated in the exchange of power and property, regulated by law, which often lay at the basis of men's networks. They could and did make some contracts, participate indirectly in feuds, and even occasionally take on clients. But they did so, according to the laws, exceptionally. As in medieval English communities, legal actions more normally consisted of the public mingling of men with men, in public spaces controlled by men, before audiences of other men.[43] Enforcement of order depended on dense, overlapping, and intimate social bonds among the freemen of a community, in whose interest it was to make contracts and treaties work.[44] Jurists' premise was that the major means and purposes of social intercourse were ordinarily denied women, although occasionally used to reward successful childbearing free women who were primary wives. Even a queen in early Ireland was, by one legal definition, *cétmuinter comcenéol,* "a chief wife [of a king] from an equally good family" rather than a ruler or lord in her own right, until at least the tenth century, if not later.[45] In a society ordered by a status hierarchy, where status derived from honor and informed both legal interactions and political ties, ordinary women had no honor and low status.[46]

Hence, not only were the principal avenues to public authority beyond the reach of women but so were most of the main reasons for being in public at all. In short, men had no logical reason to include women in their social networks except as wives and close kinswomen, whose participation was, at best, supportive. The literati cast women as supplementary to the most important ties binding man to man. And they were right: the bonds that existed between men and women or between women and women *were* unlike those among men. The uses that men and women made of social networks were not the same; when they gathered at a single event, such as a feast, women and men interpreted and used the event differently. And when women constructed networks for themselves, men's ties of blood, fosterage, and clientage were not necessarily their most important models.

Proximity and Women's Networks

Let us reverse the critical gaze of the literati, who proclaimed the unreliable participation of women in men's networks, and look upon the forest of social ties with women's eyes. For women in early Ireland, mere blood did not provide sufficient reason to seek friendship, nor did kinship or marriage automatically inspire trust and loyalty. Both blood and marriage were important in the relationships that women constructed with men but other principles, along with these, inspired women's bonds with women.

Simple physical proximity provided the opportunities for women to find friends and allies, most of whom were coworkers in the same domestic space. When men left for the day, going out to work in the fields or to visit their estates or possibly to negotiate lawsuits or burn down an enemy's house, women stayed home to perform the chores that grounded their roles as wives, mothers, daughters, and servants. Around the house and yard women spent most of their time with other working women and with their children, as was true across early medieval Europe. Houses were too small, even local travel too bothersome, and social restrictions too pervasive for women to have daily contact with any but those who lived nearest. Survival was too uncertain and daily labor too demanding for them to socialize much with any but coworkers.[47]

We have seen that the ordinary woman spent her life as part of a small household in one of several dispersed but related homesteads or, perhaps, in one of a small cluster of houses. Without censuses we can never be completely certain who lived with a woman, or recover the composition of the early Irish household. Canonists and lawyers suggested that coresidents and near neighbors were also kinfolk and that residence was patrilocal. Lawyers assumed members of a three-generational family to be coresidential or at least neighbors, with more distant kin living a little farther out.[48] Eighth-century canonists considered it normal for two generations of women to live with or near each other when they ruled that only the mother, aunts, daughters, sisters, or nieces of a cleric could live with him.[49]

Unlike men, who left home for fosterage but permanently returned to their parents' community at adolescence, women did not spend their entire lives in the same house and enclosure, peering across the fire at the same faces. Neither did they enter an entirely new group when, at fosterage or marriage, they left home for other enclosures. They took some of their primary kinship ties with them when they went, although these must have shifted form, purpose, and meaning. Legal commentators expected children to live close enough to their parents that one could bring the other food or clothing. When hagiographers also described sisters who remained in touch even when they no longer lived together, they meant sisters in neighboring farmsteads. In stories of Saint Íte, for instance, the saint was busily involved in intimate aspects of her sister's life long after the latter had married and moved out; it was Íte who got her sister a husband in the first place and who helped her sister with a difficult pregnancy.[50] It was also common for siblings to remain together in religious communities or for mother and daughter to set up housekeeping together as religious women.

Just as men needed other reasons, such as foster ties or clientage, to select an ally from the larger pool of relations-by-blood, a woman also had good reasons for choosing her allies. When the miles between them were many, the tie between a woman and her relatives stretched thin. A man, although also friendly with his neighbors, might travel some distance to support a cousin in legal trouble or to help an uncle on a cattle raid. A woman, however, who had few legal obligations or rewards, had no large stake in the affairs of a kinsman or kinswoman in the next *túath,* or even the next settlement, except indirectly, through her male relations. Women may have found their friends among kinfolk, as did men, but did not select them by swearing oaths together, dividing land among themselves, sharing farming equipment, or fighting a common foe. Instead, they chose those who worked side by side with them. Men worked together too, but theoretically, the bonds among working men were secondary to ties of kinship, fosterage, and clientage. Although the same could be said of women, they did not have even the theoretical option of dividing their loyalties between formal legal allies and working partners; even if they were taught to honor their husbands, children, and kinsmen before the other women with whom they labored, no legal tension existed between these two groups of allies. Moreover, a woman was much more likely than a man to move from one community to another when she married, making location even more important in her construction of alliances and friendships. If residence was, indeed, patrilocal, then a woman depended more upon her in-laws for companionship than any man did. For a woman, the locus of her social ties, wherever she was, had to be the site of her daily labor; mother and daughter, sisters, mistress and servant, and female in-laws labored together and formed affiliations in the process.

Material remains, along with laws, narratives, and vitae suggest that women made use of the social opportunities brought by coresidence and shared work. To begin with, women spun, wove, and sewed together, as we have seen, and may have had specifically feminine concerns to discuss as they did. Where better for women to solidify friendships and exchange their thoughts than at intellectual leisure in their homes, hands flying with spindle or needle? Continental women of the later Middle Ages often sat to spin, weave, and sew; in fact, this was an important opportunity for forming alliances and feminine subcultures, for the hours women spent together produced *chansons de toile,* romances, and even heretical theology.[51]

Wherever archaeologists find spindle whorls (small flywheels of stone or bone) today, women of the early medieval period were making cloth and weaving alliances with other women. Only a couple of references suggest separate spaces within larger buildings or separate buildings within enclosures where women might have worked. Some of the later narratives mentioned a *grianán,* literally (and optimistically, in Ireland), a "sun-chamber" or "sunny place," probably a balcony or upper story to which women could withdraw.[52] Whereas in some cultures people subdivide their houses and public spaces, relegating women or their work to special subspaces, the ubiquitous Irish spindle whorl confirms that inhabited space was women's space, and that women did not leave home to work with other women in a communal workshop,[53] except when they went to another woman's house.

But the camaraderie brought by proximity could be shattered, for more than needles could fly in such intimate quarters. Jurists paid attention to working women's alliances only when they fell apart. *Bretha Étgid,* which adjudicated cases of injury and assault, discussed the "bla bancatha ban," or battle of women's insults, in which combatants shook their distaves and wool-comb bags at each other. Things could get ugly. According to later commentary on the tract, a woman who started such a ruckus in order to reclaim a welched debt was not liable for injuries inflicted on her coworker.[54] Nonetheless, the possible disintegration of alliances among coworkers and the attention paid by the jurists only emphasized the importance of the bond among laboring women.

Other kinds of work besides cloth production brought occasions for social interaction. *Bretha Étgid* also discussed the case of the servant woman (*cumal*) at the kneading trough. If in the course of making her bread she accidentally injured *esbach ocus etarbach,* "idlers and unprofitable workers," in her vicinity, she was exempt from liability. If she happened to harm a "profitable worker" (one of the *áes comgnimraid*), however, or if she somehow damaged a domestic animal—did the bread board fly from her hands to bruise a dog? did the force of her dough pounding cause the roof to clobber the head of a wandering sow?—she had to pay a fine.[55] Whatever the improbable scene, it took place around the house and farmyard where the careless *cumal* interacted with other domestic workers. Although jurists did not specify the gender of the idle or profitable workers, given that it was women who were also spinning, weaving, and minding children in the house, chances are that the *cumal* injured a woman. *Cáin Adomnáin* took up the same theme, listing the sites of domestic accidents, which were also the places where women worked with women— "ditch and pit and bridge and fireplace and doorstep and pools and kilns," as well as the farmyard where pigs and dogs wandered.[56]

Even if women working at home in what was, by default, women's space, wove and cooked with other women, the precise identity of their coworkers remains to be clarified. Much depended upon the composition of the household. The clumsy *cumal* of *Bretha Étgid* must have labored with or near women of higher standing. In some stories, noblewomen and their servants were confidants as well as coworkers. That these relationships were often depicted as hostile, however, might indicate the intrusion of class tension into female bonds; on the other hand, it might just reflect the literati's suspicion of woman-woman ties that defied the social hierarchy. More likely it reflected the competition between women, for in the sagas and vitae, mistress and servant could also be sexual partners of the same man. The jurists conceived of a situation in which a primary wife exchanged words or blows with her competition, her husband's new *adaltrach.*[57] Both lawyers and saga writers were attuned to the inherent social drama of the situation in which more than one woman depended upon one man while being forced to live and work with their rivals. The penitentialists simply ordered a man who impregnated his female slave to set her free, which suggests yet another means by which households came to contain several women of different classes.[58] Hagiographers were also sensitive to the problems of polygyny, but were more concerned for the men involved. Saint Brénainn's hagiographer wrote of cowives who spent enough time in each other's company that their squabbling drove their mutual spouse into religious celibacy on a deserted island; Comgall's hagiographer had the dark vision of a secondary wife attempting to poison a favored primary wife.[59]

The saga writers also assumed hostility among cowives. In *Echtra Mac nEchach Muigmedóin* (Adventure of the sons of Eochaid Muigmedón), Cairenn, the secondary wife or concubine of the king suffered "great hardship . . . from the queen." Cairenn, an English princess, was forced to labor like a slave, which she may have been, during her pregnancy. She bore her son by herself on the green before the fort, after which she was forced to expose him. He grew up, nonetheless, to be Níall Noígíallach, king of Temair and eponym of the great Uí Néill dynasty. The competition and hostility of cowives, one of whom bore a heroic child, was a motif in both secular and religious literature, as we have already seen in the cases of Saint Brigit and Mugain, mother of Aed Sláine.[60]

Both kinds of relationships—cowives or mistress-servant—suggested the proximity but not amity of a nobleman's several women. Even if secondary wives were relegated to their own homesteads, where their men periodically came to call, men still had to keep their several women close enough to themselves, and thus to each other, to maintain an efficient household economy (or economies), and thus near enough for hostile interactions between the women. Nothing in any document suggests the solidarity among cospouses touted by some modern-day feminist anthropologists and Mormon defenders of polygamy, however; the legal system of inheritance set one man's women against each other, rather than allowing them to band together.[61] Even in feminine space, then, social forces driven by male solidarity and men's rules worked to damage some relationships among women and ensure their reliance on male guardians.

Beyond those they lived and worked with daily, a larger circle of potential allies awaited women at certain gathering points in their neighborhoods. There were no shops or markets where women might stop for a chat, as in modern villages. In fact, there were no villages that modern observers would recognize. Apparently ale houses existed, although not for respectable women, where people drank and quarreled together.[62] The four places where men gathered for public business—according to one tract, the fort of a ruler, the fort of a jurist, a smithy, and the chief church of a territory—were not women's places, since women were formally excluded, physically and socially, from public legal or political arenas. Women might attend and might even support parties of men involved in negotiation and conflict, but their presence was unnecessary.[63]

But certain spots appeared again and again in different kinds of sources as regular meeting places for women. Women socialized at wells and rivers, the mill, and shrines and churches; they also exchanged hospitality in their homes or the homes of others. At these sites, women had a chance to meet people familiar but less intimate than their cohabitants and to form another set of relationships with different functions and of a less intensive character than ties to kin and servants. These more distant allies also made up part of a community for women who won the economic opportunities to venture beyond the enclosure or when spiritual pursuits took them out of the house. Despite their need to get out, get the chore done, and return home, women must have derived some benefit from work-related contacts outside their own farms; indeed, perhaps women performed economic tasks partly in order to socialize.[64] The texts depicted women actually forming groups at public places and cast suspicion on what, exactly, women were doing together. The question remains, of course, what this social intercourse meant to them.

Women's interactions seem innocent enough. For instance, they went out of their houses to meet at the river or well to do the wash and to wash themselves.[65] Nonetheless, according to hagiographers, women washing in groups caused misogynist saints much annoyance. Máedóc, for instance, reprimanded women who washed their clothes or, in some versions, their hair in the stream that refreshed his monks. He did not want their filth, tangible or spiritual, leaking into his monastic enclosure.[66] The assumption that when women formed a group they did something distinctly feminine, and hence caused more trouble than a single woman, recurred in the sources, as we shall see shortly. But it also suggests that bathing and laundry might have provided work-related social occasions for women living in the same area. A few hagiographic references to groups of women crying out when their cows and calves mixed or bringing cheeses to local monks hinted that farmers' wives and daughters seized any chance in a workday to congregate and socialize.[67]

At the mill, women may have met a still larger circle of acquaintances from nearby houses. Women seem sometimes to have been responsible for taking the grain to the mill and bringing home the flour.[68] The hagiographers assumed that society's humble—women, slaves, and monks—worked the mill but that everyone in a community gathered at this recognized meeting place.[69] Mills could attract quite a crowd. According to one hagiographer, the boy Molua went to the local mill with his mother and their grain but could not get a turn at grinding. In protest, Molua miraculously brought the operations to a halt until they gave his mother a turn.[70] Even if milling was women's duty, hagiographers clearly thought it normal for both sexes to drop by the mill to see and be seen. In another vita, local farmers, monks, and a respectable married woman all happened to be at a mill when a blind wandering cleric arrived, at angelic direction, seeking a cure for his ailment.[71] The cleric knew he could get directions and help at the mill, which was one social and geographical focus of the community. The fact that mills were owned by local landlords (including churchmen) or jointly by free farmers, rather than being the private possessions of single families, guaranteed that they were meeting places.[72]

Besides wells and mills, fieldwork and trade sometimes took women out of the enclosure, as we saw in the last chapter. But when they went into the fields in seasonal time of need, it was along with, and to help, their men. They went to trade only when they gained the economic opportunity by producing enough personal surplus. It happened, but probably not often, not as often as to men, and not to every woman. Although the laws allowed for it, none of the narrative sources, secular or religious, depicted women at trade or agricultural work, with only one or two exceptions.[73] Women may also have herded animals to high ground in the summer, but it is unclear whether boolying included only women and children or whether and where it even took place in the early medieval period.[74] If women did set up temporary communities during the summer, they probably did so with the same comrades, season after season, and most likely, their summer partners were the same women with whom they spent lowland winters.

When women went into public for other than economic reasons, they were likely to meet an even larger circle of acquaintances, for the churches and shrines of the saints drew a more diverse crowd than the mills. From the arrival of Christian missionaries in the pagan hinterland, women had journeyed to these places to participate in the exchange of the good word and the celebration of Christian rituals. Some women went regularly to local monastic communities for other reasons, as did men: to get help from the local religious professionals, their saint, and the saint's God. In the vitae, stories of women visiting the saints signified women's dealings with clerics or religious women at a local church or shrine in the period when the vitae were written, particularly women seeking cures from holy healers. Munnu's hagiographer told the story of a dying woman who begged the saint to cure her. Munnu, possibly envisioning mobs of adoring but ailing fans, demanded crankily whether he was expected to cure all the women in the province. That he was tricked into healing her suggests that women did, indeed, expect him and his monastic successors to do so.[75] Women also came to the saints for aid with difficult pregnancies, advice about wayward sons, and help in retrieving children and other relatives taken hostage.[76] In fact, as we shall see, some saints gained reputations for being especially accessible to female clients, a sign that the monks of their monasteries were particularly willing to offer ritual services to female clients.

When women went to regional ecclesiastical centers, they obviously met Christians of both sexes. Since most Christian communities belonged to men rather than women, female pilgrims may even have aimed to meet holy men. None of the sources show whether women preferred the services of female saints and religious women and, hence, were more likely to choose a community of holy women for their pilgrimage. However, chances were that once they got to shrine or church, women mingled more with women than with men. For example, pilgrims of both sexes flocked to Cell Dara (Kildare), one of the greatest ecclesiastical settlements in Ireland, for the rites of priests and nuns, for fairs and festivals, and to gawk at the sheer spectacle of the great woman saint's city. Nonetheless, once they entered Brigit's church, they stood and prayed segregated by sex, for a wall divided men's and women's sections of the building. Even Brigit herself lay in a tomb separated by an altar from her comrade and bishop, Conláed, who reposed on the men's side.[77] Similarly, when female pilgrims became temporary or even permanent residents at religious communities, they probably lived with other holy women. The largest monasteries set aside separate spaces for students, ascetics, guests, and other subgroups, and had designated spots for women, too.[78] Annalists mentioned queens and daughters of kings who retired to monasteries throughout the early Middle Ages, possibly keeping their own houses within the sacred enclosure.[79]

The segregation of sexes had a firm theological foundation. Eighth-century canonists decreed that no women were to enter the holiest space of the enclosure, its sanctuary. Even when they came to church with men, women were socially segregated by their need to maintain the strictest of Pauline silences.[80] The principle on which canonists based gender segregation is not hard to detect: the old equation of women with sexual sin, which we have already encountered. Keeping women apart from men and confining them together seemed safer than turning them loose within the churchyard. At Christian sites, theologically informed misogyny was as strong a force as legal restriction or economic utility in pushing women into social spaces shared with other women, not with men.

For some women, visits to local holy places might have been as regular an outing as trips to the mill or the well. For others, pilgrimage was a rare journey for a special occasion. The different social, economic, political, and religious goals of their expeditions helped to determine the nature of women's contact with the folk they met at their destinations. At all these venues, women probably socialized with both friends and strangers, confirming some important ties, strengthening or discarding relationships with more peripheral acquaintances, and possibly making new allies of familiar faces. Men also went to many of these same places for many of the same reasons. Yet the character and purpose of social networks and interactions at these sites differed by sex. Men and women could mingle at a mill or shrine with the same group of fellow travelers and yet accomplish utterly discrete ends within their respective, diverse circles of contacts. They used social space differently, just as each sex claimed different social spaces.

Similarly, men and women made separate uses of encounters with the larger community—say, the inhabitants of related homesteads—or political group—say, a kingdom—of which they both were part. Hospitality, one of the main occasions for social interaction and creation or reinforcement of bonds among both women and men, provides an excellent example. Everyone in early Ireland provided or received many kinds of hospitality. Women, like men, were bound to offer home and hearth to those in need and to those whom they owed. In return, they received the thanks, news, and company of their guests. It was every *cétmuinter*'s specified right to host guests, although whether they were travelers chancing upon her house or people bound to her guardian as patrons or clients, the jurists did not say.[81] Indeed, the *Heptads* deprived a woman of her honor price if she refused hospitality to "every law-abiding person."[82] Hagiographers certainly believed that hospitality was a sacred duty of women as well as men; in the life of Ciarán, the saint raged at his mother for turning away hungry travelers.[83] Hostesses confirmed their importance in the domestic space over which they presided. They did not, however, rely on these fleeting contacts for any kind of support unless their guests were already bound to them by stronger ties. Women could also be guests, of course, in the house of another.

On special days, hospitality became a political event involving more than just local friends or spare travelers. On such occasions, women left their ordinary labors to meet an expanded circle of potential allies at extracommunal gatherings such as regional feasts and assemblies, and it was here that women might have achieved some sort of cohesion and some consciousness of themselves as a social group. Men certainly did.[84] Feasts were a regular part of life in early Ireland, affirming the political and social structure when offered as yearly rents or as a lord's gift to his clients[85] or marking the community's passage through time in seasonal, personal, or military celebration. One jurist listed the dates and places of major public gatherings as the festivals of Easter and Christmas, the *dáil* (glossed as *oenach*), and the gathering (*tocomracc*) of the *túath*, where legal cases might be pleaded before a king or an ecclesiastical synod.[86]

Naturally, women encountered men as well as other women at these gatherings, but their participation differed from that of men, who always organized and dominated public occasions, carrying out legal duties and confirming their political obligations. The jurists took little more interest in women's presence at these affairs than they did in women's participation in other legal maneuvers. Their rules regarding women's involvement in laws of hospitality suggest, however, that women had some formal responsibilities in this kind of ritualized socializing, too. Nonetheless, women arrived at such gatherings in their men's wake, but only to socialize with other women. The eleventh- or twelfth-century *dindsenchas* suggested that women should congregate only with women at yearly *oenaig*, although the text also hinted that some young women seized the chance to sneak away and meet boys.[87] In sagas and stories, women drifted through the shadowy background of feasts and gatherings like bit players to men's dramas, even when their actions moved the tale forward or had symbolic importance. In the feasting hall, for example, they languished on couches with their mates or appeared only to hand around the drink while men boasted of their prowess and challenged each other to fight (sometimes over women). Deirdriu's mother passed through men's company with the beer, just as her Anglo-Saxon counterpart, Wealtheow, did in *Beowulf,* and as her Scandinavian sisters did in Icelandic sagas.

Women's main function at feasts and meetings was extralegal, to support their men in whatever ways allowed by their disenfranchisement, yet to remain on the margins of formal legal and political dealings with the other women. The inevitable tension caused by this contradictory responsibility—devoted to men's formal alliances while excluded from them and pushed into the com- pany of others excluded—occasionally erupted when women moved from the audience of men's meetings into the midst of the players. The *dindsenchas* sug- gested, as did other efforts to segregate women and men, that such mixing of the sexes could lead to trouble. In stories, wars and inconvenient passions began whenever strangers met over food and drink and newcomers intruded upon the small household that formed a woman's most intimate circle.[88] It was at a feast that Gráinne enticed Diarmaid and Rónán committed his terrible kin slaying. Over their meat, surrounded by drink-dispensing women, the heroes of Ulster boasted and counterboasted themselves into duels and competitions that left comrades and strangers dead.[89] In fact, any extracommunal gathering of women or men or both could disintegrate into melodrama and violence, as narratives and monastic annals show. Annalists recorded endless fights and raids at yearly fairs and intertribal treaty meetings.[90]

Men had ways of resolving the problems of extracommunal friction. That is what many of these stories were all about: the creation and resolution of con- flict among the subgroups of early Irish society. In meetings of households, communities, branches of a kindred, tribes, or kingdoms, men either negoti- ated or fought. They relied on their laws to enforce the orderly working of their social hierarchies and to control the behavior of large groups of people in public places. But when hierarchies gave way or when social networks did not extend to everyone gathered in one place, men resorted to arms. The early Irish had no peace-keeping institutions at the national or even provincial level, but relied on linkages of kinship and clientage and local lordships to keep the peace. By and large, this strategy worked in Ireland as well as anywhere in early medieval Europe.

In the eyes of the literati, women were the volatile factor in the equation of public peace. Women had no hierarchies, no negotiating powers, and no weapons. They were attached but not necessarily committed to men's social networks. According to storytellers, despite all the rules governing social intercourse, they had a disturbing tendency to ignore men's rules, alliances, and negotiations, and to elope, seduce, argue, and generally cause mayhem. Jurists recognized the problem, too, with all their laws against elopements and women's participation in public negotiation. And gnomic writers warned men outright against the connection between women's talk and social conflict. Women were "silly counsellors," "quarrelsome in company," "dishonest in assembly," "stubborn in quarrel," "mindful of strife," "feeble in a constest," "vigorous of speech," "quick to revile," and possessed of a hundred other disagreeable, uncooperative, provocative, asocial characteristics.[91]

One of the best accounts of a melee and, at the same time, most amusing critiques of unseemly public behavior is the eighth- or ninth-century *Fled Bricrenn* (Feast of Bricriu), which comically showed the worst of what happened when men let women into the feasting hall. At a gathering of Ulster heroes and their wives, poison-tongued Bricriu, troublemaker extraordinaire, set the women to competing for entry into the feasting hall, in parodic imitation of their warrior mates. The women ended up literally racing, legs and backsides exposed below raised skirts. With a noise of fifty racing chariots, they thundered for the hall, alarming the warriors, who snatched up their arms; but soon the men hurried instead to slam the doors against the women. The ladies then began to boast of their own best qualities and those of their stud husbands in a ritual "War of Women's Words" (recalling the *bla bancatha ban* of the laws), although even that did not end what the writer called the *ráidsecha,* prattlings, of the women. Eventually, Cú Chulainn, in defense of his woman's honor, literally brought down the house. He lifted the walls to let Emer take the best seat, then dropped the house before any other women slipped inside.[92]

Bricriu's feast was funny because its slapstick represented no real damage to the Ulstermen. Its author was poking affectionate fun at much earlier Ulster sagas with their formulaic conflicts. Although the actions of both heroes and wives were meant to summon the reader's laughter, it was the women—so susceptible to Bricriu's insinuations, so undignified in their conflicts, so foolish in their boasts—who were the real subjects of the satire. But the story tickled early Irish audiences because they realized that real women would never brag or battle as the heroes' wives did. Since women's social networks were different from those of men, their public and personal interactions, even when hostile, had to be different too. Women could not duel with spears or swords but only make feeble boasts in imitation of men. Yet they could not use words as men did, either, in proper legal negotiation to resolve their differences. The Ulsterwomen did not defend their own honor against each other so much as praise their husbands' prowess; in a double dig, the author of *Fled Bricrenn* depicted women not only aping men's boasts but boasting about men. Women were not liable for their words but threw them at each other freely and desperately. Jurists knew that women threatened each other and tore each other's curls out, instead of practicing legal logic or hacking at one another with swords. It took men to resolve even a war of words. Cú Chulainn, not Emer, actually ended the word war of Bricriu's feast with his masculine feats of physical strength.

Men in a similar situation argued and fought by men's rules about proper men's matters, such as prestige; perhaps they had a little war. Usually, their violence was spent against outsiders and other tribes. But when women took over the assembly place, according to the tales, their ungovernable havoc turned inward the violence inherent in extracommmunal gatherings, as the Ulsterwomen's war of words set the Ulstermen at each other's throats. Whether gender-integrated or gender-segregated, social intercourse on an extracommunity level had its costs, but the involvement of women directed the damage toward the very core of social organization: the kin group, the bond among foster relations, and the tie between lord and client. The blood feud and kin slaying of *Fingal Rónáin, Loinges Mac nUislenn, Aided Lugdach ocus Derbforgaille,* and the *Táin* proved the point more tragically than *Fled Bricrenn.*

Men were familiar with this sort of disaster. After all, their stories created and rehearsed it. They generated rules for controlling it. But the rules did not always work. The problem, as storytellers revealed, was not simply the number of people collected in one spot, but the social concentration of women. Like the Ulsterwomen at Bricriu's feast, they were so noisy that they drowned out the words of men's rule making and negotiating. They did not conduct legal discourse as ordered by jurists or take proper turns making outrageous boasts as the literati imagined that men did or even keep quiet as the canonists demanded. Among women's fifteen bad characteristics, according to *Senbríathra Fíthail*, were *labra* (talkativeness) and *glór* (noisiness), which, coupled with another terrible defect, *cúairt*—the tendency to go visiting— were disastrous.[93] For obviously, the talkative visited the noisy; bad women went to bad women's homes to meet more bad women, where they blathered and nattered instead of doing their farmyard chores, minding their children, and spinning. Or worse, women traipsed off to men's gatherings and made both noise and trouble there.[94] And most alarming of all was when women gathered together according to their own rules, for their own ends, because there men's hierarchies and laws lost sway over them. Not only simple rules for conversation but the most crucial social relationships were forgotten in the babble—and babble it was, for woman's very name was derived from the biblical tower, according to Cormac's glossary: "*Baulūan* [recte *Bablúan*], the name of a woman, as in Babylon, that is, meaning 'confusion,' that is, the mingling in one language of many languages at the tower in Mag Senair."[95] The raucous converse of women with women might be funny, like the Ulsterwomen racing for Bricriu's hall, or lewd and tragic but it usually caused calamity.

The worries of the literati were intentionally exaggerated. Writers were making statements about conflict and its resolution, about social hierarchies and their operational flaws, and about relations between men and women—all weighty topics deserving larger-than-life plots and themes. Equally important, the literati were expressing anxieties about what happened when women gathered together with men, or assembled as men did. In reality, women had limited time and opportunity for extensive contact with other women, or with men, for that matter. The nature of settlement and their economic functions helped keep women at home, where they allied themselves with cohabitants or close neighbors. Formal laws, which restricted most public legal interactions, such as economic transactions, contracts, oath making, and suits, also limited women's contacts with the outside world. Women only occasionally had opportunities to make meaningful social contacts at wells, mills, churches, and other local sites. Feasts and fairs were the rarer times when women encountered more exotic, less familiar women and men.

But at those precious moments, women may well have considered themselves a community defined by sex. The literati worried that they did; they gnawed their lips over women entering public arenas just like men. They feared two things: that women would participate in, and so ruin, the public bonding of feasting, legal interaction, and military actions that lent communities cohesion; or that women might refuse to participate in, and instead disrupt, men's bonds and the orderly process of male negotiation, even the disorderly process of men's confrontations. Their very fears suggest that women did, indeed, achieve some kind of consciousness when they gathered together.

The Meanings of Solidarity

According to the literati, only two destinations drew more socializing women together than home, mill, shrine, or feasting hall. Like good dream and nightmare, the two venues represented everything that men both tolerated and disliked about women's alliances with women. One was the religious community, as we shall see in the next chapter. Behind the walls of the sacred enclosure existed the exemplar, in the eyes of both men and women, of women's social networks, a solidarity of women who lived and worked together, linked by male hierarchies of kin and clientage to men outside and by their women's networks to female acquaintances in lay society. Communities of religious women were tolerable to men because they did not compete with male networks or infiltrate or imitate them but intertwined with them, like tender vines on strong trees. Still, a leitmotif of suspicion and even antagonism toward women's communities and religious women pervaded some of the texts.

But antipathy combined with fascination was strong in the stories of that other bastion of female solidarity, Tír inna mBan, the legendary Land of Women, which tale-tellers placed in the seas of the otherworld. In the narratives, the community of women on Tír inna mBan was no fragile tendril but a lush and seductive creeper of vicious strength that could choke the life out of men's society. The Land of Women helps illustrate the diverse meanings of ordinary women's networks in early Ireland and women's place among the bonds between men. When the literati envisioned communities of women they saw them only in relation to men's organizations: either good and vulnerable women forming hierarchies modeled on those of men or the untidy and unanchored female mob that was the antithesis of all order and morality and that captured weak men or invaded men's community in order to perpetrate turmoil.

But Tír inna mBan also confirms that, in fact, even when women organized themselves into groups well regarded by men, they may not have relied on men's social models, but had their own models and purposes for coming together. The literati certainly believed that women looked to their own female priorities. Stories of *bantrachta,* bands of women, intimated that women in groups had a single-mindedness, even a distinct female consciousness. The implication was that women, left out when men formed public social groups, determinedly formed their own. According to the literati, the purpose of these *bantrachta* was defensive, aimed at the social survival of the woman troop itself in the face of men's exclusivity and loyalty to their own kind. But in reality, the construction of women's networks may also have been a positive act with an identifiable function.

In a sense, any place where women of the sagas and stories congregated as a *bantracht* was Tír inna mBan, although storytellers used the name only for a paradisiacal island in the seas of the otherworld. The women of literature—who were not ordinary women but princesses and *mná síde*—spent much of their time in men's company. The stories were, after all, mostly about men. But especially when gathered in spaces of their own, female characters represented everything that made women's social landscape different from that of men: their inability to speak or negotiate like men, make men's alliances and enmities, or fight. In stories of religious settlements, these differences were at once suppressed and elevated to Christian ideal. Neither monks nor nuns were supposed to emerge into the chattering, negotiating public except in the ritualized political role of mediator between warring parties; anyway, fighting was altogether unchristian, although plenty of religious professionals conversed, argued, negotiated, and clashed in public.[96] But just as the male business of legal negotiation and battle had no place within the private household dominated by ordinary women, likewise, wherever women gathered in the narratives, men's rules and relationships also lost ground.

In particular, the *bantracht* worked to maintain the social group based ultimately on the proximity of coworkers and to privilege it over either individual women or the larger community based on men's solidarities. In some episodes of the narratives, for example, women acted to preserve the membership of the group and its welfare, which were threatened by men's combat or men's courtship of women. When, for instance, Cú Chulainn's uncontrollable ardor for battle threatened his own people, it was the *bantracht* of Emain Macha that faced him, employing a distinctly feminine tactic; moving as one, they bared their breasts at the furious boy to shame him into calmness.[97]

In another Ulster tale, the sad story of Derbforgaill, the women went so far as to assault and shame a newcomer to their community, indirectly causing her death. The women were angry because Cú Chulainn had brought an outsider into the community to be his lover. According to the storyteller, the *bantracht* feared that Derbforgaill would steal their own men. They were hanging around a gathering of Ulster heroes and decided to organize a contest in which each woman pissed in the snow, to see who could piss the most and farthest. Derbforgaill, performing from the top of a snowbank, produced a prodigious quantity of urine that melted the snow. The Ulsterwomen knew immediately that her powers would attract all their husbands and lovers; so they attacked and mutilated her, and drove her to suicide from shame. That they acted in opposition to the men of the community is clear from the vengeance taken on them. Their acts were nominally a protest against an Ulsterman's union with a foreigner and that alien beauty's allure, but the *bantracht* also rebelled against men's recasting the rules of courtship and sexual union. What is more, the women acted in complete concert, without even discussing their plans (at least, not within the hearing of the tale's narrator.) They moved as one to act in a way that outraged and repulsed the men in the tale and those who heard or read the story. They were loyal to each other first, and only second to their spouses, families, and the larger community of Ulstermen. According to the literati, this was the source of their strange destructive power; for women intimate to, but not directly involved in, men's society were in the perfect position to undermine its orderly working.[98]

Not even men's institutions or the greatest of heroes could withstand the *bantracht* in action. For male protagonists of the tales, the trick was to avoid a group of women in the feminine lair. A hero was safe, at least for the moment, when he encountered a single woman or a lady with female companion on the highroad or at a well; these were public places, and his retinue or charioteer was usually within calling distance. Consider the scene in *Tochmarc Becfola*, for example, where Diarmait presented his mystery lady to the Greek chorus of his retinue, which chimed in with its own unsolicited opinions about the bargain he was making.[99] But when a hero happened on a whole *bantracht* or "women troop" gathered around the lady they attended, he was likely to encounter trouble, if not peril, because of whatever the ladies were cooking up among themselves. In *Serglige Con Culainn,* the Ulsterwomen were hanging around outside the fort at Emain Macha, doing nothing much besides nagging their husbands to hunt some birds for them. Disaster descended upon the Ulstermen when these ladies were joined by a pair of bird-women from the *síd* who, together with the human women, thrust Cú Chulainn and his charioteer, the faithful Láeg, into a series of otherworldly adventures that threatened the well-being and sanity of the hero and his wife; and of course, to weaken Cú Chulainn was to endanger the entire kingdom of Ulster.[100]

In stories, the more women in one place, doing whatever women did on their own time, the more hazardous for any hapless man who tried to make contact with them on masculine terms. Hence, the literary place most thoroughly feminine was also one of the most attractive and yet dangerous for men. The island called Tír inna mBan in the voyage tales boasted the highest sex ratio in the narratives: no men lived there. The hero Bran once sailed there in his hide-covered boat. When he approached the shore, a band of women called for him to land, but he balked; he knew trouble when he saw it, and as the author put it, "He dare not go ashore."[101] The crafty female leader threw a ball of thread at Bran's face and when the hero caught it, it stuck to his palm so that she reeled him and the boat into the harbor. What Bran and his men found did not seem so terrible: a feasting hall grand enough to hold twenty-seven couches, each ready for a romantic couple; a woman for each sailor; and a never-ending supply of food.

But the peril was subtle, for the women beguiled Bran and his men into forgetting everything that was important to them. Although it seemed that they passed only one year there, it was actually many years—decades or even centuries. When Bran finally freed himself of the women and sailed home, he found family, friends, and allies long dead and himself hardly a memory in an ancient tale.[102] The women of Tír inna mBan deprived him of his entire social network as well as his place in the vertical chain that linked him to ancestors gone before and to the sons of sons to come. They forever severed his every contact with men except his sailors, who were henceforth doomed to putter endlessly about the seas of fantasy.[103]

Tír inna mBan was conceived as a place of feminine wiles, a source of the kind of delightful trouble that women generated best when they worked together to deceive, capture, and utterly boggle men. Other otherworldly women enticed men to the *síd,* as we have seen: Oengus, Nera, and Cú Chulainn were a few of the victims. Women of the *síd,* like all the ladies of leisure and literature, conspicuously spent their time in public places, such as crowded feasting halls, not in the dark workplace where ordinary women were supposed to pass their days. Women in the narratives did not labor, unless they were serving women; in fact, the literati placed their supernatural heroines precisely in the places where they could never work, such as feasting halls. And everyone knew what happened when women did not toil, when their troublemaking hands were not occupied with needlework or their tongues not busy with household matters: they caused trouble.

Of course, such trouble could be alluring. The monk who composed *Immram Brain* created quite a lurid fantasy for his readers when he sent Bran to that otherworldly sexual playground, that island of enticements where a man might stray and, entangled in ultimate femaleness, might never return to the dull security of his own home. Indeed, when an otherworldly beauty came to fetch Conla in *Echtrae Chonlai* rather than wait around for him in the Land of the Living, he had no choice but to follow her to that irresistible, feminine stronghold, where "no people are . . . save women and maidens," much to his kinfolk's sorrow. But he put it simply: "It is not easy for me [to go,] for I love my people. However, a longing for the woman has come upon me."[104] In many respects, Tír inna mBan was the opposite of the defeminized space of the Christian monastic enclosure, where women were either excluded entirely, or where they hid in order to become better Christians. Any good man could safely visit a nuns' community, but the hero Bran himself feared to enter Tír inna mBan, and Conla, like many, never came back. Once a man was lost there, he forgot home, time, kin, friends, and everything else that mattered to normal men.

The Land of Women had no resident patriarchs to impose rules or render feminine interrelationships secondary to kinship or clientage ties. The literati could imagine such a place only as so magical that shelter and food were conjured from thin air, as otherworldly people themselves tended to appear and disappear at random. The Land of Women was not fed and protected by hardworking men who ploughed and fought; it was not ordered logically as was the real world of laws and kinship and clientage, suit, and vengeance, but was sustained by phantasms and nourished from a pagan cornucopia. In men's stories, a community completely controlled by women who were attached to each other by their own mysterious nonrules could not hope to survive without the fearsome female sorcery of the presocial, pre-Christian past.

Tomás Ó Cathasaigh has argued that the the the otherworld, *síd,* had its origins in a homonymy with *síd,* peace; that the Land of Promise, the Land of the Living, and the Land of Women, those nonfighters, were one and the same.[105] But if the *síd* was a peaceable kingdom, its accord was illusory, like the quiet, base pleasures of Circe's island. Men were taken from this world to the otherworld and held captive in a place where their status as lords and fighters, farmers and fathers became meaningless. The social ties they so carefully forged with one another dissolved into nothing.

The worst thing about such an untamed land, according to the literati, was not so much that it could exist without men as that its inherent disorder could spill out of Tír inna mBan into the public places of normal society. The lawlessness of women could erupt wherever they gathered, for no man in early Ireland could keep his woman locked up or prevent her from getting together with other women. Men tried to forbid women from speaking in men's legal language or sharing men's places and their public displays of kinship, fosterage, or clientage. Indeed, they were not content to mastermind the whole range of their own ties to women or restrict women's social opportunities; they needed to meddle with the bonds of woman to woman.

If early Irish texts did not directly address the nature of women's social networks, at least their stories of the Land of Women admitted the existence and shape of women's social networks and women's discrete social purposes. Their stories of that Land of Women revealed a literati most anxious about the effects of women's chattering disorderliness upon their own social hierarchies, which were more fluid and fragile than men liked to admit. That social ties were precious and precarious in early Ireland is obvious. That women were to blame simply because they chose their friends differently from men is less clear to modern historians than it was to early medieval writers.

Women created different kinds of social networks than men not only because men would not let them into theirs but because their needs were different from men's. Women did not simply allow themselves to be attached to men's hierarchies as wives and mothers. They manipulated their ties to men, participating in men's networks when necessary and drawing from them for their own circles of contacts. Since men kept them out of the official business of the community, women had to fend for themselves without the ready-made comforts of kin ties, in which their place was always precarious anyway, or fosterage ties, or patron-client relations. But their maneuvering of men's networks was only one dimension of a complex social world. Women made a variety of contacts at home in private and abroad in public. Many, even the majority, of such meaningful contacts must have been with other women. Women socialized with those confined by babies and jobs to the same or neighboring homes, those who carried grain to the mills, and those who were excluded from the sacred space of the monastic sanctuary. A woman surrounded and protected herself with an elaborately woven web of friendships, exchanges, and alliances just as men did; but she began by relying on the simple principle of proximity.

We must look out from the Land of Women in order to envision women's own social priorities, avoiding the male perspective that monopolized the laws, the narratives, and even recent scholarly analysis of early Irish kinship and clientage. The social relationships that women were told, by laws and other documents, to value were not necessarily the ones they held most dear or most useful. Laws instructed women to give their first loyalty to husbands, kinsmen, male foster relations, and male allies of the same. Women may well have done so, sometimes, with or without considering the alternatives. But men gave women another lesson about friends and allies, too, when they excluded women from the formal, public, legal associations that they themselves held so dear. Laws, the economy, and gender ideologies pushed women into the company of women. They spent most of their lives with other women. Their opportunities for making useful allies and meaningful relationships existed mostly in proximity to other women. Even at mixed-sex gatherings, women gathered with women; even when they were expected to follow their husbands or fathers to feasts or fairs, linger on the edges of men's socializing, and keep out of men's friendships with men, women were left with women. And the literati, if not all men, recognized what went on when women made friendships with women: trouble. Some common aim, some shared thought could lead women to prize their ties to other women over their bonds to men. More frightening, women bound to other women might work to undermine men's formal associations. If women put their minds to it, the literati worried, they could bring down the clientage, fosterage, and kinship systems that formed the very basis of order, of society, of human life. Men who had visited that dangerous territory sent back the warning: let no man stray into the Land of Women.

8

Priests' Wives and Brides of Christ

T he Irish literati wrote with unusual frankness, for once, about religious women and their relations with men. While they never defined the creature woman, clerical writers did attempt formal definitions of different types of religious women. Eighth-century canonists, after Augustine, set out two precise models for the religious life. Virgins were to imitate Mary in body and custom, and penitents were to follow her mother Anna; both were to shun social and sexual contact with men. Along with pious laywomen, these two categories made up the traditional, tripartite womanhood of Christian theology.[1]

The suggestion that women imitate Gospel exemplars encapsulated a small history. From the time of Christ until the Irish eighth century, nothing had changed for those who wished to devote themselves to Christianity; religious women secured a spot in the Christian past, thus escaping the association with pre-Patrician pagan culture that tainted their secular sisters. But the literati's historical picture of religious women was more colorful and mutable than their paraphrase of Augustine might suggest. In fact, the learned elite constantly devised and revised the history of their female colleagues in religion, using visions of the past to reorder the lives of contemporary religious women and to generate a protocol for contact with them. One clerical writer summarized it this way in the eighth or ninth century: three *ordines* of saints had accomplished the Christianization of Ireland, each *ordo* representative of a different period of relations between male and female religious professionals. The first *ordo* of bishop missionaries, which had flourished in the fifth century with Saint Pátraic, "did not spurn the administration and fellowship of women because . . . they did not fear the wind of temptation." After this brief heyday of cooperation, the second order, forty years later, "fled the administration of women and excluded them from their monasteries." The third order of monks, another forty years later, ignored women altogether and "lived in deserted places" as ascetics.[2]

The text shouted the ambivalence felt by Christian men for even the most laudable women but also whispered clues to gender relations within the sacred enclosures of early Ireland. As the three *ordines* showed, clerics came to perceive genderless interaction as a prelapsarian ideal left from the days of missionizing but no longer available to canny men of religion. Instead, the canonists assumed, women could choose the life of a professional virgin or penitent inside the protected world of the Christian settlement, as the canons allowed. Nonetheless, religious women had to be closely supervised for their good and for the benefit of men wary of their own virtue. And they had no business trying to co-opt or ape the functions of male ecclesiastics, according to the third *ordo*.

Yet the subtexts of this microcosmic ecclesiastical history also suggested that women were acceptable as religious professionals, that they tried to exercise options for the religious life, and that they were perceived as different enough from ordinary women to warrant extensive, formal discussion of their identity, behavior, and histories. Religious women were the exception to every unspoken rule about men and women in early Ireland. In practical terms, they were different for reasons obvious to even the dimmest or most unchristian of observers: they did not have sex, husbands, or babies. Of course, the potential for all these remained, lurking within the dry and untouchable breasts of every nun, as the most misogynist clercial writers insisted in their stories of lustfully wayward women of religion. But their rejection of the carnal act made it possible for them to do many things that most laywomen could not: swear legal oaths, own property, manage their own farms, even broker political treaties and work miracles. Paradoxically, abstaining from the honored roles of lover, wife, and mother, created for and by them in collusion with men, earned religious women the respect of many men, if the enmity of others.

Still, neither female saints nor other religious women eluded the ideological disagreements of Christian theorizers about woman. Nor could they evade the strictures imposed upon all women's lives by custom and politics. Religious women remained female, if exceptional, and their sex affected their experience as professional Christians. It meant that the entire range of their relations with men, both lay and ecclesiastical, had to be constantly renegotiated to take into account their perplexing, almost oxymoronic status as female religious professionals. In particular, the literati's rules and models for fraternization with religious women showed how Christian ideas both reflected and directly influenced gender relations among religious women and others in the context of sex, marriage, and family structures. In turn, ordinary social ties helped shape Christian gender ideology and the practice of religion.

Women themselves might have viewed their aims and lives not as rejections or revisions of traditional social roles but as a series of positive choices. They chose ecclesiastical superiors and consorts, Jesus and his clerical representatives, rather than husbands. They chose to pray and to conduct a life of ritual, but they also worked hard to feed, clothe, and keep house for other ecclesiastics. They were *muimmi,* nurturers, to abbots and saints. By their choices, religious women neither raised nor lowered the status of all women, as some historians have argued, nor did they affect the putative power of their lay sisters. Nuns and penitents did not enjoy any special periods of influence and freedom. Although their experience of Christianity and their relations with male colleagues fluctuated throughout the pre-Norman period, these depended more on the social contexts of marriage and family relations than on sexual attitudes and devotion to the Blessed Virgin. Religious women merely acted out more exceptions and added complications to the already complex pattern of gender relations in early Ireland.

The Foundation of Women's Communities

The Irish have traditionally held Saint Pátraic responsible for the first phase of recruitment to Christianity and for the first shrines and *eigenkirchen,* family-run churches, although most scholars now agree that he had some help. According to the seventh-century accounts of his life and deeds, Pátraic traveled the island building churches, baptizing and consecrating women and men to staff them, and distributing the necessary equipment—books, vestments, and relics, including the occasional tooth or garment of his own—to his new foundations. These seventh-century texts probably do not reflect exactly what occurred in the first century of conversion but represent instead a later memory of the earliest religious foundations. Whether or not Pátraic created them, however, archaeological evidence shows that Christian settlements were certainly in existence soon after the first missionary activity. These were probably little farms with a modest church or an oratory, normally constructed on family lands, inhabited by a daughter or a son of the landowners along with a few companions, or by brothers and sisters together. No doubt many of them served parish functions, whatever those might have been in the early centuries of Christianization.[3] Many survived for a century or two, some then disappearing from the records, and others turning into full-blown monasteries for men, women, or both.

The hagiographers held that by 700 or so the Irish had determined that their rural island was to be guided by Christian monks. Some of the monks resembled laymen rather than ascetics on the Mediterranean model, and others were also bishops and priests. Beginning in the second century of Christianization, each of the major saints, of which there were hundreds on this *insula sanctorum,* supposedly founded anywhere from several to dozens of religious communities for men or women or both. For once the hagiographers were exaggerating only slightly. It is true, as other texts and material remains confirm, that soon after the arrival of the faith, Christian officials began organizing themselves into something called, for lack of a better term, monasteries rather than parishes, and that hundreds of such settlements appeared in these early centuries, crediting saints with their foundation. It is not necessarily the case, however, that each saint founded and that his or her successors controlled all the communities claimed by the saint's hagiographer. Nor were these communities identical in size, function, or prosperity. What is more, some were women's foundations, some were men's, and many religious communities contained both sexes, either temporarily or permanently.[4]

Women were among the heroic founders, although their settlements formed a small percentage of those that dotted the island. Only ten or eleven women's communities are known surely to have existed before the Vikings came to Ireland, some officially attached to men's settlements as at Ard Macha, where, as one seventh-century scholar wrote, "both sexes are seen to live together in religion from the coming of the faith to the present day almost inseparably."[5] Maybe fifty more foundations, including hermitages, double communities, and *eigenkirchen,* were founded before 1200, but evidence for some of these amounts to little more than a stray hagiographic reference or a nineteenth-century tradition of dedication to a pre-Norman female saint.[6] Many of the foundations dispersed either when the Northmen attacked or for some other indiscernible reason at some point between 600 and 1100. In fact, the names of dozens or even hundreds of unidentifiable religious women flickered once upon the page of vitae or martyrologies, and then were snuffed out forever.

Either women's communities regularly foundered, or they did not merit the notice of the literati. Either way, the explanation may lie in the larger pattern of gender relations and property ownership. Women's relations with anyone outside their own families, including the saints and even God, were negotiated by kinsmen or husbands or by men such as monks or priests who acted in the place of kinsmen or husbands. Taking the veil did not change this situation for a woman, even a bona fide abbess of the highest nobility; the most admirably androgynous religious women could no more throw off the language of gender than they could discard Irish or Latin. Hence, the effects of traditional gender roles and ideologies upon women's choice to become religious pro-

Religious settlements mentioned in the text.

fessionals were threefold. First, custom helped determine the placement and prosperity of the community a woman joined. Second, tradition helped determine the kind of religious life a woman chose, whether at home, in a mixed or single-sex community, or in a hermitage of her own. Finally, both custom and tradition guided her relations with her clerical colleagues, with whom she formed bonds creatively modeled on those existing already in secular contexts. All these conditions helped keep women's communities in the shadows of the sources.

One of the principle differences between women's and men's communities concerned property and longevity. Historians (including me) have described how women founded fewer and less durable settlements than men did, suggesting that women's communities were ephemeral because it was harder for women to find property on which to settle and, more important, upon which a community could support itself for several generations. Unless women attracted endowments from outsiders or managed to collect noble recruits who brought gifts of land from doting parents along with them, their community could not legally last longer than the lifetime of its founding heiress, whose land returned to her kin at her death.[7]

Actually, the evidence for this neat but melancholy picture is more complex than historians have previously thought. Hagiographers recorded stories of women who turned their "dowries" of land into the basis for a community, suggesting that parents and children alike sometimes ignored property laws and gave aspiring holy women premortem inheritances, which may have become their permanent property, with which to found religious communities.[8] The impulses of affection and piety were as important to the early Irish as the profit motive, if not more so; and as the vitae of female saints demonstrated, many ordinary men respected the skills and status of religious women. Canonists knew that men wanted to honor their kinswomen's vocation when they excepted women's religious donations from inheritance rules. They maintained that heiresses could donate land to religious communities if their kinsmen raised no objections.[9]

Hence, we who have assumed that religious women generally lived in poverty or at least were less well off than men's communities may be wrong. Indeed, several references in the hagiography to religious women's handing property over to men's settlements lead to one of three conclusions: this was code for women's settlements that placed themselves under the authority of male clerics, who collected rents and dues; or these were women's foundations that then became the property of men; or these communities of women were wealthy enough to afford donations of land to more substantial male settlements whose protection they sought.[10] They could pay, in other words, for what they wanted from male colleagues.

On the other hand, the hagiographers often pleaded poverty for their female saints. Perhaps women's communities never appeared to be wealthy in the vitae because most of them were indeed smaller, more dependent on family goodwill, and less well endowed than men's communities. This hypothesis would make sense, given what we have seen of traditional social relations and laws of property.[11] But it also may be that women's communities normally grew up on the lands that a family could spare for its devout females—in other words, on marginal land or on lands best suited to women's pursuit of self-sufficency, such as pasturage for sheep, which was unfit for crops. Even men's settlements appeared on the borders of political territories; women's foundations were likely to be even more marginal, socially and politically as well as economically and geographically.[12] Thus, though they may not have been rich, religious women's communities may have endured longer than we have thought.

In fact, some communities of women could manage quite well, economically and otherwise. As we have seen, wealth in early Ireland was not necessarily measured by the amount of a person's land. More important gauges were the amount she or he had to eat and the number of clients and aristocratic privileges she or he commanded. Richer, nobler men put more elaborate walls around their farmsteads, for instance; in this context, it becomes significant that some women's communities, such as Cell Dara, supposedly had "invisible" boundaries kept by God rather than actual walls to protect against enemies.[13] But was this absence of physical walls proof of Cell Dara's poverty? Not if the seventh-century scholar Cogitosus is to be taken seriously when he described the flocks of gift-bearing pilgrims at Brigit's church. Moreover, the very ability of Cell Dara to support a scholar of his caliber attested to the community's wealth. Likewise, Saint Samthann's community of Cluain Brónaig indulged in several eighth-century building projects, according to her hagiographer, relying upon the labor of clients and tenants, which suggests extensive holdings. In fact, the nuns there collected enough donations and rents that they worried about how to divide the profits.[14] When Samthann's hagiographer, like those of Brigit, Moninne, and many other male and female saints, pleaded poverty for his subject, he must have been describing the spiritual poverty appropriate to Christian professionals rather than an actual lack of goods and land. The very vitae these women merited argue for the prosperity of their houses.

What is more, some groups of religious women made good simply by moving in with men. In some of the earliest stories about women during the conversion period—written during or soon after that same period, between the fifth and eighth centuries—women went to visit kinsmen under religious vows or joined existing communities that also included monks with inherited land or formed communities affiliated with male monasteries. Tírechán, the seventh-century hagiographer of Pátraic, described Christian women who lived with clerics in religious settlements on the pagan frontier, where they helped operate ritual centers and spread the new faith. Some of these communities were the *eigenkirchen*.[15] Even when women were able to form religious communities of their own, according to Tírechán, these were almost always located near the monasteries or churches of men, usually kinsmen. In some cases, evangelizing women supposedly established religious settlements under the direction of bishops and abbots as well as, ultimately, Pátraic himself.[16] In later stories of conversion, such as those found in post-800 hagiography, women continued to put themselves or their communities near those of kinsmen. Saint Ciarán and his mother and kinswomen inhabited adjacent settlements, according to his many vitae.[17] Several of the major monastic settlements included women's churches in their enclosures or set discretely but not too distant from them.[18] In this context, the inevitable historical debates over the nature and endurance of "double" communities lose relevance; rather, groups of male and female religious lived and labored in a whole range of situations of varying integration, some more formal than others, just as men and women lived in varying arrangements in secular life.[19]

Throughout the Middle Ages, women probably had at least a few choices about where to go to practice Christianity or how to support themselves while they did it.[20] They could join family members already settled in the neighborhood or, if maternal kin, at a little distance. If they were lucky, they could move to sites donated by male relatives or acquired by dowry or gift. These sites, however, were probably located near other family estates, some of which already supported religious settlements composed of their own kin.[21] Both economic considerations and traditional social ties placed women near their families. And like their secular sisters, religious women made use of the restrictions that kept them close to home.

The main evidence for religious women's marginality, economic or other, is simply the tendency of women and their religious communities to disappear from the sources after a reference or two. But this should not surprise anyone familiar with the documents' general treatment of the female sex. The literati, who had no interest in women's friendships and alliances, did not advertise small communities of religious women or list obscure foundations by religious men except when they played some part in the lives of larger, richer, more influential monasteries. The rolls of unidentified holy women and their settlements were, in fact, perverse propaganda for women's religious vocation. Many communities and many religious women came into the historical spotlight only when the literati tried to insert them into the larger, male-run ecclesiastical hierarchy; only in subordination to the mixed community at Cell

Dara, or when they offered their foundations to Pátraic or another Christian pioneer; only in a swift political moment in a half sentence in the annals did women surface at all. The odd references to a nun here, a holy sister there, formed an address book to the otherwise anonymous—but *not* lost—religious women of the Irish past and a testament to the flexibility of their vocation.

The Creation of Women's Religious Roles

According to the author of the three *ordines* of Irish Christianization, the history of women's religious roles was actually a history of gender relations. In the long-gone days when converts had kept themselves separate from their pagan neighbors, male and female missionaries had mingled freely. Together, men and women had led their fellow believers into an age of Christian establishment. But as the story went, once the majority had accepted at least the semblance of Christian belief, men turned back to those they trusted most—not their wives but their kinsmen and allies—to communicate God's word to the lay community and help them apply it to their lives. Archaeological evidence, the annals, the vitae, and other religious texts all suggest that men and women continued to mingle while they worked for the faith, but something happened during the long centuries of Christianization to drive them increasingly farther apart ideologically, if not physically. Conchubranus told a story in the twelfth century about Saint Cóemgen and how he determined to destroy Moninne's settlement, which could never have been written by Cogitosus or Tírechán in the seventh century.[22] When Cóemgen found out that Moninne was reading her psalms with a reformed robber and a band of hoodlums, a devil persuaded him to attack and wreck the nun's community. Moninne took the threat serenely, suggesting that Cóemgen notice the "little black boy" whose advice had inspired his jealousy. She settled the whole matter by driving off the demon and drawing Cóemgen a nice, hot bath—a reminder, perhaps, of the Ulstermen's habits of dunking Cú Chulainn in an icy-cold tub when he went a little wild. In the old days, female saints had usually competed with male colleagues more discreetly, and their companions in religion never threatened outright violence. On the contrary, they had worked with women and protected them from harm. By the twelfth century, though, Conchubranus looked back to Moninne's time and assumed an antagonism based as much on sexual difference as anything else; nevertheless, he wrote Moninne the heroine's part in the sexual contest.

The hagiographer's story recounted a history similar to that of the three *ordines*. Changes in religious women's participation in Christianity indicated shifting practices and attitudes—from the heady and dangerous days of missionizing, when women trudged off with husbands and brothers to set up Christian outposts on the pagan frontier, preaching and assisting at major rituals and struggling to maintain growing monastic communities of both men and women, to the period when religious women chose, by lack of alternatives or force of men's objections, to live quietly at home or with other sympathetic women, minding their own Christian business. Yet religious women in early Ireland never suffered what medieval historians have imposed, in retrospect, on the nuns of Francia and England. They were never snatched out of some golden age of religious influence and cloistered into oblivion. Each century of Christian history in Ireland saw female religious professionals making active, meaningful choices about their own lives with the help of, and in the company of, religious men. Their options may have grown or shrunk, depending on the social and ideological milieux in which they found themselves. They may have been pushed to make certain choices. Nonetheless, they did choose.

The heyday of missionizing ended in the seventh century. By then, not every soul in Ireland had given itself to Jesus; total conversion (in the sense of Catholic orthodoxy and orthopraxis) would not happen until the nineteenth century, if then. But by the early Middle Ages, the professional religious women of Ireland had settled into two roles, as had most of their religious sisters throughout Europe: they were either kinswomen or wives to monks, priests, bishops, and Jesus Christ. The early Irish could not imagine meaningful alternatives to these essential roles. No doubt women experienced a genuine vocation as wives of priests, mothers of saints, and brides of Christ. Many may have wielded great political influence and controlled considerable estates. But their status, like that of secular women, always depended on the status of their male guardians and their roles remained formally supportive. They played these roles, in many permutations, from the arrival of Christianity in the fourth century until the Norman invasion. Penitentials, canons, laws, annals, and genealogies all confirmed women's subsidiary relation to male clerics. While interpretations of religious women's roles changed over time, by region, by individual, and according to gendered perspective, the roles themselves remained the same.

At first, women could remain at home with their families and, from the safety of conventional context, make the radical choice of becoming a professional religious. Pátraic himself described in his fifth-century *Confessio* the young women who vowed virginity with or without the blessing of their parents before any of them knew where, exactly, such action would lead them.[23] No communities existed yet to take them in. Like the little family foundations that appeared soon after and survived throughout the Middle Ages, maintaining one's vows at home also remained an option for religious women until at least the Norman period. Conchubranus, writing in the eleventh century and drawing on a seventh-century original of the life of the sixth-century saint Moninne, described how she lived in her parents' house but *seorsum,* apart, learning her psalms from a local priest before moving later to a mixed-sex monastery run by her uncle.[24] No doubt Moninne's case represented the career of other religious women who moved easily from a private life of devotion to a place in an organized settlement run by a clerical relative, to a community set up expressly for women, and possibly, at some later date, to a permanent foundation or even a hermitage of her own.[25]

Penitent spouses and widows were also apparently able to live a religious life at home.[26] One of the few documents to legislate for widows, the eighth-century canons, made provision for their support by church officials but did not specify that they live in organized communities of nuns.[27] A woman's life cycle might parallel her itinerancy. She changed from unmarried daughter in her father's house, celibate wife of a similarly inclined man, or bereft wife living among her affines to a devout visitor among her own kin and, finally, sometimes, to a recognized religious professional enclosed by sacred space, imbued with the authority of her calling. Occasionally, as penitentials warned and hagiographic tales of fallen nuns insinuated, a religious woman returned to the *saeculum.* The variety and fluidity of religious women's lives suggested by the vitae cannot be emphasized too much. Religious professionals adapted to the available material and spiritual resources, always finding a way to distinguish themselves from the Christian mainstream. For women, it was necessary to maneuver within traditionally feminine spaces and explore subtle variations on a very few social roles.

Wives provided the third model for a professional religious life. At least in the first centuries of Christianization, some women took the possibility literally, legally becoming a priest's or bishop's wife. The sixth- and seventh-century penitentials hinted at an official function for priests' wives in new Christian communities. The so-called "First Synod of Saint Patrick," probably a sixth-century tract, ordered priests to wear Roman-style tunics and haircuts and their wives to veil themselves when going out. Violation of the dress code was a serious offense, punishable by excommunication.[28] Since priests' wives had to maintain a certain uniform that identified them as religious professionals, they may have been expected to assist with their husbands' social and ritual services.[29] The later sources said little about clerical wives, and it is clear that celibacy became an important ideal to the ecclesiastical elite in Ireland, as elsewhere. Both laws and eighth-century canons assumed that priests and bishops could be married men. Evidence from the annals also shows that clerics continued to marry well into the Norman period, fathering dynasties of monks and nuns, which suggests that their wives also held high social status if not well-defined religious functions.[30]

From as early as the eighth century, however, the role of cleric's wife took a new form that became increasingly influential in the religious literature and, the vitae suggested, in the self-conceptualization of religious women. Throughout Christendom, the discrete functions of priests' wives disappeared from orthopraxis, primarily under the influence of barbarian laws that treated women as sex objects and chattel and thus unfit for religious office, as Suzanne Wemple and others have ably demonstrated.[31] But women could still marry into the profession by becoming brides of Christ and spiritual consorts of male saints. Whereas such women appeared occasionally in conversion-era texts of the seventh century, they filled the vitae of the ninth and later centuries; and, although the theological image of Christ's bride was not well elaborated until much later, early Irish religious men and women were sensitive to all the connotations of the role.[32] Indeed, one of the words for a married woman was the very same word for a veiled nun: *caillech*.[33]

The *sponsa dei* was less a spouse than priests' wives in some crucial and crude ways, but she was a wife nonetheless. Women in early Ireland had little choice about whether to marry or form some other liaison with a man, as we have seen; however, they did have a choice among men. Some, with or without their parents' approval, chose Jesus. The hagiographers depicted women quite consciously playing this role and vigorously rejecting secular spouses for Christ, sometimes against great opposition from their families. Saint Brigit is only the most famous of women who had other good reasons for choosing Jesus and who managed to marry the man she wanted despite her kinsmen.[34] We have seen that ordinary women had only informal say in their selection of spouses, and only the goodwill of their families allowed them to choose; but women had the backing of the ecclesiastical hierarchy when they settled on Jesus. After all, once they married into a religious community women gained almost all the benefits of secular marriage—a secure place in a household, economic support, physical protection—without its disadvantages, such as competition on behalf of their children against their husbands' other women or alienation from their own kin. What is more, brides of Christ gained a superlative bride gift, better than land or cattle or jewels, and never offered to laywomen: assurance of salvation.

Nevertheless, spiritual marriage was a *lánamnas* like any other. Marriage of religious virgin and male proselytizer or deity also brought a burden of wifely duties and behavioral restrictions. This was increasingly the case from the eighth century on, as their bridegrooms more frequently were spiritual; apparently more was expected from the wife of the son of God than from the wife of the local priest. Like ordinary married women, they were not to mingle too freely with other men. Penitentialists hinted that vowed virgins who committed sexual acts were adulteresses. Eighth-century canons also forbade women to commit spiritual adultery. Quoting Paul and Isidore, canonists specifically prohibited women from speaking in Christian assemblies, teaching men, or performing priestly rituals.[35] Not only was this prohibition doctrinally correct, it also derived from the native wisdom on wives, which frowned so severely on chattering women. Both secular and ecclesiastical law allowed a man to repudiate a woman who jabbered too much, as well as one who committed adultery.[36] Just as a wife in secular life should not presume to advise her husband—as Mac Dathó's unhappy story showed—or consort with other men, so a woman spiritually wed to Christ or one of his representatives was to remain both quiet and monogamous. Their function was to support their spouses, not to presume knowledge or authority.

Some hagiographers took the wifely ideal to a disturbing extreme, sending a not-so-obscure message about the limits and purpose of women's participation in the church. Women chose marriage to Christ because it brought them union with the savior, according to the vitae, but the honeymoon was short for some holy brides. The story of the daughters of Lóegaire mac Néill, a fifth-century king, which appeared in Tírechán's seventh-century account and in the ninth-century *Vita Tripartita* of Saint Pátraic, illustrated the ambiguity of the relationship between spiritual bride and groom.

As the story goes, Pátraic happened on two princesses, Ethne and Fedelm, while they were bathing at a well. The women were husband hunting and Pátraic seemed a likely prospect; they asked him about his own social background, but he rebuked them: "You'd do better to ask about our God than our family," he scolded. Their interest piqued, they did. "Who is God?" they inquired.

> Where is God and whose God is he, and where does he live? Does he have sons, daughters, gold or silver, your God? Is he everliving? Handsome? Did many men foster his sons? Are his daughters dear and beautiful to the men of the world? Is he in heaven or on earth? In the air, in rivers, on mountains, in valleys? How can we see him? How love him? How find him? Is he young or old?

Ethne and Fedelm were interested in all the details of family, status, and appearance which normally concerned young women. When Pátraic suggested they marry [*coniungere*] Jesus, they wanted to check him out *facie ad faciem*. But their passion was spiritual as well as emotional and physical. When Pátraic demanded that they convert, be baptized, take the veil, and die for Christ, they did so unhesitatingly. Physical death replaced the sexual consummation that normally followed a wedding. The story ended with the family's reaction to the radical decision of Ethne and Fedelm; their druid foster fathers were annoyed but eventually converted as well, and the women were buried in a shrine at the well.[37]

The episode perfectly expressed the clerical elite's reinterpretation of the wifely contours of women's Christian experience. According to this paradigm, which was perfected in the vitae of the postconversion period, all women wanted was an intimate relationship with God or his representative, such as Pátraic. Once they achieved this, earthly life lost meaning for them. Salvation came, like everything else women owned, as a dowry, gift, or inheritance from men closely related to them by blood or marriage. It was personal property. Christian women had no reason to share salvation with others. Their business was not to proselytize directly but to convert by withdrawing from secular life; in hagiographic literature they then became what Jo Ann McNamara has aptly called "living sermons."[38]

In this respect, the story of Ethne and Fedelm sent an unsettling message about gender relations within the Christian hierarchy. By dying, the women helped Pátraic to convert their foster fathers. Further, they were buried in a shrine that hagiographers made sure to mention so as to attract pilgrims to it. Hence, the texts suggested that dead women helped many more Christians and converted many more pagans than the Uí Néill princesses could ever have done while alive. And Pátraic's vita was not the only text to preach by example of dead virgins; other saints' lives also described women who converted, took the veil, and died in order to consummate their unions with Christ.[39] Women in other kinds of stories had died for love, but not this way. Deirdriu had dashed out her brains on a rock, but she had not simply withered away passively at the suggestion of her lover; the nun Liadain expired for love, but only after consummating a very physical yearning for Cuirithir, not Jesus. Hagiographers made as much of the relics of male saints, who were also valuable to believers as mere bones, but men never perished for the express purpose of providing relics. They had better things to do. Ireland had no other martyrs to speak of besides its hagiographic nuns. Restricted from preaching or ministering, confined to shrines and vitae, Christ's brides were most effective when dead.[40]

Yet the story of Lóegaire's daughters also demonstrated that women could show men the way to God. Their druidic fosterers and, presumably, readers of Pátraic's vitae followed the princesses' example, choosing to sacrifice much to follow Jesus. Of course, the majority of spiritual brides in early Ireland were not sacrificial virgins but ordinary religious women. Those who married Christ were also consciously choosing to proselytize in three ways: by becoming the wife of God's son, with all the connotations of status, responsibility, and links among kin groups implied by marriage; by the behavioral example of living a religious life; and by providing the ritual and educational services common in women's communities. Considering marriage laws, with their relatively liberal rights of property and divorce granted to legally married *cétmuinter*s, spiritual marriage also carried implications of limited influence which adds complexity to the message of the Uí Néill princesses. In other words, even when limiting religious women to the roles of wife and kinswoman of Jesus and his male representatives and preaching to them through vitae about behavioral control, the clerical elite were actually, in their own way, inviting women to take active part in Christianity.

Blest Sisters, Sinless Wives

Kinship and marriage, the two principal categories of gender interaction in early Ireland, were paramount in the conceptualization of religious women's roles. Predictably, both directly influenced the relations of religious women to their ecclesiastical colleagues. The vitae depicted women operating as surrogate wives, mothers, sisters, or other kinswomen to individual monks, as well as collectively at the community level. And they were not just freeloading on hardworking husbands, either. Women expected a partnership in which they paid for what they received, offering their communities and estates in clientage (*céilsine,* the same word for clientage and marriage) to male authorities, laboring to feed and clothe their men like any good wife, and providing the kind of friendly companionship even a spiritual man needed on an occasional cold and lonely night. The most chaste bride of Christ dwelled on the same social continuum as the worldliest bishop's consort.

Religious women inserted themselves into a larger ecclesiastical hierarchy while forming a more local partnership with neighboring clergymen. Their settlements and communities joined others in a network of subordination and rule, in which some groups and their saints paid dues and obeisance to others. At the same time, female religious professionals offered camaraderie, labor, and a variety of other personal services to male clerics whom they knew intimately; as surrogate wives and kinswomen, they provided support that was expected and cherished by male colleauges. Finally, a very few venerable women gained authority and fame that rivaled those of the greatest churchmen. In fact, their achievements and virtues shone more brightly in the hagiographers' eyes for their femininity.

Women had much to give and as much to gain from the particular means by which they participated, individually and collectively, in ties to others of their profession. Historians have not given them nearly enough credit for doing far more than quietly enduring against the odds of a patriarchal society. There is no better example of the adaptability of traditional gender roles and practical gender relations, or of women simply managing, than the dense, interrelated processes by which professional religious women joined men in creating Christianity and its churches.

The vitae offered the best account of relations between male and female religious. Women's settlements that managed to survive more than a generation had to jockey for place in a sophisticated network of religious communities including everything from the oratories of recluses to major settlements such as Cell Dara. Religious communities competed among themselves for authority, status, and lay patronage, in the sense of both donations and customers. Women's communities and monasteries exchanged blessings and curses, gifts and favors, ritual services and hospitality, and in the process established their position in relation to each other.

Hagiographers' texts were the manifestoes of major religious communities in this competition. All the vitae acknowledged a few saints and their communities to be more powerful than others.[41] Ard Macha, the principle church of Saint Pátraic, and Cell Dara, Saint Brigit's major foundation, spent centuries competing for precedence and patronage, and their contest pervaded several vitae. Only in the late seventh century did one of Brigit's hagiographers concede that Pátraic outranked Brigit, largely because Cell Dara was at that time seeking political aid from some northern Ard Macha–supporting kingdoms against its own predatory southern kings.[42] Although well-known settlements founded by women were fewer than those of men, Cell Dara and a few other major women's communities and their saints attracted recruits and donations from across Ireland, just as monasteries did, making them well able to compete. Hagiographers were less explicit about how second-string communities managed in the contest, or how they related to even smaller and less prominent settlements, or how the men and women who inhabited them personally interacted.

Women's communities interacted with other religious communities in a different way than men's settlements might have. Whereas men's communities and individual clerics became clients or patrons of their brethren, women, who could never fully participate in clientage, found their place in the ecclesiastical hierarchy by playing traditional roles of wife and sister. The models for relations between women's and men's settlements and for relations between individual men and women derived directly from marriage and kinship. We have seen that polygyny flourished at elite levels in early Ireland. A well-to-do primary wife who normally resided with her husband on his major estate might well have kept a dowered farm of her own in her natal territory. Secondary wives or concubines may have lived with their mate or dwelled on his other farms or on their own family property. Legal responsibilities toward each other and property sharing of partners varied according to the type of legal union they enjoyed, as we have seen.

Similarly, the relations between communities of religious women and the abbots or bishops who claimed jurisdiction over them varied according to the formality of their ties, the degree of kinship involved, the nobility and prosperity of each, and even the affection among all parties. Some powerful communities claimed that their saintly founders had authority over smaller, poorer communities of men as well as women; such hagiographical claims, which varied by vita, reflected the constant squabble over estates, precedence, and status throughout the network of communities. But very few women's or genuinely mixed-sex communities (as opposed to men's communities with separate enclosures or related settlements for women) claimed authority over men's communities; one was Cell Dara, a "mixed" community that included an abbess with her nuns, a bishop, priests, and monks.[43] By and large, even the most prosperous and famous women's communities maintained dependent, marriage-style ties with the leader of at least one male community, observing the decorum that dictated their inferior status in the relationship.

This is not to say that religious women were at the mercy of monastic and episcopal overseers, as were continental nuns of later centuries.[44] On the contrary, just as secular *cétmuinters* maintained ownership and some authority over their own farms, so abbesses retained their positions when hosting clerics. Hospitality was as important among religious personnel as it was in the secular world; in the vitae, saints visited one another constantly to exchange ritual services and hospitality, and hagiographers used these situations to clarify the relative status of their communities. Saint Ailbe, for instance, helped some women steer a wayward fosterling back onto the path of righteousness, in exchange for which the sisters granted him their homestead at Achad Carech; the episode probably reflected the relations conducted by Ailbe's successor at Imlech with a subordinate settlement of women, who enjoyed the abbot's protection and the saint's patronage in exchange for taking them as landlords.[45] Hagiographers depicted other male saints coming to raise dead members of women's communities, cure religious women, or consecrate virgins as religious professionals, in return for which the grateful women sometimes gave them feasts, goods, or land.[46] All these exchanges signified to hagiographers and monastic readers the relationship between the husband community and a settlement of women, symbolized in the amicable ties between male saint and female colleagues.

Only in a few hagiographic instances was the formula reversed, so that an abbess saint provided ritual services to a community of men. Most of these stories involved Brigit and Íte, the two premier female saints of Ireland, but some involved more local saints. Brénainn, for examples, was happy to have the assistance of Ciar in fighting an outbreak of sulphurous hellfire in Munster; Mochuda used the services of a holy prophetess to solve a murder case.[47] The baby that would become Saint Cuimmíne Fota was abandoned at a settlement housing both a *secnab,* a male official, and a *banóircindeach,* abbess; the latter was very much in charge.[48] In very few of these cases, however, did the woman's services imply her followers' lordship over local monks, or the mens' dependence on her community; more often, the stories conveyed only the special holiness of the female saint and the reverence due her from laymen and clerics alike.

Abbots and bishops also visited friendly nuns to provide and accept more mundane services, just as a husband might help out about the house. Several of the male saints seem to have been particularly responsible for women's communities, visiting routinely, always arriving in time for dinner and always received joyously. Saint Aed, for instance visited several communities of women, moving from one of his women's farms to the next, miraculously supplying the nuns with beer, magically aborting the fetus of a pregnant nun, or preserving a nun from seduction or abduction.[49] Similarly, Saint Daig dropped in to revive dead women or to teach the nuns their letters; Saint Ailbe came by to lend women some ploughing equipment and a scribe.[50] All these episodes and dozens more in the vitae, recorded a debt owed by a particular community to a saint and his monastery for services rendered, thus justifying the dependence of wifely community on husbandly monastery.

For the relationship between monasteries and women's communities was never one-sided. Women's communities were expected to pay for men's protection and patronage, but by doing so they maintained their own dignity and some autonomy in the larger ecclesiastical hierarchy. Indeed, the traditional *cétmuinter*'s role could connote great prestige for a very few religious women and their communities. An eleventh-century poem depicted Saint Brigit happily arranging an ale feast for Jesus and "the household of heaven," which included a "great lake of ale" and "cheerfulness . . . in their drinking." Above all, the saint wished to be *císaige don flaith,* a rent payer to the lord. Humbly though she expressed herself, the Brigit of this poem imagined herself an important noble client to none other than God himself, in the form of Jesus, her holy husband, and no other cleric got in the way of this exclusive relationship.[51] While the poet may have placed Cell Dara at the top of the ecclesiastical hierarchy, most women's communities were able to balance a whole web of obligations to both Jesus and their male colleagues, which helped reinforce their personal and collective dependence on their patron communities while making them valuable clients to religious men.

Individual religious women also operated as surrogate wives for monastic officials at affiliated men's communities. Religious women practiced the same arts and performed the same tasks, except reproduction, as secular women. Women cooked for their men when they came to call. They also raised children, just like secular mothers; they fostered young boys, giving them an elementary education before the boys moved on to higher learning in a community of men.[52] Besides feeding and nurturing their visiting mates, they also seem to have been responsible for clothing their male colleagues. We have seen that women were sainted for their embroidery. Religious women also performed the homely tasks of making the cloth and clothes from it. We have seen that Samthann's nuns at Cluain Brónaig received a boatload of wool from Í, presumably for making wool.[53] Saint Mochta had a female disciple whom he had raised from the dead; she was so grateful that she became a nun and spent the next thirty years of his life making clothes for his monks.[54] The nun Ciar made special clothes for Saint Cóemgen, although she needed an angel to persuade him to give up his old animal skins; the whole episode persuaded her to submit her community and its holdings to Cóemgen's rule.[55] Buite's monastery at Mainistir Buite conducted a *fedus* (formal alliance) with Saint Moduca's nunnery, during which nuns and monks prayed for one another and nuns washed the monks' clothes.[56] All miraculous window dressing aside, the stories suggested that throughout the Middle Ages religious women, like laywomen, spent much of their time producing cloth for men.

Although the basic social model for the relationship between men's and women's communities was marriage, some communities were also linked by actual blood kinship or other sorts of ties. Rather than share the same tiny settlement—although references to settlements of siblings continued throughout the pre-Norman period—brother and sister or mother and son sometimes lived in the same or adjacent settlements, as we have seen with Saint Ciarán and his kinswomen.[57] Saint Fáenche taught her brother Saint Énna a thing or two about avoiding the pitfalls of politics and the sinfully macho code of warriors; she took him into her religious settlement as a novice until he had learned and labored enough to set up his own community.[58] The proximity of siblings in religion was more than just a result of property laws. Ciarán's hagiographers depicted him as the protector of his mother's community, reflecting a pact between Saiger and a subsidiary house of nuns. Such a mutually satisfactory arrangement not only provided property for a settlement of women but allowed Ciarán's family to maintain its ownership as landlords of Saiger and its dependencies, thus assuring the nunnery some economic stability. Further, Saiger's men could offer ritual services and all sorts of support to the women down the road, to the benefit of both establishments.

The compacts between the heroes and heroines of hagiography, so weighted with political and social messages, also implied intellectual and spiritual exchanges between women's communities and those of men. On account of their Christian mission, their chastity, and occasionally, their literacy, religious women were different enough to escape some of the distrust and suspicion leveled at their secular sisters. Yet religious women were still feminine enough to perform wifely or motherly tasks and provide comfortable companionship to their male colleagues. As a result, many religious men and women seem to have indulged in agreeable and familiar relations that signaled respect on both parts.[59] Women dispensed advice to men, and some were famous for their wisdom and prescience. Later in life, grown-up fosterlings remained loyal to their wise religious *muimmi;* Ciarán, for instance, supposedly flew miraculously to his foster mother's foundation to say Christmas mass for her every year.[60] Íte, who was not only a famous prophetess but also a particularly testy saint, supposedly maintained ties with clerics in distant communities. The abbot saints Luchtigern and Laisren were on their way to visit the abbess when a young monk with them—called "stupid and foolish" by Íte's hagiographer— demanded to know why great and wise men such as the abbots would bother to visit the old hag Íte. The abbots quickly scolded him, fearing rightly that prescient Íte had heard the exchange. When the monks arrived at Íte's community she immediately demanded to know why they had come to visit an old hag such as she, and only after the novice did penance did all three saints trade blessings.[61] The exchange between senior clerics, male and female, and their communities could clearly be one of mutual esteem despite differences in status, just like a good marriage.

In fact, many hagiographers made charmingly clear just how much pleasure religious professionals took in each other's company. It was a great day for the nuns of Cell Sléibe when the bishop came to visit, for they all got positively giddy with beer.[62] Likewise Mac Nise's monks were so downhearted one day, according to his hagiographer, that the saint wanted to give them a little pick-me-up, and so decided to arrange for a visit from Saint Brigit.[63] The Irish left behind no testimony so personal as the letters from Boniface to his female confidantes; none of the texts describes how individual men and women formed friendships or the quality of affection between them. All we know for certain is that the hagiographers envisioned male and female religious professionals as congenial spouses who, if not social equals, nonetheless were able to overcome the gender hierarchy to form close affective ties.

With help from their kinsmen, real or surrogate, women's communities functioned much as men's communities did. Religious women supported themselves through farming and donations. They filled many of the same social and political functions as men, acting as mediators in political disputes and as landlords and patrons to local farmers and providing sanctuary.[64] The vitae advertised the different kinds of political expertise practiced by abbess saints and their successors, and the texts themselves functioned as a kind of mediation. As Dorothy Africa has shown for Íte and Samthann, the very geography of their vitae suggested the authority of saints and their successors in kingdoms both local and distant, as well as religious women's abilities to broker both sacral and political powers.[65] Their communities supplied ritual services, too, as did male monasteries. When large enough to accommodate a priest, the community could offer masses and other rituals; they also provided healing services and contacted their patron saints on general behalf of the lay population.

Yet, in the hierarchy of religious settlements, women's communities were rarely leaders, with the exception of the double community at Cell Dara, and they usually depended on the kindness of kinsmen and strangers for survival.[66] They were able to compete largely because men made it possible, support-ing them in ways large and small. A father donated a back pasture on which to build a settlement; a local priest dropped by to say a mass for the sis-ters; neighboring communities engaged in give and take; an abbot protected his sister's settlement against other aggressive monasteries; devotees of Brigit gave the extravagant gifts that made Cell Dara great. When they secured the cooperation and support of men, communities of women could survive and even flourish. In any showdown with a monastery, however, women usually lost out.

Again, hagiographers' stories showed how even admirably godly women bowed to male saints. One anecdote recounted how a nun called Ciar de-manded that Saint Munnu donate his settlement site of Tech Tailli to her, on the premise that his many monks could always move off and build a new mon-astery, whereas her few companions needed a secure property with a sturdy enclosure already built upon it. Munnu's response to this reasonable request was to depart immediately, taking only his books and precious ecclesiastical equipment with him but leaving behind a prophecy that the women's com-munity would dwindle away and be taken again by monks.[67] The annalists' tales of women's property lost and their communities disappearing may have held the same lesson.

But these contests were not the serious rivalries between men's commu-nities that could and did erupt into full-scale armed encounters. With the exception of Cell Dara's battles with Ard Macha,[68] the vitae described only minor-league competition between men's and women's communities. Mo-ninne's late vita, for instance, praised her as worthy of the competition of both men and women but showed her backing down in some trials of her will. Ac-cording to one story, she and her followers spent some time in her uncle Ibar's community, where he sent her a young girl to raise. Eventually the fosterling became jealous, complaining to Ibar, "Nobody amongst the people now seeks you out. The gifts and presents of all who live in your territory are handed over to those stranger women." Ibar paid no attention, but Moninne was wise to the rivalry, telling her companions, "If they begin to do these things to us while we are together, I know that after my death you will not be able to dwell here."[69] She and her sisters moved on. As Dorothy Africa has pointed out, this episode is one of several that located Moninne and her successor abbesses of Cell Sléibe firmly in the political orbit of the kingdom of Airthir.[70] But the language of the political message was one of competition among subgroups of an ecclesiastical settlement; in general, the men of monasteries (including hagiographers) only rarely deemed women worthy of direct attack or even genuine competition, such was the acknowledged spiritual, political, and material inferiority of women's settlements. As the angel told Saint Ailbe, even the miracles of holy women were *minima miracula* compared to those of sainted men.[71] When Moninne bested a male colleague, such as Cóemgen, it was by the passive aggression of prayer, which proved a different virtue for her settlements than the dog-eat-dog miracle working or threats of physical harm, such as Cóemgen aimed at her, and which proved profoundly worldly powers.

When women's communities competed among themselves, according to the vitae, they normally reserved their hostility for Cell Dara, which the hagiographers perceived as the foremost community of women in Ireland, although it was no coincidence that Cell Dara contained a bishop and monks, as well. Again, these conflicts took the hagiographic form of saintly interactions. Moninne, according to the hagiographers, outshone Brigit in austerity and charity, and Fáenche outdid Moninne.[72] The morals: Moninne's community of Cell Sléibe was more worthy of support and donations than Cell Dara, and Fáenche's house even more so. But these very same hagiographic episodes illustrated the solidarity among women's communities which balanced this gentle competition. When they competed, holy women practiced mild, sisterly rivlary rather than the showmanship and violence that marred relations between men's communities. By and large, hagiographers did not believe women's communities capable of genuine competition, not even with each other, just as lawmakers did not deem women's fights worthy of compensation.

Hagiographers of male saints also mostly ignored the possibilities of any meaningful positive relations among women's communities, just as the entire literati ignored women's alliances with other women. Conchubranus's eleventh-century vita, as ever, was the exception, describing a touching scene enacted by Moninne and Íte. Íte sent a girl to Moninne with a book, a generous offering, but the way between the settlements was perilous and the girl fell off a plank bridge into a deep river.[73] Three days later, Íte and Moninne both set off from their respective hermitages to find the missing girl, meeting at the river, where they exchanged information. Tearfully, both prayed by the riverside, "Lord Jesus Christ, son of the living God, by the intercession of Your holy mother and of Saints Peter and Paul and Andrew and all the saints give us back our girl." Moninne summoned the girl three times, after which she answered from the depths, and in the name of the lord, Moninne raised her sister to safety. She signed the wet virgin with the cross and "handed her to Íte and said: Here is the girl."[74] In the eleventh century, Conchubranus could depict women saints working miracles together as a friendly team. Most hagiographers, including the author of a previous life of Moninne, had a more aggressive male vocabulary for ecclesiastical interrelations, which, when it included women, was muted but still evident.

Hence, lives of female saints recounted some tender abbess-disciple bonds but depicted nothing particularly feminine about them; none of the annoying and destructive characteristics of female friendships in the *saeculum* turned up among religious women. Saint Moninne's relationship with her companion Bríg, for instance, echoed the friendship between Saint Columcille and his disciple Báethán depicted in the much earlier vita by Adomnán. Just as Columcille instructed Báethán when he erred or misunderstood, Moninne gently lectured her troubled sister on the weakness and fears of women.[75] More often, women's ties to women were minor versions of the professional rivalries rife in male monasteries. The rivalry between Saint Moninne and other women, including Brigit, was much like that between Cainnech and Columcille.[76]

On the other hand, the hagiographers hinted that some ties among women were different from women's relations with male colleagues or among men themselves. When Saint Cainnech visited a nunnery and found one of the sisters pregnant, he threatened her with punishment and miraculously disposed of the fetus. This action was in keeping with the penitentials, which forbade sexual acts among monks and nuns and levied higher penances for sex resulting in pregnancy. But when Íte discovered the fallen nun who had run away in shame, she had the woman and child fetched to the loving security of her community, where the child was then raised.[77] The hagiographer meant to praise Íte. The episode suggested her motherly sanctity, support of the penitent by her sisters, and the hagiographer's acknowledgment that women interpreted men's rules of sexual conduct differently for their own groups.

Sisterly solidarity alone could not sustain a small settlement of religious women, however. Women in early Ireland must have possessed some sort of shared sensibility and determination merely in order to maintain their religious communities in a world of belligerent men. In fact, an episode in the vita of Cainnech, where women in his settlement sought not his help but that of Samthann, suggests that the accord among religious women stretched from one community to another, bypassing the men who were nominally in authority.[78] Story after story told of the nuns' tactics to outwit irreligious men, would-be thieves of their property, virtue, and communal independence.[79] Accounts of both men's monasteries and women's settlements hinted at the necessity for community morale, positing as a plus the solidarity that nuns needed in order to survive.[80] Religious women chose to model their groups on men's communities and yet to adapt men's values and practices to suit their own distinctly female requirements, altering the community structure to fit these needs and the nature of their alliances.

In effect, this meant organizing their communities by means of typically female relationships, based on proximity rather than defined exclusively by male status hierarchies. Like other homesteads, women's settlements contained a small group of women who worked and slept in the same space, spending most of each day and night together. But women's communities were also unusual because they sometimes lacked coresidential male guardians and because a group of women formed the core of the household. No matter how much interaction with male colleagues they enjoyed—or suffered—religious women were living their daily lives in a way quite different from their secular sisters: without men. An ordinary family farm might temporarily lack men, lost to war or another calamity, but nothing in the laws suggested that secular women normally lived on their own properties, gathered other women to live with them, or managed their estates without the help of men. Secular women sent their patriarchs out for the day, into the world of laws, fieldwork, and war; but religious women often had no resident patriarchs to send.

The ramifications of the very existence of women's communities on the larger society and its gender ideologies is hard to judge. Historians have claimed that the creation of self-sufficient social groups of women revolutionized gender relations, but in early Ireland at least, religious women's communities were modeled on existing households and bound by familiar social ties both internally and externally. Yet, settlements of religious women in early Ireland, as elsewhere in early medieval Europe, provided refuge for young women seeking escape from traditional ties of marriage and for widowed or aging noblewomen who refused second husbands.[81] Even elite women could not simply opt out of their homes and families for new friends and a new life unless it was within the sacred space of a Christian settlement.

The most important consequence was the affirmation of distinctly female communities. A woman's decision to live with other women rather than with a husband meant the selection of a completely different set of allies from the affines a husband might bring. She was extending the web of her own alliances, based on proximity as well as blood, rather than attach herself to a new man and his family. Jesus demanded a different kind of marriage, although not

a completely exotic one; he did not return to the enclosure at sunset or demand to be petted or bedded, although he did involve his consorts indirectly
in his family ties and clientage relationships. But to wed the son of God was
like marrying into a woman's own family; her in-laws were the same kinsmen
who donated the property for her settlement or oversaw her community's
well-being. Instead of leaving home for a foreign territory, a religious woman
moved into a Christian Land of Women, bringing her divine spouse with her.

Male Imitators and Cloistered Nuns

To a certain extent, even the most famous religious women conformed
to the roles of wife and mother prescribed by secular and clerical elites. The
communities of famous saints acted as way stations and second homes to male
saints, just as did the settlements of lesser-known religious women, according
to hagiographers. Female saints of the fifth and sixth centuries, like all other
religious women in the age of conversion, had been kinswomen of clerics and
spiritual consorts of Christ and were depicted as such in the religious literature.[82] They were intimately related to monks and bishops and worked under
the supervision of paternalistic clerics. Each of them supposedly engaged in a
battle with her family in order to marry Christ.

Yet the heroines of the vitae also aimed for a higher male standard of sanctity
inconsistent with traditional female roles. From this contradiction of ideals
springs the explanation of religious women's lives in early Ireland. For signifi-
cantly, hagiographers of the ninth and later centuries admired female saints for
committing acts that they condemned in ordinary wives and religious women.
In the vitae, saintly women proselytized by behavioral example and by helping their male colleagues, but they also played a third and far more aggressive
role. Hagiographers depicted a small number of women as charismatic nuns
and abbesses who preached to clergymen, bargained with God for privileges,
and fought to protect devotees. In the vitae, these saintly heroines did not
merely symbolically marry or mother men; they also imitated men, preaching
and proselytizing directly. For example, according to the vita of Saint Énna, he
might never have become a saint if not for his sister, Fáenche, who preached
to him about damnation until she made him cry. Under Fáenche's guidance,
Énna gave up a perfectly good kingdom to become a monk, a recluse, and a
famous saint.[83]

According to the post-800 vitae, other female saints of olden times performed almost all the functions of male saints. These abbess saints politicked
with local leaders, protected innocent victims of violence, helped the wronged
to achieve justice, brought punishment to the wicked, and opened heaven to

the deserving. One woman even became a bishop, although by mistake. The anonymous ninth-century *Bethu Brigte* described how, when Brigit knelt before Bishop Mel to take the nun's veil, the bishop became "so intoxicated with the grace of God" that he recited the wrong service and accidentally made Brigit a bishop too. Mel justified his mistake with a prophecy. "This virgin alone in Ireland," he proclaimed, "will hold the episcopal ordination."[84]

Everything historians know about religious women in the age of conversion makes it unlikely that Brigit or any other woman actually became a bishop, and no other document described a woman performing recognizable episcopal duties. The literary incident in which Brigit became a bishop is hard to reconcile with the wives and sisters of historical reality, but it was no accident. Brigit's hagiographer meant for Mel to bungle the ordination, for although male hagiographers described women saints of the conversion period as wifely surrogates, they also sometimes cast them as ecclesiastical chiefs, landowners, and the lords of clients. What better illustration of the complex, contradictory ideas about gender interaction flourishing among the early Irish: most women were guided into traditional roles of wife and mother, and Christian theology limited its female professionals to chaste imitations of these real-life roles; yet the most admirable and saintly nuns were not real women at all, at least by early Irish standards, but ersatz men.[85]

To a certain extent, female saints in the vitae were larger-than-life reflections of abbesses familiar to the hagiographers.[86] The vitae that took women as their protagonists naturally emphasized not only their founders' skills and influence but also those of successor abbesses.[87] Both hagiography and the annals suggested that aristocratic nuns did indeed perform some of the same clientage and peacemaking functions as abbots. Yet the clerical literati were not using Bishop Brigit and her proselytizing sisters to create a third legitimate role model for religious women. Instead, they employed Brigit and her like to consolidate gender boundaries and reinforce the two models already available to women (as well as, in Brigit's case, making political claims for the community of Cell Dara.) In the first place, these powerful male imitators appeared only in postconversion vitae, some of them written long after the saints themselves had actually lived. The only pre-ninth-century vitae of women, two lives of Brigit, cast her in a somewhat less aggressive role.[88] Second, the majority of religious women in the saints' lives—the ordinary nuns, bit players to the heroic protagonists of the texts—took the traditional guise of wives and kinswomen. These incidental hagiographical characters provide a more accurate picture, when compared with other sources, of the functions and status of female religious professionals in early Ireland than do the saints themselves. Finally, ecclesiastical canons specifically prohibited women from many of the activities in which female saints indulged, such as preaching.[89]

The major female saints were a creation of ninth-century literati and their intellectual successors, who manufactured a Christian history paralleling the teleology of the three *ordines*. In the early years of Christianization, they wrote, women had attained sainthood just as men did, by working many of the same kinds of wonders, filling the same sacral roles, and interacting with the secular community in the same ways. Through their extraordinary holiness, they overcame the normally arrested development of women, growing into complete humans, even superhumans, who could touch God on behalf of others. After that marvelous missionizing age, however, female religious professionals had ceased to grow beyond womanhood (with the exception of Samthann, an eighth-century saintly figure related hagiographically to the *céli dé* reformers).[90] They were good women, to be sure, obediently following canon laws and society's customs, but they remained thoroughly female nonetheless. No longer could they participate in the promulgation of the faith as equal partners to male coworkers; no more preaching, direct proselytizing, or cohabitation with men. At best, early medieval nuns could support their husbandly colleagues while trying vainly to imitate male impersonators of the lost past, who were held up as hagiographic exemplars.

The change in women's functions and relations with male clerics did not coincide with any obvious historical change in the experience of religious women. However, a couple of major developments in Irish society between the fifth and ninth centuries help place the shift in historical context. First and best documented was the establishment of the clerical elite. As elsewhere in the barbarian north, social customs had temporarily lost force in the first rush of enthusiasm for the new faith. Traditional rules about the behavior of women had relaxed when missionaries such as Pátraic were desperate for converts of both sexes.[91] Pátraic was thrilled to attract women, who gave him gifts of their jewelry as well as their souls, but by the time his hagiographers began to record and revise his deeds in the seventh century, Pátraic was made to demand more of his female converts. In the story of the Uí Néill princesses, Ethne and Fedelm had to accept his catechism, follow his instructions for a religious life, and even yield their own lives at his command in order to attain salvation. Further, they had to accept an ecclesiastical hierarchy among religious professionals based on gender, closely modeled on secular custom. They were to define their spiritual status in relation to the men who directed and protected them as kinsmen and husbands. Finally, Ethne and Fedelm taught religious women that to proselytize effectively they must submit to the symbolic death of supportive roles in the Christian hierarchy, if not to actual physical death.

The second related major social development was the increasing solidarity of monastic families. As with all social groups, the extended kin group, the *fine,* was the major organizational principle behind Irish monastic communities. But monasteries were families with a difference. Theoretically, they included no women. At least secular families acknowledged the need for wives and mothers. The vitae and monastic rules envisioned a group of men born of no mothers, bound to no wives, but linked by affective ties to other men and, occasionally, to chaste *muimmi.* The annals and laws revealed that these monastic *familiae* were also commonly bound by actual blood ties between siblings, cousins, uncles and nephews, and even fathers and sons. Even when monastic officials and so-called monks married and produced children—and they often did—their wives and daughters had no formal place in the organization of this highest form of Christian community. Unlike the priests' wives of earlier generations, real married women could no longer be religious professionals or proselytizers, even by example, except unofficially.

Nonetheless, women could and did form communities of their own based on the same familial model, as we have seen, and may have found a genuine feminine solidarity there. Still, even the Christian Land of Women needed at least the son of God. No community of religious women could never be physically or conceptually complete without men; nuns needed priests to perform rituals, warriors to protect them, laborers to feed them, and kinsmen's land to live on. No matter how charismatic the saintly patroness of a nunnery, her disciples remained unable to compete with male clerics for property and endowments in the way that she could compete with brother saints in hagiographical accounts. They were relegated to performing *minima miracula* rather than the blockbuster wonders of major male performers such as Ailbe, Cóemgen, Ciarán, and Pátraic, and to providing gentle reminders and passive behavioral models.[92]

But exceptions to this gendered ecclesiastical hierarchy abounded. The whole web of relations among early Irish men and women complicates any easy explanation of the gender teleology dreamed up by religious writers. Changes in the gender system are difficult to chart; by and large, my argument in this book has focused on the *longue durée* of attitudes and practices rather than the subtle shifts of years and decades, or even centuries; this is mostly because the evidence itself points more to stasis than to change, or to such variety of custom and thought that quick, specific change is too difficult to detect. Stories about powerful female saints, such as Bishop Brigit, taught no facile lesson about sharp turnabouts in the status of women in Christianizing Ireland.

On the contrary, the absorption of Christian ideas by the political and intellectual elites brought no long-term gender-specific benefits or disadvantages to early medieval women. As we have seen, *Cáin Adomnáin* had little effect on the status—whatever that was—of women; we do not even know whether its declared purpose, to protect women from murder, was accomplished. The reverence for mothers which permeated Irish attitudes was no guarantee of good treatment for women but an indication of the society's desire for babies, which had preceded and outlasted conversion. Christian writers of theology, canons, penitentials, and vitae all remained divided, at best, about the souls of women and conservative about their social status. As late as the seventeenth century and beyond, writers continued to debate the nature, worth, and purpose of women in Irish society, sometimes in amusing and sexy literature, such as Brian Mac Giolla-Meidhre (Merriman)'s *Cúirt an Mheadhon Oidhche* (The midnight court). Even the clerical push for monogamy did not necessarily alter the material life of most women, who were probably largely monogamous anyway; among the nobility, some men persisted in taking more than their share of women, and some women continued to move from man to man well into the early modern period.

The heroic female saints of the post-ninth-century vitae provided no clues to improved conditions for women but merely revealed the concerns of the androcentric genre of medieval hagiography. The major female saints were heroes first, saints second, and women last. Their hagiographers wanted above all to teach the value and efficacy of their cults, rather than to present Brigit and her sisters as attainable models of specifically feminine virtues; neither women nor men could choose to become saints. In fact, at the same time that female saints became most powerful in the vitae, women actually lost ground in Christian ideology. The misogyny for which Irish clerics are famous did not manifest itself in the earliest texts, but did so more and more after 800, by which time many of the vitae had achieved their present form. The anecdote, for example, about Saint Moling and his lecherous neighbor could not have appeared in the days when Pátraic freely invited virgins into the religious profession. The story, which tells how the lady caught Moling in the bathtub and the saint then stabbed himself in the erect penis with an awl, reflected the sensibilities of the twelfth century; it contains the charming poem about concupiscence chanted by Moling as he pinned himself to the tub: "My lad, the dog-faced one, a little thing pleases him greatly; he wishes to stray from his own private place to the private place of neighbors."[93]

Related to the increasing misogyny of the clerical attitudes articulated in later texts was the spiritual and physical segregation of religious professionals by gender, which slowly but inexorably became more common, although the trend began soon after initial conversion and was never really complete. The spiritual marriage of religious woman to Christ continued to represent simultaneously an ideal of the relations between communities of women and their clerical protectors and between women and God himself, but increasingly the marriage went sour. Even when it worked best, the bond between religious women and religious men was always potentially unstable, not just from men's point of view but for both sexes. The strain of suspicion was obvious from the beginning of Christianization, but the ambivalence of some clerics towards the functions of religious women was heightened by other factors between the eighth and twelfth centuries, in particular by the arrival of the Vikings and the clerical push for monogamy.

Suspicion of the other sex afflicted men and women alike, but derived from different sources. For one thing, although many texts acknowledged the heroic efforts of some women to deny their inherent weaknesses, religious men feared the taint and temptation of women's sexuality. Saint Cóemgen, for instance, fled the bleating of sheep, reasoning that where there were sheep there were shepherdesses, where shepherdesses temptation, where temptation sin, and where sin damnation.[94] And as we have seen, the danger became greater when women congregated in groups, even in pious groups behind the sacred walls of a nuns' enclosure. It was not women so much as their threat to men's ascetic purpose that scared monks. When thirty young girls fell in love with the good-looking Saint Mochuda, he saved himself by tranforming their affection into something platonic and recruiting them as nuns, also altering the women from sexual threat to spiritual dependents.[95]

But not every cleric was happy with Mochuda's solution. Misogynous episodes peppered the hagiographical material along with criticism of less suspicious clerics, showing that some monks were happier without any direct relations with dependent women's communities. Cú Chuimne, who composed a hymn to the Blessed Virgin, supposedly turned to religion after a bad marriage; apparently, all it took to transform him into a fierce ascetic was a little time with the little woman.[96] The preface to his hymn and his eighth-century obituary in the annals was a curious poem about his leaving female colleagues in religion:

> Cú Chuimne
> Has read the learned authors right through;
> The other half of the fosterage fee
> He has let go for the sake of nuns.
>
> All [the distraction] Cú Chuimne had
> Has left him so that he became sage;
> He has abandonned nuns
> And read the remainder which was before him.[97]

Saint Daig's hagiographer also illustrated men's suspicion of women with a story about the mixed-sex community run by the saint. According to his hagiographer, rumors flew among other abbots about what exactly went on there. When Abbot Oengus of Cluain Moccu Nóis sent messengers to investigate, it took a miracle to convince them that hanky-panky was not endemic to such communities. Only after Daig's female companions carried burning coals in their garments without harm did Oengus concede their sinlessness. Nonetheless, Daig decided to set up an affiliated community for his nuns rather than risk having them with him any longer.[98] Another solution was for abbots to oversee a discrete enclosure of nuns within a larger community, as we have seen.

Not every cleric came to hate women, nor was every ecclesiastic content to shun and denigrate them. There were degrees of misogynous suspicion about which men even quarreled. The ascetic *céli dé* (clients fo God) of eighth-century Tamlachta, for example, seem to have been constantly negotiating a protocol for their contact with women. But anecdotes about these reformers, which registered a variety of polite disagreements, taught other monks how to interact with women, primarily through a sensitive use of physical spaces and boundaries. In one story, the complex ritual process by which a monk and religious woman might cautiously interact was played out. The holy man might converse with her about the faith, but only if he met her in the neutral, protected space by the cross in front of her sacred enclosure and in the company of a senior cleric and an older nun; his eyes could not cross the boundary that kept back the rest of his body, either, for he was not to look at her.[99] In another tale, in the open space before their monastery, a monk named Dublitir and his confessor encountered a visiting nun who asked permission to sleep in the separate women's enclosure. Her supplications annoyed Dublitir, who ordered her to begone. His confessor immediately rebuked him, calling the nun back and giving her a place in the women's house as well as the compensation of a cloak and a cow and assigning a penance to Dublitir.[100] Like clerics elsewhere in Christendom, the *céli dé* and their female associates tried to arrange their shared space in order to reinforce the rules of contact between the sexes.[101]

The *céli dé*, a fairly unified group of reform-minded monks who consciously set themselves apart from ordinary Christians and clerical slackers, clearly gave much discussion to the problem of women. In particular, they looked to their sisters as models of good and bad behavior. In another Tamlachta episode, a nun from Cell Uaitne "endowed with the grace of God" was cited as an exemplar of prayer, and in another a monk was advised to ignore his mother's pleas for her son's support until she reformed her sinful ways.[102] One more story described Saint Molaise putting a nun on a diet designed to reduce her innate lust because desire was "a third part as strong again in women as in men."[103] Finally, the woman saint Samthann advised the *céli dé* leader Máel-

ruain never to bestow friendship or confidence upon a woman, even herself.[104]
The *céli dé* were trying hard to include women in their revision of the Christian life but could devise no single attitude toward women's nature, religious vocation, proper place, or the proper mode of relations with them. Other less organized clerics registered an even wider range of conflicting views, although misogynous themes pervaded their literature. And no matter how severe the pronouncements of prosegregationists, it is clear from the vitae that women continued to move in and out of men's communities and over their boundaries with ease.

Women, unlike men, did not fear seduction so much as abduction into the secular life. Unlike men, while they could shun the opposite sex, they could not refuse to deal with men who were kinsmen, clients, or sponsors of their religious vocations. Whereas the kinds of sins committed by religious women in the vitae were largely sexual and brought about the downfall of monks, the crime most often committed against religious women was their removal from a community by rape or murder. The episode contained in all versions of Saint Ciarán's life about the saint's foster daughter, Bruinech, suggests that it was not simply violation and violence that women worried about but being taken from the enclosure. When a local king carried her off, taking her home to sleep with her *in coniugem* (for he "loved her greatly"), it took a miracle and, in one version, material restitution to make the king give Bruinech back. By that time she was pregnant, although Saint Ciarán miraculously aborted the fetus.[105] But neither superior political power nor military force nor secular laws of marriage nor even rape and pregnancy could keep Bruinech from her vocation.

The story taught a lesson to the men who would drag women out of the sacred enclosure as well as to the women who might stray out by themselves. But the lesson also congratulated the dedicated religious women whose vocation was confirmed by Bruinech's misfortune. Bruinech's story resonated with the themes, so prominent in hagiography, of violence done to religious women and parental objections to their daughters' vocations. Some in the society disapproved of religious women, seeing in them a waste of precious childbearers and a misuse of political tools. Yet women continued to take up religion, and women's communities, although they occasionally dwindled in number, continued to exist, adapting to changing social and political circumstances. If anything, clerical doubt and secular objections to nuns may have increased after the ninth century; these themes certainly became more pronounced in the literature.

The Vikings may have had something to do with that. Despite the continuing debate among historians about the effects of the Viking presence in early Ireland, one thing seems clear: they arrived at the end of the eighth century, wreaking destruction on women's settlements in Ireland, as in England.[106] Both women's and men's communities were hard hit in the first attacks, as the annals' reports of burnings and killings attested. If the most prosperous and populated men's communities suffered the Northmen, how much more vulnerable was a little family nunnery? References in the vitae to women surrendering their property to male saints may well reflect the dissolution of their communities in this period or at least a need for increased protection from, and dependence upon, male neighbors and authorities. The Vikings were not the only predators on women's communities. And as archaeological investigation at Dublin and elsehwere is beginning to show, no matter what trouble the Northmen caused at first, they did not remain heathen raiders but settled down as traders, craftsmen, and mercenaries in the proto-urban centers of the island.[107] Meanwhile, religious women were at risk of assault, theft, and intimidation throughout the Middle Ages, and the Vikings were only one of the authors of harm.[108]

Another, probably more important influence on the life of religious women and their communities was the clerical push for monogamy. The attitudes of the clerical elite toward female religious were always fraught with tension, but when some churchmen began to agitate for monogamy among the laity, one of the comfortable models for relations between monks and nuns became problematic. The preference for formal monogamy appeared in ecclesiastical sources soon after Christian establishment. Seventh-century penitentialists laid down penalties for adultery, by which they meant men having sex with concubines as well as sex between people married to others.[109] The eighth-century canonists referred to Paul and made it quite clear that good Christians got married once and forever and refrained from sexual relations with others. Reforming churchmen even insisted that marriage was more a spiritual partnership than a social union and ordered married Christians to refrain from having sex with each other except on canonically safe days.[110]

But such teachings challenged the kinship and property structures of early Irish society, which were based on the elite male's ability to gather as many women to him as he liked or needed and to produce as many heirs as possible. This may explain why the reforming push for monogamy was never extremely successful. Anglo-Norman bishops were still complaining about polygamy in the twelfth century, and even the Irish hagiographers took disparate points of view on the subject, as demonstrated by the story of the monkish ex-polygamist in the later vita of Brénainn.[111] Although the story taught that the celibate life was better than married life, it also assumed that a man with two wives could be a good Christian. Certainly Saint Brénainn revealed no qualms about polygamy per se.

Ultimately, however, the challenge to polygyny must have damaged the

marriage of cleric and religious woman. Women and monks had other models
to fall back on, such as blood kinship; on the Continent, professional religious
men and women were spiritual kindred in the early Middle Ages and became
spiritual husbands and wives only in the Gregorian period. But in Ireland, the
easy exchanges of ritual and more mundane services between a visiting abbot
and friendly religious women must have become more strained as the partners
in the exchange sought to establish the exact nature of their tie.

In this context, Conchubranus's eleventh-century picture of Saint Moninne
and her communities showed nunneries on the defensive and abbesses growing
more aware of gender-based status differences than before. For the religious
women depicted in Moninne's vita, this awareness meant self-imposed segregation. After Moninne left her parents' home and went to the monastery
of Bishop Ibar, she began to attract female recruits there, according to the
vita, and eventually moved with the women to an independent community at
Fochard. There, however, the sounds of the *saeculum*—especially the noise of
wedding revelry—were so disturbing to the nuns that they fled farther north
to a more remote site at Cell Šléibe.[112] Other episodes in the vita echoed
this representation of the secular world as both male and sexual. Priest-killing
bandits tried to debauch the nuns, Saint Cóemgen criticized Moninne's vocation, and Moninne herself decided never again to look at men, going out
only at night to perform her parish functions or covering her head entirely in
public.[113]

In fact, religious women's very identity as women left them vulnerable to
men. When Moninne determined to leave one nun named Orbile behind to
guard Fochard, the sister pleaded that the saint turn her youthful beauty into
the ugliness of an aged hag, to protect her from sexual violation.[114] And Moninne herself was as much man as woman, going beyond imitation to take "a
man's spirit in a woman's body."[115] Moninne severely lectured her own right-
hand woman on the sinful weaknesses of the female sex, which was more
vulnerable to demons than men because "a little thing can upset a woman."[116]
The only answer was enclosure and isolation, willingly imposed by Moninne's
community upon itself; what was for male overseers of women's communities
claustration became, for women themselves, a spirituality.

It is hard to say whether Conchubranus, writing for a women's community,
transmitted any kind of uniquely female ideology of segregation. It is possible
that any difference in male and female attitudes lay not in the writing so much
as the reading of his work. Although Moninne's vita mimicked the rest of
the genre in most ways, nonetheless, the nuns of Cell Šléibe may have sensed
different emphases from, say, a monk of Glenn Dá Locha reading the same
story. The nuns may, for instance, have found the episode of Cóemgen and
his murderous imp (retold earlier in this chapter) more humorous than did

Cóemgen's successors at Glenn Dá Locha. What is more, merely to describe the dilemma of women beset by the characteristics of their own gender as well as by truculent colleagues may have been instructive or even empowering to religious women in a way that men could never understand; at the same time, the rhetoric of misogyny reminded clerics that, horrible as women could be, good men still faced the trial of coexisting with them.[117]

Whether at the impetus of hagiography, or whether vitae reflected their determination, women resisted attempts to erode their spiritual validity simply by continuing to exist in Ireland, adapting to whatever changes, good or bad, occurred. But they did not endure by chance, neglect, or the greater goodwill of their male colleagues. Women chose to become religious professionals, and they chose how they would live the Christian life, year after year, no matter whether their kinfolk, neighbors, and the larger society supported them or not. Religious women occasionally lost some autonomy or status as the waves of clerical reform advanced and receded, and in some centuries their numbers declined, but they never entirely lost the impetus for religious life. When Anglo-Norman reformers came to do away with the old-style monastic communities of Ireland, replete with the polygamous sins of the secular social structure as they were, women formed new-style communities. They became cloistered nuns in formal continental orders in Norman-controlled urban centers.

But the older forms of female religious life did not completely disappear either. As late as the seventeenth century, English officials of the dissolution were complaining about ancient clerical families that hung on to bits and pieces of formerly monastic property. And later medieval hagiographers continued to record attitudes about religious women which had been around since Pátraic first attracted young girls to the celibate life. So the thirteenth-century hagiographer of Saint Sénán made clear in his story of the holy woman Canair. When Canair walked on water to get to his island hermitage, Sénán tried to keep her out, but Canair challenged him eloquently: "Christ is no worse than you. Christ came to redeem women no less than men. . . . women have served and administered to Christ and his Apostles. Indeed, no less than men do women enter the heavenly kingdom. Why then shouldn't you take women on your island?"[118] When Sénán refused his traditional role as Christ's surrogate and Canair's husbandly protector, Canair was right to be angry, according to Sénán's own hagiographer. Nevertheless, the saint never did take her in but sent her off to found her own community elsewhere.

Postconversion literature taught the women of Ireland a paradoxical lesson. Women brought pollution and sin to men, and so had to be kept apart from clerical colleagues and contained away from secular society. Yet women could only pursue religious vocations in close proximity to their husbands in Christ and their blood kin. Monks could seek the pious life by leaving society and its women altogether, but religious women remained dependent on men despite the theoretical segregation of religious professionals by sex. The dilemma became acute as early Irish society became more Christianized, lost its initial missionizing zeal, and restored the gender assymetry that constituted social equilibrium. After that, the annals attested to the increasing indifference of Irishmen to their women's religious vocations with the frequent disappearance of women's religious communities from the sight and the sources of the literati—although not necessarily from existence—after 800. In the eyes of men, religious women and their communities became fewer and fewer and proselytizing women such as the major female saints left real life for literature.

So, how did Brigit manage to become a bishop? Where did Fáenche find the gumption to preach to Énna? Such anomalous behavior could occur only in hagiography, a literary genre that crossed gender boundaries and treated its heroines as slightly less than male and much more than female. Like Bishop Mel, the male literati of the ninth and later centuries endowed the proselytizing women of conversion-era Ireland with the powers of the clerical elite. Earlier, Cogitosus had written of a Brigit who gently spoke her mind and guided her community as partner to her bishop; Conláed did not "spurn her administration and fellowship," as the historian of the *ordines* put it, because he did not contest her right and status as religious professional. Brigit was a woman and a public figure who governed her city of Cell Dara and lay, when dead, at the front of her church in a tomb next to that of her bishop (although discreetly segregated by an altar). Later vitae of women sent them home to their settlements where they prepared for the visits of bishops and other men with good hot meals and baths; they did not dare perform in public. Yet they carried on their religious careers with admirable fortitude, as the hagiographers acknowledged. Conchubranus saw Moninne's house as a remote haven of Christianity so pure that even as great a man as Saint Cóemgen could not fully appreciate it without the holy nun's help.

The response of the Irish to their professional religious women varied by period, by place, even by the temper of local male ecclesiastics. No particular period was worse than any other for the nuns of early Ireland, except possibly the first decades of the Viking incursions. The three *ordines* of Irish Christianization had no historical validity. Male-female clerical relations did not degenerate over time but changed in tone, fluctuating throughout the pre-Norman period. Historians are accustomed to looking for long-term improvements or declines in women's status during the Middle Ages.[119] But what does it mean when those major changes occurred only symbolically on the pages of certain kinds of documents written by men? If we give up the notion that for a few happy decades women almost enjoyed social equality with men, then we need not assume that women became men's victims in succeeding periods or that they submitted passively to an involuntary claustration—with occasional breakouts by belligerent sisters—which lasted through the Catholic Reformation. Although good evidence exists for changes in the situation of religious women between 600 and 1200, it is not the case that women everywhere lost religious importance to their societies or that they found Christian religious life less meaningful or satisfying as the Middle Ages progressed. Their religious experience varied widely according to local social organization, cultural contours, and the strategies of women themselves.[120]

Religious women, like men, adapted their vocations and their communities to accommodate social and political changes. When abbots and bishops were content to protect and respect communities of nuns, religious women enjoyed exchange relationships with the monks based on native models of marriage and kinship. In times or places when the male clerical elite decided that religious women were more seductive than useful, women adapted to this misogynous ideology as well. And when the secular world seemed more threatening than supportive, women such as Saint Moninne voluntarily chose to isolate themselves from the noise of the *saeculum:* this voluntary segregation is the closest that Irish nuns came to claustration in the pre-Norman period.

We shall never be sure how much of women's maneuvering around social and political restrictions, economic problems, and disapproving male colleagues was merely reaction to external circumstances and how much was an inspired, continuous refashioning of gender roles. We do know that women on the Continent and in England as well as in Ireland continued to join religious communities and take up independent lives of religion in the most repressive of times, although perhaps fewer than before. It was this remarkable ability to adapt their spiritual needs to the whimsical contours of the patriarchy that enabled women to enjoy exemplary, purposeful, meaningful Christian lives.

9

Warriors, Hags, and Sheelanagigs

Of all the contradictory attitudes toward women articulated in a canon of ambivalence, the most profoundly paradoxical was this: Queen Medb, the spear-toting, free-speaking, sexually independent virago, ruled the sagas while, in reality, the women of Ériu were coaxed or coerced into restrictive social roles. Real women were lovers, wives, mothers, and kinswomen to their men while in the sagas and histories shape-shifting raven goddesses haunted the battlefields, dealing terror and bloodlust to men in combat. Images of hostile and powerful women were commonplace in all genres of the literature of this society, which otherwise cast its women as physically flawed, legally subordinate, and spiritually inferior. Female fighters instructed male heroes of saga in the arts of war. Hags turned up to prophesy, and even bring about, the heroes' downfall. Vicious sorceresses battled the saints in the vitae. Jurists even ruled on the legal rights of female werewolves and spell casters to compensation. "Save us," pleaded a prayer attributed to Saint Pátraic, "from the spells of women and smiths and druids."[1]

Despite all sorts of limits on women's authority and status and despite the very real and constant risk of violence to women, the men and women of early Ireland were fascinated by a veritable pornography of powerful females. Their stories of women warriors, war goddesses, and witches included everything modern pornographers offer their audiences: sex, violence, and political conflict, with magic thrown in to mark this peculiarly premodern genre.[2] The early Irish were obsessed with arms-bearing woman warriors in contest with men, otherworldly *dominatrices* demanding sex from handsome heroes, insolent queens ordering soldiers around, or—best of all—any of these ill-humored females being beaten in combat or sexually subdued by other warriors.

Of course, there are important differences between what I am calling an early Irish "pornography" and more recent forays into the skin trade. Modern pornography bears a direct, if debated, relation to both gender ideologies and sexual relations. At its mildest, it facilitates relations between willing partners or enables a loner to achieve sexual stimulation. At its worst, it is the product of a sexual hierarchy that persuades men to dominate or even harm women; some theorists argue that it betrays a hatred of women, which smolders in sleazy magazines and X-rated films and sometimes flames into actual violence.[3] Whatever the precise connection between the modern literature and mundane sexual relations among real men and women, pornography derives from, and influences, the very definition of sex and sexuality in our own society, especially from a legal point of view.[4] Similarly, early Irish stories bear a collection of messages from the past about once-living women's relations with once-living men, but so encoded are those messages, so wrapped in brown paper by the passage of centuries, that we must struggle to uncover them.

Like modern pornography, these tales concerned the most fundamental ties between men and women and the kind of society that was built upon those ties in early Ireland. I have tried in this book to show how the early Irish created formal social roles for women, how women maneuvered within and around them, and how men and women sometimes colluded in maintaining these roles and at other times joined in modifying or even subverting them. Tales of Queen Medb and other powerful women represented, on one level, a literary subversion of formal social roles: women turning men's weapons against men, taking on men's characteristics, becoming and doing everything that women could and should not. Yet, on a deeper level, the tales were part of the larger discussion of sex, gender conflict, and politics which underlay the sources. If productive, legal sexual alliances between men and women formed the basis of the early Irish family, community, and society, then the war between hostile females and their male enemies illustrated the worst threat to social order. The literature limned, in contorted and fabulous outline, the entire gender system of early Ireland.

Specifically, in the Irish texts, a combination of sex, evil, violence, and social politics inspired and empowered dangerous females. This heady mix made the fictions compelling for both writers and audiences. Two kinds of powerful females invaded the texts, both of whom drew strength from the uncontrolled sexuality so frightening and fascinating to the early Irish: militant women and magic-making women. Differences between the two were crucial, even if the literati did not always carefully distiguish between bloodthirsty females and those who cast spells, for goddesses of war were also sometimes fighters or spell casters, and the sorceresses of saints' lives sometimes resembled the prophesizing hags of secular tales.

Nonetheless, the literati and their readers sorted violent women from female magicians in several highly instructive ways. First, they distinguished between the goals and methods of fighters and spell casters. Fighters sought political dominance over men; spell casters aimed their magic at manhood and its proper products, the family and patrilineage. Second, in many of these stories, when warrior women tried to dominate or destroy men, male heroes tamed them with rape or seduction. In fact, forcible or illicit sex acts, which shamed or killed virtuous women, transformed and civilized battle goddesses and women warriors. Spell casters and magic makers, on the other hand, employed magic for ends that were always evil, almost always sexual, and often violent. Such women were irredeemable by civilizing sex or any other cure. They were ultimately far more terrifying to the Irish than any woman with a sword.

Finally, and most important, tale-tellers cast their stories of women warriors and war goddesses in the pre-Christian past, whereas magicians, werewolves, and necromancing hags continued to haunt the Christianizing Middle Ages. Women warriors rampaged through narratives and mythological histories but rarely entered either secular or religious legal material. Penitentialists, canonists, and secular jurists, however, all warned against actual, living, evil women who used sexually charged magic to manipulate and harm their lovers, husbands, families, neighbors, and property.

Hags with magic were real to the early medieval Irish; women warriors were not. But stories of both point to the literati's obsession with the war between the sexes, and the disasters it could cause. In short, Medb ruled in the fictional past of the *Táin* for the very same reason that spell casters threatened the early Irish: not because many like them invaded real life but because their opposites—obedient, cautious, cagey, childbearing *cétmuinters*—were the most highly valued and influential women in Ireland, from the iron age to the industrial age.

Warrior Women

Violent female figures took many guises in the tales, often quite literally. The shapeshifting crow woman, the prophesizing crone, and the deranged princess were all related to the militant *ban-láech* (female warrior) who threatened and titillated her readers. All were strong but ambiguous figures, often simultaneously attractive, repellent, and sexual.

The most powerful female figures in early Irish literature were hardly women at all but goddesses, numinous abstracts in sagas and myths who signified war with its terrors and exhilarations. It is no coincidence that a Christian literature should link destruction with the female and all her life-giving properties. Nor is it surprising that the literati actively summoned phantoms of the pagan past for this purpose.[5] More than any other characters in the tales, the *badb*, the Morrígan, Nemain, and their many manifestations most clearly derived from pagan deities.

It seems fairly certain that Celts in Gaul once worshiped goddesses as well as male deities and that these beliefs accompanied Celtic immigrants to Ireland. As far as any modern scholar can tell, goddesses sometimes presided over war and death. They were also tribal patronesses and sources of fertility for their land and its people. Inscriptions and carvings from Roman Gaul—harder evidence than medieval Irish monks' renditions of sagas—recorded a devotion to territorial goddesses who as consorts to male divinities gave the land plenty and protected it from enemies. In double or triple form, with or without male consorts, they were *matres* or *matrones,* bearing fruits, cornucopias, babies, and other explicit symbols of fertility. Several of these nurturing goddesses also stood with ravens, scavengers of the dead, perched about them, symbolizing their simultaneous rule over life and its limits. So powerful were some, such as the horse goddess Epona, that their fame reached deep into the heart of the Roman Empire.[6]

Over a hundred years ago, the Celticist William Hennessy first linked a Gaulish deity, the CATHVBODUA chiseled into a pillar in Haute-Savoie, to a figure in early Irish texts, the *badb-chatha* ("hooded crow of battle") of *Tochmarc Emire*.[7] Since then, scholars have rarely hesitated to assimilate female figures from Irish and Welsh medieval texts to continental images of early Celtic deities, thus (re)creating entire pantheons of pre-Christian worship. The question of the goddesses' origins in the undocumented pan-Celtic past, their literary links to fertility and sovereignty figures, and their multivalent meanings in the literature of a Christianizing Ireland have panicked and misled many otherwise cautious examiners of the sources.[8] Despite the foolishness of hastily linking the material evidence of iron-age Gaul to the texts of early medieval Ireland and bearing in mind the kind of reinterpretation that accompanies such an inheritance, it may be safe to suggest some conceptual continuity between the deities of old Gaul and the battle phantoms or war goddesses of early medieval texts. But the Christian writers of the early Middle Ages used goddess figures for a different purpose from that of earlier worshipers.

In fact, scribes carried out a war of their own, a war of interpretations, in the margins and between the lines of their manuscripts. To begin with, the war goddesses of early medieval stories were often triple in manifestation, like the *matrones* of Gaul, but writers did not always distinguish between the *badb,* the Morrígan (the "phantom queen" who was sometimes actually three Morrígans),[9] and Nemain ("frenzy"). In the *Tochmarc Emire* reference, for instance, the Morrígan was glossed as "the *badbcatha,* and she is called the Woman of

Néit, that is, the goddess of battle, for Néit is the same as the god of battle."[10] In Cormac's eighth-century glossary, *Bé Néid* was glossed as *badb,* and Néit, which was glossed "goddess of war of the Goidel," was linked to Nemon; and *crú fechto,* "battle gore," was glossed as the *badb.*[11] Equally confusing, Macha, Crunniuc's wife who raced at Emain and cursed the Ulstermen, was only one of three Machas who appeared in Irish texts, all of whom seem to have been associated with the Morrígan, the *badb,* death, and physical conflict, but only one of whom was a war leader.[12] The battle goddesses mixed almost interchangeably; by the early Middle Ages they had lost any distinguishing functions they might once have had, any specific territorial identities given them by earlier Celts.

In the texts, all these female figures performed the same misdeeds. In sagas, annals, and histories, they descended ominously before an impending conflict to shriek at warriors, either to fire them for the fray or to terrorize them into defeat and death. Before the first battle of Mag Tuired, according to the eleventh- or twelfth-century account (possibly based on a ninth-century original), when men raised their weapons, poised to slaughter, "the *badb*s and monsters [*bledlochtana*] and witches [*ammaiti*] shouted so that they were heard in clefts and cascades and caves of the earth."[13] Nemain's cry in the night felled a hundred warriors of the *Táin* from sheer terror, and the Morrígan chanted warnings to bloodcurdling effect:

> Ravens gnawing
> men's necks
> blood spurting
> in the fierce fray
> hacked flesh
> battle madness
> blades in bodies
> acts of war.[14]

The goddesses were not warriors themselves; they rarely attacked directly, although the Morrígan took the forms of eel, wolf, and heifer to duel with Cú Chulainn.[15] Mostly, like the crows they were named for, the *badb* and her bloody counterparts "hopped over the points of spears and shields," inciting men to slaughter and picking over their gory remains.[16]

The *badb,* the Morrígan, and Nemain remained goddesses. Cormac named them as such, calling them *dea,* and one glossator on the Vulgate translated the *lamia* of Isaiah 34 as "monstra in feminae figura, that is, as Morrígain."[17] Yet their meanings to the monks who used them in stories and histories remained various as well as difficult to decipher. They were more than simple symbols, yet less than pagan deities. According to the conceits of annalists and historians, the goddesses continued to descend onto the battle plains of early medieval history. In 870 when Laigen and Osraige went to war, the *badb* "raised her head among them, and there was much slaughter among them everywhere."[18] And the "wild, impetuous, precipitate, mad, inexorable, furious, dark, lacerating, merciless, combative, contentious *badb*" was there when Brian Bóruma fell at the Battle of Clontarf, along with a whole host of devils and phantoms who were inciting and overwhelming the combatants.[19] In both of these instances, the war goddesses seem to have imparted and embodied the berserker spirit of men at battle.

If the chroniclers used the *badb* and her vicious sisters as straightforward metaphors for bloodlust and its effects, the goddesses must have meant more to the authors and audiences of secular narratives. Their presence in sagas and stories was too varied and unsettling to be reduced to a metaphor of one meaning. For one thing, their multiple mixed identities were confusing; and the Morrígan, at least, betrayed a schizophrenic affection for Cú Chulainn which belied her fierce nature. What is more, the war goddesses bore too much resemblance to other females in the tales, both evil crones and warrior women, not to mention sovereignty figures in their hag form, to be dismissed as facile tropes for violence or as pale descendants of fully realized Celtic deities.[20]

Certain continuities in the functions of all these female figures within the tales betrayed implicit connections between women, violence, access to power, and gender relations. To begin with, the *badb*s shared unpleasant traits with the prophesying crones who foretold or even caused the strife that brought the death of heroes and kings.[21] Just as the presence of the war goddesses meant certain death, so the appearance of a particular second-sighted old woman brought catastrophe to men. This is not to say anything so absurdly simple as that men believed women to be the only cause of political misfortune or the ruin of other good men, but the vocabulary of political power and the vocabulary of violence (and, as we have seen, the vocabularies of sex and disorder) were female. An assortment of overlapping feminized symbols expressed the literati's ideas about politics, sex, and death. In Irish tales, sovereignty came as a luscious beauty dispensing the drink of lordship;[22] likewise, disaster arrived with the words of a hideous old woman. Sometimes, the two were one and the same.[23]

Such a hag helped bring about the destruction of Da Derga's hostel (*Togail Bruidne Da Derga*) and the legendary king of Temair, Conaire Mór, along with it. Conaire was already in trouble for having violated several of his *gessa* (arbitrary ritual prohibitions), but the woman who appeared at his door forced him to break yet another, his *geis* against admitting a single woman to his house after sunset. She was a distasteful figure, as the tale-teller put it, whose beard—not the beard of her chin—"reached her knees, and her mouth was on one side of her head." When Conaire asked her to look into his future, she replied, "I see that neither hide nor hair of you will escape from this house, save what the birds carry off in their claws." And when Conaire asked her name, she replied, in one breath, standing on one foot:

> Cailb . . . Samuin, Sinand, Seiscleand, Sodb, Saiglend, Samlocht, Caill, Coll, Díchoem, Díchuil, Díchim, Díchuimne, Díchuinne, Dáirne, Dáirine, Der Úaine, Égem, Agam, Ethamne, Gním, Cluichi, Cethardam, Nith, Nemuin, Noenden, Badb, Blosc, Bloar, Uaet, Mede, Mod.[24]

Her mysterious posture gave away her destructive identity. She was Destruction (*coill*), Oblivion (*díchuimne*), the *badb*, and Nemain, whose words of prophecy realized the very future she predicted.[25]

Elsewhere in the texts, hags, sometimes identified as the *badb* and her sinister analogues, actively caused the destruction of valorous men. It took a whole trio of hags to kill Cú Chulainn, despite the efforts of the Morrígan, who actually attempted to warn him of his coming destruction. She broke the axle cast of his chariot trying to prevent him from going out to fight that day, but the Cú was determined to prove his prowess, as usual, and so went off to battle. En route, he encountered three old mothers hovered over a cook fire.[26] They invited him to eat, invoking the rules of hospitality to force his acceptance, but they served him dogmeat, the one food forbidden the Hound of Culann, since the dog was his totem. He reluctantly ate it, violating his *geis* and sealing his fate. As he died in combat just hours later, the *badb* settled on his shoulder in raven form and his horse kept watch "while his soul was in him and his warrior's light remained shining from his brow."[27]

The worst things that could happen to a man in early Ireland were the loss of his honor, his lordship, his patrimony, and his life, not necessarily in that order. When the *badb* turned against him, a man might lose them all in the single stroke of a sword. Even in her metaphorical crone's rags, the *badb* remained female because of her fickleness. Just as sovereignty whimsically selected men to rule, the war goddess chose to cut them down. Given the volatile and violent nature of politics in early Ireland and the frequency with which lordship passed from one man's hands to another's, it made sense for the literati to cast power as female, although not to endow women with power. Ordinary people died of accidents, casual assaults, or illness, but the noblest, strongest, and manliest of men fell to the curse of a female, albeit a supernatural, symbolic, textual female.

We have seen in an earlier chapter how sex killed men, or at least how the literati said that it did. The war goddesses, along with other supernaturally powerful females in early Irish narratives, confirmed this cause and effect on a more abstract level. They were not incidentally female; their power derived from their sexuality. And just as femaleness on the battlefield drove men to kill each other, a dose of virility could cure an amazon of her viciousness or transform a wandering sovereignty figure from hag to trophy wife. Sex in the arsenal of women brought men down, but men could use sex as a weapon to tame war goddesses, beautify and domesticate hags, and reduce women warriors to docile concubines. Thus, the ninth-century prologue to *Cáin Adomnáin* suggested that every woman of the pagan past had been a potential warrior; in that unforgiving past, only sexual domination by a man had kept her in her place as his servant.[28] Even the Morrígan fell in amorous thrall to Cú Chulainn, approaching him in the form of a delectable princess and begging him to sleep with her; only when he refused did she change herself into the vicious beasts that attacked him in outrage.[29] Even the literati used sex to keep their female creations under control, endowing the *badb* and other goddesses and warriors with a more benign and fertile aspect that tempered their fierceness.

The sexual aspect of war goddesses, and the nature of their taming, is most obvious in tales of blatant sovereignty figures, such as Mór Muman and her sister, Suithchern or Ruithchern.[30] Ruithchern and Mór were outcast princesses made haglike by their rootlessness. Sex with kings cured each of them, changing them from ugly, demented, threatening outcasts to pliable, desirable wives and lovers. An early modern tale, based on a lost medieval exemplar, made the process even clearer. In the tale of Mis and Dub Ruis, Mis went mad when she witnessed her royal father's death at Cath Finntrága (the Battle of Ventry).[31] She drank his blood, so wild from grief was she, and took to the mountains, where she grew hairy and lived like a beast, devouring all men who attempted to capture her. Dub Ruis, the harper to Feidlimid mac Crimthainn (king of Munster, d. 847) found her on Slíab Mis. He tamed her first with memories of her father's court, then with sex, which she had never experienced before. "That's a good trick, do it again," Mis demanded coyly in this ribald text.[32] Memory and sex were the fundamentals of her civilization, which Dub Ruis completed with music, cooked food, and a bath. Eventually Mis lost her fur, returned with Dub Ruis to the community of humans, and married him.

Mis was a faint reflection of Mór and her sister; like them, she carried her father's political power with her and kept it from men until one seduced her into yielding it. Mis was a combination of a woman warrior and a sovereignty figure, and she also resembled Suibne, the lunatic (*geilt*) warrior who grew feathers and flew like a bird among trees.[33] Her layers of meaning were many, and the date of her story was very late. Nonetheless, the tale of Mis is an inverted beauty-and-the-beast narrative of a she-animal who represented raw power, which was captured and contained by means of sex with a man, the ultimate civilizing act. In this she resembled many other militant females of early Irish texts.[34]

The sexy warrior women whom Christian authors recalled from the pagan past retained some of the goddess's powers and some of the hag's ferocity and sexuality. Like the princesses and the *badb,* who disguised themselves as hags, female warriors were cross-dressing symbols of sex and politics, not historical representations of real fighting women. Nevertheless, Celticists and romantic historians have sought vainly for the militants' historical origins in the scrolls of prurient Greek and Roman ethnographers.[35] But the theme of aggressive, militaristic Celtic women is too formulaically pervasive in classical literature to be very credible. Romans and Greeks wanted an upside-down world for the barbarians, who frightened and fascinated their sophisticated neighbors, and a standard ingredient in such a world was the manly warrior woman.[36]

Mis and the *badb* had no historical ancestresses. In neither pagan nor Christian times did Irish women go to war against men. Irish writers of the early Middle Ages may have pilfered images of warrior women from old stories or classical reports, but in their hands, the images gained new meaning for Christian audiences. Fierce women of the pagan past had titillatingly undesirable qualities that good women of the early medieval period did (or should) not: aggression, blatant sexuality, a tendency to speak their minds, and a habit of tossing spears at men. Storytellers were recreating a cosmos that, however attractively heroic, was organized on what they imagined to be exotic pagan principles.[37] In that lost and mixed-up past, women had escaped the control of men, got out of the house and into the battlefield, and crossed the boundaries of the feminine. This is why the author of *Cáin Adomnáin* told his story of women enslaved and forced to fight until Adomnán, the Lord's servant, rescued them with Christianity. And with Christianity came an end to cross-dressing and the violation of gender roles. The new social order both protected and restricted women. In most texts, the warrior women of ancient Ireland had imitated men not in order to become better, less feminine human beings in the Christian sense, like Brigit or Íte; they aped men because they dwelled in a pagan era that was morally and sexually out of control.

In story, belligerent women fought to threaten, harm, and dominate men; and men overcame them with sex. In a sense, so did the men who knew their histories, for the warrior women fought before three different audiences of men simultaneously: the male characters in the tales who vanquished them, the men who tamed and contained them by writing their stories, and male readers and audiences of the texts, who must have found excitement and relief in their defeat. Just as tales of rape sometimes narrated men's political play with men (at least, on one level), so the warrior women of narratives fought both to arouse and to instruct good Christian men.[38]

The warrior women of sagas and stories functioned on many levels for the early Irish, but unlike the more ambiguous war goddesses or sovereignty figures, they almost always represented trouble. Medb, as she appeared in *Táin Bó Cuailnge* offered a classic example. According to the early medieval version contained in the twelfth-century manuscript, the great war between Connacht and Ulster began because of nothing more than a marital spat between Medb and Ailill. As they lay in bed together, instead of making babies like a good wife, Medb began totting up her flocks and clients, trying to prove that her wealth and status outweighed his. She attacked the Ulstermen to even things up by stealing a bull, but her war ran awry because Medb herself led the army, introducing distinctly feminine thinking into the male game of war. She tried, for example, to kill off unreliable allies, chose the wrong routes for her troops, and bought soldiers with offers of her daughter's and her own sexual services.[39] One of her hirelings praised her in decidedly ironic terms, given the attitudes expressed in contemporary texts, calling her proud, uncontrollable in her own house, and noisy:

> A Medb co méd búafaid
> nít cerb caíme núachair
> dearb leam is tú is búachail
> ar Crúachain na clad.
> Art glor is art gairgnert.

O Medb great in boastfulness! The beauty of a bridegroom does not touch you. I am certain that you are master in Crúachu of the mounds. Loud your voice, great your fierce strength.[40]

She was also adulterous, carrying on with Fergus mac Róich almost in front of her husband's eyes. And she finished the unsuccessful *táin* in disgrace, a wayward mare leading her herd astray, caught pissing in the dust.

In short, Medb was everything the literati feared in a woman. Yet she was also devilishly clever, quick with her tongue, beautiful, and lethal, at least in her twelfth-century manifestation. One of her victims described her as "a tall beautiful woman with pale tender face and long cheeks" who carried a shield, a sword, and "in her hand a javelin, keen, sharp-edged and light."[41] What is more, according to the tale-tellers, as we have seen, men wanted her. The author of the *Táin* made sure that Medb was attractive as well as dangerous.[42] She seemed an authentic combination of female faults and follies, writ large as a sword-wielding siren.

In fact, the writer was using ideas as old as the Gaulish *matrones* to make specific points with his sexy Medb and all she represented to his audiences. Daring women who overstepped the boundaries of prescribed social roles were kinkily attractive. In other stories, where Medb gave more evidence of her divine origins, she was less fallible, less desirable, and more paradigmatic. Authors of these texts presented Medb as at once a personification and patroness of war, of fertility, and of sovereignty, who both sustained and snuffed out life and lordship at her pleasure. Medieval storytellers drew on this figure from their collective and literary past, more or less consciously, to describe gender's infiltration of issues of power on both symbolic and actual levels.

In *Cath Bóinde,* for instance, Medb's purpose was to conduct a series of *lánamnasa,* legal sexual unions, with royal consorts. She first accepted Conchobar mac Nesa, king of Ulster; along with her sisters, she constituted the *éraic* (compensation) for the murder of Conchobar's father. But she wearied of Conchobar and left him for Tinde mac Conrach. She was installed as queen of Connacht by her father, the king of Temair, giving her the right to confer kingship on her consort; this event had no historical counterpart but has been used as evidence for Medb's previous importance as a sovereignty goddess.[43] En route to the yearly feast of Temair, Conchobar caught her in the Boyne River and raped her in revenge for abandoning him. Tinde was killed trying to take vengeance for the rape. Medb then married Eochaid Dala but left him for their foster son, Ailill, to whom she bore seven sons in hopes that one of them would finally murder Conchobar.[44] It was Conchobar, of course, against whom she led a *táin.* The story made points, simultaneously, about the history of war between Connacht and Ulster; the cause of the *Táin Bó Cuailnge;* the whimsical nature of political power; and the limits of tolerable conflict between men and women, husbands and wives.

As a woman of many meanings, Medb resembled other female figures who marched and marauded through early Irish tales (or they resembled her). According to *Tochmarc Emire,* Cú Chulainn learned all his warrior's tricks from a woman called Scáthach and her daughters. All the ladies were fighters, although Cú Chulainn managed to seduce at least one of them and subdue them all. Scáthach's rival was another woman, Aífe, whom her protégé dueled with, raped, and impregnated.[45] Women took up arms in other stories, too. Mes Búachalla, mother of Conaire Mór, led her men to battle. Macha, in one of her manifestations, fought off would-be assailants one by one to take the kingship of Ireland. And in the Middle Irish *Tochmarc Delbchaime,* the monstrous Coinchend Cendfada had the strength of one hundred men when she defended her daughter's honor against abductors.[46]

All these figures were queens or rulers of territory, all were at least a match for male attackers and competitors, and all had more than a little trouble, to say the least, in managing normal gender relations. Not coincidentally, moreover, every one of these militant, manly women was threatened with forcible sex or actually raped. Perhaps these characters symbolized a form of rule which, like Medb, had to be captured and forced; women were excluded from rule, but marriage and sex with them secured rule for men. Therefore, women necessarily became potential threats to lordship. To lose them was to lose power, just as, we have seen, to lose control over their sexuality was to endanger a patrilineage. Hence the sagas' trope of the violent female raped.

But sex and power were inextricably bound. Stories of women warriors were not just about power, as some scholars have insisted; nor was gender merely a lens for viewing the political games of men. These hostile females were at war with men over sexual issues as well as issues of dominance and control. Although they triumphed for a time, brandishing their spears and threatening men, eventually women warriors fell to rape or some other retribution at a warrior's hands. In a sense, the war goddesses were far less dangerous than women warriors, because they were less female, less sexual, and less real. The *badb* never fell by a man's hand because she usually stuck to the acceptable female violence of incitement (although she did duel with Cú Chulainn). Women had to be rough enough to inspire political conflict, but not manly enough to take part in it. In real life, they would never take up arms.

Nonetheless, there was anarchic and even erotic pleasure in reading about things no good Christian woman would ever do, as the literati well knew. Good women could and did witness and incite violence in both tales and real life, watching men's battles from safe hills and sidelines, screaming either courage or death, depending on their loyalties. In early Irish tales, as in Icelandic sagas, the inciter played an important supportive role in violent conflicts between men.[47] When Cú Chulainn went to his death, he was encouraged by several Ulsterwomen, who urged him to take up arms; women played similar roles in the death tales of Conchobar and Celtchair.[48] The presence of a female audience charged men's duels with eroticism, further betraying the sexual connotations of violence; just as rape was politics, so politics could be a contest of virility.[49] But real women never participated in the contest as aggressors. Like the *badb,* they merely hovered over the consciousness of men at war.

From days of old, the war goddesses, hags of prophecy and sovereignty, and militant females arose to tell stories of men and women at war. Taletellers rendered no subtle and realistic portraits of female fighters. They were, like Medb, parodies of men summoned from a remote past. In Christian Ireland, women no longer practiced such overt hostility against men. If women of the historical period actually took up arms and went to war against the opposite sex, we have no evidence for it. Christian Ireland needed its *Cáin Adomnáin* both to protect its unarmed women and to explain why warrior women became docile mothers.[50]

The idea beckoned the literati and their audiences, leading them to fill pages with lady warriors, gruesome crones, tales of rape, and terrifying goddesses. Once, in the pagan past, both men and women had been able to indulge their impulses for violence against each other. Once, aspirants to political power might have seized what they wanted and prospered for it. Now, in the Christianizing present, laws and Christian mores bound both men and women to proper social roles with more limited opportunities for violence, chaos, and sex. Sexy warrior queens no longer incited a transfer of political rule. In the orderly present, men who took women by force were dangerous to the peace. They also violated the Christian sexual standard, which penalized male fornicators and adulterers along with, although less severely than, female sinners. A real man had no need to subdue a *ban-láech* with rape, which, although not uncommon, was no longer an honorable means of seizing what he wanted.

Chaos and desire ran rampant in that sex-driven, violent, pre-Christian long-ago. Tales of women warriors were fables "for the delectation of fools," as the author of the *Táin* put it in his famous colophon, to be read by early Irish audiences as a code for other conflicts.[51] For despite the dangers of male violence and despite legal and customary limits on women's autonomy and influence, real women—not war goddesses or women warriors—sometimes sought to harm or kill their men in other, more insidious ways. They poisoned or betrayed, destroyed families or offspring, dishonored or stole, and conspired with blood kin against their husbands' or stepsons' political success. By the literati's tamer time, both men and women had to watch out for a more subtly dangerous female: the maker of evil magic. The *badb* of olden days had yielded to the spell casters of the Christian present.

Spell Casters and Werewolves

Everyone knew that the *ban-láech* had disappeared with the days of Cú Chulainn or at least with the coming of the Christian saints and the law of Adomnán. But the female magician had not gone with her, nor had she been banished with the druids. Magic-making women were not products of the tumultuous pagan past, as were war goddesses, prophesizing hags, and women warriors—all of whom were safely contained in the literati's narratives. In the estimation of the early medieval Irish, magicians were real. They practiced a different kind of violence. They had no swords, fought no battles, and sought no direct political sway. Instead, they subversively aimed the devious weapon of spells and potions at the patrilineal kin group, the community, and all orderly, congenial gender relations.

Of course, women had always had magic, not all of it bad. In the literati's construction of the pre-Christian Irish past, both male and female inhabitants of the island had been skilled at "fesa ocus fithnasachta ocus druídechtai ocus amaidechtai ocus amainsechta" (occult lore, sorcery, druidic arts, witchcraft, and magical skill).[52] In historical stories of the Túatha Dé Danann (tribe of the goddess Danu), former deities became supernaturally skillful men and women, some of whom were adept at healing spells; the son and daughter of Dían Cecht (the same Dían Cecht who lent his name to the medicolegal tract), for example, sang spells over a well into which the dead of the Túatha Dé were cast so that they might climb out alive again.[53] Early medieval healing spells and Christian prayers still invoked supernatural females such as the three daughters of the goddess Flidais and the seven daughters of the sea.[54] The Morrígan, too, patrolled these stories as an enchantress, imbued with prophetic knowledge and the power to bring men to bloody conflict by her spells as well as her shrieks: "I shall pursue what was watched," she chanted; "I will be able to kill; I will be able to destroy those who might be subdued."[55] And it was no coincidence that Bríg was the name, at one and the same time, of the three spell-casting daughters of the great god Dagda—one a seer, one a healer, and one a smith—and the first sainted Irishwoman, Brigit, also a miraculous healer.[56]

The syncretistic histories were not the literati's only stories of female magicians from long ago. In the narratives the otherworld produced a whole horde of spooky, magical, shapeshifting women, as well as female seers and wielders of love charms. Some of these, such as the seer Fedelm in the *Táin*, were morally neutral figures.[57] More often, as with the character Fuamnach in the love story of Étaín and Midir, such females were evil and dangerous. Fuamnach was Midir's first wife, who turned her competitor Étaín into a fly.[58]

The most explicit connection between women and magic, sex, danger, and paganism appeared in the Middle Irish tale of Muirchertach mac Erca's death.[59] Muirchertach, the legendary sixth-century king of Ireland, was already married to Duaibsech, a princess of Connacht, when he met an otherworldly beauty named Sín. She agreed to live with him if only he would satisfy three conditions: he could never utter her name; he must evict Duaibsech and her children; and he must never bring Christian clerics into the house, for her powers were clearly anathema to Christian men. The love-besotted king agreed. Although Sín claimed to be a Christian herself, she also boasted of being capable of miracles. She could create her own sun, moon, and stars; she could conjure realistic visions of attacking armies; she could make wine from water, sheep of stones, swine of ferns, and precious metals from nothing.

Eventually, she charmed Muirchertach with magic wine, first into believing himself attacked, then into a physical decline, into pronouncing her forbidden names, and finally into a combat with imaginary demons and genuine foes, which got him killed. Sín ultimately revealed to the local clergy that her aim had been revenge. Muirchertach had long ago killed her father, Sige mac Déin meic Triuin, her mother, and her sister in battle. Sín then made her confession and died of grief for Muirchertach.

Sín was human and inhuman, Christian confessant and wielder of female magic. She fought against her competitor, Duaibsech, for Muirchertach's affections and inheritance, as a wife ought, but bore no children to Muirchertach. She avenged her family, as a decent woman should, but at the cost of her husband's life. Although she died a Christian, ultimately, her many names gave her away—Osnad, Easnadh, Sín, Gaeth Garb, Gem-adaig, Ochsad, Iachtad, Taetean: Sigh, Sough, Storm, Rough Wind, Wind-at-night, Cry, Wail, and (possibly) Groan.[60] Like the prophesizing hags and the *badb,* the very multiplicity of her names and her nature brought destruction to men. She combined war goddess and spell caster in her ability to incite violence and cast spells. She symbolized everything inherently pagan about women of all eras, everything dangerous about paganism and the past, and everything potentially destructive about sexual liaisons. But to the early medieval Irish, Sín was nonetheless a woman of the tangible, recent past. Whatever her other significance, she destroyed a purportedly historical king with magic. She was not transformed and subdued by sex, but used her attractions and her magic to play politics and avenge her kin. In the end, she was herself redeemed by magic's foe, Christianity.[61]

Just as women warriors had made pagan Ireland a dangerous place for men, so had pagan magic, whether wielded by men or women. But it was women who carried that danger into the Christian present.[62] Druids had troubled the missionizing saints by wielding pagan wizardry against the superior power of God and his religion. In hagiography, saints triumphed over druids and rid Ireland of them, but magic continued to annoy the Christian clergy long after Saint Pátraic had dispersed the druids of Temair. In the hands of women, it became a tool with which they could harm good men, their kin, and their property. Saints' lives and other religious texts described the mischief intended by women magic makers; prayers called on God's help to defend against women's magic. An early Irish invocation found in a continental manuscript calls for God's protection "ar upt[h]aib ban ṁb[á]eth," against the spells of wanton women.[63] Laws limited the social effects of female conjurers. According to penitentials, laws, and narratives alike, spell casters went for a man's most vulnerable spot: his legitimate babies or his ability to produce them. The earliest penitentials forbade the belief in what modern translators have understood as vampires or witches (*lamia*) but, at the same time, denounced the use of magic by women or those other wonder workers, Christian clerics, or, at any rate, clerics without the sanction of religious colleagues—for the saints made magic constantly, according to the vitae.[64] The penitentialists interpreted magic specifically as abortifacients or love potions. Whereas one penitentialist set high penalties for a woman or cleric who "led astray anyone by their magic" ("malifica uel malificus"), another set more precise penances for a woman who, by her *maleficium*, killed an unwanted child.[65] Columban's penitential forbade magic that killed as well as magic *pro amore* even when no one got hurt.[66] Elsewhere the penitentialists ruled against the practice of magic along with murders, adulteries, heresies, and other serious sins.[67] Sorcery was no casual leftover of pre-Patrician Ireland. It was instead a well-defined threat to Christian social order, like any of the other heinous deeds condemned by penitentialists.

Laws, prayers, and narratives also assumed women's specialization in the magics of love and sex. Jurists included female magicians among women who had transgressed fundamental behavioral rules and hence lost what relative status society accorded them. Thieves, harlots, violent women, and magic makers were often grouped together by the jurists and turned up in other lists of women excluded from ordinary social relations. Three women who had no right to compensation or health care when injured were "a woman who cares not with whom she sleeps," "a woman who robs everybody," and "a sorceress who traffics in charms," the last glossed by a later commentator as a woman "who does death to somebody" by magic.[68] Likewise, three special women deserved reduced compensation for injuries, scheduled according to the sorts of sexual unions they were in; they received smaller portions of their mates' honor prices because of their "crimes" (*cin*). Jurists explained this as a situation in which their men were responsible for preventing these despicable women from injuring anyone or anything, as was their natural inclination. The women were "the sharp-tongued virago," the werewolf (*confail conrecta,* glossed as "the woman who likes to stray in wolf-shapes"), and the vagrant "who goes off with *síd*-folk." These females were likely, respectively, to satirize someone into injury, kill livestock, and summon demons.[69] *Cáin Adomnáin* also legislated against women who killed other women with charms or spells (*epthai*).[70] And the legal tract on distraint (*Di Chetharslicht Athgabála*) allowed prosecution of anyone who practiced "bed magic," glossed as having something to do with love spells and preventing coition between a woman and man joined in *lánamnas;* the law also pronounced against anyone practicing love charms or, according to the commentary, trying out charmed (poisoned?) morsels on a dog.[71] Magic, love, and sex were inextricable in the jurists' eyes.[72]

Any woman who damaged her people's property or reputation, whether by word or by deed, lost her fragile right to membership in their group.[73] But only two of these female perpetrators, the whore and the violent woman, transgressed physically. The rest offended by harsh, false, or spell-casting words (and we have already seen what trouble a noisy woman could cause). Yet none of these women, not even the spell caster or werewolf, was a killer of other adult humans. None were so dangerous to people that they were exiled or executed; the jurists just ordered their husbands to keep an eye on them.[74] Jurists realized that bad and magic-making women had limited means by which to express their antisocial and antimale impulses. They could employ men's violence in imitation of men, but in the Christian days of the early Middle Ages, such violence was directed at surrogate victims instead of men: livestock, female competitors for their men, or babies. Magic makers hated the babies of the future, not the adults of the present.

Christian prayers, which protected ordinary people against both the great and tiny evils of everyday life, sought supernatural aid against the female spell casters who threatened the fertility of land, creatures, and human womb. Pátraic pleaded for help against the spells of smiths, women, and druids. Another incantation from the Saint Gall glosses prayed for assistance against urinary diseases and sorceresses (or, possibly, assistance *from* sorceresses).[75] The tradition was older than Christianity apparently; evidence from one Celtic site in Gaul shows that women were casting spells for the harm of others, using words that eerily echoed the *brichtu ban* (spells of women) in Pátraic's prayer: *bnamon b[r]ictom*.[76] And women went right on working charms, according to two very late (seventeenth- and eighteenth-century) manuscripts of saints' lives, which were probably composed closer to our period. The hagiographers told the story of a truly despicable witch named Cainech, the stepmother (*les-máthair*) of Fáelán mac Colmáin, who was son of the king of Leinster. Cainech, who was one of at least two wives of Colmán, tried to hex the child to death. When Fáelán was born, Cainech became consumed with jealousy for fear that "the kingdom would be conferred on Fáelán to the exclusion of her own children." So she came to Glenn Dá Locha, where Fáelán was being fostered, with her *banntracht cumachta* (literally, "woman troop of power") in order to "ply druidism, and (magic) craft, and paganism, and diabolic science upon the boy to destroy him." These skills sound remarkably like the magic practiced by the Túatha Dé Danann in the histories of the premortal past of Ireland. Cainech was clearly a descendant of the amoral otherworldly women of the pagan past, but her devlish aims were very much of the present.

But Saint Cóemgen, abbot of Glenn Dá Locha, was Fáelán's protector and fosterer and, with his henchman, Saint Berach, clearly more than a match for the evil stepmother. Cóemgen sent Berach to confront Cainech. When he caught her on a mountaintop casting druidic spells, Berach fell to the ground and prayed that Cainech and her band be swallowed by the earth, which, the hagiographer announced, came to pass. What is more, the dogs of Glenn Dá Locha would "shit on her head" until doomsday.[77] In the less colorful version of the story, Cóemgen's own vita, the saint cursed the stepmother and her women, who were turned into stones.[78]

By the time female magicians made their way into these early modern hagiographic manuscripts, their diabolical counterparts were being burned on the Continent. No doubt the Irish notion of spell casters had begun to be influenced by the whole construct of the satanic witch borrowed from abroad; although the Irish, to their credit, tried only one witch, and she somehow escaped the island.[79] Nonetheless, the idea that women's magic was both evil and sexual, aimed jealously at the other lovers of their men or at their men's babies borne by other women, endured over ten centuries, from the days of the penitentialists to the difficult years of Elizabethan and later conquests.[80] And it is no coincidence, given the literati's ambivalence toward women of influence and early Irish society's uncertainty regarding nuns, that the same word—*caillech*—came to stand for wife, nun, crone, and witch. The same law that limited legal compensation to female werewolves also limited compensation to such demonstrably real and influential women as abbesses.[81]

Before the saints had brought Christianity to Ireland, women warriors had fought men with swords and spears. In the sympathetic view of the *Cáin Adomnáin,* this had been a miserable past when women were made to disregard all their maternal instincts in order to march into battle. In the less pious view of the sagas and pseudohistories, women had enthusiastically entered the fray, thirsty for men's blood. But with Pátraic and his cohort had come the domestication of the woman warrior and the cloaking of her violence in the magic of spells and potions. Both before and after conversion, evil women sought to harm men and those who colluded with them in upholding the family, the community, and the entire society. In the past, warriors had attacked men directly with spears; sorceresses of the Christian Middle Ages aimed their magic not only at men but at their progeny, their animals, and their love.

Either way, women were doomed to failure. Male heroes and kings of saga occasionally fell prey to violent women; yet, if a king died after a visit by an ugly old prophesizing hag, it was not because of her arbitrary and vicious whim, but because he was weak and unfit to rule. By and large, heroes were able to subdue the amazons, often by civilizing them sexually. In Christianizing Ireland, men and women protected themselves against magicians with the help of penitentials, laws, prayers, and the superior power of the saints. In either case, the outcome was never uncertain. The suspense of witnessing the contest of man against woman was only temporary. Everyone knew how the story ended, and everyone read or heard the story in the context of the violent society around them, where real women were assaulted, maimed, and killed.

Violence against Women

The same men who gave life to fictional *badb*s and magic makers also assumed that women were liable to harm every day of their lives. According to *Cogadh Gaedhel re Gallaibh* (War of the Gael and the Gall), written around 1100, it was only at the end of our period, when Brian Bóruma took the high kingship of Ireland, that the land finally became safe for women:

> Thoraigh co Clíodhna cais
> is fail óir aice re a hais
> i sé briain taoibhghil nar tím
> do thimchil aoinbhen Erinn.[82]

> From Torach to pleasant Clíodhna,
> And carrying a golden ring
> During the reign of bright-sided, fearless Brian
> A lone woman could make the circuit of Ireland.

When Brian died in the Battle of Clontarf in 1013, Ireland's cows lost their bulls, women their modesty, the land its homesteads, and kings their rightful tribute.[83] When Brian put society right, then, women neither gave sex freely nor had it violently taken from them. Only in exceptionally good times, as when a strong man managed to assume the high kingship, did women escape assault, and only in disastrous times, as at the death of a high king, did they willingly lose their virtue. On an ordinary day, under normal political conditions of fragmented authority and constant warfare among chieftains and kings, the assault of women was common the length of Ireland, from Tory Island down to Cork. Women could not defend against it, nor could their men protect them from other men.

Many different texts suggest that violence against women in early Ireland was casual and common, but in fact, all kinds of violence among men, women, and children were endemic in early medieval Europe. This is not to suggest that everyone north of Rome was an axe-wielding maniac, but people employed force more freely and suffered fewer legal or social consequences for it than in our own society. They assumed that when negotiation failed, war was the solution to conflict between political units, and violence a legitimate punishment for civil and criminal violations.[84]

But women were not warriors and could not participate directly in a feud. Men did not ordinarily go to war against women, nor did they normally aim their revenge at women although, to be sure, women could be casualties of war.[85] Violence directed specifically at women had other causes and took other forms, such as rape, assault, and abduction. As in other legal codes of the period, Irish laws defined crimes against women as injuries to the male guardian of the victim, analogous to theft or abuse of his property.[86] When an Irishwoman was murdered, her guardian could claim a proportion of his own honor price from the slayer.[87] The amount of reparation for any crime committed against a woman depended upon the seriousness of the damage and the value of the goods. For a marriageable virgin, a *cétmuinter,* or a nun, a rapist had to pay the honor price of the woman's guardian, plus compensation (*éraic*) for the damage.[88] Rape of an *adaltrach* cost only half the normal *éraic.* For women of dubious quality, no payment was necessary; a prostitute, an adulteress, or any woman on her way to a lover's tryst was fair game for sex-hungry assailants.[89]

The literati did not take a unified stance on offenses against women. Some texts treated the abuse or rape of women more severely. *Bretha Nemed toísech* suggested that a man who kissed an unwilling woman should pay her full honor price to her guardian.[90] The *Heptads* even allowed a woman to leave her abusive husband if he inflicted blows that permanently blemished her.[91] *Cáin Adomnáin,* as we have seen, decreed much higher penalties than secular laws for rape as well as other sexual violations and murder. To kill a woman cost a man his hand, his foot, and his life, and his heirs seven *cumals* (or seven years' hard penance and fourteen *cumals*).[92] A man who touched a woman against her will or stuck his hand in her clothes owed seven *cumals,* the equivalent of full *éraic,* to her guardian; for violating her by hand, he owed the same fine plus an additional penalty of three ounces of silver.[93]

But who can say whether anyone paid attention to *Cáin Adomnáin?* The annalists recorded the *cáin*'s promulgation, but whether families involved in a legal dispute over the alleged rape of a woman invoked the saint's law is another question. The *cáin* attributed to Saint Adomnán may have influenced local perspectives on the seriousness of rape and the assault of women in areas where it had been recently proclaimed and where clerical influence kept the memory of the *cáin* fresh and forceful. The text took a unique stance on the issue of rape, however, just as it did on the subject of motherhood; it seems unlikely that the law itself contributed to any islandwide reevaluation of crimes against women or the penalties men paid for committing them.

The laws were, after all, nothing but guidelines for negotiating conflicts in order to avoid (further) violence. The jurists who wrote and used the laws assumed that many of the same injuries afflicted men and women and that many of the rules they voiced applied to other people besides the adult male standard. Just because specific rules regarding the murder and injury of women did not appear in the law tracts does not mean that women in early Ireland were never or rarely murdered or injured. Nor did the legal texts on rape and sexual abuse necessarily imply that these crimes were more common than other kinds of injury to women.

On the other hand, the prominence of sexual assault in secular and religious narratives suggests a genuine concern about the vulnerability of women to sexual violation. In other words, the men who produced the documents—the men who formally articulated the culture's ideas about women and their relations to men—represented women as more susceptible to rape than to other injuries. What is more, the meaning of stories of sexual assault varied by genre of texts. Rape subdued and civilized the sagas' viragos, but hagiographic accounts of abducted nuns represented the laity's aversion to the waste of potential childbearers in a life of chastity. Hagiographers recognized society's ambivalence toward religious women and made it a theme in stories of nuns beheaded, raped, seduced, and generally ruined for the religious life, as we have seen. But hagiographers also used rape stories to remind religious women that the world beyond the sacred enclosure was perilous for devout and virtuous ladies and that their protectors should be aware of the danger.[94] If the famous rape of the abbess of Cell Dara is anything to judge by, nuns were right to worry. In 1132 the henchmen of Diarmait mac Murchada assaulted the abbess in order to make her unfit to rule; Diarmait then installed his own kinswoman as abbess.[95] For the king of the Laigin, then, the rape held yet another meaning. It was like burning down a church—a shrewd political move and an act of aggression against the religious hierarchy.

In secular narratives, which had a less explicitly didactic function than hagiography, rape was told as a different story, or stories. Sexual assault, or the threat of it, usually had one of two effects. Either the victim suffered shame even to the point of death, or the victim manfully took no notice. In the narratives, forcible sex was not an evil aimed at a woman's body and mind but a tool for other conflicts and larger events involving both men and women, often a way for men to insult other men. In *Tochmarc Luaine*, for instance, King Conchobar's betrothed died of shame when three satirists tried unsuccessfully to verbally coerce her into sleeping with them.[96] Deirdriu, too, the headstrong heroine of *Loinges mac nUislenn*, killed herself rather than be forced to have sex with her lover's murderer. In these tales, sexual advances to unwilling women became a means by which men played one-upmanship with men. Luaine fell victim to poets trying to co-opt the property of a king; Deirdriu, who instigated defiance of Conchobar's authority, eventually became the pawn in a game of retribution aimed at the sons of Uisliu and those who supported them.

But in still other stories, sexual assault was merely the form that violence took between a man and a woman of almost equal strength. In *Cath Bóinde*, as we have seen, Conchobar met Medb bathing in a river and raped her; she responded by initiating the *Táin*. If Medb had been another male warrior, Conchobar might have dueled with him to the death. In the *Táin*, Cú Chulainn used the symbolic violation of Medb's daughter Finnabair to strike at the queen herself. When Finnabair came to seduce the hero into ambush, he snipped off some of her hair and thrust a pillar up her gown, leaving her stuck, exposed, and shamed.[97] In the tale of Aífe's only son (*Aided Óenfir Aífe*), Cú Chulainn overcame the woman warrior Aífe and demanded, among his rewards, the right to impregnate her. Aífe had to concede defeat or die; so she had intercourse with the victor.[98] It was no coincidence that these women were militant figures from the pagan past, which added to the sexual charge of their stories.

Still other women took no notice at all of their rapes, at least not so far as author and audience could tell. The victims in these tales confirmed the subordinate role of women in men's political machinations. In the ninth- or tenth-century story of Buchet's hostel, Eithne was raped by the king, Cormac mac Airt, who coveted her as a bride. Although the text did not specify whether she colluded in her violation, she did cheerfully settle down with Cormac as his wife. Her foster father prospered as a result of his relationship with his new ally, the king.[99] The story of another Eithne used rape—simultaneously by her three brothers—as the premise for the heroic birth of a future king, Lugaid Réoderg.[100] Rape advanced these plots, which is to say, men's conflicts with men. In Buchet's tale, the rape confirmed his subordination to the rapist; in *Cath Bóinde*, it validated Lugaid's claim to rule. The rapes were a bit of background which justified or facilitated men's actions, confirming the social hierarchy and the important but subordinate roles of women.

Of course, we should not expect the literature of early Ireland to include any fierce condemnations of men's aggression toward women. By and large, sexual assault figured as an abnormal but not at all unusual event. Yet the laws took it for an offense, even if an offense to property or Christian morality. People clearly thought it wrong. It was wrong, however, because it reflected ordinary social relations tipped askew and sexuality out of control, rather than personal injury to an individual woman. In the laws rape represented the stealing or damaging of one man's property by another. In the narratives rape occurred because a man sought power over another. Sometimes, it simply confirmed a man's virility and strength, as in the story of MacCecht, whom no woman would approach because she knew that he would rape her.[101]

More often, though, rape occurred when the normal social order was already upset somehow, as when a man had been injured and sought to avenge himself on another. It allowed male characters to get what was coming to them, be it justice, revenge, or a wife. Used against nuns, rape was an attempt to stop clerics from seducing young women into the religious life. In the case of Diarmait mac Murchada and the abbess of Cell Dara, it enabled Diarmait to regain a valuable property. Rape was a means to injure a prominent woman of a competing dynasty and restore the political balance among male leaders; Diarmait's men might also have accomplished their goal with the theft of cattle or the seizure of territory. As with feuds and warfare, women were formally excluded from the larger issues that eventually brought them harm.

Nonetheless, as in the case of other social and political restrictions imposed upon women, men suspected women of maneuvering around their exclusion from political conflict, too. Lawyers worried about the issue of consent and women's complicity in sexual abduction and assault, or at least their responsibility for their victimization. On the one hand, lawyers recognized the possibility that a woman might collude in her own abduction; on the other hand, they worried about the harm, even violent death, that could befall a victim of abduction.[102] As we saw earlier, jurists distinguished among *forcor,* forced intercourse; *sleth,* nonconsensual intercourse; and willing fornication. If a woman was drunk when a man assaulted her, that was punishable *sleth,* but if she got drunk by visiting an alehouse without a male chaperone, the rapist could take her with no legal consequences to himself.[103] She was asking for it, too, if she did not cry out during the assault when the crime took place *i cathair,* in a settlement where others might hear.[104] The *Triads* advised potential victims not to tempt rapists by venturing into the "three darknesses: the darkness of mist, the darkness of a wood, the darkness of night."[105] Like modern urbanites who fear to walk the streets at night, good girls were to stay safely at home in early Ireland or suffer the consequences. According to *Bretha Crólige,* it was folly to allow a woman even to visit another household without a companion to guard her virtue.[106]

But most men must have tried to protect their women from harm, including sexual abuse. No one condoned rape, at least not when committed against their own women. Laws forbade it; tales of women maimed, shamed, and killed showed what resulted from it. When women had not the strength or wiles or strategies or networks with which to defend themselves against male violence, good women—other men's daughters, wives, and mothers— suffered and died. The literati were not oblivious nor their audiences cold to the tragedy of a lost woman. But if families mourned a girl's harm and condemned her violator, it was not because the deed was criminal and the victim terrorized; they all felt the insult to collective prestige and property. The most basic alliance of Irish society, upon which the entire social order rested, was the sexual union of man and woman. The alliance of kin groups depended on the movement of a woman from one family to another, her consensual sexual union with a man, and their production of legitimate offspring. Conflict between two groups could be expressed through the seizure and violation of a woman and the subsequent pollution of her reproductive potential. Just as spell casters struck men where it hurt most, in their progeny, rapists attacked the source of a kin group's future. In their assaults on each other, according to the literati, men and women chose exactly the same kind of target.

It may be, as one Celticist has improbably argued, that "the primary role of women in any male-oriented literature is a sexual one," hence, that the rape and assault of women depicted in narratives were merely incidental and no indication either of hostility toward women in real life or of gendered political issues.[107] But to dismiss an entire palimpsest of messages about women and gender relations as single-minded maleness, incidental to plot and message, is a reductionist (if not tautological) approach to a complex problem. Likewise, to dismiss literary references to sexual assault as straightforward reports of the actual deed is to miss the literati's points.

The frequent presence of sexual assault in all kinds of texts suggests two things. First, rape was not just a tale in manuscripts but a script regularly acted out. Second, whatever the actual frequency of its occurrence compared with other offenses to women, violent sexual conflict was a recognized code for other battles at the same time that it was both a political and sexual assault on women. The texts contained ideas, not always coherent, about the potentially violent nature of gender relations and the sexual nature of violence, all of which were built into the early Irish social structure. When women struck at men they used swords or spells. When men tamed dangerous women they used sex. When men harmed good women, they used sex. Men could redistribute power and property among themselves, either legitimately or illegitimately, by striking at women. Violence against women sliced at the very heart of everything both men and women held dear.

The corollary to this political use of violent sex, as we have seen, was that women could manipulate their subordinate sexual and social roles. They could refuse to marry the right men, have sex with men, bear legitimate children, or nurture their offspring, or they could even kill babies. As tales of fallen nuns and the legal distinction between *forcor* and *sleth* revealed, women could collude in their violation to the detriment of their kinsmen. And most outrageous of all, women could attack directly, as they once had with weapons. In the era of Pátraic and Brigit the weapons of choice were wicked words of magic.

The literati described an endemic war between the sexes, but the profound political symbolism with which they charged sexual conflict—and, vice versa, the way they read politics as sexual, erotic, even pornographic—makes clear the literati's most precious assumption about the society around them. They believed that men and women, working amiably together, created not only a couple, a family, and a community, but a kin group, a kingdom, and an entire cosmos. As a result, neither man nor woman was less responsible for, valuable, or dangerous to the working of the world.

Nothing makes this view more evident or sums up the war between the sexes more aptly than the *dindsenchas,* place-name stories and poems of the tenth through the twelfth centuries. The *dindsenchas* described a landscape of Ireland steeped in history, myth, and fancy, where places had meaning and names only after some violent interaction of men or women took place there.[108] For the authors of the *dindsenchas,* Ireland's surface was made memorable by a map of betrayal, assault, and combat; a pass or lake named without reference to some sort of mayhem, be it man's or woman's, lacked pizzazz. The Irish named the very land around them, which nourished them as only a mother could, for the perpetrators and victims of violence, coloring the landscape with blood.

And women committed their share of the toponymic terror. The texts are full of mythic feminine brutality. There was, for instance, the story of Carman; she had three marauding sons named Dian, Dub, and Dothur (Violent, Black, and Evil) who raided and burned while she herself cast evil spells on the crops of Ireland.[109] There was Duirgein, who slept with a slave and was then ambushed by a soldier employed by her mother, upon whom she inflicted fifty wounds before falling.[110] Duiblind, a third virago, sang a sea spell to kill her husband's other wife.[111]

One of the most unearthly tales was of Rúad mac Rigduind, prince of Fir Muirig, who sailed with his men in three ships across the sea. Suddenly their boats were caught and held still in the waves. When they peered into the depths, nine mysterious women gazed back. Rúad went with the women to an otherworld beneath the water, where he slept each night with a different woman, leaving one pregnant, and although he promised to return, he never did. Seven years later, when he sailed back again to Ireland, the women chased after him in a bronze boat, bringing Rúad's son and singing magic as they came. They did not catch him, but without comment or cry, the child's mother slashed off the head of the boy and hurled it after Rúad. The place where it happened was called Inber nAilbine because everyone hearing the story declared, "is ollbine," "it is an awful crime."[112]

The *dindsenchas* told neither the most appalling nor uncommon stories of men and women locked in violent conflict, but their themes and meanings added heavy emphasis to the message of an entire canon of gender ideologies. Men hurt women in one way, and women hurt men in another. Both methods had to do with sex and politics, both threatened the perceived natural order of society and the cosmos, and both had to be protected against by men and women working together. And yet, there was something so organic and inevitable about the war between the sexes that it permeated the rocks and rivers and earth itself. It made the land intelligible to the people who occupied and organized it into a human landscape.

Sheelanagigs

At the end of our period, when the Normans came to Ireland and Continental influence started to weigh heavy on the literati, stoneworkers began to carve sheelanagigs above the doors of the churches of Ireland. Sheelanagigs are naked female grotesques who spread their legs and expose their genitals to the world. Some leer, some grimace; some gesture impudently to their pudenda, some hold their arms akimbo; many crouch, some recline. Most are bony and emaciated. Several are scarred or tatooed or marked by generations of pilgrims' fingers caressing them, ritually, again and again in the same places.

In Irish, she is *síle-na-gcíoch,* a name of imprecise meaning. It may come from Sighe na gCioch, "old hag of the paps," or Síle na Giob, "Sheela on her hunkers," from the squatting that many of them do.[113] Archaeologists used to think that sheelas were direct descendants of pre-Christian idols, fertility goddesses related to the hags of ancient tales—hence the "old hag" interpretation of their name. But it seems more likely that they came from France. Similar exhibitionist figures were carved on Continental churches in the eleventh century, and probably reached Ireland via Anglo-Norman England. The first sheela (or acrobatic prototype of a sheela) appeared in Ireland during the 1160s, with the earliest wave of Romanesque architectural influence, on the nun's church at Cluain Moccu Nóis.[114] From Cluain, they spread across Ireland, although most of the surviving sheelas are concentrated in the south, especially County Tipperary. They range in date from the twelfth to the seventeenth century.[115]

On the Continent and in England, carved grotesques at ecclesiastical sites represented God's use of evil to combat evil, and the fundamental humor of God's gross enemies.[116] But in Ireland, where the minds of men and women were more receptive to the duality and fundamental paganism of the female form, the grotesques became sexy sheelas. They, too, were humorous figures, surely—the Ballylarkin sheela, with her bald head, jug ears, and almost goofy smile; or the sheela of Cavan with her rude squat and childishly stuck-out tongue.[117] Again, the joke was on women, for the menace of the sheelas was just silly; still, menace it was, for the figures were reminders of fruitful, womanly evil. They bore distinct resemblances to both the hags of sagas and the magic makers of hagiography. Like both kinds of hostile women in the texts, they were ugly, frightening, amusing, fertile, and erotic all at once. And

Sheelanagig, Seirkieran, County Offaly. Photograph: National Museum of Ireland.

Sheelanagig, Ballylarkin, County Kilkenny. Photograph: National Museum of Ireland.

Sheelanagig, County Cavan. Photograph: National Museum of Ireland.

like the hostile women of story, they loitered where they had no proper feminine business: over the entrances to the most sacred space of the Christian landscape, where they reminded the pious of the most profane of human activities. They stared observers right in the eyes (they still do), casting spells and taking them captive by horrified fascination.[118] Sheelas were another chapter in that peculiar Irish pornography of sex and political power expressed in, of all things, church decor.

Many modern interpreters have suggested an apotropaic function for the sheelanagigs. Although they were threatening, rude, and exciting, their danger was harnessed and put to good use by the Christian clergy, for the sheelas guarded churches and churchgoers from worse evils. Sheelas thus became totems for devout Christians. This interpretation makes sense because, as we have seen, the texts of early Ireland had already established a tradition in which militant women were always eventually contained and domesticated, as the Morrígan ultimately was by Cú Chulainn, so that they might turn their strength to the support of men. The early Irish, who had enjoyed tantalizing themselves with unruly females imprisoned within texts, could easily make the leap to visualizing such women caged in stone above the doors of churches. And it also makes sense that the Irish should have used women, denied power, to express threats to both spiritual and political power; as with hags of sovereignty, so with sheelas. But the guardian function of sheelas also seems likely because, well into the early modern period, they continued to pop up on the protective walls of fortified buildings and at particularly important structural points on houses and towers. They also leered from bridges and watched over the boundaries of territories or towns.[119]

However, the precise relation of sheelas to their literary antecedents and, more distantly, to Celtic goddesses of life and death, is far more complex than Celticists once thought. The image of the woman creature that inspired the sheelas sprang from the same minds that had produced the baby killers of the *dindsenchas* and Medb of the *Táin*. It had taken the Irish literati centuries to refine that image, in all its gleeful, disruptive, shocking, fertile amgibuity. Much had changed during the long generation of the sheelas, everything from basic political structures of kingship and clientage to tiny details of dress and written expression. But the *longue durée* of gender ideologies had not changed so much as gained greater expression in a wider variety of written and visual media, allowing the literati and their audiences more room to ponder the troubling meaning of the female.[120]

Men and women related in much the same ways from the beginning of Ireland's early Middle Ages to the time when the Normans came with their newfangled laws, their castles, and their French talk. The rigors of daily life did not allow for much variation. There were only so many ways in which men and women could organize themselves in pairs and groups. Men were bound by the social and political structures of kinship, clientage, and fosterage; women were stuck with those they spent the most time with and with subsidiary roles in men's social networks and politics. Both did the best they could to maneuver around the formalities of law and custom to form meaningful ties with each other. Together, they worked to make prosperous households, simply in order to get by. And each struggled to understand the flaws and strengths of the other.

Whether or not most Irish men and women of the pre-Norman period considered the problem of woman at any length or cogitated on the meaning of gender relations in any formal terms remains unlikely. But this does not mean that the ideologies of the literati did not trickle down to ordinary farmers and their women, for the learned men of Ireland expressed themselves not in complicated theory but in vivid tales of ancient kingdoms, myths of the otherworld, jurists' handbooks, tales of saints, and other accessible forms. If people could not read the theories of the literati, they certainly encountered them as repeated around the fire or told along the road. Everyone knew what women were supposed to be and do, and everyone understood that women did not always obey.

Indeed, women sometimes rebelled outright. From the explicit attacks of sorceresses to the subtle politicking of a clever *cétmuinter,* from the solidarity of homebound weavers to the chattering mob of the Land of Women, from the threat of sexual virago to the refusal of all females to be categorized and defined, women found ways to survive and even to defy the gender ideologies of the learned men of Ireland. The tensions, confusions, and quarrels of the texts showed that the literati were not always unsympathetic. Disagreements among different sources revealed a conflict between ideologies and social realities; and that conflict, often expressed by the texts as a war between the sexes, helped the Irish think about all the things, including that fundamental alliance between man and woman, that were most precious to them.

The women of Ériu may be long gone, but the men who hated and loved them also captured them for us in sagas, saint's lives, laws, and poems. And captured is precisely the right word for the process by which women of such a distant past have come to us. They have not offered themselves willingly to modern historical examination, although a few of them colluded. But I have dragged them from the manuscripts and the bits of bone and stone that provide our evidence. I have held them hostage while I, like the literati of early Ireland, have told their story, not in their words but in my own. May they forgive and bless my efforts.

Notes

1. The Texts and the Tellers of Women's Tales

1. Yeats's Maeve in *The Celtic Twilight* (1893) is typical: "The woman had a sword by her side and a dagger lifted up in her hand, and was dressed in white, with bare arms and feet. She looked 'very strong, but not wicked' . . . she had no stomach on her, and was slight and broad in the shoulders, and was handsomer than any one you ever saw; she looked about thirty."

2. Rosalind Clark, *The Great Queens: Irish Goddesses from the Morrígan to Cathleen Ní Houlihan*, Irish Literary Studies 34 (Gerrards Cross, U.K., 1991), 153–85.

3. Tomás Ó Máille, ed. and trans., "Medb Cruachna," *ZCP* 17 (1927): 129–46; T. F. O'Rahilly, *Early Irish History and Mythology* (Dublin, 1946; repr. 1976), 269-71; O'Rahilly, "On the Origins of the Names Érainn and Ériu," *Ériu* 14 (1943), 7–28, esp. 15–16; Rudolf Thurneysen, "Allerlei Keltisches: 7 Göttin *Medb*," *ZCP* 18 (1929), 108–10; 19 (1933), 352. See also Mary Condren, *The Serpent and the Goddess: Women, Religion, and Power in Celtic Ireland* (New York, 1989), 70.

4. Proinsias Mac Cana, "Women in Irish Mythology," *Crane Bag* 4.1 (1980), 10. See also Patrick Ford, "Celtic Women: The Opposing Sex," *Viator* 19 (1988), 417–38; Patrick Power, *Sex and Marriage in Ancient Ireland* (Dublin, 1976), 10; James Doan, *Women and Goddesses in Early Celtic History, Myth, and Legend*, Northeastern University Working Papers in Irish Studies 87—4/5 (Boston, 1987), esp. 32, 35. But for a fresh perspective, see Patricia Kelly, "The *Táin* as Literature," in J. P. Mallory, ed., *Aspects of the Táin* (Belfast, 1992), 69–102, esp. 76–85.

5. Donnchadh Ó Corráin, "Women in Early Ireland," in Ó Corráin and Margaret MacCurtain, eds., *Women in Irish Society: The Historical Dimension* (Westport, Conn., 1980), 10–11.

6. Population estimates vary wildly. See A. P. Smyth, *Celtic Leinster: Towards an Historical Geography of Early Irish Civilization, A.D. 500-1600* (Blackrock, Éire, 1982), 4–5; Harold Mytum, *The Origins of Early Christian Ireland* (London, 1992), 16–17, 48. But see Dáibhí Ó Cróinín's response to Mytum's estimates: *Linen Hall Review* 9.1 (1992), 23–25.

7. D. A. Binchy, "Secular Institutions," in Myles Dillon, ed., *Early Irish Society* (Dublin, 1954), 52–65.

8. C. J. Lynn, "Deer Park Farms, Glenarm, Co. Antrim," *Archaeology Ireland* 1.1 (1987), 11–15.

9. Others, working from the evidence of dendrochronology, have hypothesized two periods of intense enclosure construction, ca. 581 and ca. 843. Michael Baillie, "Marker Dates: Turning Prehistory into History," *Archaeology Ireland* 2 (1988), 154–55; Matthew Stout, "Ringforts in the South-west Midlands of Ireland," *PRIA* 91 C 8 (1991), 202.

10. C. J. Lynn, "An Early Christian Period Site in Ballybrolly, County Armagh," *UJA* 46 (1983), 47–51; but cf. Lynn, "A Rath in Seacash Townland, County Antrim," *UJA* 41 (1978), 70, where he suggests that a combination of dating techniques can lead to more precise dating of sites; also Stout, "Ringforts in the South-west Midlands," 202–3. The possible exceptions are the Scandinavian settlements at Dublin and elsewhere. See John Bradley, "The Interpretation of Scandinavian Settlement in Ireland," in Bradley, ed., *Settlement and Society in Medieval Ireland* (Kilkenny, Éire, 1988), 49–78; P. F. Wallace, "The Origins of Dublin," in B. G. Scott, ed., *Studies on Early Ireland* (Belfast, 1981); Wallace, "The Archaeology of Viking Dublin," in Howard B. Clarke and Anngret Simms, eds., *The Comparative History of Urban Origins in Non-Roman Europe,* BAR International Series 255 (Oxford, 1985), 103–45.

11. Stout's study of distribution in Tipperary and Offaly suggests a mean distance between ring forts of 1,000 meters: "Ringforts in the South-west Midlands," 210–12. The extensive laws of trespass, neighborhood, joint responsibility, and the sheer bulk of legal interaction suggested by the legal tracts confirm a certain concentration of the rural population. See, for example, laws on trespass: *CIH,* 64–79, 191–205 = *ALI* 4:69–159.

12. Nancy Edwards, *The Archaeology of Early Medieval Ireland* (Philadelphia, 1990), 27.

13. David Herlihy, *Medieval Households* (Cambridge, Mass., 1985), 68–72.

14. This is certainly the pattern considered traditional in modern times. See Hugh Brody, *Inishkillane: Change and Decline in the West of Ireland* (London, 1973), 113–16; Conrad Arensberg, *The Irish Countryman: An Anthropological Study* (1937; repr. New York, 1968), 87–93.

15. *CIH,* 299 = *ALI* 2:332–34; *CIH,* 215–17 = *SEIL,* 144–45, which seems to refer to a *gelfine* consisting of five members, each with his own household; see also Thomas Charles-Edwards, *Early Irish and Welsh Kinship* (Oxford, 1993), 55–60, 413–30.

16. Lynn, "Deer Park Farms," 11–15.

17. Chris Lynn, "Ulster's Oldest Wooden Houses," in Ann Hamlin and Chris Lynn, eds. *Pieces of the Past: Archaeological Excavations by the Department of the Environment* (Belfast, 1988), 44–47. For reports of other sites where enclosures contain more than one house or sites with related enclosures, see Conleth Manning, "Archaeological Excavation of a Succession of Enclosures at Millockstown, Co. Louth," *PRIA* 86 C (1986), 135–81; Seán P. Ó Ríordáin, "Excavations at Cush, Co. Limerick," *PRIA* 45 C (1939–40), 83–181; Ó Ríordáin, "Lough Gur Excavations: Three Marshland Habitation Sites," *JRSAI* 79 (1949), 126–45; D. M. Waterman, "A Group of Raths at Ballypalady, Co. Antrim," *UJA* 35 (1972), 29–36; Lynn, "An Early Chris-

tian Site in Ballybrolly"; C. J. Lynn, "Two Raths at Ballyhenry, Country Antrim," *UJA* 46 (1983), 67–91, where Lynn cautions that we cannot adduce any relationship between the two raths, unlike the site at Ballypalady.

18. B. B. Williams, "Excavations at Ballyutoag, County Antrim," *UJA* 47 (1984), 37–49.

19. Edwards, *Archaeology of Early Medieval Ireland,* 29–32; see also Stout, "Ring-forts in the South-west Midlands," 213–41, esp. 238–39.

20. *CIH,* 1769, 1770; Fergus Kelly, *Guide to Early Irish Law* (Dublin, 1987), 89–90.

21. *CIH,* 505 = *ALI* 2:356–57.

22. *SEIL,* 16–75; Kelly, *Guide,* 70–71.

23. *CIH,* 511–12 = *ALI* 2:378, 384. For similar situations elsewhere in early medieval Europe, see Suzanne Foney Wemple, *Women in Frankish Society: Marriage and the Cloister, 500 to 900* (Philadelphia, 1981), 38–42, 56, 73, 75–96; Jenny Jochens, "The Church and Sexuality in Medieval Iceland," *Journal of Medieval History* 6 (1980), 377–92; Ruth Mazo Karras, "Concubinage and Slavery in the Viking Age," *Scandinavian Studies* 62.2 (1990), 141–62.

24. *CIH,* 443–44; Rudolf Thurneysen, *Irisches Recht,* Abhandlungen der Preussischen Akademie der Wissenschaften, Phil.-Hist. Klasse. 2 (Berlin, 1931), 35–37; Kelly, *Guide,* 76.

25. Kelly, *Guide,* 68–79; see also Kuno Meyer, ed. and trans., *The Triads of Ireland,* Todd Lecture Series 13 (Dublin, 1906), 20 (150, 151, 159, 160).

26. *CG,* 11, l. 280; Kelly, *Guide,* 14.

27. *Can. Hib.,* 122; *CIH,* 45 = *ALI* 5:284.

28. Ó Corráin, "Women in Early Irish Society," 1–13; Nerys Patterson, *Cattle-Lords and Clansmen: Kinship and Rank in Early Ireland,* Harvard Studies in Sociology (Cambridge, 1991), 272–75. See, however, Katherine Simms, "The Legal Position of Irishwomen in the Later Middle Ages," *Irish Jurist* n.s. 10 (1975), 96–111, where she points out correctly that divorce was not to women's advantage.

29. Neil McLeod, *Early Irish Contract Law,* Sydney Series in Celtic Studies 1 (Sydney, 1992), 71–80.

30. On the laws, see Liam Breatnach, "Lawyers in Early Ireland," in Daire Hogan and W. N. Osborough, eds., *Brehons, Serjeants, and Attorneys: Studies in the History of the Irish Legal Profession* (Blackrock, Éire, 1990), 1–13; Kelly, *Guide,* 225–63. The language of the sagas and other tales often appears to be early medieval though the manuscripts are much later in date. Whether individual texts pertain to the period of their language or their manuscripts is as contentious an issue as the supposed oral origins of texts. See Kim McCone, *Pagan Past and Christian Present in Early Irish Literature* (Maynooth, Éire, 1990), 29–53; Cecile O'Rahilly, ed., *Táin Bó Cúailnge: Recension I* (Dublin, 1976), vii–xxiii.

31. Breatnach, "Lawyers in Early Ireland," 4–5.

32. Kenneth H. Jackson, *The Oldest Irish Tradition: A Window on the Iron Age* (Cambridge, 1964); Gerard Murphy, *Saga and Myth in Ancient Ireland* (Dublin, 1961), esp. 5–14; Proinsias Mac Cana, "Conservation and Innovation in Early Celtic Literature," *ÉC* 13 (1971), 61–118; all cited in McCone, *Pagan Past and Christian Present,* 4–6.

33. On Brigit, see Donál Ó Cathasaigh, "The Cult of Brigid: A Study of Pagan-

Christian Syncretism in Ireland," in James J. Preston, ed., *Mother Worship: Theme and Variations* (Chapel Hill, N.C., 1982), 75–94; on saints as deities, see Charles Plummer, ed., *Vitae Sanctorum Hibernae* (Oxford, 1910), 1:clxxix–clxxxviii.

34. The debate goes on: Seán Ó Coileáin, "Oral or Literary: Some Strands of the Argument," *Studia Hibernica* 17-18 (1977–78), 7–35; Edgar Slotkin, "Medieval Irish Scribes and Fixed Texts," *Éigse* 17 (1978–79), 437–50; Gearóid Mac Niocaill, "Orality and Literacy in Some Middle-Irish King-Tales," in Stephen N. Tranter and Hildegard L. C. Tristram, eds., *Early Irish Literature—Media and Communication* (Tübingen, 1989), 149–83; McCone, *Pagan Past and Christian Present*, 12. The definitive work on the early Irish literati, their collective identity, and their very self-conscious literature is about to be Joseph Falaky Nagy, *Conversing with Angels and Ancients* (forthcoming).

35. Donnchadh Ó Corráin, "Legend as Critic," in Tom Dunne, ed., *The Writer as Witness: Literature as Historical Evidence* (Cork, 1987), 26; Ó Corráin, "Nationality and Kingship in Pre-Norman Ireland," in T. W. Moody, ed., *Nationality and the Pursuit of National Independence* (Belfast, 1978), 18–19; Ó Corráin, "The Early Irish Churches: Some Aspects of Organisation," in Ó Corráin, ed., *Irish Antiquity* (Cork, 1981), 328–31; Lisa M. Bitel, *Isle of the Saints: Monastic Settlement and Christian Community in Early Ireland* (Ithaca, N.Y., 1990), 94–114.

36. McCone, *Pagan Past and Christian Present*, 22.

37. Kelly, *Guide*, 55–57; Meyer, *Triads*, 2 (12, 16, 21); McCone, *Pagan Past and Christian Present*, 23. But see Thomas Charles-Edwards, "Review Article: The Corpus Iuris Hibernici," *Studia Hibernica* 20 (1980), esp. 158–62. See also Breatnach, "Lawyers in Early Ireland."

38. *AU*, 256 (802), 328 (871), 432 (1004), 492 (1056); McCone, *Pagan Past and Christian Present*, 24.

39. *CIH*, 348–49, 1616.

40. Liam Breatnach, ed., *Uraicecht na Ríar* (Dublin, 1987), 91; *CIH*, 2150; both cited in McCone, *Pagan Past and Christian Present*, 23.

41. McCone, *Pagan Past and Christian Present*, esp. 22–28; Ó Corráin, "Legend as Critic," 23–38; John Ryan, *Irish Monasticism: Its Origins and Early Development* (Dublin, 1931), 167–90; Kathleen Hughes, *The Church in Early Irish Society* (Ithaca, N.Y., 1966), 57–90; Bitel, *Isle of the Saints*, 141 n. 26; Joseph F. T. Kelly, "Christianity and the Latin Tradition in Early Medieval Ireland," *Bulletin of the John Rylands University Library of Manchester* 68.2 (1986), 410–33.

42. McCone, *Pagan Past and Christian Present*, esp. 18–28 and 256–67.

43. Emmet Larkin, "The Devotional Revolution in Ireland, 1850–75," *American Historical Review* 77.3 (1972), 625–52. For the social, political, and cultural functions of lay-clerical relations in the early Middle Ages, see Bitel, *Isle of the Saints;* Megan McLaughlin, *Consorting with Saints: Prayer for the Dead in Early Medieval France* (Ithaca, N.Y.: 1994).

44. Ó Corráin, "Nationality and Kingship," 1–35.

45. T. J. Jackson Lears, "The Concept of Cultural Hegemony: Problems and Possibilities," *American Historical Review* 90.3 (1985), 567–93, esp. 568.

46. As the Russian literary critic Mikhail Bakhtin put it for the novel, each text constitutes a cultural conversation between the authorial voice and other voices (or languages, social groups, or heteroglossia). See Mikhail Bakhtin, *The Dialogic Imagi-*

nation: Four Essays by M. M. Bakhtin, ed. Michael Holquist (Austin, Tex., 1981), esp. the fourth essay, "Discourse in the Novel." See also Joan Cadden, *The Meanings of Sex Difference in the Middle Ages: Medicine, Science, and Culture* (Cambridge, 1993), esp. 218–27, where she explains how the very diversity of ideas about sex and gender strengthened medieval gender constructs.

2. The Wisdom on Women

1. Gregory of Tours, *Historia francorum, MGH* Scriptorum rerum Merovingicarum 1, 8.20. See also Albert Demyttenaere, "The Cleric, Women, and the Stain: Some Beliefs and Ritual Practices Concerning Women in the Early Middle Ages," in Werner Affeldt and Ursula Vorwerk, eds., *Frauen in Spätantike und Frühmittelalter: Lebensbedingungen, Lebensnormen, Lebensformen* (Berlin, 1990), 141–45; Manfred P. Fleischer, "Are Women Human? The Debate of 1595," *Sixteenth-Century Journal* 12 (1981), 108–22.

2. The secondary literature on medieval European clerical attitudes toward women grows threateningly greater almost daily. Some standard contributions include Rosemary Ruether, ed., *Religion and Sexism: Images of Women in the Jewish and Christian Traditions* (New York, 1974); Wemple, *Women in Frankish Society,* esp. 19–25; Jacques Dalarun, "Regard des clercs," in Michelle Perrot and Georges Duby, gen. eds., *Histoire des femmes en occident,* vol. 2: *Le Moyen Age,* ed. Christiane Klapisch-Zuber (Paris, 1991), 31–54; Alcuin Blamires, ed., *Woman Defamed and Woman Defended: An Anthology of Medieval Texts* (Oxford, 1992).

3. Simone de Beauvoir posited that women in all societies are a passive, oppressed Other: *The Second Sex* (New York, 1949). However, this proposition is untrue of early Irish society as well as many other societies, as the subsequent debate on gender constructs has shown. Sherry B. Ortner, "Is Female to Male as Nature Is to Culture?" in M. Z. Rosaldo and Louise Lamphere, eds., *Woman, Culture, and Society* (Stanford, Calif., 1974), 67–88; Edwin Ardener, "Belief and the Problem of Women," and "The Problem Revisited," in Shirley Ardener, ed., *Perceiving Women* (London, 1972), 1–18, 19–28; Carol MacCormack and Marilyn Strathern, eds., *Nature, Culture, and Gender* (Cambridge, 1980); Peggy Reeves Sanday and Ruth Gallagher Goodenough, eds., *Beyond the Second Sex: New Directions in the Anthropology of Gender* (Philadelphia, 1990).

4. Kelly, *Guide,* 225–86.

5. Ibid., 68–79; also the more detailed articles in *SEIL.*

6. D. A. Binchy, ed. and trans. "Bretha Crólige," *Ériu* 12 (1938), 8 (7); *CIH,* 2288; *CA,* 24–27; Kelly, *Guide,* 83; Christopher McAll, "The Normal Paradigms of a Woman's Life in the Irish and Welsh Law Texts," in Dafydd Jenkins and Morfydd E. Owen, eds., *The Welsh Law of Women: Studies Presented to Professor Daniel A. Binchy* (Cardiff, 1980), 7. For a discussion of honor price, see Kelly, *Guide,* 8; also Charles-Edwards, *Early Irish and Welsh Kinship,* 25.

7. *CIH,* 777, 778; *CG,* 1–2 (ll. 23–46), 3–4 (ll. 63–86, 89–90); Kelly, *Guide,* 82; McAll, "Normal Paradigms of a Woman's Life," 7–8. See also Shulamith Shahar, *Childhood in the Middle Ages* (London, 1990), 21–31.

8. *CIH,* 519, 779; but see *CA,* 24–25, 26–31; Kelly, *Guide,* 79.

9. Pactus Legis Sal. 24. 8–9, *MGH* Legum Sectio I, 4/1. 92; Lex Rib. 12–13, *MGH* Legum Sectio I, 3/2, 78–79; Wemple, *Women in Frankish Society,* 28–29.

10. Katherine Walsh, "Scholarship and the Natural Sciences in Early Medieval Ireland," *Studies* 74 (1985): 214–15. Joan Cadden discusses the complex of ideas, scientific and other, that allowed later medieval Europeans to construct genders, but her references to Isidore and her general conclusions are directly relevant to the early Irish: *Meanings of Sex Difference,* esp. 169–227.

11. D. A. Binchy, ed. and trans., "Bretha Déin Chécht," *Ériu* 20 (1966), 1–66; Binchy, "Bretha Crólige," 24–25, 44–45; Lisa M. Bitel, " 'Conceived in Sins, Born in Delights': Stories of Procreation from Early Ireland," *Journal of the History of Sexuality* 3 (1992), 181–202; Penelope Johnson, *Equal in Monastic Profession: Religious Women in Medieval France* (Chicago, 1991), 54 n. 153.

12. Binchy, "Bretha Crólige," 10–11, 30–31, and see 58n.

13. Ibid., 30–33; see also Exodus 21:22.

14. Wemple, *Women in Frankish Society,* 29–30.

15. *CIH,* 502–504 = *ALI* 2:345; see also Kelly, *Guide,* 70; *SEIL,* 16–75.

16. Cf. Cormac, *Glossary,* 40 (Y473): "druth .i. merdreach"; *CIH,* 522, 536 = *ALI* 3:10, 58.

17. Everywhere in barbarian Europe women's legal and social positions depended upon those of their men. See Joel Rosenthal, "Anglo-Saxon Attitudes: Men's Sources, Women's History," in Joel T. Rosenthal, ed., *Medieval Women and the Sources of Medieval History* (Athens, Ga., 1990), 259–84; Herlihy, *Medieval Households,* 44–52; Mary P. Richards and B. Jane Stanfield, "Concepts of Anglo-Saxon Women in the Laws," in Helen Damico and Alexandra Hennessey Olsen, eds., *New Readings on Women in Old English Literature* (Bloomington, Ind., 1990), 89–99; Jo Ann McNamara and Suzanne Wemple, "The Power of Women through the Family in Medieval Europe, 500–1100," in Mary Erler and Maryanne Kowalski, eds., *Women and Power in the Middle Ages* (Athens, Ga., 1988), 83–101.

18. *CIH,* 538–39, 1890, 546–47, 1894–95, 41, 955, 1845 = *ALI* 5:176, 199, 203, 273. See also Binchy, "Bretha Crólige," 26–29; Meyer, *Triads,* 21 (160), 25 (185). According to early Irish laws and secular literature, satirizing someone with verbal assaults could not only damage the victim's reputation but also cause physical blemish or injury. See Kelly, *Guide,* 137–39; Rolf Baumgarten, ed., *Bibliography of Irish Linguistics and Literature, 1942–1971* (Dublin, 1986), 550.

19. One exception is the list of women excluded from sick maintenance, which includes the *rechtaid géill,* ruler entitled to hostages, glossed "such as was Medb of Cruachain": Binchy, "Bretha Crólige," 26–27 (32).

20. Kelly, *Guide,* 284–85; Meyer, *Triads,* v–xv.

21. Meyer, *Triads,* 16 (126).

22. Ibid., 24 (180; cf. 181). See also Kelly, *Guide,* 69.

23. Meyer, *Triads,* 8 (72, 73).

24. Ibid., 10 (87, 88).

25. Ibid., 12 (91), 32 (238); see also 12 (95), 16 (124).

26. Ibid., 20 (148).

27. Deuteronomy 23:18 suggests the connection among women, animals, and sexual pollution, but the connection is an intentionally created and specifically West-

ern concept. See the essays in MacCormack and Strathern, *Nature, Culture, and Gender,* especially MacCormack, "Nature, Culture, and Gender: A Critique," 1–14; and Strathern, "No Nature, No Culture: The Hagen Case," 174–222. See also Glenda McLeod, *Virtue and Venom: Catalogs of Women from Antiquity to the Renaissance* (Ann Arbor, Mich., 1991), 11–48.

28. Meyer, *Triads,* 10 (85); Bitel, *Isle of the Saints,* 32–35.

29. *CIH,* 9–11, 38, 41 = *ALI* 5:153–57, 261, 269.

30. *CIH,* 7–9, 151 = *ALI* 5:5, 141, 151. See also a Welsh analogue: S. J. Williams and J. E. Powell, eds., *Cyfreithiau Hywel Dda yn ôl Llyfr Blegywryd* (Cardiff, 1942; 2d ed. 1961), 116 (ll. 27–29); McAll, "Normal Paradigms of a Woman's Life," 21.

31. Some penitentialists allowed a husband to kill his wife and her lover caught *in flagrante delicto.* Ludwig Bieler, ed. and trans., *The Irish Penitentials* (Dublin, 1963), 138.

32. Kuno Meyer, ed. and trans., *The Instructions of King Cormac Mac Airt,* Todd Lecture Series 15 (Dublin, 1909), 35; the text also calls women "waves," "fire," "weapons," "leeches," "serpents," and "darkness."

33. Tomás Ó Cathasaigh, "The Semantics of *Síd,*" *Éigse* 17 (1977–78), 127–54; Patrick Sims-Williams, "Some Celtic Otherworld Terms," 57–81.

34. Myles Dillon, ed., *Serglige Con Culainn* (Repr. Dublin, 1975), 2–3; Charles Plummer, ed. and trans., *Bethada Náem nÉrenn* (Oxford, 1922), 1:81–83, 2:79–80. Dobarchú's story has a specific etymological purpose, but this does not affect its use of the shapeshifter motif. See also O'Rahilly, *Táin Bó Cúailnge,* 57, trans. 176–77; Eleanor Knott, ed., *Togail Bruidne Da Derga* (Repr. Dublin, 1975), 3.

35. O'Rahilly, *Táin Bó Cúailnge,* 64–67, trans. 184–85. For the literature of *immrama,* sea journeys to the otherworld, see Kathleen Hughes, *Early Christian Ireland: An Introduction to the Sources* (Ithaca, N.Y., 1973), 210–16; Alwyn Rees and Brinley Rees, *Celtic Heritage* (London, 1961), 314–25; James Carney, *Studies in Early Irish Literature and History* (Dublin, 1955), 276–323; David Dumville, "Echtrae and Immram: Some Problems of Definition," *Ériu* 27 (1976), 73–94.

36. Lisa M. Bitel, "*In Visu Noctis:* Dreams in Early Medieval Hagiography and Histories, 500–900," *History of Religions* 31 (1991), 39–59. See also David N. Dumville, "The World of the *Síd* and the Attitude of the Narrator in *Táin bó Fraích,*" *Studia Celtica Japonica* 7 (1995), 21–25.

37. John Carey, "The Location of the Otherworld in Irish Tradition," *Éigse* 19 (1982), 36–43.

38. John Carey, "Sequence and Causation in *Echtrae Nerai,*" *Ériu* 39 (1988), 67–74; Carey, "Time, Space, and the Otherworld," *PHCC* 7 (1987), 1–27.

39. Proinsias Mac Cana, "The Sinless Otherworld of *Immram Brain,*" *Ériu* 27 (1976), 95–115; but see also Carney, *Studies in Early Irish Literature and History,* 1–65. The otherworld as abundant, peaceable kingdom of pleasure-seeking immortals appears in *Echtrae Chonlai,* where it is represented by a seductive woman and called *tír béo,* land of the living. See H. P. A. Oskamp, ed. and trans., "Echtra Condla," *ÉC* 14 (1974), 212, 221.

40. As Joseph Nagy has repeatedly pointed out to me, Étaín of *Tochmarc Étaíne* may be the exception. She is described as a woman of the Ulaid when the otherworldly Mider takes her in *lánamnas,* and he does eventually woo her to the other-

world. However, Étaín's multiple transformations and rebirth suggest that she is not your ordinary Ulsterwoman. Several Celticists have identified her with other Étaíns and interpreted her as a sovereignty or fertility figure, for example, Christian-J. Guyonvarc'h, *Textes mythologiques irlandais* (Rennes, 1980), 1:43: "Etain n'est ni légère ni 'amoureuse' au sens humain du terme, elle est la Souveraineté, divinité féminine unique, épouse polyandre des dieux souverains." See also McCone, *Pagan Past and Christian Present,* 110–13; Proinsias Mac Cana, *Celtic Mythology* (Repr. Feltham, Middlesex, 1986), 90–92.

41. Dillon, *Serglige Con Culainn;* O'Rahilly, *Táin Bó Cúailnge,* 57, 61–63, trans. 176–77, 180–82. Male seducers from the otherworld also took animal or bird form.

42. Frances Shaw, ed., *Aislinge Oenguso* (Dublin, 1934); Dillon, *Serglige Con Culainn;* Kuno Meyer, ed., "Echtra Nerai," *RC* 10 (1889): 212–28.

43. Oskamp, "Echtra Condla," esp. 225, 228, where the otherworld is described: "Ní fil cenél ann nammá acht mná 7 ingena," "No people are there save women and maidens"; A. G. Van Hamel, ed., *Immrama* (Dublin, 1941), 18 (62); Mac Cana, "Sinless Otherworld of *Immram Brain,*" 110–13; Doan, *Women and Goddesses,* 58–61. But see also McCone, *Pagan Past and Christian Present,* 79–80.

44. As in *Echtrae Chonlai,* where the seductress steals a king's son, for Conla, the choice is between a people whom he loves ("ní réid dam sech caraim mo daini") and the woman for whom he longs and her promise of immortality ("rom gab dono eulcaire immon mnaí"): Oskamp, "Echtra Condla," 224, 227.

45. See Carey, "Location of the Otherworld," 36–43; Bitel, "*In Visu Noctis.*"

46. Knott, *Togail Bruidne Da Derga,* 1–2; trans. in Jeffrey Gantz, *Early Irish Myths and Sagas* (Repr. New York, 1985), 62–63.

47. In one Middle Irish tale, a *síd* woman seduces, charms, and kills the king by her magic. See Lil Nic Dhonnchadha, *Aided Muirchertaig Meic Erca* (Dublin, 1964); trans. Whitley Stokes, "The Death of Muirchertach mac Erca," *RC* 23 (1902): 395–437. On the date of the story, which is probably older than its manuscript forms, see introductions to both versions.

48. Roland Mitchell Smith, "The *Speculum Principum* in Early Irish Literature," *Speculum* 2 (1927), 411–45; McCone, *Pagan Past and Christian Present,* 31, 121–26, 140–43. For editions of *tecosca,* see Kelly, *Guide,* 284–86; also Fergus Kelly, ed., *Audacht Morainn* (Dublin, 1976); Meyer, *Instructions of Cormac;* R. I. Best, M. A. O'Brien, and Anne O'Sullivan, eds., *The Book of Leinster* (Dublin, 1954–83), 6:1503–23.

49. Blamires, *Woman Defamed and Woman Defended,* 1–82; McLeod, *Virtue and Venom,* 35–46.

50. Fíthal is identified in James Carney, ed. and trans., "Nia Son of Lugna Fer Trí," *Éigse* 2 (1940), 192.

51. Roland M. Smith, ed. and trans., "The *Senbriathra Fithail* and Related Texts," *RC* 45 (1928), 53. See also E. J. Gwynn's corrections to Smith: "*Senbriathra Fithail,*" *RC* 46 (1929), 268–71; and Roland M. Smith, "Fithal and Flann Fina," *RC* 47 (1930), 30–38.

52. Proverbs 31.

53. Meyer, *Instructions of Cormac,* 28–34; *Can. Hib.,* 187; *CIH* 538 = *ALI* 5:177.

54. Smith, "*Senbriathra Fithail,*" 52; see also Meyer, *Triads,* 10 (86).

55. Smith, "*Senbriathra Fithail,*" 53–57.

56. Ibid., 58. See also commentary on the *Heptads* in *CIH* 42 (ll. 10–12) = *ALI* 5:274.

57. Smith, "*Senbriathra Fithail,*" 55.

58. Ibid., 56. These categories echoed secular narratives. Deirdriu, a famous femme fatale of saga, was described as "bé find fota foltlebor," "a fair tall long-haired woman." See Best and O'Brien, *Book of Leinster* 5:1163, l. 34343.

59. Smith, "*Senbriathra Fithail,*" 57–58.

60. Ibid., 58–59.

61. Meyer, *Instructions of Cormac,* 38–39.

62. Ibid., 32–33.

63. Kuno Meyer, ed. and trans., *Hail Brigit: An Old-Irish Poem on the Hill of Alenn* (Dublin, 1912); trans. by P. L. Henry, *Dánta Ban: Poems of Irish Women, Early and Modern* (Cork, 1991), 47; F. E. Warren, ed. and trans., *The Antiphonary of Bangor* (London, 1895), pt. 2, 28; "Brigit Bé Bithmaith," in Whitley Stokes, ed. and trans., *Lives of the Saints from the Book of Lismore* (Oxford 1890), 51–52, 198–99, 332–34. See also James Good, "The Mariology of the Early Irish Church," *Irish Ecclesiastical Record* 100 (1963): 73–79; Peter O'Dwyer, *Mary: A History of Devotion in Ireland* (Dublin, 1988), 32–72.

64. For example, Ambrose, *De Cain et Abel* 1, 4, where he argues that Rebecca carried within her the seeds of both good and evil; Jerome, *Epistolae,* 130, 17; both cited in Ruether, "Virginal Feminism in the Fathers of the Church," in Ruether, ed., *Religion and Sexism,* 181.

65. Eriugena thought that the distinction between male and female would disappear at the Resurrection, when each good Christian would arise as *homo: Periphiseon* V, in *PL* 122:893. He followed a well-established theological tradition; see Carolyn Bynum, *The Resurrection of the Body in Western Christianity, 200–1336* (New York, 1994), 143–46; Ruether, "Virginal Feminism," 160–61; Peter Brown, *The Body and Society: Men, Women, and Sexual Renunciation in Early Christianity* (New York, 1988), 382–84.

66. Kelly, *Guide,* 231–50; Donnchadh Ó Corráin, Liam Breatnach, and Aidan Breen, "The Laws of the Irish," *Peritia* 3 (1984), 382–438; Liam Breatnach, "Canon Law and Secular Law in Early Ireland: The Significance of *Bretha Nemed,*" *Peritia* 3 (1984), 439–59; Ó Corráin, "Irish Law and Canon Law," in Proinséas Ní Chatháin and Michael Richter, eds., *Irland und Europa: Die Kirche im Frühmittelalter* (Stuttgart, 1984), 157–66.

67. *Can. Hib.,* 191–92. Isidore, *Etymologiarum Libri XX,* ed. W. M. Lindsay (Oxford, 1911), 11.1.141, 148; 11.2.17; 20.2.18, 22. See also *CIH,* 504, which derives *fer* from *virtus* and *ben* from *bonum*.

68. *Can. Hib.,* 180.

69. Ibid.

70. McLeod, *Virtue and Venom,* 39–47.

71. *Can. Hib.,* 185, 187.

72. Ibid., 180–81; Bieler, *Penitentials,* 76–77, 160–61.

73. Kuno Meyer, ed. and trans., "Eve's Lament," *Ériu* 3 (1907), 148; trans. Henry, *Dánta Ban,* 81.

74. Brown, *Body and Society,* esp. 241–84; Joyce E. Salisbury, "Latin Doctors of the Church on Sexuality," *Journal of Medieval History* 12 (1986), 279–90; Vern L. Bullough, "Formation of Medieval Ideals: Christian Theory and Christian Practice," in Bullough and James Brundage, eds., *Sexual Practices and the Medieval Church* (Buffalo, N.Y., 1982), 14–21; Jo Ann McNamara, "Chaste Marriage and Clerical Celibacy," in Bullough and Brundage, *Sexual Practices,* 22–33.

75. Kuno Meyer, ed. and trans., "Daniel Húa Liathaide's Advice to a Woman," *Ériu* 1 (1904), 67–71; Best and O'Brien, *Book of Leinster* 5:1221.

76. *Can. Hib.,* 28.

77. Ibid., 184.

78. Ibid., 175.

79. Ibid., 183.

80. Bieler, *Penitentials,* 92–93, 116–17, 222–23; *Can. Hib.,* 187–88; Brundage, *Law, Sex, and Christian Society,* 160–63.

81. Bieler, *Penitentials,* 56, 70, 76–78, 86–88, 116, 222.

82. Lisa Bitel, "Women's Monastic Enclosures in Early Ireland: A Study in Female Spirituality and Male Monastic Mentalities," *Journal of Medieval History* 12 (1986), 32–33; Bieler, *Penitentials,* 70 (5, 11), 72 (15), 88 (37), 116 (24), 222 (5, 6). The exception is 56 (17).

83. Plummer, *Bethada* 1:47 (19); Plummer, *Vitae* 2:119; but cf. *FO,* 44–45, where Íte nurses Jesus.

84. Donncha Ó hAodha, ed. and trans., *Bethu Brigte* (Dublin, 1978), 4–5, trans. 23. See also the case of Orbile, USMLS, "The Life of St. Monenna by Conchubranus," I, *Seanchas Ard Mhacha* 9 (1979), 258–61.

85. USMLS, "Life of St. Monenna," I, 258–61; E. J. Gwynn and W. J. Purton, eds. and trans., "The Monastery of Tallaght," *PRIA* 29 C (1911), 149, 150–51.

86. Ludwig Bieler, ed. and trans., *Patrician Texts in the Book of Armagh* (Dublin, 1979), 142–45; *VT,* 98–104; W. W. Heist, ed., *Vitae Sanctorum Hiberniae,* Subsidia Hagiographica 28 (Brussels, 1965), 109, 141; Plummer, *Vitae* 2:61. See also Heist, *Vitae,* 172–73, 223, 394; Plummer, *Vitae* 1:38; Plummer, *Bethada* 1:164–65; cf. Bieler, *Penitentials,* 188: "A dead body does not harm another's dead body."

87. *Can. Hib.,* 183.

88. Bieler, *Patrician Texts,* 98–101; Heist, *Vitae,* 109, 141; Plummer, *Vitae* 2:61; Jo Ann McNamara, "Living Sermons: Consecrated Women and the Conversion of Gaul," in John A. Nichols and Lillian Thomas Shank, eds., *Medieval Religious Women,* vol. 2: *Peaceweavers* (Kalamazoo, Mich., 1987), 19–37.

89. Kirsten Hastrup, "The Semantics of Biology: Virginity," in Shirley Ardener, ed., *Defining Females: The Nature of Women in Society* (London, 1978); Hastrup, "The Sexual Boundary—Purity: Heterosexuality and Virginity," *Anthropological Society of Oxford* 5 (1974), 137–47.

90. Cf. Brigitte Bedos-Rezak, "Medieval Women in French Sigillographic Sources," in Rosenthal, *Medieval Women and the Sources of Medieval History,* 10–11.

91. The exception was men's co-opting of procreative powers. See Bitel, "Conceived in Sins"; also Roberta Valente, "Gwydion and Aranrhod: Crossing the Borders of Gender in *Math,*" *Bulletin of the Board of Celtic Studies* 35 (1988), 1–9.

92. For one saintly example, Plummer, *Bethada* 1:47 (10–11), 2:47.

93. Meyer, *Instructions of Cormac*, 28–29 (l. 21). See also *Aided Oenfir Aífe*, in which Cú Chulainn needs no advice from his wife, in A. G. Van Hamel, ed., *Compert Con Culainn and Other Stories* (Repr. Dublin, 1968), 14 (9): "Coisc, a ben! . . ." See also Whitley Stokes and Ernst Windisch, eds., *Irische Texte mit Übersetzungen und Wörterbuch*, 3d ser. (Leipzig, 1897), 1:123 (from Egerton 1782, l. 18): "ni dat maithe banruna."

94. Rudolf Thurneysen, ed., *Scéla Mucce Meic Dathó* (Repr. Dublin, 1975); trans. Gantz, *Early Irish Myths and Sagas*, 179–87.

3. *The Canon of Coupling*

1. David Greene and Frank O'Connor, eds. and trans., *A Golden Treasury of Irish Poetry, A.D. 600 to 1200* (London, 1967), 111–14, 202–3.

2. Suzanne Wemple suggests that Germanic barbarians distinguished among love, sex, and formal marriage, rarely linking all three. See *Women in Frankish Society*, esp. 12–15. Historians' discussions of gender relations in early Ireland, as well as supposedly more general discussions of women, tend to focus on formal legal relationships of marriage and concubinage. See Kelly, *Guide*, 70–75; Donnchadh Ó Corráin, "Marriage in Early Ireland," in Art Cosgrove, ed., *Marriage in Ireland* (Dublin, 1985), 5–24; Nancy Power, "Classes of Women Described in the *Senchas Mar*," in *SEIL*, 81–108; D. A. Binchy, "The Legal Capacity of Women in Regard to Contracts," in *SEIL*, 207–34; Ó Corráin, "Women in Early Irish Society," 2–8; Wendy Davies, "Celtic Women in the Early Middle Ages," in Averil Cameron and Amelie Kuhrt, eds., *Images of Women in Antiquity* (Detroit, 1983), 153–57; D. B. Walters, "The European Legal Context of the Welsh Law of Matrimony and Property," in Jenkins and Owen, *Welsh Law of Women*, 115–31; McAll, "Normal Paradigms of a Woman's Life"; T. M. Charles-Edwards, "Nau Kynywedi Teithiauc," in Jenkins and Owen, *Welsh Law of Women*, 23–39. The exception, with its own unique biases, is Condren, *The Serpent and the Goddess*, esp. 79–94.

3. *CIH*, 502–19; *Can. Hib.*, 185–95. See also Charles-Edwards, *Early Irish and Welsh Kinship*, 462–63, where he discusses the nonjural "fact" (rather than jural relationship) of Irish sexual unions.

4. *CIH*, 1117.

5. At least one penitentialist insisted that both bride and groom give prior consent to the union; see Bieler, *Penitentials*, 184. This position is consistent with that of later medieval canonists on the Continent; see James Brundage, *Law, Sex, and Christian Society in Medieval Europe* (Chicago, 1987), 92, 94, 236–38. See also Jenny Jochens, "Consent in Marriage: Old Norse Law, Life, and Literature," *Scandinavian Studies* 58 (1986), 142–76; Jochens, "'Med Jákvæði Hennar Sjálfrar'": Consent as Signifier in the Old Norse World," in Angeliki Laiou, ed., *Consent and Coercion to Sex and Marriage in Ancient and Medieval Societies* (Washington, D.C., Dumbarton Oaks, 1993), 271–87.

6. *CG*, 2, ll. 30–34, describes the legal actions of a family on behalf of a male minor; see also McAll, "Normal Paradigms," 8.

7. Cf. the *Triads:* Three "sparks that kindle love" are "face, bearing, speech." Meyer, *Triads,* 10. The motif of love-by-rumor is extremely well attested in the early Irish narratives. See, for just a few examples, R. I. Best, ed. and trans., "The Adventures of Art Son of Conn and the Courtship of Delbchaem," *Ériu* 3 (1907), 152; Liam Breatnach, ed., "Tochmarc Luaine ocus Aided Athairne," *Celtica* 13 (1980), 6–10; Carl Marstrander, ed. and trans., "The Deaths of Lugaid and Derbforgaill," *Ériu* 5 (1911), 208; Best and O'Brien, *Book of Leinster* 5:1164 (34388–94).

8. William G. Lockwood, "Bride-Theft and Social Maneuverability in West Bosnia," *Anthropological Quarterly* 47.3 (1974), 267.

9. No such scenes remain in the literature, although there are scenes in which the allies or retainers of a king discuss or criticize his choice of mate. See, for example, Máire Bhreathnach, ed. and trans., "A New Edition of *Tochmarc Becfhola,*" *Ériu* 35 (1984), 72, 81; Best and O'Brien, *Book of Leinster* 5:1164: "Marbthar ind ingen ar ind óic" (34380).

10. *Can. Hib.,* 46 (sec. 16); *CIH,* 189–90, 725–26, cited in Ó Corráin, "Marriage in Early Ireland," 18–20.

11. *CIH,* 25 = *ALI* 5:214: "coibce mna nad urnuidet" glossed as "coibce doberar don mnai nad hurnaidenn gu dligtech .i. int urnaidm nidnaide no urnaidm ar adhall." See also *CIH,* 47 = *ALI* 5:292; Adomnán, *Adomnán's Life of Columba,* ed. A. O. Anderson and M. O. Anderson (London, 1961), 436–40, for an unusual example of such an arranged union; Kelly, *Guide,* 71 n. 21.

12. *CIH,* 294 = *ALI* 3:314. See also Kelly, *Guide,* 71–73; Charles-Edwards, *Early Irish and Welsh Kinship,* 463–69; Patterson, *Cattle-Lords and Clansmen,* 266–67. Still the best discussion of marriage exchanges is Diane Owen Hughes, "From Brideprice to Dowry in Mediterranean Europe," *Journal of Family History* 3 (1978), 262–96.

13. *CIH,* 1235–37; Kelly, *Guide,* 72; McAll, "Normal Paradigms," 11; Ó Corráin, "Marriage in Early Ireland," 15–16; *SEIL,* 112–25.

14. On betrothal, see Charles-Edwards, *Early Irish and Welsh Kinship,* 315; *SEIL,* 112–25. On guardianship, see the *díre* text at *CIH,* 443–44; trans. Kelly, *Guide,* 76. On exceptions, see *CIH,* 515–16; see also Wemple, *Women in Frankish Society,* 29–31.

15. Wemple, *Women in Frankish Society,* 33.

16. Breatnach, "Tochmarc Luaine," 12–13.

17. Bieler, *Penitentials,* 196; *Can. Hib.,* 189.

18. Ó Corráin, "Marriage in Early Ireland," 15. See also Wemple, *Women in Frankish Society,* 35. See also *CIH,* 515 = *ALI* 2:390 (*SEIL,* 56), which suggests temporary unions.

19. Kelly, *Guide,* 72–73; but see *Can. Hib.,* 185: *dotata legitime.* See also Ó Corráin, "Marriage in Early Ireland," 17; Patterson, *Cattle-Lords and Clansmen,* 281–83.

20. *DIL,* 28. By extension, *banais* came to be used for the inaugural feasts of kings and for feasts or celebrations generally. See Proinsias Mac Cana, "Aspects of the Theme of King and Goddess in Early Irish Literature," *ÉC* 7 (1955–56), 85–86.

21. *Can. Hib.,* 185: "evangelium publicis nuptiis"; Ó Corráin, "Marriage in Early Ireland," 14.

22. Plummer, *Vitae* 2:78. See also Máirín O Daly, ed. and trans., *Cath Maige Mucrama* (Dublin, 1975), 66–67, for the exchange between Art Mac Cuinn and the daughter of Olc Aiche.

23. Kuno Meyer, ed., "Scél Baili Binnbérlaig," *RC* 13 (1892), 223.

24. Proinsias Mac Cana, *The Learned Tales of Medieval Ireland* (Dublin, 1980), esp. 74–75, 78. For an extended analysis of the folkloric import of "wooings" and "elopements," see Rees and Rees, *Celtic Heritage*, 259–95, esp. 291. Vincent Dunn interprets *tána* (cattle raids) and *tochmarca* as related treatments of the theme of initiation. He argues (222–23) that the stories lost relevance as behavioral models when they became amalgamated into a formal cycle of written stories, and as their audience began to "misunderstand" them: Vincent A. Dunn, *Cattle-Raids and Courtships: Medieval Narrative Genres in a Traditional Context* (New York, 1989).

25. Bhreathnach, "A New Edition of *Tochmarc Becfhola*." Earlier editions are Bryon O'Looney, "Tochmarc Bec-Fola," *PRIA*, Mss. Series 1, 1 (1870), 172–83; Standish O'Grady, ed., *Silva Gadelica* (London, 1892), 1:85–87, 2:91–83. See also Myles Dillon, "The Wooing of Becfhola and the Stories of Cano Son of Gartnan," *Modern Philology* 43 (1945), 11–17.

26. Cf. Suithchern's response: Gearóid Mac Eoin, "Suithchern and Rónán Dícolla," *ZCP* 36 (1978), 67; cited in Bhreathnach, "A New Edition of *Tochmarc Becfhola*," 64 n. 35.

27. Nic Dhonnchadha, *Aided Muirchertaig Meic Erca*.

28. Breatnach, "Tochmarc Luaine," 9–10; Whitley Stokes, "The Wooing of Luaine and Death of Athirne," *RC* 24 (1903): 274. See also Wolfgang Meid, ed., *Táin Bó Fraích* (Repr. Dublin, 1974), 1.

29. "Tochmarc Emire," in Van Hamel, *Compert Con Culainn*, 16–68, esp. 23–24; R. I. Best and Osbern Bergin, eds., *Lebor na hUidre* (Dublin, 1929), 307–19. The same convention occurred in Icelandic narratives: Jenny Jochens, "The Illicit Love Visit: An Archaeology of Old Norse Sexuality," *Journal of the History of Sexuality* 1 (1991): 357–92.

30. Van Hamel, *Compert Con Culainn*, 31; see Thomas Kinsella's loose but apt translation, in *The Tain* (Oxford, 1970), 27. Note that Cú Chulainn is offered Emer's older sister but refuses her because of a rumor that she has been the lover of another man. Emer's virginity is clearly part of the marriage bargain.

31. Meid, *Táin Bó Fraích*, x–xvi.

32. *Táin Bó Fraích* is translated in Gantz, *Early Irish Myths and Sagas*, 114–26. Meid and others see a late Middle Irish tale, *Tochmarc Treblainne*, as a double of the first half of *Táin Bó Fraích*. In that tale, Fráech loves Treblainne, a fosterling of Coirpre mac Rosa Ruaid, who forbids her marriage to Fráech on the grounds that she could make a better match. Treblainne sends word that she is willing to elope. Fráech eventually wins her by force, but Treblainne then dies on account of Coirpre's revenge, although she seems to end happily with Fráech in the *síd*. Kuno Meyer, ed., "Tochmarc Treblainne," *ZCP* 13 (1921), 166–75; Carney, *Studies in Early Irish Literature and History* 206–10.

33. Best, "Adventures of Art Son of Conn," 149–73; Best and Bergin, *Lebor na hUidre*, 323–32. Although the earliest version of the tale exists in a twelfth-century manuscript, the story I have paraphrased comes from the fifteenth-century Book of Fermoy, and is late in style and narrative convention; however, its title, *Echtra Airt*, is included in the earlier tale lists: Mac Cana, *Learned Tales*, 53.

34. Dunn, *Cattle-Raids and Courtships*, 69–96.

35. Kuno Meyer, ed. and trans., "Reicne Fothaid Canainne," in Meyer, ed., *Fianaigecht*, Todd Lecture Series 16 (Dublin, 1910), 1–9; Vernam Hull, ed. and trans., "The Death of Fothath Canainne," *ZCP* 20 (1936), 400–404.

36. Best and Bergin, *Lebor na hUidre*, 331; Gantz, *Early Irish Myths*, 56.

37. A late Middle Irish story similar in some of its themes is *Serc Duibe-Lacha do Mongán* (Dubhlacha's love for Mongán), which tells how Mongán, the semi-supernatural son of Manannán mac Lir, unthinkingly trades his wife to Brandub mac Echach, king of Leinster, for some very nice cattle. Through a variety of tricks, including Mongán's shapeshifting, love charms, and Dubhlacha's sharp negotiating with Brandub, Mongán eventually wins her back. The story is full of jokes and erotic touches. See Kuno Meyer, ed., *The Voyage of Bran, Son of Febal, to the Land of the Living* (London, 1895), 1:58–84.

38. Illicit love of various sorts also had disastrous effects in Norse literature. Jochens, "Illict Love Visit," 357–92.

39. E. J. Gwynn, ed., *The Metrical Dindsenchas*, Todd Lecture Series 8–12 (Dublin, 1913–35), 3:18 (l. 225), modified trans.; Mac Cana, *Learned Tales*, 74.

40. Nessa Ní Shéaghdha, ed., *Tóruigheacht Dhiarmada agus Ghráinne* (Dublin, 1967); Joseph Falaky Nagy, *The Wisdom of the Outlaw: The Boyhood Deeds of Finn in Gaelic Narrative Tradition* (Berkeley, 1985), 73–74. The tale of Diarmaid and Gráinne exists only in early modern form, although it derives from a tenth-century or earlier tale; see Mac Cana, *Learned Tales*, 40. The elopement of Fothad Canainne with another man's wife also causes *fíana*, war bands, to clash and Fothad to lose his head (which does not stop the head from singing a lament). See Meyer, "Reicne Fothaid Canainne," 1–21.

41. Mac Eoin, "Suithchern and Rónán Dícolla," 63–82, points out that the original *Aided Cuanach Meic Ailchine* was probably a tenth-century tale derived from others, listed in the late lists as *Nemain Fír Móire Muman* and *Aided Ruithcheirne la Cuana Mac Cailchín*; T. P. O'Nolan, ed. and trans., "Mór of Munster and the Tragic Fate of Cuanu Son of Cailchín," *PRIA* 30 C (1912–13), 261–82. See also Mac Cana, "Aspects of the Theme of King and Goddess," 91–114; Seán Ó Coileáin, "The Structure of a Literary Cycle," *Ériu* 25 (1974), 88–125, esp. 114–25.

42. Best and O'Brien, *Book of Leinster* 5:1162–70. See also Mac Cana, *Learned Tales*, 46.

43. The translation in Kinsella, *Táin*, 9–11, is evocative although not exact; Best and O'Brien, *Book of Leinster* 5:1163–64.

44. Best and O'Brien, *Book of Leinster* 5:1164–65; Kinsella, *Táin*, 12.

45. But see Máire Herbert's interpretation: "Celtic Heroine? The Archaeology of the Deirdre Story," in Toni O'Brien Johnson and David Cairns, eds., *Gender in Irish Writing* (Philadelphia, 1991), 13–22.

46. Máire Herbert, "The Universe of Male and Female: A Reading of the Deirdre Story," in Cyril J. Byrne et al., eds., *Celtic Languages and Celtic Peoples*, Proceedings of the Second North American Congress of Celtic Studies (Halifax, 1989), 54–64.

47. Best and O'Brien, *Book of Leinster* 5:1168; Kinsella, *Táin*, 17. See also Maria Tymoczko, "Animal Imagery in *Loinges mac nUislenn*," *Studia Celtica* 20–21 (1985–86), 145–66.

48. A similar situation in Scandinavian literature occurred in the depiction of women's consent to marriage. Jochens, "Consent as Signifier," 271–89.

49. D. A. Binchy, ed., *Scéla Cano Meic Gartnáin* (Dublin, 1963), represents a variation on the elopement theme in which the lovers Cano and Créd arrange a tryst, escape another jealous suitor of Créd, but eventually come to bad ends. The key event seems to be a feast at which Créd hands around drugged drink to everyone but Cano, giving herself the opportunity to initiate the affair.

50. Dillon, *Serglige Con Culainn.*

51. O'Rahilly, *Táin Bó Cúailnge,* 79: "comaidom sliasaid-sea"; Kinsella, *Tain,* 169. See also Joseph O'Neill, ed. and trans., "Cath Bóinde," *Ériu* 2 (1905), 174–85; Ó Máille, "Medb Cruachna"; Marie-Louise Sjoestedt, *Gods and Heroes of the Celts* (London, 1949), 233–34; Mac Cana, *Celtic Mythology,* 84–86.

52. O'Neill, "Cath Bóinde," 182.

53. Kuno Meyer, ed. and trans., *Liadain and Cuirithir: An Irish Love Story of the Ninth Century* (London, 1902); trans. Henry, *Dánta Ban,* 52–59.

54. R. A. Stewart Macalister, ed. and trans., *Lebor Gabála Érenn,* part 3 (Dublin, 1940), 62–71.

55. Herbert, "Celtic Heroine," esp. 16–21.

56. O'Rahilly, *Táin Bó Cúailnge,* 8; Van Hamel, *Compert Con Culainn,* 50–51, 55.

57. "Esnada Tige Buchet," in David Greene, ed., *Fingal Rónáin and Other Stories* (Dublin, 1955), 27–44. The fornication in the story, while an important plot device and symbol of all sorts of political events and ideals, had no deeper social meaning beyond the consummation of the coupling and the procreation of a famous heir. See also the case of Finnabair, offered to and taken by a series of warriors in the *Táin.*

58. O'Neill, "Cath Bóinde," 174. See also Plummer, *Vitae* 1:65.

59. Plummer, *Vitae* 2:4, 121; Heist, *Vitae,* 350.

60. Ó Corráin, "Marriage in Early Ireland," 1; *SEIL,* 85–86; Kelly, *Guide,* 70–71; Mac Cana, "Sinless Otherworld of *Immraim Brain.*"

61. Lisa Bitel, "Sex, Sin, and Celibacy in Early Christian Ireland," *PHCC* 7 (1987), 67–68.

62. On *adaltrach: CIH,* 7–8 = *ALI* 5:142–44, 1296, 1847 = *ALI* 5:286; Binchy, "Bretha Crólige," 44. On monogamy: *Can. Hib.,* 185–87, 189–90. On the marriage of man and *cétmuinter: CIH,* 505, 1483, 2301; Kelly, *Guide,* 70–72; Ó Corráin, "Marriage in Early Ireland," 10–11; Bitel, "Sex, Sin, and Celibacy," 78–80.

63. *CIH,* 505 = *ALI* 2:357: "fer tathaigte cen urgram cen urail cen tarcud cen tinol lanamnas foxail lanamnas amsa for faeniul lanamnas fothla lanamnas ecne lanamnus genaige."

64. *CIH,* 505, 518. See also Power, "Classes of Women," 88–90; Rebecca Colman, "The Abduction of Women in Barbarian Law," *Florilegium* 5 (1983), 62–75.

65. See the special issue of *Anthropological Quarterly* 47.3 (1974): "Kidnapping and Elopement as Alternative Systems of Marriage," especially the introduction by Daniel Bates, Francis Conant, and Ayse Kudat; Barbara Ayres, "Bride-Theft and Raiding for Wives in Cross-Cultural Perspective," 238–52; Lockwood, "Bride-Theft and Social Maneuverability," 253–49; Jan Bruckman, "Stealing Women among the Koya of Southern India," 304–13.

66. *CIH,* 1296; Kelly, *Guide,* 102–103; *SEIL,* 94–95.

67. Bieler, *Pententials,* 102, 115, 220–22.

68. *CIH,* 21–22, 31, 232, 442, 2194; Kelly, *Guide,* 6, 85–86, 102–3. The eighth-century *Críth Gablach* insists on marriage between those of the same class. *CG,* 8 (ll. 198–200). See also Patterson, *Cattle-Lords and Clansmen,* 259.

69. Although the laws refer to a secondary wife as *adaltrach,* she is a legitimate secondary wife or formal concubine, sometimes taken even when a man had no primary wife (*cétmuinter*): *CIH,* 7–8 = *ALI* 5:142–44. On the legal definition of incest, see Charles-Edwards, *Early Irish and Welsh Kinship,* 315–16.

70. *Can. Hib.,* 46 (sec. 8–10); *CIH,* 4 = *ALI* 4:132; *CIH,* 47 = *ALI* 5:292; *CIH,* 2198; Kelly, *Guide,* 73–75; Bitel, "Sex, Sin, and Celibacy," 76, 77–79.

71. Bieler, *Penitentials,* 56, 90, 100, 102, 104, 116, 222; but see also 194.

72. Joan Radner, ed. and trans., *The Fragmentary Annals of Ireland* (Dublin, 1978), 132–33; James Doan, "Sovereignty Aspects in the Roles of Women in Medieval Irish and Welsh Society," *PHCC* 5 (1985):90–91.

73. Cf. the confusing situation at 838, 840, where another Gormflaith, married to another Uí Néill king was kidnapped by another Munster king: Seán Mac Airt, ed. and trans. *The Annals of Inisfallen* (Repr. Dublin, 1977), 128. The literature on Gormflaith, wife of Níall Glúndub, is extensive. See W. Ann Trindade, "Irish Gormlaith as a Sovereignty Figure," *ÉC* 23 (1986), 143–56, esp. the notes.

74. Bitel, "Sex, Sin, and Celibacy," 78. Germanic laws take a varied stand on men divorcing for no good reason but generally agree that adulteresses and women who want divorces be punished severely, often with death. The Burgundian code, for instance, suggested that a woman who left her husband be "smothered in the mire." See Katherine Fisher Drew, *The Burgundian Code* (Repr. Philadelphia, 1988), 45.

75. Bieler, *Penitentials,* 68, 70, 102, 114, 194, 196, 220; *Can. Hib.,* 46 (35).

76. The incestuous origin of heroes was a standard motif in Irish king-tales. See Best and O'Brien, *Book of Leinster* 3:539 (37620–24), explained in Max Nettlau, "On the Irish Text *Togail Bruidne Da Derga* and Connected Stories," *RC* 12 (1891):237; Whitley Stokes, ed., *Cóir Anmann,* in Stokes and Windisch, *Irische Texte* 2:333; see also Rees and Rees, *Celtic Heritage,* 233–35. Such a tradition surrounded Saint Cuimmíne Fota; see *FO,* 242; Gearóid Mac Eoin, ed. and trans., "A Life of Cumaine Fota," *Béaloideas* 39–41 (1971–73), 198, 201; M. A. O'Brien, *Corpus Genealogiarum Hiberniae* (Repr. Dublin, 1976), 226:15; Ó Coileáin, "Structure of a Literary Cycle," 93–95.

77. *CIH,* 744 (l. 28); Kelly, *Guide,* 220–21. For references to infanticide or abandonment, see also Heist, *Vitae,* 118, 219–20; Plummer, *Vitae* 1:183, 250, 2:18; *FO,* 180, 242; Plummer, *Bethada* 1:30, 40, 2:29, 39; Gantz, *Early Irish Myths and Sagas,* 64; *CIH,* 2198; *Can. Hib.,* 180–81; Bieler, *Penitentials,* 76, 160. See also John T. Noonan, *Contraception: A History of Its Treatment by the Catholic Theologians and Canonists* (Cambridge, Mass., 1965), 161. Infanticide does not seem to have been gender-specific in early Ireland. But see Emily R. Coleman, "Infanticide in the Early Middle Ages," in Susan Stuard, ed., *Women in Medieval Society* (Philadelphia, 1976), 47–70; John Boswell, *The Kindness of Strangers: The Abandonment of Children in Western Europe from Late Antiquity to the Renaissance* (New York, 1988), 181–266.

78. *Can. Hib.,* 115–16; Bieler, *Penitentials,* 196.

79. Lanfranc, archbishop of Canterbury, was particularly exercised about Irish marriage customs. As he wrote to Guthric, Viking king of Dublin, in 1073–74: "There are reported to be men in your kingdom who take wives of either their own kindred or that of their deceased wives; others who by their own will abandon the wives who are legally married to them." He wrote in similar terms to Toirrdelbach Úa Briain, king of Munster in 1074: Helen Clover and Margaret Gibson, ed. and trans., *The Letters of Lanfranc, Archbishop of Canterbury* (Oxford, 1979), 68–69, 70–73. See also John Watt, *The Church in Medieval Ireland* (Dublin, 1972), 6, 8–9, 24, 27.

80. *CIH*, 47–48 = *ALI* 5:292; Kelly, *Guide*, 74.

81. Bieler, *Penitentials*, 74, 114, 126–28, 265; Bitel, "Sex, Sin, and Celibacy," 76–77.

82. Best and O'Brien, *Book of Leinster* 5:1202–3; David Greene, "The 'Act of Truth' in a Middle Irish Story," *Saga och Sed* (1976), 30–37.

83. Brundage, *Law, Sex, and Christian Society*, 56–61, 136.

84. For example, the conjugal relationship depicted in Adomnán, *Life of Columba*, 436–41.

85. *CIH*, 47–48 = *ALI* 5:292.

86. On the other hand, "lust begets contempt," and "due consideration is better than desire." Smith, "*Senbriathra Fithail*," 28 (10), 23.

87. Jerome, *Adversus Jovinianum* 1.49. There is nothing in the Irish sources to suggest that Jerome's advice to women themselves about the dangers of sex and childbirth was ever taken very seriously.

88. But see Joseph F. Nagy's interpretation in "Fenian Heroes and Their Rites of Passage," in Bo Almquist et al., eds., *The Heroic Process: Form, Function, and Fantasy in Folk Epic*, Proceedings of the International Folk Epic Conference (Dublin, 1985), 161–82, esp. 179–82.

89. Meyer, *Triads*, 31.

90. Hastrup, "The Sexual Boundary."

91. Mac Airt, *Annals of Inisfallen*, 128; Doan, "Sovereignty Aspects in the Roles of Women," 94–97.

4. Procreation Tales

1. Helen Callaway, "'The Most Essentially Female Function of All': Giving Birth," in Ardener, ed., *Defining Females*, 163–65; Thomas Laqueur, "Orgasm, Generation, and the Politics of Reproductive Biology," *Representations* 14 (1986), 1–41.

2. Paola Tabet, "Fertilité naturelle, reproduction forcée," in Nicole-Claude Mathieu, ed., *L'arraisonnement des femmes: Essais en anthropologie des sexes*, Cahiers de l'homme: Ethno.-géog.-ling. n.s. 24 (Paris, 1985), 61–146.

3. Bronislaw Malinowski, *Argonauts of the Western Pacific* (Repr. New York, 1950), 52–55, 71–72; Callaway, "Most Essentially Female Function," 167.

4. Patterson, *Cattle-Lords and Clansmen*, 271–75; Ó Corráin, "Women in Early Irish Society," 1–13; Patrick Power, *Sex and Marriage in Ancient Ireland* (Dublin and Cork, 1976).

5. Medieval Scandinavians made up their own revealing and culturally specific

birth stories. See Grethe Jacobsen, "Pregnancy and Childbirth in the Medieval North: A Topology of Sources and a Preliminary Study," *Scandinavian History Journal* 9 (1984), 91–111.

6. It is likely, but not certain that Galenic ideas reached Ireland through Isidore of Seville. See Jocelyn Hillgarth, "Ireland and Spain in the Seventh Century," *Peritia* 3 (1987), 1–16; also Owsei Tewkin, *Galenism: Rise and Decline of a Medical Philosophy* (Ithaca, N.Y., 1973), 95–96; Danielle Jacquart and Claude Thomasset, *Sexuality and Medicine in the Middle Ages* (Princeton, 1988), 48.

7. Meyer, *Instructions of Cormac,* 28.

8. Binchy, "Bretha Crólige," 24–25. The premise of *Bretha Crólige* is that the victim of violence, along with his or her retinue, be supported by the assailant until recovery.

9. Ibid., 10–11.

10. Ibid., 18–21, 34–35.

11. Plummer, *Vitae* 1:224–25.

12. Gwynn and Purton, "The Monastery of Tallaght," 149, also 149–51, for a similar story about Samthann, and see 152 (66) for the case of a monk seduced by a shameless woman.

13. Shaw, *Aislinge Oenguso;* see also R. I. Best and Osbern Bergin, ed. and trans., "Tochmarc Étaíne," *Ériu* 12 (1938), 137–96; Dillon, *Serglige Con Culainn.* All three tales are translated in Gantz, *Early Irish Myths and Sagas.*

14. Best and O'Brien, *Book of Leinster* 5:1164–65; Kinsella, *Tain,* 11–13; Nagy, "Fenian Heroes," 179–80.

15. Pádraig Ó Riain, "A Study of the Irish Legend of the Wild Man," *Éigse* 14 (1972), 192–93, 202–3.

16. Mac Eoin, "Suithchern and Rónán Dícolla"; O'Nolan, "Mor of Munster." See also the story of Níall Noígíallach in Whitley Stokes, ed. and trans., "The Death of Crimthann Son of Fidach and the Adventures of the Sons of Eochaid Muigmedón," *RC* 24 (1903), 190–207; see also Mac Cana, "Aspects of the Theme of King and Goddess."

17. Hippocratic thinkers also believed in the sexual healing of young women; see Aline Rousselle, *Porneia: On Desire and the Body in Antiquity* (Oxford, 1988), 67–69.

18. Ó Máille, "Medb Cruachna"; Sjoestedt, *Gods and Heroes of the Celts,* 233–34; Mac Cana, *Celtic Mythology,* 84–86.

19. O'Neill, "Cath Bóinde."

20. Ó Máille, "Medb Cruachna," 143–44.

21. Best and O'Brien, *Book of Leinster* 2:262; Kinsella, *Tain,* 53.

22. O'Rahilly, *Táin Bó Cúailnge,* 33; Kinsella, *Tain,* 103–5.

23. Cf. the scene in which the Ulsterwomen cool Cú Chulainn's fury by baring their breasts at him. Cecile O'Rahilly, ed. and trans., *The Táin Bó Cúailnge from the Book of Leinster* (Dublin, 1984), 32–33, 170–71 (ll. 1186–1207).

24. Charles Bowen, "Great-Bladdered Medb: Mythology and Invention in the *Táin Bó Cúailnge,*" *Éire-Ireland* 10 (1975): esp. 26–33. A woman's skills at urinating are not necessarily sexy only because, as Bowen puts it, "a woman's sexual power [is measured] by the capacity of her 'inner space,' with the bladder undoubtedly serving as an analogue for the vagina and uterus," but also because a woman who can con-

trol urination clearly has well-developed vaginal muscles. For a woman who got in trouble over her skills at urinating, see Marstrander, "Deaths of Lugaid and Derbforgaill," 208–9, 214–15. On the connection among fertility, sexuality, and death, see Ford, "Celtic Women," 429–32. See also Jacquart and Thomasset, *Sexuality and Medicine,* 73–76; James H. Dunn, "Síle-na-gCíoch," *Éire-Ireland* 12 (1977), 68–85.

25. John Strachan and J. G. O'Keeffe, eds., *The Táin Bó Cúailnge from the Yellow Book of Lecan* (Dublin, 1912), 121: "Dolotar do fasguba fairseom o Meidb conroimsitis a fuile fair"; Best and O'Brien, *Book of Leinster* 2:396, l. 12320: "fúal fola for Meidb." See also Kelly, "The Táin as Literature," 82; Bowen, "Great-Bladdered Medb," 31–33. On manuscripts and recensions of the *Táin,* see O'Rahilly, *Táin Bó Cúailnge,* vii–xxii.

26. Isidore of Seville, *Etymologiarum Libri xx,* 11.1, quoting Pliny, *Historia naturalis*; Demyttenaere, "The Cleric, Women, and the Stain," 161, and see 158–62. See also Noonan, *Contraception,* 16, 54. Jews and Christians were forbidden intercourse during menstruation. Noonan, *Contraception,* 35, 93, 165. See also Charles T. Wood, "The Doctor's Dilemma: Sin, Salvation, and the Menstrual Cycle in Medieval Thought," *Speculum* 56 (1981), 710–27.

27. Kelly, "The Táin as Literature," 79–80.

28. Kuno Meyer, ed. and trans., *Death Tales of the Ulster Heroes,* Todd Lecture Series 14 (Dublin, 1906), 8–9.

29. Ní Shéaghdha, *Tóruigheacht Dhiarmada agus Ghráinne.* Heroes' deaths often began with their seduction of or by an illicit lover; see the *aideda* of other early Irish heroes contained in Meyer, *Death Tales* and in Maria Tymoczko, trans., *Two Death Tales from the Ulster Cycle* (Dublin, 1981).

30. *Can. Hib.,* 180; Bieler, *Penitentials,* 60–61, 66–67, 68–69, 70–73, 76–77, 82–83, 96–97, 100–101, 112–15, 188–89, 218–21, 262–63.

31. Brown, *The Body and Society,* esp. 140–59.

32. Bitel, "Sex, Sin, and Celibacy."

33. Brundage, *Law, Sex, and Society,* 160–63; Bieler, *Penitentials,* 92–93, 116–17, 222–23; *CIH,* 187–88.

34. Brown, *Body and Society,* 361–64, 401–8; Noonan, *Contraception.*

35. *CIH,* 1883 = *ALI* 5:292.

36. *CIH,* 42 = *ALI* 5:272; *CIH,* 519 = *SEIL,* 71; *CIH,* 779 = *CG,* 5.121–24; see also *CIH,* 20 = *ALI* 5:198; Kelly, *Guide,* 134–35. Sex accomplished by means of love magic was also repugnant to rule makers; see Bieler, *Penitentials,* 78, 100, 160; *CIH,* 48 = *ALI* 5:292.

37. *Can. Hib.,* 187–88; Bieler, *Penitentials,* 90–92, 116, 222, 264; Bitel, "Sex, Sin, and Celibacy," 80.

38. See the metaphorical use of *sringce* (umbilical cord) in *Immacallam in Dá Thúarad:* Best and O'Brien, *Book of Leinster* 4:819: "Iar srinci oic . . . nomen alicuius partis paruae quae sit in ore infantis in utero matris. cuius nomen est srinci." My thanks to John Carey for this reference.

39. Plummer, *Vitae* 1:4–5; Adomnán, *Life of Columba,* 434–37. See also O Daly, *Cath Maige Mucrama,* 50–51; Whitley Stokes, ed. and trans., "The Violent Deaths of Goll and Garb," *RC* 14 (1893), 408–9 (19).

40. Plummer, *Vitae* 1:107.

41. Plummer, *Bethada* 1:319, 2:310.

42. Smyth, *Celtic Leinster,* 4–5. See also J. C. Russell, "Late Thirteenth-Century Ireland as a Region," *Demography* 3 (1966), 500–512.

43. Josiah Cox Russell, *Late Ancient and Medieval Population Control* (Philadelphia, 1985), 153–58; David Herlihy, "Life Expectancies for Women in Medieval Society," in R. T. Morewedge, ed., *The Role of Woman in the Middle Ages* (Albany, 1975), 1–22; Emily R. Coleman, "Medieval Marriage Characteristics: A Neglected Factor in the History of Medieval Serfdom," *Journal of Interdisciplinary History* 2 (1971), 205–21. See also William Petersen, "A Demographer's View of Prehistoric Demography," *Current Anthropology* 16 (1975): 207–26.

44. Nicholas D. Kristof, "Stark Data on Women: 100 Million Are Missing," *New York Times,* Nov. 5, 1991, B5, C1.

45. Herlihy, "Life Expectancies for Women," 5–7.

46. Coleman, "Infanticide in the Early Middle Ages"; see also Carol Clover, "The Politics of Scarcity: Notes on the Sex Ratio in Early Scandinavia," in Damico and Olsen, *New Readings on Women,* 100–134; Nancy L. Wicker, "Mortuary Evidence of the Scarcity of Women in Early Medieval Scandinavia," presented to the Medieval Academy, Tucson, Ariz., 1993.

47. Coleman, "Medieval Marriage Characteristics," 213–16.

48. Herlihy, "Life Expectancies for Women," 8–9. There is little reason to assume, with Patterson, that young adult sex ratios were high: *Cattle-Lords and Clansmen,* 284.

49. Bitel, "Women's Monastic Enclosures," 22–23.

50. Best and O'Brien, *Book of Leinster* 5:1162; Kinsella, *Tain,* 8–9; Plummer, *Vitae* 1:65–66; and see 1:53, 217, 234; Plummer, *Bethada* 1:11, 2:11; Heist, *Vitae,* 334.

51. Heist, *Vitae,* 366; Adomnán, *Life of Columba,* 464–67; Plummer, *Vitae* 1:98, 171, and see 2:131.

52. Plummer, *Bethada* 1:191, 2:185.

53. Best and O'Brien, *Book of Leinster* 5:1162; Kinsella, *Tain,* 9.

54. Binchy, "Bretha Crólige," 20.

55. *Can. Hib.,* 186–87; *CIH,* 47–48, 1848.

56. The origins of this peculiar rule may lie in the levirate. *CIH,* 294; Kelly, *Guide,* 75. See also Nancy Power's description of polygamous unions, "Classes of Women," *SEIL,* 81–108; also *SEIL* 228–32; Ó Corráin, "Women in Early Irish Society," 4–7.

57. *CIH,* 294; Kelly, *Guide,* 75.

58. *Can. Hib.,* 186–89, 192–95; *CIH,* 47, 451, 2198.

59. *Can. Hib.,* 181; Bieler, *Penitentials,* 78–79; see also *CIH,* 2198.

60. Brundage, *Law, Sex, and Christian Society,* 80–93; Noonan, *Contraception,* 143–70; Herlihy, *Medieval Households,* 29–78.

61. Heist, *Vitae,* 348.

62. Plummer, *Bethada* 1:105, 2:101; see also Heist, *Vitae,* 172, 197.

63. Van Hamel, *Compert Con Culainn,* 6; Best and Bergin, eds., *Lebor na hUidre,* 321; Gantz, *Early Irish Myths and Sagas,* 133. See also Tomás Ó Concheanainn, "The Textual Tradition of *Compert Con Culainn,*" *Celtica* 21 (1990), 441–55.

64. Bieler, *Penitentials,* 116 (17, 24, 26, as compared to 32).

65. Binchy, "Secular Institutions."

66. Heist, *Vitae,* 234.

67. *FO,* 242; Plummer, *Bethada* 1:173–74, 2:167–68; Bieler, *Penitentials,* 56, 70, 90, 92, et passim; *Can. Hib.,* 192–93; *CIH,* 4–5, 20–22, 519.

68. See, for example, the birth of Lugaid Riab nDerg in O'Neill, "Cath Bóinde," 174–75.

69. Vernam Hull, ed. and trans., "The Conception of Conchobor," *Irish Texts* 4 (1934), 4–12; Kinsella, *Tain,* 3; see also O Daly, *Cath Maige Mucrama,* 64–67.

70. Meyer, *Liadain and Cuirithir,* 23; see also Plummer, *Vitae* 1:96, for a similar but happier situation.

71. Leviticus 12:1–8; Bieler, *Penitentials,* 200–201; see also Plummer, *Vitae* 1:53.

72. *Can. Hib.,* 175.

73. Heist, *Vitae,* 178–79, 239; Plummer, *Bethada* 1:195, 217–18, 2:180, 211.

74. Mary Douglas, *Purity and Danger* (New York, 1966), esp. 140–58.

75. Averil Cameron, "Virginity as Metaphor: Women and the Rhetoric of Early Christianity," in Cameron, ed., *History as Text: The Writing of Ancient History* (London, 1989), 184–205; *FO,* 22; see also Wood, "The Doctor's Dilemma," 717–21.

76. Best and Bergin, "Tochmarc Étaíne," 156–57; Gantz, *Early Irish Myths and Sagas,* 47. See also Ó Concheanainn, "Textual Tradition of *Compert Con Culainn,*" 445 n. 17; Lucius Gwynn, "The Two Versions of *Tochmarc Étaíne,*" *ZCP* 9 (1913), 354–56; Wendy Doniger O'Flaherty, *Women, Androgynes, and Other Mythical Beasts* (Chicago, 1980), 149–90, esp. 170–71. At least one theologian of the period believed that conception was physiologically possible without intercourse. See Hincmar of Reims's argument in *PL* 125:690–707.

77. *FO,* 86, 87, 112, 134.

78. O'Grady, *Silva Gadelica* 1:82–84, 2:88–91.

79. Tabet, "Fertilité naturelle," 62–63.

80. Jan Van Baal, "The Part of Women in the Marriage Trade," *Bijdragen* (Leiden) 126.3 (1970); Hastrup, "Semantics of Biology," 56–57.

81. Plummer, *Bethada* 1:319–20, 2:310–11. Only one female saint specialized in birthings, and she imitated male models in the kinds of miraculous assistance she offered. See Plummer, *Vitae* 2:166; also *FO,* 36, where Íte is said to succor "many grievous diseases."

82. *CIH,* 2295; Binchy, "Bretha Crólige," 26; Kelly, *Guide,* 77 n. 66. See also Vernam Hull, ed., "Geneamuin Chormaic," *Ériu* 16 (1952), 82–83.

83. Best and O'Brien, *Book of Leinster* 5:1163–64; Kinsella, *Tain,* 10; Heist, *Vitae,* 167–68; Plummer, *Vitae* 1:53, 96, 98–99, 200, 217; Plummer, *Bethada* 1:190, 2:184.

84. Best and O'Brien, *Book of Leinster* 2:467–68; Kinsella, *Tain,* 6–8.

85. For debate on *cess noínden,* see Tomás Ó Bróin, "What Is the 'Debility' of the Ulstermen?" *Éigse* 10 (1963), 286–99; Ó Bróin, "The Word *Noínden,*" *Éigse* 13 (1969–70), 165–76; J. F. Killeen, "The Debility of the Ulstermen—a Suggestion," *ZCP* 33 (1974), 81–86; Edgar M. Slotkin, "*Noínden:* Its Semantic Range," in A. T. E. Matonis and Daniel F. Melia, eds., *Celtic Language, Celtic Culture* (Van Nuys, Calif., 1990), 137–50.

86. On Macha, see Jean Puhvel, "Aspects of Equine Functionality," in Puhvel, ed., *Myth and Law among the Indo-Europeans* (Berkeley, Calif., 1970), 159–72; Georges Dumézil, "Le trio des Macha," *Revue de l'Histoire des Religions* 146 (1954): 5–17; Sjoestedt, *Gods and Heroes,* 204–26; O'Flaherty, *Women, Androgynes,* 166–204.

87. Fertility and birth came to signify other concepts fundamental to the patri-

archal organization of Irish society. Two classic examples of the sovereignty figure are contained in Rudolf Thurneysen, ed., "Baile in Scáil," *ZCP* 20 (1935), 213–27; Stokes, "Death of Crimthann," 190–205. See also Mac Cana, "Women in Irish Mythology," 8–9.

5. Mothers, Mothering, and Motherhood

1. *CA,* 2; the translation is Máirín Ní Dhonnchadha's, from her forthcoming edition for the Dublin Institute for Advanced Studies. This passage appears in Máirín Ní Dhonnchadha, "The *Lex Innocentium:* Adomnán's Law for Women, Clerics, and Youths, 697 A.D.," in Mary O'Dowd and Sabine Wichert, eds., *Chattel, Servant, or Citizen* (Belfast, 1995), 66. Cormac's glossary derives the term *cumal,* female slave, from the sluice gate of the mill where she worked (*comla*) (Y.324): Cormac, *Glossary,* 28. Meyer translates, "the end of the great cooking spit was set on top of her till the cooking was done."

2. *CA,* 2.

3. *CA,* 4–5; Ní Dhonnchadha, *"Lex Innocentium,"* 67–68.

4. *CA,* 8.

5. *CA,* 4. The last epithet is *tustigud talman,* literally "earth's propagation," as Ní Dhonnchadha translates, *"Lex Innocentium,"* 68.

6. Ní Dhonnchadha argues for the precise historical origins of the *cáin* in the events of the late seventh century in Brega and northern Britain, specifically, Ecgfrith of Northumbria's taking of Irish captives, Adomnán's release of the same, and the synod at Birr. *"Lex Innocentium,"* 58–69.

7. Máirín Ní Dhonnchadha, "The Guarantor List of *Cáin Adomnáin,* 697," *Peritia* 1 (1982), 178–215; Daniel Melia, "Law and the Shaman Saint," in Patrick K. Ford, ed., *Celtic Folklore and Christianity* (Santa Barbara, Calif., 1983), 113–28; Máire Herbert, *Iona, Kells, and Derry: The History and Hagiography of the Monastic Family of Columba* (Oxford, 1988), 50–51.

8. Kelly, *Guide,* 86–87.

9. *CIH,* 507; *SEIL,* 26, 187.

10. *CIH,* 1760 = *ALI* 2:151. But see Máirín Ní Dhonnchadha, *"Inailt,* Foster-Sister, Fosterling," *Celtica* 18 (1986), 185–91, where she suggests that some girls were fostered up as companions or servants to women of superior status.

11. *SEIL,* 191.

12. *CIH,* 1761.

13. *CIH,* 375. Cf. the English evidence. Bede complained of unloving mothers who resorted to wet nurses in order to resume carnal relations with their husbands. *Historia Ecclesiastica Gentis Anglorum* 1:27, in J. E. King, ed. and trans., *Baedae Opera Historica* (Cambridge, Mass., 1979). Irish vitae refer to babies nursed with cow's milk: Heist, *Vitae,* 361; Plummer, *Bethada* 1:29, 126, 2:28, 122.

14. *CIH,* 20–22, 375, 1575, 2193; *SEIL,* 191–200. See also Stephen Wilson, "The Myth of Mothering a Myth: The Historical View of European Child-Rearing," *Social History* 9 (1984), 186; Clarissa Atkinson, " 'Your Servant, My Mother': The Figure of Saint Monica in the Ideology of Christian Motherhood," in Atkinson,

Constance H. Buchanan, and Margaret R. Miles, eds., *Immaculate and Powerful: The Female in Sacred Image and Social Reality* (Boston, 1985), 139–72, esp. 139–40.

15. But the laws also discussed a biological father's need to ransom his child from the mother married to another man. *CIH*, 546, 1894 = *ALI* 5:200–201; *CIH*, 294 = *ALI* 3:310–15: "Saer bru beiris brith do tabairt cli cid do cet colla cumscaithi." The poem suggests that custody decisions were rendered by the men who argued about parentage, not by the mother.

16. *CIH*, 375.

17. Bieler, *Pentientials*, 160 (11).

18. Charles-Edwards, *Early Irish and Welsh Kinship*, 85–87; Patterson, *Cattle-Lords and Clansmen*, 215; Kelly, *Guide*, 12–13.

19. Charles-Edwards, *Early Irish and Welsh Kinship*, 313–24; Patterson, *Cattle-Lords and Clansmen*, 274–88.

20. The major legal tracts on kinship groups are *D'Fodlaib Cineoil Tuaithi* (or *Fodla Fine*), *CIH*, 429–32; and *Córus Fine, CIH*, 728–46; see also *CIH*, 215–217; Kelly, *Guide*, 12–14; Charles-Edwards, *Early Irish and Welsh Kinship*, esp. 44–73.

21. *CIH*, 411, 2015; Kelly, *Guide*, 13, 100–101, 102–5.

22. *SEIL*, 84–95; Kelly, *Guide*, 70–71; McAll, "Normal Paradigms of a Woman's Life," 11–16.

23. Smith, *"Senbriathra Fithail* and Related Texts," 58: "Fer doda-beir i cormthech coa chenél," literally "the man who brings her into an ale-house to his kin."

24. Such is the situation described in a legal gloss in Trinity College H.3.17 regarding a man who is *anfine*, not of the *fine*, trying to claim membership through his father. Despite a formal contract of union between the parents, their retaining a formal guarantor from the father's own territory, and the support of the mother and her kin, the child is required to find thirty oath helpers to swear to his membership in the paternal *fine*. Myles Dillon, ed. and trans., "Stories from the Law-tracts," *Ériu* 11 (1932), 47–48, 57–58.

25. Patterson, *Cattle-Lords and Clansmen*, 297. But see Charles-Edwards, *Early Irish and Welsh Kinship*, 313–16, where he argues that the *máithre*'s recognition of a union determined the child's status.

26. Charles-Edwards, *Early Irish and Welsh Kinship*, 84–87; Kelly, *Guide*, 14; *SEIL*, 182.

27. *CIH*, 441–42; Kelly, *Guide*, 14.

28. Patterson, *Cattle-Lords and Clansmen*, xxvii.

29. *CIH*, 856; Kelly, *Guide*, 103.

30. O Daly, *Cath Maige Mucrama*, 76–77.

31. *CIH*, 915, 232 = *ALI* 5:454–55, "mad bean indric . . ." See also *SEIL*, 199.

32. *CIH*, 294 = *ALI* 3:314–15.

33. Ó hAodha, *Bethu Brigte*, 14–15, 31. But see *CIH*, 744, re the abandonment of *mac scríne*, literally, "child of the shrine," that is, the illegitimate son of a cleric (cited in Kelly, *Guide*, 220; also *Can. Hib.*, 168), and the incidents described in the *Book of Leinster* involving Saint Moling and two women, one a nun (translated by Hull as "an old woman"), who gave him their babies: Vernam Hull, ed. and trans., "Two Anecdotes Concerning St. Moling," *ZCP* 18 (1930), 90–99; also Carney, *Studies in Early Irish Literature and History*, 138–42. But see Máirín Ní Dhonnchadha, "*Caillech*

and Other Terms for Veiled Women in Medieval Irish Texts," *Éigse* (199), 74–75.

34. Kelly, *Guide,* 102; *CIH,* 1296. A similar situation applied in Anglo-Saxon England and Scandinavia. See Margaret Clunies Ross, "Concubinage in Anglo-Saxon England," *Past and Present* 108 (1985): 13–28; Karras, "Concubinage and Slavery."

35. *CIH,* 232–33 = *ALI* 5:452–59; Kelly, *Guide,* 103–4; Charles-Edwards, *Early Irish and Welsh Kinship,* 61–62, 70. A child's inheritance was limited or prevented if the father was a landless man not already a member of the community. *CIH,* 308 = *ALI* 3:390–93.

36. Kelly, *Guide,* 104–5; *SEIL,* 129–79.

37. Tomás Ó Cathasaigh, "The Sister's Son in Early Irish Literature," *Peritia* 5 (1986), 128–60; Jan Bremmer, "Avunculate and Fosterage," *Journal of Indo-European Studies* 4 (1976), 65–76. The jurists understood the difficulties involved, as the story of Dorn and her son illustrate. See D. A. Binchy, ed. and trans., "The Saga of Fergus Mac Léti," *Ériu* 16 (1952), 33–48.

38. *CIH,* 512; Kelly, *Guide,* 76–77.

39. The exception was the heiress, *banchomarbae,* who married out of the *túath* (tribe). She could give her son the *orbae niad,* inheritance of a sister's son. *CIH,* 431 = *ALI* 4:284; Kelly, *Guide,* 104; *SEIL,* 226–27; Charles-Edwards, *Early Irish and Welsh Kinship,* 82–84.

40. Charles-Edwards, *Early Irish and Welsh Kinship,* 87, 313–16.

41. Still useful is Kathleen Mulchrone's discussion of fosterage, "The Rights and Duties of Women with Regard to the Education of Their Children," in *SEIL,* 187–205.

42. The exception, mentioned briefly in the laws, is *altramm serce,* fosterage for affection: *CIH,* 1764. See 1762 where commentators discuss fosterage within the *gelfine;* see also Mulchrone in *SEIL,* 187 n. 2.

43. *CIH,* 904, 1764.

44. *CIH,* 1760–21, Kelly, *Guide,* 87.

45. *CIH,* 440, 2014; Kelly, *Guide,* 89.

46. *CIH,* 1761, 1762; Kelly, *Guide,* 87.

47. *CIH,* 1760–61. See also François Kerlouegan, "Essai sur la mise en nourriture et l'éducation dans les pays celtiques d'après le témoignage des textes hagiographiques latins," *ÉC* 12 (1968–69), 101–46.

48. *CIH,* 1760.

49. *CIH,* 1761.

50. Ní Dhonnchadha, *"Inailt,* Foster-Sister, Fosterling," maintains that female fosterlings were educated to service.

51. Kelly, *Guide,* 90.

52. Georges Duby, "Youth in Aristocratic Society: Northwestern France in the Twelfth Century," in Duby, *The Chivalrous Society* (Berkeley, 1977), 114–15; Shahar, *Childhood in the Middle Ages,* 209–24, 227–29, 232–35; Helena Wall, *Fierce Communion: Family and Community in Early America* (Cambridge, Mass., 1990), 95–101.

53. Charles-Edwards, *Early Irish and Welsh Kinship,* 79–82.

54. For examples, see *CIH,* 45, 227, 489, 536, 1348, on the dissolution of contracts perceived as unfair by sons, fathers, or kinsmen. See also Kelly, *Guide,* 159–63.

55. *CIH,* 1296; Kelly, *Guide,* 102.

56. Plummer, *Vitae* 1:250–51; see other versions in Plummer, *Bethada* 1:128–29, 164. See also the more colorful story of Cainnech, Fáelán, and Saint Berach in Plummer, *Bethada* 1:30, 2:29.

57. Heist, *Vitae*, 2–3; Stokes, "Death of Crimthann," 172–89. The famous exceptions are the story of Sín (Nic Dhonnchadha, *Aided Muirchertaig Meic Erca*, 1–6) and the story of Bécuma (Best, "Adventures of Art").

58. *Can. Hib.*, 185–95; Bieler, *Penitentials*, 88, 148.

59. Herlihy, *Medieval Households*, 38–43.

60. *SEIL*, 174–75.

61. Ó hAodha, *Bethu Brigte*, 4–5, 23.

62. Ó Cathasaigh, "Sister's Son," 133–35.

63. Ibid., 152–60. Cf. Kelly, "The *Táin* as Literature," 73–74.

64. The vitae suggest close ties between saints and maternal kin, sometimes reinforced by fosterage. Plummer, *Vitae* 2:166–69; see also Heist, *Vitae*, 169 (7), and 234–35, where Máedóc, although supposedly fostered at home, minds his maternal aunt's sheep.

65. *CG*, 2 (ll. 89–90): *fer midboth*.

66. *CIH*, 1769, 1770; Kelly, *Guide*, 89–90.

67. *CIH*, 411, 442: "altruma o matrem," "fosterage by mother's kin."

68. Van Hamel, *Compert Con Culainn*, 6; trans. Kinsella, *Tain*, 23.

69. Plummer, *Bethada* 1:26, 2:25.

70. Plummer, *Vitae* 2:164–67.

71. The vitae describe bishops, abbots, and abbesses who baptized or named babies, which seems to have constituted some sort of spiritual parentage. See, for example, Plummer, *Vitae* 2:167, 262. But Charles-Edwards suggests that fosterage supplanted godparentage in Celtic cultures. *Early Irish and Welsh Kinship*, 79 n. 132.

72. Meyer, *Instructions of King Cormac*, 31.

73. Best and O'Brien, *Book of Leinster* 5:1162; but for an exception, see Van Hamel, *Compert Con Culainn*, 6–8; trans. Kinsella, *Tain*, 11, 23–25.

74. As Mulchrone puts it, "We may regard her as practically identical with the mother once she has undertaken to act as fostermother." *SEIL*, 200–201.

75. *CIH*, 503 = *ALI* 2:349.

76. See "Scéla Eogain," in O Daly, *Cath Maige Mucrama*, 70, where a foster father mourns his adult fosterling and transfers his affections to the fosterling's baby son.

77. O'Rahilly, *Táin Bó Cúailnge*, 8 (ll. 28–29), 41 (ll. 1312–19), 43 (ll. 1369–70), 83 (ll. 2726–32), 123 (ll. 4097–4107).

78. Despite Jack Goody's contention that the church opposed fosterage, Irish clerics seem to have practiced it with enthusiasm. See Jack Goody, *The Development of the Family and Marriage in Europe* (Cambridge, 1983), 68.

79. *VT*, 9 n. 2, 10.

80. *VT*, 10.

81. *VT*, 10, 12, 14.

82. For a similar relationship between a boy saint and his *máthair*, see Ciarán of Cluain Moccu Nóis, in Plummer, *Vitae* 1:201–3.

83. *VT*, 12.

84. *VT*, 12.

85. Plummer, *Vitae* 1:145; Plummer, *Bethada* 1:45–46, 2:45–46; see also Plummer, *Vitae* 1:226.

86. Plummer, *Bethada* 1:192, 2:186.

87. Ibid., 1:173, 2:168.

88. Ibid., 2:22, 33; see also the anecdote concerning Ultán: *FO*, 200; and Berach: Plummer, *Vitae* 1:76.

89. *FO*, 83; Rudolf Thurneysen, ed., "Brigit Buadach," in Stokes and Windisch, *Irische Texte* 3:71.

90. E. G. Quin, ed. and trans., "The Early Irish Poem *Ísucán*," *Cambridge Medieval Celtic Studies* 1 (1981), 39–52.

91. On spiritual motherhood, see Clarissa Atkinson, *The Oldest Vocation: Christian Motherhood in the Middle Ages* (Ithaca, N.Y., 1991), 92–96. When the author of *Suidigud Tellaig Temra* (Settling of the manor of Tara) sought a metaphor for the deepest affection, he chose a *muimme* and her *daltae*, which he likened to Ireland and its people: "ocus is tairise . . . hÉri": R. I. Best, ed. and trans., *Ériu* 4 (1910), 128–29.

92. Heist, *Vitae*, 257; Plummer, *Vitae* 1:66, 2:3.

93. Philippe Ariès, *Centuries of Childhood: A Social History of Family Life* (New York, 1962); Shahar, *Childhood in the Middle Ages*, esp. 1–7. See also the medieval Irish poem on the mother's lament at the massacre of the innocents. Kuno Meyer, ed. and trans., "The Mothers' Lament at the Slaughter of the Innocents," *Gaelic Journal* 4 (1891), 89–90; trans. Henry, *Dánta Ban*, 80–85.

94. Heist, *Vitae*, 383.

95. One eighth-century legal tract mentions the possibility of a young adult taking his mother with him when being offered formal medical care in another man's house. *CG*, 3 (l. 63).

96. *CIH*, 1109; Kelly, *Guide*, 121.

97. *CIH*, 503.

98. *CIH*, 451, 534–36 = *ALI* 3:52–59; but see also some of the jurists' qualifications, *CIH*, 1817 = *ALI* 3:62–65. See also Kelly, *Guide*, 80, also 11.

99. Plummer, *Bethada* 1:104, 2:100; Plummer, *Vitae* 1:220–21; Heist, *Vitae*, 250, 347–48. See also Heist, *Vitae*, 186, where a distressed mother approaches Saint Cainnech for help with a disobedient adult son. The mother was concerned for her son, but interestingly, both she and the hagiographer clearly thought she needed the assistance of a male authority in order to mother her son properly.

100. Charles-Edwards, *Early Irish and Welsh Kinship*, 81.

101. On Mary, see Atkinson, *Oldest Vocation*, 101–43.

102. We also have a tenth-century vita of Adomnán: Máire Herbert and Pádraig Ó Riain, eds. and trans., *Betha Adamnáin: The Irish Life of Adamnan* (Dublin, 1988).

103. Ní Dhonnchadha, "Guarantor List of *Cáin Adomnáin*."

104. *AU*, 156; Ní Dhonnchadha, "*Lex Innocentium*," esp. 59–64.

105. Ní Dhonnchadha, "*Lex Innocentium*," 67. For parallels in continental thought, see Wemple, *Women in Frankish Society*, 103.

106. *CA*, 12, 4.

107. Kelly, *Guide*, 21–22, 281–82, 305.

108. *CA*, 8.

109. *CA*, 10.

110. Melia, "Law and the Shaman Saint," 118.

111. A *cumal* was worth six *séts*. See *CA*, 25. But see the *díre* tract, which sets the honor price of a few elite mothers of kings, bishops, and some learned men at that of their sons. *CIH*, 1964.

112. *CA*, 12.

113. *CA*, 24–25.

114. *CA*, 24–25.

115. O'Dwyer, *Mary*, 32–72; O'Brien, *Corpus Genealogiarum Hiberniae*, 80.

116. Warren, *Antiphonary of Bangor*, pt. 2, 28; O'Dwyer, *Mary*, 33.

117. James Carney, ed. and trans., *The Poems of Blathmac, Son of Cú Brettan* (Dublin, 1964); Brian Ó Cuív, ed. and trans., "Some Early Devotional Verse in Irish," *Ériu* 19 (1959), 13–17; James Good, "The Mariology of the Blathmac Poems," *Irish Ecclesiastical Record* 104 (1965), 1–7; O'Dwyer, *Mary*, 42–63.

118. *CA*, 28.

119. *CA*, 30.

6. The Domestic Economy

1. Cf. the gloss on the *Lebor Gabála Érenn* (Book of the invasions of Ireland), which comments on the purposes of marriage, citing the precedent of Adam and Eve: "arāi grādha, no ar tusmidh cloindi," "for love or for creating progeny:" Mac-Alister, *Lebor Gabála Érenn* 1:62–63.

2. Compare the situation in the medieval English village of Brigstock, where both spouses labored in the conjugal economy, but only husbands won the opportunity to move out to external markets. Judith Bennett, *Women in the Medieval English Countryside: Gender and Household in Brigstock before the Plague* (Oxford, 1987), 110–29.

3. *CIH*, 294–95 = *ALI* 3:314–17, states that the father kept the bride gift (*coibche*) from his daughter's first marriage but that she got a proportion of the *coibche* from subsequent unions. See also *SEIL*, 114–25; Charles-Edwards, *Early Irish and Welsh Kinship*, 462–68; Ó Corráin, "Marriage in Early Ireland," 15; Patterson, *Cattle-Lords and Clansmen*, 281. Later legal commentators confused *tinól* (marriage portion consisting of cattle) with *tinchor* (marriage contribution or household goods); see *DIL*, 591, 592.

4. Charles-Edwards, *Early Irish and Welsh Kinship*, 464–69, esp. 469; Hughes, "From Brideprice to Dowry," 266–72, 275–76; Herlihy, *Medieval Households*, 49–50, 77; Christine Fell, *Women in Anglo-Saxon England* (London, 1984), 56–57; McNamara and Wemple, "Power of Women through the Family," 86–87.

5. *DIL*, 616.

6. Patterson, *Cattle-Lords and Clansmen*, 220, insists on separate residences for men and women connected by formal *lánamnasa*, hence separate property, arguing from divorce laws and one reference to the interactions of primary and secondary wives. But as the next chapter shows in more depth, very little evidence exists to support such an interpretation. See *ALI* 2:396–99, which miscites Domnall O'Davoren,

the sixteenth-century legal commentator, in a comment on a woman who maintains her own house.

7. *CIH*, 512 = *ALI* 2:380–81; Charles-Edwards, *Early Irish and Welsh Kinship*, 466.

8. *CIH*, 505–6 = *ALI* 2:356; *SEIL*, 18–21; Charles-Edwards, *Early Irish and Welsh Kinship*, 465.

9. *SEIL*, 133–79, esp. 134–38; *CIH*, 736; Kelly, *Guide*, 104–5; David Herlihy, "Land, Family, and Women in Continental Europe, 701–1200," *Traditio* 18 (1962), 90–91; McNamara and Wemple, "Power of Women," 89–90.

10. *CIH*, 1154–55, comment.; also *SEIL*, 155–56, 168–71; Kelly, *Guide* 104–5. Kelly values the *cumal* at approximately 34.23 acres, or 13.85 hectares (*Guide*, 99) although he admits this to be a highly tentative figure.

11. Donnchadh Ó Corráin, citing Jack Goody, suggests that 20 percent of estates devolved to *banchomarbai* (heiresses): "Marriage in Early Ireland," 10–11. But given probable female longevity and sex ratios, this is surely an inflated percentage.

12. *Can. Hib.*, 115–16; *SEIL*, 150–51.

13. *SEIL*, 143, 168–71; unless he were a member of her *fine* or a foreigner, in which case her son could receive "the inheritance of a sister's son." See *CIH*, 431 = *ALI* 4:284; *SEIL*, 150–53; Kelly, *Guide*, 104–5; Charles-Edwards, *Early Irish and Welsh Kinship*, 467.

14. Thurneysen, *Irisches Recht*, 34; *SEIL*, 174–75. See *CIH*, 378 = *ALI* 1:148, where *orba cruib* is equated with *orba feirtsi*, "spindle-land."

15. See the fragment of a story contained in the law tracts regarding a woman landholder (*banchoairt mná*) whose wealth was still measured in cattle, 700 of them. Dillon, "Stories from the Law-Tracts," 51.

16. McNamara and Wemple, "Power of Women," 88–89; Fell, *Women in Anglo-Saxon England*, 75–78. See also Gregory of Tours's account of the quarrel between Ingitrude and her daughter Berthegund over family property. *Hist. franc.* 10.12.

17. *CIH*, 591, 2201.

18. See, for example, Heist, *Vitae*, 397. See also Kathleen Hughes's argument about women's communities established on family property. *Early Christian Ireland*, 234–35.

19. Robin Fox, *The Tory Islanders: A People of the Celtic Fringe* (Cambridge, 1978), esp. 122–26, 156–85. The alternative model of Clare and elsewhere made famous in Arensberg, *The Irish Countryman*, is a postfamine model. See esp. 71–106.

20. Bitel, *Isle of the Saints*, 39–40, and n. 40.

21. *CIH*, 214, 224–29, 244–45, 247, 533; *ALI* 3:48, 5:510; see also Kelly, *Guide*, 100.

22. Bitel, *Isle of the Saints*, 40, 98. See also Goody, *Development of the Family and Marriage*, esp. 103–13, 122–25.

23. *CG*, 4.

24. *CG*, 18–19; Georges Duby, *The Early Growth of the European Economy: Warriors and Peasants from the 7th to the 12th Century* (London, 1974), 36–37. See also Francis J. Byrne, *Irish Kings and High-Kings* (London, 1973), 28–47.

25. Bitel, *Isle of the Saints*, 39–40 n. 99.

26. *CA*, 2–3, 14–15.

27. See *CG*, 4, for the equipment owned by an *ócaire;* see *CIH*, 319 = *ALI* 1:150–53 for women's cloth-making equipment.

28. *SEIL*, 133, 171 n. 3; *Can. Hib.*, 116; Lisa Bitel, "Women's Donations to the Churches in Early Ireland," *JRSAI* 114 (1984), 9–11.

29. *CIH*, 472 = *ALI* 5:406–7.

30. *Bretha im Fuillema Gell* lists the items in a queen's *íadach*, workbag, and suggests the value of women's clothing and other possessions. *CIH*, 464–66 = *ALI* 5:382–89.

31. Gregory of Tours, *Hist. franc.* 4.28; Wemple, *Women in Frankish Society*, 47.

32. See, for example, Knott, *Togail Bruidne Da Derga*, 1–2: "con-accai in mnaí . . . Cáem cach co hÉtaín."

33. Plummer, *Vitae* 2:78.

34. *CIH*, 515 = *ALI* 2:392.

35. Meyer, *Instructions of King Cormac*, 28 ("báetha comairle"), 32 ("dulbaire torbai"). See also O'Rahilly, *Táin Bó Cúailnge*, 6, 74, 129, 192; Kelly, "The *Táin* as Literature," 78–79.

36. Dorothy Africa, "Armagh, Bangor, and Bans(h)enchas," paper presented to the American Conference for Irish Studies, April 11, 1991.

37. Charles-Edwards argues, however, that a woman's relations with her in-laws were profoundly different from those of a man (*clemnas*). *Early Irish and Welsh Kinship*, 85.

38. *Can. Hib.*, 191; *CIH*, 504 = *ALI* 2:391; see also *CIH*, 517, comment. = *ALI* 2:398, which describes a *lánamnas* based primarily on periodic sexual liaisons.

39. *CA*, 4.

40. *Can. Hib.*, 186–87; *CIH*, 47–48, 1848.

41. Friedrich Engels, *The Origins of the Family, Private Property, and the State* (New York, 1972); see also Claude Lévi-Strauss, "The Family," in Harry L. Shapiro, ed., *Man, Culture, and Society* (New York, 1956), 333–57; Gerda Lerner, *The Creation of Patriarchy* (Oxford, 1986).

42. Ester Boserup, *Women's Role in Economic Development* (Aldershot, U.K., 1986); see also Jack Goody and Joan Buckley, "Implications of the Sexual Division of Labor in Agriculture," in J. Clyde Mitchell, ed., *Numerical Techniques in Social Anthropology* (Philadelphia, 1980), 33–47; Rae Lesser Blumberg, "Rural Women in Development: Veil of Invisibility, World of Work," *International Journal of Intercultural Relations* 3 (1979), 447–72.

43. Mina Davis Caulfield, "Equality, Sex, and Mode of Production," in Gerald D. Berreman, ed., with Kathleen M. Zaretsky, *Social Inequality: Comparative and Developmental Approaches* (New York, 1981), 201–19.

44. Ellen Lewin, "By Design: Reproductive Strategies and the Meaning of Motherhood," in Hilary Homans, ed., *The Sexual Politics of Reproduction* (Aldershot, U.K., 1988), 123–38.

45. Tabet, "Fertilité naturelle," 61–146.

46. O'Grady, *Silva Gadelica* 1:82–84, 2:88–91; Lewin, "By Design," 125.

47. Daniel W. Amundsen and Carol Jean Diers, "The Age of Menarche in Medieval Europe," *Human Biology* 45 (1973), 363–69; Rose E. Frisch, "Population, Food Intake, and Fertility," *Science* 199 (1977), 22–30.

48. Bitel, "Sex, Sin, and Celibacy," 80–81.

49. Russell, *Late Ancient and Medieval Population Control,* 144–46.

50. Ibid., 147–48; but see the caveats in Petersen, "A Demographer's View of Prehistoric Demography."

51. Russell, *Late Ancient and Medieval Population Control,* 150–53.

52. Smith, *"Senbriathra Fithail,"* 19.

53. Plummer, *Bethada* 1:40, 2:39.

54. *CIH,* 511–12, 513 = *ALI* 2:378, 384.

55. Janet Siskind, "Kinship and Mode of Production," *American Anthropologist* 80.4 (1978), 864.

56. Cf. the situation in later medieval England. Barbara Hanawalt, *The Ties That Bound: Peasant Families in Medieval England* (Oxford, 1986), 141–55.

57. Cooking: *CIH,* 285–86 = *ALI* 3:274–77; quern work: *CIH,* 467–68 = *ALI* 5:274–75; O'Rahilly, *Táin Bó Cúailnge,* 40 (ll. 1269–70); *CIH,* 287 = *ALI* 3:280–83, discusses milling but does not assign the work exclusively to women. However, the term used in the laws for a female slave *cumalach,* derives fr. **com–muala.* Slave women probably had the genuinely hazardous job of working the grindstones, where they might crush an arm or fall into the millworks to their deaths. *CA,* 28–29, sets work-related penalties for accidents that occurred to female servants in various venues. Mill work was so hazardous that Saint Ciarán of Cluain Moccu Nóis used his miraculous wiles to free a slavewoman condemned to it. At first, Ciarán tried to trade his services for hers with the king who owned her, but when refused, he simply made the woman invisible and led her away. Plummer, *Vitae* 1:206–7. The hagiographer wrote that this particular slave was held *iniuste,* the implication being that other women worked the mills without saints to liberate them. See also 203–4.

58. Several passages in the laws pair a dairymaid or milker (*bligre*) with a male cowherd (*buachall*) as legal prototypes: *CIH,* 1886 (l. 38) = *ALI* 5:152–53; *CIH,* 1276. See also *CG,* 6 (l. 155), which requires a freeman (*bóaire febsa*) to grind "for his household and followers," but of course, the *bóaire* would not necessarily have done the grinding himself.

59. *CIH,* 507–8 = *ALI* 2:362–65.

60. *CIH,* 508 = *ALI* 2:364–67.

61. *CIH,* 508 = *ALI* 2:366–67.

62. *VT,* 12; Plummer, *Vitae* 2:135, 192–93; Plummer, *Bethada* 1:212–13, 2:206–7.

63. Cogitosus, *PL* 72:777B; Plummer, *Bethada* 1:166–67, 2:161.

64. *CIH,* 43 = *ALI* 5:277; cited in Patterson, *Cattle-Lords and Clansmen,* 290.

65. Finbar McCormick, "Dairying and Beef Production in Early Christian Ireland," in T. Reeves-Smyth and F. Hamond, eds., *Landscape Archaeology in Ireland,* BAR 116 (Oxford, 1983), 253–68; A. T. Lucas, "Cattle in Ancient and Medieval Irish Society," *O'Connell School Union Record* (Dublin, 1958); Micheál Ó Sé, "Old Irish Cheeses and Other Milk Products," *JCHAS* 53 (1948), 82–87; Ó Sé, "Old Irish Buttermaking," *JCHAS* 54 (1949), 61–67.

66. *CG,* 6 (l. 160), 8 (l. 203), et passim; see 75–76 (*bés*) for discussion. See also J. O'Loan, "Livestock in the Brehon Laws," *Agricultural History Review* 7 (1959), 65–74.

67. When hagiographers depicted monks milking, it was probably a sign of their

humble, nonwarrior status, in the same sense that *Cáin Adomnáin* included clerics with women and children among noncombatants. See the lesson about the sexual division of labor taught to Saint Ailbe by an angel in Heist, *Vitae*, 129 (sec. 47). See also Plummer, *Bethada* 1:46, 164, 2:46, 159. Patterson suggests that women drove the herds to summer pastures, but her evidence is slight and late: *Cattle-Lords and Clansmen*, 73–75.

68. Nuala Cullen, "Women and Preparation of Food in Eighteenth-Century Ireland," in Margaret MacCurtain and Mary O'Dowd, eds., *Women in Early Modern Ireland* (Edinburgh, 1991), 267–68.

69. *CIH*, 509; *ALI* 2:366–67. *Crud*, which the legal commentators took for *crod*, "stock," should be read, with Thurneysen, as *cróud*: "penning." See *SEIL*, 34. Just possibly the word could also mean *crúd*, "milking," instead; see *DIL*, 161.

70. Proinséas Ní Chatháin, "Swineherds, Seers, and Druids," *Studia Celtica* 14–15 (1979–80), 200–211; Patterson, *Cattle-Lords and Clansmen*, 81–82.

71. *CIH*, 509; *ALI* 2:367–69.

72. *VT*, 198; Dillon, "Stories from the Law-Tracts," 44–45, 53.

73. Patterson, *Cattle-Lords and Clansmen*, 82–86.

74. Heist, *Vitae*, 137. See also *Táin Bó Fraích* (Meid, ed., 14 [l. 338]), where the hero and companions encounter a woman (*fraccnatan*), possibly a slave, herding sheep.

75. Heist, *Vitae*, 234–35 (where the sheep belong to the saint's aunt), 361, 383; see also episodes in which boys minded calves: Heist, *Vitae*, 357; Plummer, *Vitae* 1:6, 201–3; 172–73 for pigs. Adomnán mentioned women herding sheep: *Life of Columba*, 248–51. Plummer, *Vitae* 2:42, refers to a noblewoman who was keeping sheep on an island pasture, but she certainly did not mind them herself. See also *CA*, 14, which refers to women's flocks. One of the few exceptional shepherdesses was Saint Brigit who claimed to love herding sheep in the rain (Ó hAodha, *Bethu Brigte*, 16), but her mythic associations with sheep make her case problematic as evidence.

76. *CIH*, 207–9 = *ALI* 4:8–17; Kelly, *Guide*, 187–88.

77. See the similar formula regarding these signifiers of a woman's possessions and functions at *CIH*, 378–79 = *ALI* 1:146–49.

78. *CG*, 8 (ll. 197–98): "He owns a green [before his homestead] in which there are always sheep."

79. See the story in the Additamenta to the *Book of Armagh*, where a woman exchanges a mantle for a horse. Bieler, *Patrician Texts*, 174.

80. *CIH*, 510; *ALI* 2:371–75; *CIH*, 176–77 = *ALI* 2:414–21. Linen production is labor-intensive work well suited to families, since some of the labor is difficult for women. W. H. Crawford, "Women in the Domestic Linen Industry," in MacCurtain and O'Dowd, *Women in Early Ireland*, 255–64.

81. *CA*, 24. See also the long antiquarian discussion of cloth and clothes making in Eugene O'Curry, *On the Manners and Customs of the Ancient Irish* (Dublin, 1873), 3:112–23.

82. *Glaisen: CIH*, 510 = *ALI* 2:373–74; *róid: CIH*, 177 = *ALI* 2:420–21; *seip: CA*, 32. See also Plummer, *Vitae* 1:95.

83. *CIH*, 510 = *ALI* 2:373–74; see also *CIH*, 176 = *ALI* 2:416–17, where the long and complicated commentary suggests that it was unusual for a man to partici-

pate in any step of the cloth-making process (except, possibly, some initial steps in the harvesting and preparation of flax).

84. Kelly, *Guide,* 177.

85. *CIH,* 378–39 = *ALI* 1:146–51. For a thorough discussion of the entire process, see D. A. Binchy, "Distraint in Irish Law," *Celtica* 10 (1973), 22–71; Kelly, *Guide,* 178.

86. *CIH,* 422 = *ALI* 1:268–69; Kelly, *Guide,* 179.

87. *CIH,* 379–81 = *ALI* 1:151–57.

88. David Herlihy, *Opera Muliebria: Women and Work in Medieval Europe* (New York, 1990), 28–29, argues against an Irish *gynaeceum* in the continental style.

89. Edwards, *Archaeology of Early Medieval Ireland* 80–83; Nanna Damsholt, "The Role of Icelandic Women in the Sagas and in the Production of Homespun Cloth," *Scandinavian Journal of History* 9.2 (1984), 83.

90. Edwards, *Archaeology of Early Medieval Ireland,* 83; also 65–66 on "burnt mounds" (*fulachta fiadh*); Herlihy, *Opera Muliebria,* 28; Damsholt, "Role of Icelandic Women," 82; Stokes, *Lives of the Saints,* 121, 266–67.

91. Plummer, *Bethada* 1:120, 2:116.

92. But see Cormac, *Glossary,* 15, where the goddess Bríg/Brigit's craftwork is referred to as *frithgnam,* a term normally applied to men's work.

93. Later in the Middle Ages the Irish exported large quantities of woolen cloth; if the Scandinavian and continental evidence provides useful analogues, women may have been excluded from cloth making once wool became a profitable object of long-distance trade. See T. B. Barry, *The Archaeology of Medieval Ireland* (London, 1987), 103–5; Herlihy, *Opera Muliebria,* 185–91; Damsholt, "Role of Icelandic Women," 84–86.

94. Mary E. Byrne, ed., "Airec Menman Uraird Maic Coisse," in O. J. Bergin, et al., eds., *Anecdota from Irish Manuscripts* (Halles 1908), 2:56. Cormac's eighth-century glossary identifies *lámthorad* with *abras,* spinning or cloth production, but with class connotations. *Abras* was the *lámthorad* of an *inailt,* a serving girl. Cormac, *Glossary,* 10.

95. Heist, *Vitae,* 366. The weaver's rod was a magical talisman in a woman's hand at the moment of childbirth. Plummer, *Bethada* 1:191; 2:185; but cf. Patricia Lysaught, *The Banshee: The Irish Supernatural Death-Messenger* (Dublin, 1986), 204.

96. *CIH,* 53 = *ALI* 5:312–15; Binchy, "Bretha Crólige," 26–27. *Ben lámtoruid* is glossed as "an embroideress and women who perform the steeping and dressing [of flax]."

97. *CIH,* 464 = *ALI* 5:382–83.

98. A few of the vitae hinted that nuns were responsible for producing the vestments of clerics and decorative cloths for churches. See *VT,* 266, also 252; *FO,* 42; also Plummer, *Vitae* 2:259, where the monks of Í send a boatload of raw wool to the nuns at Samthann's community, presumably so that the women can produce cloth for them. (My thanks to Dorothy Africa for this reference.)

99. *CIH,* 1721.65 = *ALI* 2:156–57.

100. Smith, "*Senbriathra Fithail,*" 56. Just because *druinecha* were admired for their handiwork does not mean that they escaped the usual accusations leveled at

women. *Senbríathra Fíthail* also reported (ibid.): "Milbéla druinecha," "Embroideresses are honey-mouthed."

101. Dillon, *Serglige Con Culainn*, 25. See also Knott, *Togail Bruidne Da Derga*, 1936), 3. Étaín was raised "co mbo druinech maith, ocus ní buí i nHérind ingen ríg bad chaímiu oldás." Best, "Adventures of Art," 168 (l. 25).

102. Whitley Stokes, ed., "The Colloquy of the Two Sages," *RC* 26 (1905), 34, 42. For another prophetic text that mentions embroidery, see Kuno Meyer, ed., "Mitteilungen aus Irischen Handschriften," *ZCP* 9 (1913), 170: "druinech cechla bean."

103. One attribute of holy women and goddesses seems to have been the ability to milk wild animals. See Heist, *Vitae*, 129; *VT*, 72; also the supernatural figure of Flidais in Ernst Windisch, ed., "Táin Bó Flidais," in Stokes and Windisch, *Irische Texte*, ser. 2, pt. 1, 215; Stokes, *Cóir Anmann*, 294–95, secs. 25–26. See also Clark, *The Great Queens*, 29–32.

104. Women grinding, Heist, *Vitae*, 391; women washing clothes, Plummer, *Vitae* 1:96; Plummer, *Bethada* 1:217, 2:211; women baking, *CIH*, 1766.14 = *ALI* 2:176.

105. Bitel, *Isle of the Saints*, 128–44.

106. *CIH*, 509 = *ALI* 2:366–67.

107. Binchy, "Bretha Crólige," 26; Kelly, *Guide*, 49, 77; O'Brien, *Corpus Genealogiarum*, 154; see also Plummer, *Vitae* 2:53; and Seán Connolly, ed., "Vita Prima Sanctae Brigitae," *JRSAI* 119 (1989), 25, for references to women practicing medicine. See also Wendy Davies, "The Place of Healing in Early Irish Society," in Donnchadh Ó Corráin et al., eds., *Sages, Saints, and Storytellers: Celtic Studies in Honour of Professor James Carney* (Maynooth, Éire, 1989), 49–50. For *banfile*: Meyer, *Liadain and Cuirithir*.

108. Binchy, "Bretha Crólige," 28; *CIH*, 233 = *ALI* 5:456; Kelly, *Guide*, 50.

109. Adomnán, *Life of Columba*, 434; H. d'Arbois de Jubainville, "Documents irlandais publiés par M. Windisch," *RC* 12 (1891), 154-55. Alexander Carmichael collected several Highland songs about blessings and charms on clothwork, as well as milking and other domestic labors. See Carmichael, ed. and trans., *Charms of the Gaels: Hymns and Incantations with Illustrative Notes on Words, Rites, and Customs, Dying and Obsolete; Orally Collected in the Highlands and Islands of Scotland by Alexander Carmichael* (1901; repr. Edinburgh, 1992), esp. 112–16, also 92–102.

110. Stokes, *Lives of the Saints*, 121, 266–67.

111. Damsholt maintains that Icelandic women derived high status in both literature and everyday life from their control of cloth production because cloth formed a principal export of Iceland. Damsholt, "Role of Icelandic Women."

112. For the equation of divorce rights with high social status, see Ó Corráin, "Women in Early Irish Society," 1–13; Patterson, *Cattle-Lords and Clansmen*, 272–75. See also Wemple, *Women in Frankish Society*, 112–13; Simms, "Legal Position of Irishwomen," 111.

113. Neil McLeod, *Early Irish Contract Law* (Sydney, 1992), 71–80.

114. *CIH*, 506–7 = *ALI* 2:358–60.

115. *CIH*, 507 = *ALI* 2:360–62.

116. *CIH* 507, 512–13 = *ALI* 2:362, 380–82.

117. *CIH*, 443 (l. 43) = *ALI* 5:284; *SEIL*, 211-15; Kelly, *Guide*, 75–76.

118. *CIH,* 505–6 = *ALI* 2:356–58.

119. The particulars are unclear, but for comparative purposes, see William Jordan, *Women and Credit in Premodern and Developing Societies* (Philadelphia, 1993), 13–49.

120. *CIH,* 511, 513 text and comm. = *ALI* 2:378, 384 comm., 386.

121. *CIH,* 515 = *ALI* 2:390–93; Kelly, *Guide,* 76.

122. *CIH,* 511–12 = *ALI* 2:378, 384. See also Patterson, *Cattle-Lords and Clansmen,* 278–81.

123. Cf. Patterson, *Cattle-Lords and Clansmen,* 286–88.

124. *CIH,* 517–18 = *ALI* 2:396–404.

125. Bitel, "Women's Donations," 9–10.

126. Bieler, *Patrician Texts,* 174–75; Bitel, "Women's Donations," 10.

127. Bitel, "Women's Donations," 8–9.

128. Herlihy, "Land, Family, and Women," 106–10.

129. Charles Doherty, "Exchange and Trade in Early Medieval Ireland," *JRSAI* 110 (1980), 67–89; Doherty, "Some Aspects of Hagiography as a Source for Irish Economic History," *Peritia* 1 (1982), 300–328. Doherty also says that monastic settlements functioned much like towns. "Monastic Towns in Early Medieval Ireland," in H. B. Clarke and Anngret Simms, eds., *The Comparative History of Urban Origins in Non-Roman Europe* (Oxford, 1984), 47–75. For the relations between Viking town dwellers and residents of the surrounding countryside, see John Bradley, "The Interpretation of Scandinavian Settlement in Ireland," in John Bradley, ed., *Settlement and Society in Medieval Ireland: Studies Presented to F. X. Martin, O.S.A.* (Kilkenny, Éire, 1988), 50–88.

130. *Can. Hib.,* 181–83, but see 188.

131. Patterson, *Cattle-Lords and Clansmen,* 285–86, argues that *adaltracha* may have functioned as slaves, sexual and otherwise. The vitae refer to the slave women of kings, but this may be the hagiographers' way of describing secondary wives or concubines who were not necessarily forced to labor. See Adomnán, *Life of Columba,* 398–403; Plummer, *Bethada* 1:11, 2:11.

132. The son of a prostitute was *mac raite,* literally "son of the road." *CIH,* 741. Promiscuous women, along with slaves, aliens, and madmen, could not give oaths or legal witness. Kelly, *Guide,* 206.

133. Adomnán, *Life of Columba,* 290–93.

134. Donncha Ó hAodha, "The Lament of the Old Woman of Beare," in Ó Corráin et al., *Sages, Saints, and Storytellers,* 308–31; Gerard Murphy, ed., *Early Irish Lyrics* (Oxford, 1956), 208; Tomás Ó Cathasaigh, "The Eponym of Cnogba," *Éigse* 23 (1989), 27–38.

135. Heist, *Vitae,* 102, 127; Plummer, *Vitae* 2:118; Bitel, "Women's Monastic Enclosures," 25.

136. Bitel, "Women's Monastic Enclosures," 30; Plummer, *Vitae* 2:128.

137. *CIH,* 174 = *ALI* 2:410–11.

138. Coleman, "Medieval Marriage Characteristics," 213–17.

139. Best and Bergin, *Lebor na hUidre,* 133–34; Philip O'Leary, "The Honour of Women in Early Irish Literature," *Ériu* 38 (1987): 39.

140. McLeod, *Early Irish Contract Law,* 77–79.

141. Caulfield, "Equality, Sex, and Mode of Production," 202–3.

7. The Land of Women

1. O'Leary, "Honour of Women."

2. Ibid., 40.

3. Bennett, *Women in the Medieval English Countryside,* 42–47; Renée Hirschon, "Open Body, Closed Space: The Transformation of Female Sexuality," in Ardener, *Defining Females,* 66–87.

4. *CIH,* 350–51 = *ALI* 1:51; see also *CIH,* 522, where the jurist says that tithes, first fruits, and alms are necessary to maintain *cairde* (amity or treaty) between king and tribe; also *CIH,* 1897.

5. John V. Kelleher, "The Pre-Norman Irish Genealogies," *Irish Historical Studies* 16 (1968), 138–53.

6. Donnchadh Ó Corráin, "Dál Cais—Church and Dynasty," *Ériu* 24 (1973), 52–63; Ó Corráin, "Irish Regnal Succession: A Reappraisal," *Studia Hibernica* 11 (1971), 7–39.

7. Marc Bloch, *Feudal Society* (Chicago, 1961; repr. 1968), 123–42.

8. Bitel, *Isle of the Saints,* 223–28; Jacques LeGoff, "The Symbolic Ritual of Vassalage," *Time, Work and Culture in the Middle Ages* (Chicago, 1980), 257–58.

9. Charles-Edwards, *Early Irish and Welsh Kinship,* 47–48, 138–40.

10. Ibid., esp. 47–61, 486–514, 515–16. See also his valuable glossary of kinship terms, 33–36.

11. Kelly, *Guide,* 101–2. In general, the jurists' discussions of inheritance make clear that kinsmen owned land together. It also seems unlikely that most nonnobles owned an entire plough team. Thus, joint agriculture among kinsmen seems certain, at least for the earliest period of the laws. See, e.g., *CIH,* 506 = *ALI* 2:358–59; Charles-Edwards, *Early Irish and Welsh Kinship,* 415–30, 453 n. 89–91.

12. Alexander Murray, *Germanic Kinship Structure: Studies in Law and Society in Antiquity and the Early Middle Ages* (Toronto, 1983), esp. 135–62, 217–19.

13. Charles-Edwards, *Early Irish and Welsh Kinship,* 59–61, 76–77.

14. *Can. Hib.,* 105–13.

15. Bloch, *Feudal Society,* 132.

16. Patterson, *Cattle-Lords and Clansmen,* xxvii.

17. *AU,* 321.

18. *AU,* 333; Kelly, *Guide,* 128 n. 20.

19. Kelly, *Guide,* 127.

20. See the index entry in the old edition of *AU:* "Brother, respective, slew" and "Brothers, respective, slew," in W. M. Hennessy, ed. and trans., *The Annals of Ulster* (Dublin, 1901), 4:43. However, what MacCarthy took for "brothers" did not always mean the sons of the same parents but simply "kinsman."

21. Charles-Edwards, *Early Irish and Welsh Kinship,* 87.

22. *CIH,* 515 = *ALI* 2:390–91.

23. *CIH,* 208, 966, 2197, 2296, all cited in Kelly, *Guide,* 207. See also Neil McLeod, *Early Irish Contract Law,* 71–79.

24. *CIH,* 515–16 = *ALI* 2:390–93.

25. Muireann Ní Bhrolcháin has made the most expert use of the *bansenchas* in recent papers, deriving information about women's place in political dynasties and marriage patterns. "The Prose Bansheanchas" (Ph.D. thesis, Coláiste na hOllscoile, Gaillimh, 1980). See also Margaret E. Dobbs, "The Ban-senchus," *RC* 47 (1930), 282–339; 48 (1931), 163–234; 49 (1932), 437–89.

26. See the analysis of *Gíslasaga* in Preben Meulengracht Sørensen, "Murder in the Marital Bed: An Attempt at Understanding a Crucial Scene in *Gíslasaga,*" in John Lindow et al., eds., *Structure and Meaning in Old Norse Literature: New Approaches to Textual Analysis in Literary Criticism* (Odense, Denmark, 1986), 235–63. Cf., in the Irish tradition, *Aided Muirchertaig Meic Erca* and *Aided Con Roí.*

27. Cf. Wemple, *Women in Frankish Society,* 58–59.

28. *CIH,* 503 = *ALI* 2:346–47. Dorothy Africa contends that women took conscious, active part in constructing networks connecting their blood kin and their affines; it is a tempting but unsupported hypothesis, resting mainly on the literati's depiction of women's collusion in men's politics. However, see Art Cosgrove's description of a medieval O'Toole who mediated between her kin and her affines. Cosgrove, ed., *New History of Ireland,* vol. 2: *Medieval Ireland, 1169–1534* (Oxford, 1993), 265 n. 5.

29. Charles-Edwards, *Early Irish and Welsh Kinship,* 85.

30. Plummer, *Vitae* 1:100; Plummer, *Bethada* 1:46, 2:46.

31. Ní Dhonnchadha, "*Inailt,* Foster-Sister, Fosterling"; see *Geneamuin Chormuic,* where the *inailt* acts as midwife and nurse for a noblewoman and her child, in Vernam Hull, ed., "Geneamuin Chormuic," *Ériu* 16 (1952), 83.

32. Greene, *Fingal Rónáin* 2–3.

33. Van Hamel, *Compert Con Culainn,* 23, 44. Cú Chulainn was not the only male with vexed fosterage relations, as Joseph Nagy has pointed out to me, similarly problematic relations appear in *Togail Bruidne Da Derga* and *Cath Maige Mucrama.* Foster sisters serve a similar function in the Middle Irish tale *Altram Tige Dá Medar.* Lilian Duncan, ed. and trans., *Ériu* 11 (1932), 193–94, 198, but see 200, where the loss of a foster sister grieves the otherworldly women.

34. *CG,* 80. For ecclesiastical clientage, see Bitel, *Isle of the Saints,* 115–44; also Doherty, "Some Aspects of Hagiography," 313–16.

35. *CIH,* 428, 535 = *ALI* 3:52–55; cf. Bloch, *Feudal Society,* 260–64.

36. *CG,* 23 (l. 594); Kelly, *Guide,* 33.

37. *CIH,* 1770–78; *CG,* 23, 107; Kelly, *Guide,* 32–33.

38. *CIH,* 1116; Kelly, *Guide,* 29.

39. *CIH,* 486; Kelly, *Guide,* 26–33.

40. In fact, the tract, purportedly about unfree clientage, celebrates the solidarity of the *fine* and often assumes a clientage tie between the *cenn fine* and its other men. *CIH,* 489–90 = *ALI* 2:280–84; also *CIH,* 432–37; Kelly, *Guide,* 29.

41. Smith, "*Senbriathra Fithail,*" 22.

42. Mac Eoin, "Suithchern and Rónán Dícolla," 68; O'Nolan, "Mór of Munster," 271–77.

43. Bennett, *Women in the Countryside,* 129–41; see also Wendy Davies, *Small Worlds: The Village Community in Early Medieval Brittany* (London, 1988), 77–79; Margaret Clunies Ross, "Women and Power in the Scandinavian Sagas," in Barbara Garlick et al., eds., *Stereotypes of Women in Power: Historical Perspectives and Revisionist Views* (New York, 1992), 105–19; Robin Stacey, *The Road to Judgment: From Custom to Court in Medieval Ireland and Wales* (Philadelphia, 1994), 33–38.

44. Stacey, *Road to Judgment,* esp. 55–81.

45. *CIH,* 347–48 = *ALI* 1:40–43. See John Carmi Parsons, "Family, Sex, and Power: The Rhythms of Medieval Queenship," in Parsons, ed., *Medieval Queenship* (New York, 1993), 1–11.

46. Philip O'Leary, "Contention at Feasts in Early Irish Literature," *Éigse* 20 (1984), 115–27.

47. Cf. Judith Jesch, *Women in the Viking Age* (Woodbridge, Suffolk, 1991), esp. 38–41.

48. See the poem on kinship and inheritance edited by Myles Dillon in *SEIL,* 135–49, and again by Charles-Edwards, *Early Irish and Welsh Kinship,* 516–19; see also *CIH,* 299 = *ALI* 3:332–34.

49. *Can. Hib.,* 28.

50. Plummer, *Vitae* 2:121–22.

51. Cf. the picture of heretical feminine solidarity described by Emmanuel LeRoy Ladurie in *Montaillou: The Promised Land of Error* (1975; repr. New York, 1979), 251–58; see Roszika Parker, *The Subversive Stitch: Embroidery and the Making of the Feminine* (London, 1984); Elizabeth Wayland Barber, *Women's Work: The First 20,000 Years* (New York, 1994).

52. Best and O'Brien, *Book of Leinster* 5:1138 (l. 33512); Duncan, "Altram Tige Dá Medar," 212; Patrick S. Dinneen, ed. and trans., *The History of Ireland by Geoffrey Keating: Foras Feasa ar Éirinn* (London, 1908), 3:558. On gendered space, see Susan Kus and Victor Raharijaona, "Domestic Space and the Tenacity of Tradition among Some Betsileo of Madagascar," in Susan Kent, ed., *Domestic Architecture and the Use of Space: An Interdisciplinary and Cross-Cultural Study* (Cambridge, 1990), 21–33; Lucienne A. Roubin, "Espace masculin, espace féminin en communautés provençales," *Annales, E.S.C.* 26.2 (1970), 537–60; Roberta Gilchrist, "Women's Archaeology? Political Feminism, Gender Theory, and Historical Revisionism," *Antiquity* 65 (1991), 495–501.

53. It seems unlikely that noblemen purposely kept mistresses in semislavery on isolated farmsteads where they might have labored in groups, as David Herlihy has shown of the late Roman Empire and the Carolingians. Herlihy, *Opera Muliebria,* 8–12, 18–20, 34–38, 78–83. The Irish laws made provision for a single woman set up on a farm by her man, but they suggested no workshops or harems of the kind run by the Eastern emperors or fantasized about by Chrétien de Troyes in *Yvain* (ll. 5185–5346).

54. *CIH,* 289 = *ALI* 3:290.

55. *CIH,* 285–86 = *ALI* 3:274–77. See also *CIH,* 265 = *ALI* 3:174–81, which exempts servants generally.

56. *CA,* 28–29.

57. *CIH,* 7–8 = *ALI* 5:142–47.

58. Bieler, *Penitentials,* 88, 116. For a general treatment, see A. T. Lucas, *Cattle in Ancient Ireland* (Kilkenny, Éire, 1989), esp. 41–55.

59. Plummer, *Vitae* 1:147–48, 2:19.

60. Stokes, "Death of Crimthann," 190–93. Cf. *CA,* 30, which treats women's assaults on women.

61. But see the variety of attitudes among cowives observed by the anthropologist Sally Price in modern Suriname. *Co-Wives and Calabashes,* 2d ed. (Ann Arbor, 1993), esp. 53–57.

62. *CIH,* 401 = *ALI* 1:230–33; *CIH,* 335–36 = *ALI* 3:532–33, where an elopement from an alehouse was considered to be legitimate because publicly witnessed and consented to; see also *CG,* 23 (l. 593), which refers to a king's need for bodyguards or bouncers against the typical "confusion" or "strife of [in] an alehouse." The alehouse was not necessarily a discrete institution or structure, but may just refer to the place where the drinking was taking place.

63. *CIH,* 577–78.

64. Cf. Rena Lederman, "Contested Order: Gender and Society in the Southern New Guinea Highlands," *American Ethnologist* 16 (1989), 230–47, where she explains that women participated in economic exchange for different reasons than men.

65. Tírechán refers to women washing at a well *more mulierum.* Bieler, *Patrician Texts,* 142–43.

66. Heist, *Vitae,* 239; Plummer, *Bethada* 1:186, 217–18, 2:180, 211.

67. Heist, *Vitae,* 136; Plummer, *Bethada* 1:166, 2:161.

68. For example, Heist, *Vitae,* 391–92. But see *CG* 6 (l. 1550), which refers to a *bóaire,* an ordinary freeman, who owns a share in a mill and grinds grain to supply a household and a retinue. It is unlikely that the farmer himself worked the mill.

69. Plummer, *Vitae* 1:207; but cf. 203–4, where slavery for the saint means working in a mill.

70. Ibid., 2:209.

71. Ibid., 2:165–66.

72. See the legal tract on joint ownership with its elaborate schemes for cooperation by all those who lived near a mill. D. A. Binchy, ed. and trans., "Irish Law Tracts Re-edited: I. Coibnes Uisci Thairidne," *Ériu* 17 (1955), 52–85.

73. Bieler, *Patrician Texts,* 174–75.

74. Patterson, *Cattle-Lords and Clansmen,* 75–77, argues for boolying on the basis of postmedieval evidence, but only a few archaeological sites suggest the possibility of high-pasture seasonal habitations. Williams, "Excavations at Ballyutoag"; Edwards, *Archaeology of Early Medieval Ireland,* 47, 57. See also Lucas, *Cattle in Ancient Ireland,* 58–67.

75. Heist, *Vitae,* 206.

76. Adomnán, *Life of Columba,* 434–47; Heist, *Vitae,* 222–23; Plummer, *Vitae* 1:4–5, 2:256; Plummer, *Bethada* 1:319–20, 2:310–11.

77. Cogitosus, *PL* 72:790; Seán Connolly and J.-M. Picard, trans., "Cogitosus' Life of St. Brigit," *JRSAI* 117 (1987), 27.

78. Gwynn and Purton, "Monastery of Tallaght," 130: *les caillech; AU,* 527, 553; Bieler, *Patrician Texts,* 186.

79. *AU,* 345 (890.5), 378 (928.2); cf. John O'Donovan, ed. and trans., *Annals of*

the Kingdom of Ireland by the Four Masters (Dublin, 1856), 2:620, 394 (948.5), 514 (1080.4); Mac Airt, *Annals of Inisfallen,* 216 (1058.2), 232 (1076.7), 286 (1126.6).

80. *Can. Hib.,* 175, 184.

81. *CIH,* 513–14 = *ALI* 2:386–89.

82. *CIH,* 15 = *ALI* 5:176; Kelly, *Guide,* 139; cf. Smith, "*Senbriathra Fithail,*" 68: "brugaid cach co heithlind."

83. Plummer, *Vitae* 1:204. Bríg *briugu* (hospitaller) was a legendary provider of food and drink who appears in the laws as a jurist: *CIH,* 377, 380; Kelly, *Guide,* 358.

84. For one treatment of male consciousness as a shared ethical code, see Philip O'Leary, "*Fír Fer:* An Internalized Ethical Concept in Early Irish Literature?" *Éigse* 22 (1987), 1–14. See also Temma Kaplan, "Female Consciousness and Collective Action: The Case of Barcelona, 1910–1918," *Signs* 7 (1982), 545–66, where she maintains that men, conscious of themselves as a group by sex, project the same consciousness on women.

85. *CG,* 9 (l. 237), 15 (l. 384), 81.

86. *CIH,* 468–69 = *ALI* 5:396–97. *Corus Béscnai* details the legal responsibility of providing feasts and hospitality. *CIH,* 524–25 = *ALI* 3:18–23; see also Katherine Simms, "Guesting and Feasting in Gaelic Ireland," *JRSAI* 108 (1978), 67–100.

87. Gwynn, *Metrical Dindsenchas* 3:18 (l. 225). The seventeenth-century historian Keating mentions marriage at the *oenach* of Tailtiu. Dinneen, *History of Ireland* 2:248–49.

88. O'Leary, "Contention at Feasts."

89. Two examples are Thurneysen, *Scéla Mucce Meic Dathó;* J. Carmichael Watson, ed., *Mesca Ulad* (Dublin, 1941).

90. Radner, *Fragmentary Annals of Ireland,* 58 (717); *AU,* 172, 230, 246, 284, 398. See also D. A. Binchy, "The Fair of Tailtiu and the Feast of Tara," *Ériu* 18 (1958), 118–22.

91. Meyer, *Instructions of King Cormac,* 28–32.

92. *Fled Bricrend,* in Best and Bergin, *Lebor na hUidre,* 246–77; the "briatharcath na mban" and its immediate consequences: 252–53, trans. by George Henderson in *Fled Bricrend* (London, 1899), 22–31. On the date of *Fled Bricrenn,* see Kelly, "*Táin* as Literature," 71 n. 4; Gearóid Mac Eoin, "The Dating of Middle Irish Texts," *ÉC* 7 (1983), 121.

93. Smith, "*Senbriathra Fithail,*" 61. Cf. Meyer, *Instructions of King Cormac,* 22: "milbéla druinecha / dálacha drochmná," "skilful women [or embroideresses] are honey-mouthed / bad women are given to trysting."

94. Cf. Meyer, *Triads,* 10 (79), 14 (109, 114).

95. Cormac, *Glossary,* 12 (Y116).

96. A few saintly abbesses performed the function of political negotiator, as did male saints and abbots; see, for example, Plummer, *Vitae* 2:255, 256, 259; Ó hAodha, *Bethu Brigte,* 7.

97. O'Rahilly, *Táin Bó Cúailnge,* 25, 147–48.

98. Marstrander, "Deaths of Lugaid and Derbforgaill." Cf. O'Leary, "Honour of Women," 27–44. Women working together were able to threaten men and their interrelations even when men created an antisociety, such as that of the *fíanna,* homeless mercenaries. See the late medieval story of Garad mac Morna in E. J.

Gwynn, ed. and trans., "The Burning of Finn's House," *Ériu* 1 (1904), 13–33; Nagy, *Wisdom of the Outlaw*, 73–74.

99. Bhreathnach, "New Edition of *Tochmarc Becfhola*," 72, 81.

100. Dillon, *Serglige Con Culainn*, 1–2.

101. Van Hamel, *Immrama*, 57.

102. Ibid., 18–19.

103. Mac Cana, "The Sinless Otherworld," 95–115, esp. 112; McCone, *Pagan Past and Christian Present*, 57–58; Séamus Mac Mathúna, ed. and trans., *Immram Brain: Bran's Journey to the Land of Women* (Tübingen, 1985), 44–45, 57–58. Cf. H. P. A. Oskamp, ed. and trans., *The Voyage of Máel Dúin: Study in Early Irish Voyage Literature* (Groningen, 1970), 59–60, 152–59. See also Whitley Stokes, ed. and trans., "The Voyage of Mael Duin," *RC* 9 (1888), 486–93; Stokes, ed. and trans., "The Voyage of the Huí Corra," *RC* 14 (1893), 46–47.

104. Oskamp, "Echtra Condla," esp. 225–28.

105. Ó Cathasaigh, "Semantics of *Síd*," esp. 139–41, 144; Sims-Williams, "Some Celtic Otherworld Terms," 61–62; Eric Hamp, "Irish *Síd* 'Tumulus' and Irish *Síd* 'Peace'," *ÉC* 19 (1982), 141.

8. Priests' Wives and Brides of Christ

1. *Can. Hib.*, 183; Ní Dhonnchadha, "*Caillech* and Other Terms," 71–72.

2. Heist, *Vitae*, 81–83.

3. Richard Sharpe, "Churches and Communities in Early Medieval Ireland: Towards a Pastoral Model," in J. Blair and Richard Sharpe, eds., *Pastoral Care before the Parish* (Leicester, 1992), 81–109; Thomas Charles-Edwards, "The Pastoral Function of the Church in the Early Irish Laws," in Blair and Sharpe, *Pastoral Care*, 63–80; Edwards, *Archaeology of Early Medieval Ireland*, 114–18.

4. Ryan, *Irish Monasticism*; cf. Roberta Gilchrist, *Gender and Material Culture: The Archaeology of Religious Women* (London, 1994), 25–32.

5. Bieler, *Patrician Texts*, 186–87.

6. Aubrey Gwynn and R. Neville Hadcock, *Medieval Religious Houses: Ireland (with an Appendix to Early Sites)* (London, 1970), 18–46, 307–26; Heist, *Vitae*, 347–48, 392–93; Plummer, *Vitae* 1:88, 96, 185, 2:268. Some hagiographic references are unclear as to whether they mean actual mixed-sex communities or women's settlements under the authority of a male saint's community.

7. Bitel, *Isle of the Saints*, 98–99; Kathleen Hughes and Ann Hamlin, *Celtic Monasticism: The Modern Traveler to the Early Irish Church* (New York, 1981), 7–9.

8. For example, Flandnait, daughter of Cuanu mac Cailchín: Plummer, *Vitae* 1:184–85. Cf. Karl J. Leyser, *Rule and Conflict in an Early Medieval Society: Ottonian Saxony* (London, 1979), 59–73.

9. *Can. Hib.*, 116; Bitel, "Women's Donations to the Churches," 9–10.

10. Heist, *Vitae*, 115, 126, 250–51.

11. Cf. Gilchrist, *Gender and Material Culture*, 66–90, where she says that, by nature, women's communities were never wealthy or even self-sufficient. See also Bernadette Barrière, "The Cistercian Convent of Coyroux in the Twelfth and Thirteenth Centuries," *Gesta* 31 (1992), 76–82.

12. Pádraig Ó Riain, "Boundary Association in Early Irish Society," *Studia Celtica* 7 (1972), 12–29; Dorothy Africa on Cluain Brónaig, "Other Than Brigit: The Cultural and Historical Context of Three Early Irish Female Saints," Kalamazoo, May 7, 1994, session 430.

13. Cogitosus, *PL* 72:790.

14. Plummer, *Vitae* 2:254–55, 256, 260. Cf. Cell Dara: Cogitosus, *PL* 72:789.

15. Bieler, *Patrician Text*, 132.

16. Ibid., 40–42.

17. Heist, *Vitae*, 347–38; Plummer, *Bethada* 1:104, 2:100.

18. Gwynn and Hadcock, *Medieval Religious Houses: Ireland*, 40 (Kilskeer = Cell Scíre), 312 (Addrigoole = Etaragabáil), 312–13 (Armagh = Ard Macha), 319–20 (Kildare = Cell Dara), 315 (Clonmacnoise = Cluain Moccu Nóis).

19. Besides the classic Mary Catherine Bateson, "Origin and Early History of Double Monasteries," *Transactions of the Royal Historical Society* n.s. 13 (1899), 137–98, see Susan Ridyard, "Anglo-Saxon Women and the Church in the Age of Conversion," in Edward B. King et al., eds., *Monks, Nuns, and Friars in Medieval Society* (Sewanee, Tenn., 1989), 110–11; Stephanie Hollis, *Anglo-Saxon Women and the Church: Sharing a Common Fate* (Woodbrige, Suffolk, 1992), esp. chaps. 8 and 9, 243–300; Constance H. Berman, "Men's Houses, Women's Houses: The Relationship between the Sexes in Twelfth-Century Monasticism," in Andrew MacLeish, ed., *The Medieval Monastery* (St. Cloud, Minn., 1988), 43–52.

20. Jo Ann McNamara describes the situation in late antiquity, which is probably more apt for the Middle Ages, too, than historians have previously supposed. "Muffled Voices: The Lives of Consecrated Women in the Fourth Century," in John A. Nichols and Lillian Thomas Shank, eds., *Medieval Religious Women*, vol. 1: *Distant Echoes* (Kalamazoo, Mich., 1984), 18–24.

21. Hughes, *Early Christian Ireland*, 234–35; Jane T. Schulenberg, "Women's Monastic Communities, 500–1100: Patterns of Expansion and Decline," in Judith M. Bennett et al., eds., *Sisters and Workers in the Middle Ages* (Repr. Chicago, 1989), 221–23.

22. USMLS, "Life of St. Monenna," I, 267–69.

23. A. B. E. Hood, *Saint Patrick: His Writings and Muirchu's Life* (Chichester, 1978), 31.

24. USMLS, "The Life of St. Monenna" I, 256–57; see also the earlier version in Heist, *Vitae*, 84; Dorothy Africa, "Moninne, Armagh, Killevy," presented to the Harvard Celtic Colloquium, April 10, 1994.

25. Heist, *Vitae*, 84–85.

26. *Can. Hib.*, 193; Máirín Ní Dhonnchadha, "*Caillech* and Other Terms for Veiled Women in Medieval Irish Texts," *Éigse* 28 (1994–95), 91–92.

27. *Can. Hib.*, 181–83; Ní Dhonnchadha, "*Caillech* and Other Terms," 83–85.

28. Bieler, *Penitentials*, 54; cf. 1 Corinthians 11:5–15.

29. McNamara, "Chaste Marriage and Clerical Celibacy," 23–25. The "First Synod of Saint Patrick" also refers to nuns traveling under the protection of monks, presumably on religious business; so the texts clearly conceive of both married women and virgins as professionally active in the Christian community. See Bieler, *Penitentials*, 54.

30. *Can. Hib.*, 5; Ní Dhonnchadha, "*Caillech* and Other Terms," 75–76; Robin

Stacey, "Translation of the Old Irish Tract *Berrad Airechta*," in T. M. Charles-Edwards et al., eds., *Lawyers and Laymen: Studies in the History of Law Presented to Professor Dafydd Jenkins on His Seventy-fifth Birthday* (Cardiff, 1986), 211; Hughes, *Church in Early Irish Society*, 161–65. Richard Sharpe has suggested in his review of my *Isle of the Saints* that ecclesiastical administrators came to be a purely secular class of landlords. *English Historical Review* 109 (1994), 679–80. But rather than label monastic rulers as either laymen or ecclesiastics, it seems more appropriate to the early medieval perspective to consider a group with an identity that fell somewhere in between. See *Isle of the Saints*, 104–7. The women attached to these semiclerics seem to have retained reflected prestige throughout the Middle Ages, judging by the reference to the *comarbae*'s daughter in the late Irish life of Máedóc. Plummer, *Bethada* 1:203, 2:196.

31. McNamara, "Chaste Marriage," 22–33; Wemple, *Women in Frankish Society;* Brown, *The Body and Society,* esp. 90, 154.

32. See, for example, the story of Saint Mochuda and the thirty virgins in Plummer, *Bethada,* 1:295, 2:286; also in Plummer, *Vitae* 1:173. Saint Cainnech was particularly friendly with nuns. Heist, *Vitae,* 192–93, 197. See also Roger Reynolds, "Virgines Subintroductae," *Harvard Theological Review* 61 (1968), 547–66; Ní Dhonnchadha, "*Caillech* and Other Terms," 76–77.

33. Ní Dhonnchadha, "*Caillech* and Other Terms," esp. 71–77.

34. Ó hAodha, *Bethu Brigte,* 5, 23.

35. Bieler, *Irish Penitentials,* 56–57, 70–71. *Can. Hib.,* 184; Ní Dhonnchadha, "*Caillech* and Other Terms," 8–9.

36. *CIH,* 48, 2198; Kelly, *Guide,* 73–75; *Can. Hib.,* 187.

37. Bieler, *Patrician Texts,* 142–45; *VT,* 98–104 = Kathleen Mulchrone, ed. and trans., *Bethu Phátraic* (Dublin, 1939), 1:60–64.

38. McNamara, "Living Sermons."

39. Bieler, *Patrician Texts,* 98–101; Heist, *Vitae,* 109, 141; Plummer, *Vitae* 2:61.

40. Many more references in the vitae describe nuns who were killed (and often decapitated) and then raised by male saints, as well as women who were killed, raised, and then became nuns. Although this kind of ritual death signifies the transition from carnal to spiritual life, it is clearly linked to the theme of dead virgins described here. See Heist, *Vitae,* 172–73, 223, 394; Plummer, *Vitae* 1:38; Plummer, *Bethada* 1:164–65, 2:159.

41. Bitel, *Isle of the Saints,* 194–221.

42. Kim McCone, "Brigit in the Seventh Century: A Saint with Three Lives?" *Peritia* 1 (1982), 107–45.

43. Heist, *Vitae,* 111; cf. 124, where Ailbe offers Brigit one hundred sheep "ante ianuam civitatis," in a kind of public, ritual payment.

44. Johnson, *Equal in Monastic Profession,* esp. 62–102; Jane Tibbetts Schulenberg, "Strict Active Enclosure and Its Effects on the Female Monastic Experience (ca. 500–1100)," in Nichols and Shank, *Medieval Religious Women* 1:51–86.

45. Heist, *Vitae,* 126.

46. Ibid., 102, 192, 175, 402; Ó hAodha, *Bethu Brigte,* 5–6, 24; USMLS, ed., "Life of St. Monenna," I, 254–57.

47. Plummer, *Vitae* 1:145–46; Plummer, *Bethada* 1:301, 2:292. See also Heist, *Vitae*, 111; Plummer, *Vitae* 2:120; Plummer, *Bethada* 1:45–46, 64, 2:45–46, 62–63.

48. Mac Eoin, "A Life of Cumaine Fota," 198, 201.

49. Heist, *Vitae*, 172, 173–74, 178.

50. Ibid., 127, 392, 394.

51. David Greene, ed., "St. Brigit's Alefeast," *Celtica* 2 (1952), 150–53.

52. Plummer, *Vitae* 1:99, 102–3, 2:60, 61–62, 166, 167.

53. Ibid., 2:259–60.

54. Heist, *Vitae*, 397.

55. Plummer, *Vitae* 1:256.

56. Ibid., 1:96. See also Doherty, "Some Aspects of Hagiography," 311–12.

57. Heist, *Vitae*, 347–49; Plummer, *Vitae* 1:220; Plummer, *Bethada* 1:104, 2:100.

58. Plummer, *Vitae* 2:60–62.

59. According to Rosemary Rader, Christian celibacy made these heterosexual friendships possible. *Breaking Boundaries: Male/Female Friendship in Early Christian Communities* (New York, 1983), 86–117.

60. Plummer, *Vitae* 1:226–27; Plummer, *Bethada* 1:108–9, 2:104–5.

61. Plummer, *Vitae* 2:127–28; see also the parallel in the vita of Samthann, 259–60.

62. USMLS, "Life of St. Monenna," III, 448–49.

63. Heist, *Vitae*, 408.

64. Binchy, "Bretha Crólige," 26–27, where "a woman who turns back the streams of war" is glossed as "such as the abbess of Kildare or the female *aíbellteóir*, one who turns back the manifold sins of wars through her prayers."

65. Africa, "Other Than Brigit."

66. The twelfth-century *Book of Leinster* contains a list of the *virgines sanctae* whose communities and foundations were supposedly subject to Brigit's community at Cell Dara. Best and O'Brien and O'Sullivan, *Book of Leinster* 6:1580 (48,496).

67. Heist, *Vitae*, 201. Cf. the version at 250–51.

68. *AU*, 292, 296, 306, 430.

69. USMLS, "Life of St. Monenna," II, *Seanchas Ard Mhacha* 10 (1980–81), 124–25.

70. Africa, "Moninne, Armagh, Killevy." See also Mario Esposito, ed., "Conchubranus Vita Sanctae Monennae," *PRIA* 28 C (1910), 244–45, for the list of Moninne's successors.

71. Heist, *Vitae*, 129.

72. The lessons are carefully couched in terms of ritual gifts and hospitality. Heist, *Vitae*, 85; cf. USMLS, "Life of St. Monenna," II, 126–29; Plummer, *Vitae* 2:63–64; see also Bitel, *Isle of the Saints*, 194–221.

73. This is one of the very few bits of evidence that women's settlements actively engaged in literate pursuits. Dorothy Africa has argued for abbesses who were patronesses of hagiographical compositions. "Other Than Brigit." See also the ninth-century poem on the Virgin Mary where she is hailed as *ecnae,* learned, because she had "read the Prophets and the Law": James Carney, ed. and trans., "Two Old Irish Poems," *Ériu* 18 (1958), 26–27.

74. USMLS, "Life of St. Monenna," II, 130–31.

75. Heist, *Vitae,* 92–93. See also USMLS, "Life of St. Monenna," III, 436–39.

76. Heist, *Vitae,* 86, 87.

77. Plummer, *Vitae* 2:129, also 121. See also Dorothy Ann Bray, "Motival Derivations in the *Life of St. Samthann,*" *Studia Celtica* 20-21 (1985-86), 82–83.

78. Plummer, *Vitae* 2:258.

79. Cogitosus, *PL* 72:782; Plummer, *Vitae* 2:61–62, 256; USMLS, "Life of St. Monenna," I, 264–67; II, 132–35.

80. Bitel, *Isle of the Saints,* 94–96, esp. n. 59.

81. McNamara, "Living Sermons," 19–38.

82. For Brigit's kin, see Dorothy C. Africa, "The Politics of Kin: Women and Preeminence in a Medieval Irish Hagiographical List" (Ph.D. thesis, University of Toronto, 1990), 103–49.

83. Plummer, *Vitae* 2:61.

84. Ó hAodha, *Bethu Brigte,* 6, 24. As Jocelyn Hilgarth has pointed out to me, the episcopal episode is a long Latin interpolation into the Irish text and is not necessarily datable to the ninth century. It may well be an earlier episode, Professor Hilgarth has suggested, which could be related to the *céli dé* reform movement and its female spiritual guides.

85. Cf. USMLS, "Life of St. Monenna," III, 428–29.

86. For a general study of gender and sanctity in Ireland, see Dianne P. Hall, "Gender and Sanctity in the Hagiography of Early Medieval Ireland" (M.A. thesis, University of Melbourne, 1992). Some of the recent material on Brigit emphasizes her place within "native" culture, especially her pre-Christian origins as a goddess or the similarity of her characteristics to those of figures from secular literature. See Margaret MacCurtain, "Towards an Appraisal of the Religious Image of Women," *Crane Bag* 4 (1980); Dorothy Ann Bray, "The Image of St. Brigit in the Early Irish Church," *ÉC* 24 (1984), 209–15; Dorothy Ann Bray, "*Secunda Brigida:* Saint Ita of Killeedy and Brigidine Tradition," in Cyril J. Byrne et al., eds., *Celtic Languages and Celtic Peoples* (Halifax, 1989), 27–38; Ó Cathasaigh, "The Cult of Brigid"; Condren, *The Serpent and the Goddess,* 47–78; Edward B. Sellner, "Brigit of Kildare—a Study in the Liminality of Women's Spiritual Power," *Cross Currents* 39 (1989–90), 402–19; McCone, *Pagan Past and Christian Present,* 162–66, 175–76, 180–83, et passim; Séamas Ó Catháin, "Hearth-Prayers and Other Traditions of Brigit: Celtic Goddess and Holy Woman," *JRSAI* 122 (1992), 12–34.

87. This practice raises the question of the gender of writers and readers of vitae. See Jane T. Schulenberg, "Saints' Lives as a Source for the History of Women, 500–1100," in Rosenthal, *Medieval Women and the Sources,* 238–320, esp. 286–92.

88. For editions of Brigit's vitae, see James F. Kenney, *The Sources for the History of Early Ireland,* vol. 1: *Ecclesiastical* (Repr. Dublin, 1979), 359–63; see also Richard Sharpe, "*Vitae Sanctae Brigidae:* The Oldest Texts," *Peritia* 1 (1982), 81–106; McCone, "Brigit in the Seventh Century."

89. *Can Hib.,* 68.

90. Bray, "Motival Derivations," 84. See also Hughes, *Church in Early Irish Society,* 173–93.

91. Schulenberg, "Women's Monastic Communities," 217–20.

92. Heist, *Vitae,* 129.

93. Hull, "Two Anecdotes Concerning St. Moling"; trans. James Carney, *Studies* 62 (1973), 240.

94. Heist, *Vitae,* 136–37.

95. Plummer, *Bethada* 1:295.

96. J. H. Bernard and Robert Atkinson, eds. and trans., *The Irish Liber Hymnorum* (London, 1898), 1:32, 2:17. Ní Dhonnchadha interprets *caillecha,* translated here as "nuns", as "hags," meaning wives or concubines: "*Caillech* and Other Terms," 6–7.

97. *AU,* 200–201.

98. Heist, *Vitae,* 392–93.

99. Gwynn and Purton, "The Monastery of Tallaght," 151.

100. Ibid., 130.

101. Cf. Loraine N. Simmons, "The Abbey Church at Fontrevaud in the Later Twelfth Century: Anxiety, Authority, and Architecture in the Female Spiritual Life," *Gesta* 31.2 (1992), 99–107.

102. Gwynn and Purton, "Monastery of Tallaght," 140, 144.

103. Ibid., 149.

104. Ibid., 150–51.

105. Heist, *Vitae,* 347–49; Plummer, *Vitae* 1:220–21; Plummer, *Bethada* 1:104–5, 2:100–101.

106. *AU,* 276 (821), when a "great prey of women" was taken; Plummer, *Vitae* 2:115, for the Viking destruction of Mag Eó; Donnchadh Ó Corráin, *Ireland before the Normans* (Dublin, 1972), 30–110; Hughes, *Church in Early Irish Society,* chap. 18: "The Church and the Viking Terror," 197–202, 203–14; Jesch, *Women in the Viking Age,* 106–9; Schulenberg, "Women's Monastic Communities," 222–24.

107. Edwards, *Archaeology of Medieval Ireland,* 172–92; John Bradley, "The Interpretation of Scandinavian Settlement in Ireland," in Bradley, *Settlement and Society,* 49–88.

108. A. T. Lucas, "The Plundering and Burning of Churches in Ireland, 7th to 16th Century," in Etienne Rynne, ed., *North Munster Studies* (Limerick, 1967), 16–54.

109. Bieler, *Irish Penitentials,* 88, 116, 148, et passim.

110. Gwynn and Purton, "Monastery of Tallaght," 132, 145–46.

111. Plummer, *Bethada* 1:90, 2:87–88.

112. USMLS, "Life of St. Monenna," I, 258–59.

113. Ibid., I, 256–69, III, 136–39.

114. Ibid., I, 258–61. This solution is interesting in light of other vitae, where saints turn girls into boys to please parents seeking heirs.

115. USMLS, "Life of St. Monenna," III, 428–29.

116. Ibid., III, 438–39.

117. Cf. Jocelyn Wogan-Brown, "Saints' Lives and the Female Reader," *Forum for Modern Language Studies* 27 (1991), 314–32.

118. Stokes, *Lives from the "Book of Lismore,"* 72–73, 219–20.

119. Wemple, *Women in Frankish Society,* 154–74; Schulenberg, "Women's Monastic Communities," esp. 215–17; Schulenberg, "Strict Active Enclosure"; Hollis, *Anglo-Saxon Women and the Church,* esp. 1–14.

120. Schulenberg, "Women's Monastic Communities," 235–36.

9. Warriors, Hags, and Sheelanagigs

1. *VT* 1, 50–51.

2. Early modern historians have argued for a sixteenth-century Western European creation of pornography. See Lynn Hunt, ed., *The Invention of Pornography: Obscenity and the Origin of Modernity, 1500–1800* (New York, 1993), especially Hunt's introduction, 9–45. Hunt admits, however (10), that an art or literature of "desire, sensuality, eroticism, and even the explicit depiction of sexual organs" could probably be found in every culture and every period.

3. For example, Andrea Dworkin, *Pornography: Men Possessing Women* (New York, 1981).

4. Catharine MacKinnon, *Only Words* (Cambridge, Mass., 1993); MacKinnon, *Feminism Unmodified: Discourses on Life and Law* (Cambridge, 1987), esp. 127–213.

5. Máire Bhreathnach, "The Sovereignty Goddess as Goddess of Death?" *ZCP* 39 (1982), 249–50; O'Flaherty, *Women, Androgynes,* esp. 262–80.

6. Miranda Green, *Symbol and Image in Celtic Art* (London, 1989), 9–73 (esp. 64–73), 188–205; Anne Ross, *Pagan Celtic Britain* (London, 1967), 205–18.

7. William Hennessy, "The Ancient Irish Goddess of War," *RC* 1 (1870–72), 32–55; Van Hamel, *Compert Con Culainn,* 42; Ross, *Pagan Celtic Britain,* 224–26; F. Benoit, *L'héroisation équestre* (Aix-en-Provence, 1954); Jaan Puhvel, "Aspects of Equine Functionality," in Puhvel, *Myth and Law,* 159–72.

8. Whitley Stokes, "The Ancient Irish Goddess of War: Corrections and Additions," *RC* 2 (1873–75), 489–92; Mac Cana, *Celtic Mythology;* Jaan Puhvel, *Comparative Mythology* (Baltimore, 1987), 166–88, et passim; James Doan, "Women and Goddesses in Early Irish History, Myth, and Legend," Northeastern Working Papers in Irish Studies 87, 4/5 (Boston, 1987); Ross, *Pagan Celtic Britain,* 230–33, 244–49; Condren, *The Serpent and the Goddess,* 35–36; John Carey, "Notes on the Irish War-Goddess," *Éigse* 19 (1983), 263–75; Rosalind Clark, "Aspects of the Morrígan in Early Irish Literature," *Irish University Review* 17 (1987). Patricia Lysaght sensibly traces the *badb* in the other direction, to modern folklore: *The Banshee,* esp. 198–210.

9. *DIL,* 173; Cormac puts it: "Gudemain .i. uatha ocus morrignae," "spectres, that is horrors and Morrígans," *Glossary,* 58.

10. Van Hamel, *Compert Con Culainn,* 42.

11. Cormac, *Glossary,* 16, 82; 26. See also Elizabeth A. Gray, ed. and trans., *Cath Maige Tuired: The Second Battle of Mag Tuired* (Naas, Éire, 1982), 118.

12. Mac Cana, *Celtic Mythology,* 86–89; Dumézil, "Le trio des Macha." The story of Macha the warrior can be found in Best and O'Brien, *Book of Leinster,* 1:79–80; see also Whitley Stokes, ed. and trans., "The Prose Tales in the *Rennes Dindsenchas,*" *RC* 16 (1895), 44–47.

13. J. Fraser, ed. and trans., "The First Battle of Moytura," *Ériu* 8 (1916), 44–45, mod. trans.; on the translation of *amaite,* see Stokes, "Ancient Irish Goddess," 489.

14. O'Rahilly, *Táin Bó Cúailnge,* 117, 118; trans. Kinsella, *Tain,* 238.

15. O'Rahilly, *Táin Bó Cúailnge,* 57.

16. Fraser, "First Battle of Moytura," 44–45. See also Kenneth H. Jackson, ed., *Cath Maighe Léna* (Dublin, 1938), 16, where the *badb,* called *ban-ghaisgedach* (woman warrior) arrives in a chariot.

17. Whitley Stokes and John Strachan, eds. and trans., *Thesaurus Paleohibernicus* (London, 1901), 1:26.

18. Radner, *Fragmentary Annals of Ireland*, 142–43; see also Cath Almaine (Battle of Allen) in 722, where "Brigit was seen over the Laigin," but so was a male saint, Columcille: Radner, *Fragmentary Annals*, 70–71; Pádraig Ó Riain, ed., *Cath Almaine* (Dublin, 1978), 6–7.

19. J. H. Todd, ed. and trans., *Cogadh Gaedhel re Gallaibh*, Rolls Series (London, 1867), 174.

20. See the early modern Irish glossary which defines *Badhb* as *feannóg*, "scald-crow," and *túath thíre*, a district or lordship: Arthur W. K. Miller, "O'Clery's Irish Glossary," *RC* 4 (repr. 1967), 369. That is, even as late as the seventeenth century, writers maintained the tradition that the *badb* was a tutelary or sovereignty figure. On sovereignty goddesses in all their manifestations, see Mac Cana, "Aspects of the Theme of King and Goddess"; Anne Ross, "The Divine Hag of the Pagan Celts," in Venetia Newall, ed., *The Witch Figure* (London, 1973), 139–64.

21. Lysaght, *The Banshee*, 198–210; Carey, "Notes on the Irish War-Goddess," 264–65.

22. As just two examples from many: Thurneysen, "Baile in Scáil"; Stokes, *Cóir Anmann*, 320–23.

23. Brendan O Hehir, "The Christian Revision of *Eachtra Airt Meic Chuind ocus Tochmarc Delbchaime Ingine Morgain*," in Ford, ed., *Celtic Folklore and Christianity*, 159–79; Clark, "Aspects of the Morrígan"; Clark, *The Great Queens*, 21–52; Bhreathnach, "Sovereignty Goddess."

24. Knott, *Togail Bruidne Da Derga* 16–17; trans. Gantz, *Early Irish Myths and Sagas*, 76. See also *Bruiden Da Choca*, where Cormac Conn Loinges meets a fate similar to that of Conaire after encountering a bloody washerwoman who turns out to be the *badb* at the ford. Whitley Stokes, ed. and trans., "Da Choca's Hostel," *RC* 21 (1900), 150–65; McCone, *Pagan Past and Christian Present*, 132.

25. Cf. Cú Chulainn's meeting with a red hag with an equally long name in *Táin Bó Regamna*. Ernst Windisch, ed., in Stokes and Windisch, *Irische Texte*, 239–47.

26. Whitley Stokes, ed. and trans., "Cuchulainn's Death Abridged from the *Book of Leinster*," *RC* 3 (1876–78), 175.

27. See Maria Tymoczko's evocative translation in *Two Death Tales*, 60–61.

28. *CA*, 2–5. See Condren, *Serpent and Goddess*, 52–56, who seems to credit the prologue with reality on this point.

29. O'Rahilly, *Táin Bó Cúailnge*, 176–77.

30. Ó Coileáin, "Structure of a Literary Cycle"; Mac Eoin, "Suithchern and Ró-nán Dícolla"; O'Nolan, "Mór of Munster"; Mac Cana, "Aspects of the Theme of King and Goddess," *ZCP* 7:91–114.

31. T. F. O'Rahilly, "Varia II: Lost Legends of Mis and Dubh Ruis," *Celtica* 1.2 (1950), 382–84; Brian Ó Cuív, ed., "The Romance of Mis and Dubh Ruis," *Celtica* 2.2 (1954), 325–33. See also Pádraig Ó Riain, "A Study of the Irish Legend of the Wild Man," *Éigse* 14 (1972), 179–206, esp. 202–3.

32. Ó Cuív, "Romance of Mis and Dubh Ruis," 330.

33. J. G. O'Keeffe, ed., *Buile Suibhne* (Dublin, 1931); Joseph Falaky Nagy, *The Wisdom of the Outlaw: The Boyhood Deeds of Finn in Gaelic Narrative Tradition* (Berkeley, 1985), 132.

34. Cf. modern stories of man-eaters in Máire Mac Neill, *The Festival of Lugh-nasa: A Study of the Survival of the Celtic Festival of the Beginning of Harvest* (London, 1962), 400, 519–20, 521.

35. Posidonius and Strabo described an island of women at the Celtic edge of the northern seas, where men could not venture for fear of death, and women ripped each other apart. Ammianus Marcellinus, Dio Cassius, and Tacitus mentioned Celtic women inciting, participating in, and even leading battles. See J. J. Tierney, "The Celtic Ethnography of Posidonius," *PRIA* 60 C (1959–60), 189–275.

36. Doan, *Women and Goddesses*, 2–23.

37. Cf. the situation in Scandinavia. Jochens, "Illicit Love Visit."

38. Cf. the lessons of lady fighters and of rape in medieval French literature. Kathryn Gravdal, "Chrétien de Troyes and the Medieval Romance of Sexual Violation," *Signs* 17.3 (1992), 558–585; Helen Solterer, "Figures of Female Militancy in French Literature," *Signs* 16.3 (1991), 522–49.

39. O'Rahilly, *Táin Bó Cúailnge*, 5–6, 36, 44, 79. See also Kelly, "The *Táin* as Literature," 77–85.

40. O'Rahilly, *Táin Bó Cúalinge*, 81, 197.

41. Ibid., 97, 121, 210, 234.

42. Ibid., 97.

43. Ó Máille, "Medb Cruachna."

44. O'Neill, "Cath Bóinde."

45. Van Hamel, *Compert Con Culainn*, 48–60.

46. Lucius Gwynn, ed., "De Síl Chonairi Móir," *Ériu* 6 (1912), 130–43; Kuno Meyer, ed., "The Dindsenchas of Emain Macha," *Archiv für Celtische Lexikographie* 3 (1907), 325–26; R. I. Best, ed., "Adventures of Art." An exceptional interpretation occurs in the story of Creidne, the daughter of an Ulster king who rapes her and begets sons on her, whom he eventually exiles. Creidne becomes a *banfén-nid*, woman warrior, in order to regain her sons' proper status and inheritance. See Meyer, *Fianaigecht*, xi–xii; Nagy, *Wisdom of the Outlaw*, 46–47.

47. Proinsias Mac Cana, "*Laíded, Gressacht,* Formalized Incitement," *Ériu* 43 (1992), 84–85; O'Leary, "Honour of Women," 29–31. Penitentialists forbade grief-stricken women to keen their dead probably to prevent incitement of survivors to violence. E. J. Gwynn, "An Irish Penitential," *Ériu* 7 (1914), 121–31, 170.

48. Stokes, "Cuchulainn's Death"; Meyer, *Death Tales*, 6–7, 24–25.

49. Solterer, "Figures of Female Militancy," 527–28.

50. Nancy Huston, "The Matrix of War: Mothers and Heroes," in Susan Rubin Suleiman, ed., *The Female Body in Western Culture: Contemporary Perspectives* (Cambridge, 1986), 126–29; Condren, *Serpent and Goddess*, 54–55, takes a unique view.

51. Best and O'Brien, *Book of Leinster* 2:399.

52. Gray, *Cath Maige Tuired*, 24.

53. Ibid., 54.

54. Kuno Meyer, ed. and trans., "An Old Irish Prayer for Long Life," in *A Miscellany Presented to John Macdonald MacKay, LL.D.* (Liverpool, 1914), 226–32; see also Macalister, *Lebor Gabála Érenn* 4:122–23.

55. Gray, *Cath Maige Tuired*, 52.

56. Kim McCone discusses the tripartite functions of Bríg in connection with

other Christian symbols of fire and the arts in *Pagan Past and Christian Present*, 161–78; see also Cormac, *Glossary*, 15; also Donál Ó Cathasaigh, in James J. Preston, ed., *Mother Worship: Theme and Variations* (Chapel Hill, N.C., 1982), 75–94.

57. O'Rahilly, *Táin Bó Cúailnge*, 2–4, 126–28.

58. Best and Bergin, "Tochmarc Étaíne," 156–61.

59. Nic Dhonnchadha, *Aided Muirchertaig*; trans. Stokes, "Death of Muirchertach."

60. Nic Dhonnchadha, *Aided Muirchertaig Meic Erca*, xvi–ii, 2.

61. McCone, *Pagan Past and Christian Present*, 132–34, 147, calls the narrative (with O Hehir, "Christian Revision of *Eachthra Airt Meic Cuind*," 168–69) an "anti-goddess" story.

62. Elsewhere in Europe, Christian leaders identified women with magic. See Gregory of Tours, *Hist. Franc.*, 10.8; also the canons of the 743 Council of Leptinnes regarding the popular belief that connected women with magic because women "surrender to the moon" once a month. Trans. J. T. McNeil and H. M. Gamer, *Medieval Handbooks of Penitentials* (New York, 1938), 419–21. On women's magic, see Valerie Flint, *The Rise of Magic in Early Medieval Europe* (Princeton, 1991), 226–39, 291–301; Michel Rouche, "The Early Middle Ages in the West," in Paul Veyne, ed., *History of Private Life* (Cambridge, 1987), 1:481–82, 519–24.

63. Whitley Stokes, ed., "The Klosterneuberg Incantation," *RC* 2 (1873–75), 112–15. See also R. I. Best, ed., "Some Irish Charms," *Ériu* 16 (1952), 27–32.

64. Bieler, *Irish Penitentials*, 56; Flint, *Rise of Magic*, esp. chap. 9, "Encouraged Magic," 254–328; Clark, *Great Queens*, 23.

65. Bieler, *Irish Penitentials*, 78, 80.

66. Ibid., 100.

67. Ibid., 160, 204, 272.

68. Binchy, "Bretha Crólige," 34–37.

69. Ibid., 26–27.

70. *CA*, 30.

71. *CIH*, 387–88 = *ALI* 1:174–81.

72. The connection endures. See Richard P. Jenkins, "Witches and Fairies: Supernatural Aggression and Deviance among the Irish Peasantry," *Ulster Folklife* 23 (1977), 33–56.

73. The only blows struck by women in the legal tracts were, as we saw in an earlier chapter, aimed at other women. The only murder committed by women and discussed in the legal tracts was infanticide. *CIH*, 2198. *Cáin Adomnáin*, however, provides for murder by women, along with poisoning, arson, and robbing a church, as well as death-causing magic. *CA*, 30. See the discussion in Kelly, *Guide*, 75, 78–79, 220.

74. One narrative, *Echtra Airt*, mentioned an otherworldly female judged a spell caster by her community. They would have burned her but this punishment was *geis* to them and would have brought pollution and damage to the community; so they set her adrift in a boat instead. R. I. Best, ed. and trans., "Echtra Airt Meic Cuinn," *Ériu* 3 (1908), 149–73.

75. Stokes and Strachan, *Thesaurus Paleohibernicus*, 248–49. Cf. Best, "Some Irish Charms."

76. Michel Lejeune, with Léon Fleuriot et al., "Textes gaulois et gallo-romains en cursive latine: 3. Le plomb de Larzac," *Études Celtiques* 22 (1985), 95–177. My thanks to Joseph Eska for this reference.

77. Plummer, *Bethada* 1:28–9, 2:31.

78. Ibid., 1:164, 2:158–59. See also Plummer, *Vitae* 1:251.

79. Cosgrove, *New History of Ireland* 2:299, 712.

80. An 1830s catechism forbids Catholics to believe in the "cure of a wise-woman . . . the voice of birds, or anything else that hasn't efficacy from God, the Church, and nature." William J. Mahon, ed. and trans., *Doctor Kirwan's Irish Cate-chism by Thomas Hughes* (Cambridge, 1993), 88–89. As Mahon points out, the phrase echoes the fifteenth-century *Leabhar Breac,* which prohibits "the charms of women, or the voice of birds." Robert Atkinson, ed. and trans., *The Passions and the Homilies from the Lebar Breac* (Dublin, 1887), ll. 7315–18. Cf. the St. Gall gloss: *énlaithi ad-mai,* "birdflocks of witches." Stokes and Strachan, *Thesaurus Paleohibernicus,* 248–49. See also Eleanor Hull, "The Ancient Hymn-charms of the Irish," *Transactions of the Folk-lore Society* 21 (1910), 417–46.

81. *DIL,* 95; see also Ní Dhonnchadha, "*Caillech* and Other Terms," 85–86; Ó Cathasaigh, "Eponym of Cnogba."

82. Todd, *Cogadh Gaedhel re Gallaibh* 138–39.

83. Ibid., 206–7.

84. The articles in Wendy Davies and Paul Fouracre, eds., *The Settlement of Dis-putes in Early Medieval Europe* (Cambridge, 1986), argue to the contrary; but to demonstrate judicial process is not to deny the violence so common in early Europe, as one glance at the Irish annals shows. See also Stacey, *Road to Judgment,* 6–9.

85. For just two examples from the literature, see Greene, *Fingal Rónáin,* 9; Nic Dhonnchadha, *Aided Muirchertaig Meic Erca,* 31.

86. *MGH, Leges nationum Germanicarum* 2/1:51; 3/2:90–91; 4/1:63, 70; 5/1:111; 5/2:356–57; *LL* 4:44–45; see also Brundage, *Law, Sex and Christian Society,* 209–10.

87. *CIH,* 779–80 = *CG,* 121–27; *CIH,* 519 = *SEIL,* 71 (l. 35); Kelly, *Guide,* 79.

88. *CIH,* 519, 779 = *SEIL,* 71; *CG,* 121–24; but see Kelly, *Guide,* 135 n. 76.

89. *CIH,* 42–43 = *ALI* 5:272; Kelly, *Guide,* 135.

90. *CIH,* 2229; Kelly, *Guide,* 136–37.

91. *CIH,* 48–49 = *ALI* 5:292–97. Cf. Hincmar, *De Divortio* 5, *PL* 125:657, re-garding men abusing or murdering their wives. See also *MGH, Capitularia regum Francorum* 2:239–40: regarding the Council of Tribur's making churches sanctuaries for women. See also Wemple, *Women in Frankish Society,* 104. Cf. Binchy, "Bretha Crólige," 48 (61): "Neither women nor men [should] exchange blows."

92. *CA,* 24.

93. *CA,* 32; Kelly, *Guide,* 137.

94. On the complex concerns regarding religious women traveling, see Hall, "Gender and Sanctity," 46–58. Late antique and medieval theorists often took an un-sympathetic view of women's participation in rape. See Wolfgang P. Müller, "Lucre-tia and the Medieval Canonists," *Bulletin of Medieval Canon Law,* n.s. 19 (1989), 13–32.

95. Cosgrove, *New History of Ireland* 2:22–23.

96. Breatnach, "Tochmarc Luaine ocus Aided Athairne," 12–13.

97. O'Rahilly, *Táin Bó Cúailnge*, 49.

98. Van Hamel, *Compert Con Culainn*, 11.

99. Greene, *Fingal Rónáin*, 27–44.

100. O'Neill, "Cath Bóinde," 174; Vernam Hull, ed. and trans., "*Aided Medb:* The Violent Death of Medb," *Speculum* 13 (1938), 55, 59.

101. Knott, *Togail Bruidne Da Derga*, 45.

102. *CIH*, 337 = *ALI* 3:540–47 (n.b., the passage breaks off in the middle of *ALI* 3:542.) Cf. *CIH*, 335–36 = *ALI* 3:532–33, regarding witnesses' tacit acknowledgment of a rape and abduction.

103. Meyer, *Triads*, 20; *CIH*, 975–96 = *ZCP* 16:225; *CIH*, 2198 = *ZCP* 15:351; cf. *CIH*, 827; Kelly, *Guide*, 35.

104. *CIH*, 1090; Kelly, *Guide*, 136; cf. Deuteronomy 23–27.

105. Meyer, *Triads*, 12; cf. Greene, *Fingal Rónáin*, 5 (ll. 90–92).

106. Binchy, "Bretha Crólige," 30.

107. Carey, "Notes on the Irish War-Goddess," 269.

108. Some of the principal edited texts include Stokes, "*Rennes Dindsenchas*"; E. J. Gwynn, *Poems from the Dindsenchas*, Todd Lecture Series 7 (Dublin, 1900); Gwynn, *Metrical Dindsenchas;* Best and O'Brien, *Book of Leinster* 3:699–760, 4:842–958, 1018–60; see also Hughes, *Early Christian Ireland*, 166–70.

109. Stokes, "*Rennes Dindsenchas*," 311–14; cf. Gwynn, *Metrical Dindsenchas* 3:2–25.

110. Stokes, "*Rennes Dindsenchas*," 323–24.

111. Ibid., 326–27.

112. Ibid., 294–95; Gwynn, *Metrical Dindsenchas*, 26–35.

113. Dunn, "Síle-na-gCíoch"; Jørgen Andersen, *The Witch on the Wall: Medieval Erotic Sculpture in the British Isles* (Copenhagen, 1977), 22–23.

114. Andersen, *Witch on the Wall*, esp. 32–57, 37–39. Cf. Etienn Rynne, "A Pagan Celtic Background for Sheela-na-gigs?" in Rynne, ed., *Figures from the Past: Studies on Figurative Art in Christian Ireland in Honour of Helen M. Roe* (Dublin, 1987), 189–202.

115. Stella Cherry, *A Guide to Sheela-na-Gigs* (Dublin: National Museum of Ireland, 1992).

116. Andersen, *Witch on the Wall*, 58–71.

117. Vivian Mercier, *The Irish Comic Tradition* (Oxford, 1962), 53–56.

118. Andersen, *Witch on the Wall*, 96–103, 120–37.

119. Ibid., 104–12. But see J. A. Jerman, "The 'Sheela-na-gig' Carving of the British Isles: Suggestions for a Re-classification and Other Notes," *County Louth Archaeology and History Journal* 20 (1981), 10–24.

120. For women's status in the Anglo-Norman and later periods, see Simms, "Legal Position of Irishwomen"; MacCurtain and O'Dowd, *Women in Early Modern Ireland.*

Selected Bibliography

Primary Sources

Adomnán. *Adomnán's Life of Columba*. Ed. A. O. Anderson and M. O. Anderson. London, 1961.

Bernard, J. H., and Robert Atkinson, eds. and trans. *The Irish Liber Hymnorum*. 2 vols. London, 1898.

Best, R. I., ed. and trans. "The Adventures of Art Son of Conn, and the Courtship of Delbchaem." *Ériu* 3 (1907): 149–73.

——, ed. and trans. "Some Irish Charms." *Ériu* 16 (1952): 27–32.

—— and Osbern Bergin, eds. *Lebor na hUidre*. Dublin, 1929.

—— and Osbern Bergin, eds. and trans. "Tochmarc Étaíne." *Ériu* 12 (1938): 137–96.

—— and M. A. O'Brien, and Anne O'Sullivan (vol. 6), eds. *The Book of Leinster*. 6 vols. Dublin, 1954–83.

Bhreathnach, Máire, ed. and trans. "A New Edition of Tochmarc Becfhola." *Ériu* 35 (1984): 59–81.

Bieler, Ludwig, ed. and trans. *The Irish Penitentials*. Dublin, 1963.

——, ed. and trans. *Patrician Texts in the Book of Armagh*. Dublin, 1979.

Binchy, D. A., ed. and trans. "Bretha Crólige." *Ériu* 12 (1938): 1–77.

——, ed. and trans. "Bretha Déin Chécht." *Ériu* 20 (1966): 1–66.

——, ed. *Corpus Iuris Hibernici*. 6 vols. Dublin, 1978.

——, ed. *Críth Gablach*. Dublin, 1941.

——, ed. and trans. "Irish Law Tracts Re-edited: I. Coibnes Uisci Thairidne." *Ériu* 17 (1955): 52–85.

——, ed. and trans. "The Saga of Fergus Mac Léti." *Ériu* 16 (1952): 33–48.

——, ed. *Scéla Cano Meic Gartnáin*. Dublin, 1963.

Blamires, Alcuin, ed. *Woman Defamed and Woman Defended: An Anthology of Medieval Texts*. Oxford, 1992.

Breatnach, Líam, ed. "Tochmarc Luaine ocus Aided Athairne." *Celtica* 13 (1980): 1–31.

——, ed. *Uraicecht na Ríar.* Dublin, 1987.

Byrne, Mary E. "Airec Menman Uraird Maic Coisse." In O. J. Bergin et al., eds., *Anecdotae from Irish Manuscripts* 2 (1908). 42–76.

Carmichael, Alexander, ed. and trans. *Charms of the Gaels: Hymns and Incantations with Illustrative Notes on Words, Rites, and Customs, Dying and Obsolete; Orally Collected in the Highlands and Islands of Scotland by Alexander Carmichael.* 1901; repr. Edinburgh, 1992.

Carney, James, ed. and trans. "Nia Son of Lugna Fer Trí." *Éigse* 2 (1940): 187–97.

——, ed. and trans. *The Poems of Blathmac, Son of Cú Brettan.* Dublin, 1964.

Clover, Helen, and Margaret Gibson, ed. and trans. *The Letters of Lanfranc, Archbishop of Canterbury.* Oxford, 1979.

Connolly, Seán, ed. "Vita Prima Sanctae Brigitae." *JRSAI* 119 (1989): 5–49.

—— and J.-M. Picard, trans. "Cogitosus' Life of St. Brigit." *JRSAI* 117 (1987): 5–27.

Dillon, Myles, ed. *Serglige Con Culainn.* Repr. Dublin, 1975.

——, ed. and trans. "Stories from the Law-tracts." *Ériu* 11 (1932): 42–65.

——, trans. "The Wooing of Becfhola and the Stories of Cano Son of Gartnan." *Modern Philology* 43 (1945): 11–17.

Dinneen, Patrick S., ed. and trans. *The History of Ireland by Geoffrey Keating: Foras Feasa ar Éirinn.* 4 vols. London, 1908.

Duncan, Lilian, ed. and trans. "Altram Tige Dá Medar." *Ériu* 11 (1932): 184–225.

Esposito, Mario, ed. "Conchubranus Vita Sanctae Monennae." *PRIA* 28 C (1910): 202–51.

Fraser, J., ed. and trans. "The First Battle of Moytura." *Ériu* 8 (1916): 1–63.

Gantz, Jeffrey. *Early Irish Myths and Sagas.* Repr. New York, 1985.

Gray, Elizabeth A., ed. and trans. *Cath Maige Tuired: The Second Battle of Mag Tuired.* Naas, Éire, 1982.

Greene, David, ed. *Fingal Rónain and Other Stories.* Dublin, 1955.

——, ed. and trans. "St. Brigit's Alefeast." *Celtica* 2 (1952): 150–53.

—— and Frank O'Connor, eds. and trans. *A Golden Treasury of Irish Poetry, A.D. 600 to 1200.* London, 1967.

Gregory of Tours. *Historia francorum. MGH* Scriptorum rerum Merovingicarum 1.

Gwynn, E. J., ed. and trans. "The Burning of Finn's House." *Ériu* 1 (1904): 13–37.

——, ed. and trans. "An Irish Pentitential." *Ériu* 7 (1914): 121–95.

——, ed. and trans. *The Metrical Dindsenchas.* Todd Lecture Series 8–12. Dublin, 1913–35.

——. *Poems from the Dindsenchas.* Todd Lecture Series 7. Dublin, 1900.

——, and W. J. Purton, eds. and trans. "The Monastery of Tallaght." *PRIA* 29 C (1911): 115–79.

Hancock, W. N., et al., eds. and trans. *The Ancient Laws of Ireland.* 6 vols. Dublin, 1865–1901.

Heist, W. W., ed. *Vitae Sanctorum Hiberniae.* Subsidia Hagiographica 28. Brussels, 1965.

Henderson, George, ed. and trans. *Fled Bricrend.* London, 1899.

Hennessy, W. M., ed. and trans. *The Annals of Ulster.* 4 vols. Dublin, 1887–1901.

Henry, P. L., ed. and trans. *Dánta Ban: Poems of Irish Women, Early and Modern.* Cork, 1991.

Hull, Vernam, ed. and trans. "*Aided Meidbe:* The Violent Death of Medb." *Speculum* 13 (1938): 52–61.

———, ed. and trans. "The Conception of Conchobor." *Irish Texts* 4 (1934): 4–12.

———, ed. and trans. "The Death of Fothath Canainne." *ZCP* 20 (1936): 400–404.

———, ed. "Geneamuin Chormaic." *Ériu* 16 (1952): 79–85.

———, ed. and trans. "Two Anecdotes Concerning St. Moling." *ZCP* 18 (1930), 90–99.

Isidore of Seville. *Etymologiarum Libri XX.* Ed. W. M. Lindsay. Oxford, 1911.

Jackson, Kenneth H., ed. *Cath Maighe Léna.* Dublin, 1938.

Kelly, Fergus, ed. *Audacht Morainn.* Dublin, 1976.

King, J. E., ed. and trans. *Baedae Opera Historica.* 2 vols. Cambridge, Mass., repr. 1979.

Kinsella, Thomas. *The Tain.* Oxford, 1970.

Knott, Eleanor, ed. *Togail Bruidne Da Derga.* Repr. Dublin, 1975.

Mac Airt, Seán, ed. and trans. *The Annals of Inisfallen.* Repr. Dublin, 1977.

———, and Gearóid Mac Niocaill, eds. and trans. *The Annals of Ulster to A.D. 1131.* Dublin, 1983.

Macalister, R. A. Stewart, ed. and trans. *Lebor Gabála Érenn.* 5 vols. Dublin, 1938–56.

Mac Eoin, Gearóid. "A Life of Cumaine Fota." *Béaloideas* 39–41 (1971–73): 192–205.

———. "Suithchern and Rónán Dícolla." *ZCP* 36 (1978): 63–82.

Mac Mathúna, Seán, ed. and trans. *Immram Brain: Bran's Journey to the Land of the Women.* Tübingen, 1985.

Marstrander, Carl, ed. and trans. "The Deaths of Lugaid and Derbforgaill." *Ériu* 5 (1911): 201–18. '

Meid, Wolfgang, ed. *Táin Bó Fraích.* Repr. Dublin, 1974.

Meyer, Kuno, ed. "Anecdotae from Irish MSS, III: The Mothers' Lament at the Slaughter of the Innocents." *Gaelic Journal* 4 (1891): 89–90.

———, ed. and trans. *Cáin Adamnáin: An Old-Irish Treatise on the Law of Adamnán.* Oxford, 1905.

———, ed. and trans. "Daniel Húa Liathaide's Advice to a Woman." *Ériu* 1 (1904): 67–71.

———, ed. and trans. *Death Tales of the Ulster Heroes.* Todd Lecture Series 14. Dublin, 1906.

———, ed. "De Síl Chonairi Móir." *Ériu* 6 (1912): 130–43.

———, ed. and trans. "The Dindsenchas of Emain Macha." *Archiv für celtische Lexicographie* 3 (1907): 325–26.

———, ed. "Echtra Nerai." *RC* 10 (1889): 212–28.

———, ed. and trans. "Eve's Lament." *Ériu* 3 (1907): 148.

———, ed. and trans. *Fianaigecht.* Todd Lecture Series 16. Dublin, 1910.

———, ed. and trans. *Hail Brigit: An Old-Irish Poem on the Hill of Alenn.* Dublin, 1912.

———, ed. and trans. *The Instructions of King Cormac Mac Airt.* Todd Lectures Series 15. Dublin, 1909.

———, ed. and trans. *Liadain and Cuirithir: An Irish Love Story of the Ninth Century.* London, 1902.

——, ed. and trans. "The Mothers' Lament at the Slaughter of the Innocents." *Gaelic Journal* 4 (1891): 89–90.

——, ed. and trans. "An Old Irish Prayer for Long Life." In *A Miscellany Presented to John Macdonald MacKay, LL.D.,* 226–32. Liverpool, 1914.

——, ed. and trans., "Reicne Fothaid Canainne." In Meyer, ed. *Fianaigecht,* 1–21. Todd Lecture Series 16. Dublin, 1910.

——, ed. *Sanas Cormaic.* Anecdota from Irish Manuscripts, IV. Dublin, 1912: i–128.

——, ed. and trans. "Scél Baili Binnbérlaig." *RC* 13 (1892): 220–27.

——, ed. "Tochmarc Treblainne." *ZCP* 13 (1921): 166–75.

——, ed. and trans. *The Triads of Ireland.* Todd Lecture Series 13. Dublin, 1906.

——, ed. and trans. *The Voyage of Bran Son of Febal to the Land of the Living.* Vol. 1. London, 1895.

Migne, J. P., ed. *Patrologia Latina.* 221 vols. Paris, 1844–64.

Mulchrone, Kathleen, ed. and trans. *Bethu Phátraic.* 2 vols. Dublin, 1939.

Murphy, Gerard, ed. *Early Irish Lyrics.* Oxford, 1956.

Nic Dhonnchadha, Lil, ed. *Aided Muirchertaig Meic Erca.* Dublin, 1964.

Ní Shéaghdha, Nessa, ed. *Tóriugheacht Dhiarmada agus Ghráinne.* Dublin, 1967.

Ó hAodha, Donncha, ed. and trans. *Bethu Brigte.* Dublin, 1978.

O'Brien, M. A., ed. *Corpus Genealogiarum Hiberniae.* Repr. Dublin, 1976.

Ó Cuív, Brian, ed. "The Romance of Mis and Dubh Ruis." *Celtica* 2.2 (1954): 325–33.

——, ed. and trans. "Some Early Devotional Verse in Irish." *Ériu* 19 (1959): 13–17.

O Daly, Máirín, ed. *Cath Maige Mucrama.* Dublin, 1975.

O'Donovan, John, ed. and trans. *Annals of the Kingdom of Ireland by the Four Masters.* 7 vols. Dublin, 1856.

O'Grady, Standish, ed. *Silva Gadelica.* 2 vols. London, 1892.

O'Keeffe, J. G., ed. *Buile Suibhne.* Dublin, 1931.

O'Looney, Bryon, ed. "Tochmarc Bec-Fola." *PRIA,* Mss. series 1, 1 (1870): 172–83.

Ó Máille, Tomás, ed. and trans. "Medb Cruachna." *ZCP* 17 (1927): 129–46.

O'Neill, Joseph, ed. and trans. "Cath Bóinde." *Ériu* 2 (1905): 174–85.

O'Nolan, T. P., ed. and trans. "Mór of Munster and the Tragic Fate of Cuanu Son of Cailchín." *PRIA* 30 C (1912–13): 261–82.

O'Rahilly, Cecile, ed. *Táin Bó Cúailnge: Recension I.* Dublin, 1976.

——, ed. and trans. *The Táin Bó Cúailnge from the Book of Leinster.* Dublin, 1984.

O'Rahilly, T. F., ed. "Varia II: Lost Legends of Mis and Dubh Ruis." *Celtica* 1.2 (1950): 382–84.

Ó Riain, Pádraig, ed. *Cath Almaine.* Dublin, 1978.

Oskamp, H. P. A., ed. and trans. "Echtra Condla." *ÉC* 14 (1974): 207–28.

——, ed. and trans. *The Voyage of Máel Dúin: A Study in Early Irish Voyage Literature.* Groningen, 1970.

Plummer, Charles, ed. and trans. *Bethada Náem nÉrenn.* 2 vols. Oxford, 1922.

——, ed. *Vitae Sanctorum Hiberniae.* 2 vols. Oxford, 1910.

Quin, E. G., gen. ed. *Dictionary of the Irish Language.* Compact ed. Dublin, 1983.

——, ed. and trans. "The Early Irish Poem *Ísucán.*" *Cambridge Medieval Celtic Studies* 1 (1981): 39–52.

Radner, Joan, ed. and trans. *The Fragmentary Annals of Ireland.* Dublin, 1978.

Shaw, Francis, ed. *Aislinge Oenguso.* Dublin, 1934.

Smith, Roland M., ed. and trans. "The *Senbriathra Fithail* and Related Texts." *RC* 45 (1928): 1–92.

Stokes, Whitley, ed. and trans. *Cóir Anmann.* In Stokes and Ernst Windisch, eds. *Irische Texte mit Übersetzungen und Wörterbuch.* 3d ser. Leipzig, 1897. 2:285–444.

———, ed. and trans. "The Colloquy of the Two Sages." *RC* 26 (1905): 4–64.

———, ed. and trans. "Cuchulainn's Death Abridged from the *Book of Leinster.*" *RC* 3 (1876–78): 175–85.

———, ed. and trans. "Da Choca's Hostel." *RC* 21 (1900): 150–65.

———, ed. and trans. "The Death of Crimthann Son of Fidach and the Adventures of the Sons of Eochaid Muigmedón." *RC* 24 (1903): 172–207.

———, ed. and trans. "The Death of Muirchertach mac Erca." *RC* 23 (1902): 395–437.

———, ed. and trans. *Félire Óengusso Céli Dé.* London, 1905.

———, ed. and trans. "The Klosterneuberg Incantation." *RC* 2 (1873–75): 112–15.

———, ed. and trans. *Lives of the Saints from the Book of Lismore.* Oxford, 1890.

———, ed. and trans. "The Prose Tales in the *Rennes Dindsenchas.*" *RC* 15 (1894): 272–336, 418–84; 16 (1895): 31–83, 135–67, 269–312.

———, ed. and trans. "The Violent Deaths of Goll and Garb." *RC* 14 (1893): 396–449.

———, ed. and trans. "The Voyage of Mael Duin." *RC* 9 (1888): 447–95; 10 (1889): 50–95.

———, ed. and trans. "The Voyage of the Huí Corra." *RC* 14 (1893): 22–69.

———, ed. and trans. "The Wooing of Luaine and Death of Athirne." *RC* 24 (1903): 270–87.

———, and John Strachan, eds. and trans. *Thesaurus Paleohibernicus.* 2 vols. London, 1901.

———, and Ernst Windisch, eds. *Irische Texte mit Übersetzungen und Wörterbuch,* 3d ser. Leipzig, 1891.

Strachan, John, and J. G. O'Keeffe, eds. *The Táin Bó Cúailnge from the Yellow Book of Lecan.* Dublin, 1912.

Thurneysen, Rudolf, ed. "Baile in Scáil." *ZCP* 20 (1935): 213–27.

———. *Irisches Recht.* Abhandlungen der Preussischen Akademie der Wissenschaften. Phil.-Hist. Klasse. 2. Berlin, 1931.

———, ed. *Scéla Mucce Meic Dathó.* Repr. Dublin, 1975.

Todd, J. H., ed. and trans. *Cogadh Gaedhel re Gallaibh.* Rolls Series. London, 1867.

Tymoczko, Maria, trans. *Two Death Tales from the Ulster Cycle.* Dublin, 1981.

Ulster Society for Medieval Latin Studies, ed. "The Life of Saint Monenna by Conchubranus." I: *Seanchas Ard Mhacha* 9 (1979): 250–73; II: 10 (1980–81): 117–40; III: 10 (1982): 426–53.

Van Hamel, A. G., ed. *Compert Con Culainn and Other Stories.* Repr. Dublin, 1968.

———, ed. *Immrama.* Dublin, 1941.

Warren, F. E., ed. and trans. *The Antiphonary of Bangor.* London, 1895.

Wasserschleben, Herrmann, ed. *Die irische Kanonensammlung.* Leipzig, 1885.

Watson, J. Carmichael, ed. *Mesca Ulad.* Dublin, 1941.

Williams, S. J., and J. E. Powell, eds. *Cyfreithiau Hywel Dda yn ôl Llyfr Belgywryd.* Cardiff, 1942; 2d ed. 1961.

Secondary Sources

Africa, Dorothy. "The Politics of Kin: Women and Preeminence in a Medieval Irish Hagiographical List." Ph.D. thesis, University of Toronto, 1990.

Amundsen, Daniel W., and Carol Jean Diers. "The Age of Menarche in Medieval Europe." *Human Biology* 45 (1973): 363–69.

Andersen, Jørgen. *The Witch on the Wall: Medieval Erotic Sculpture in the British Isles.* Copenhagen, 1977.

Ardener, Shirley, ed. *Defining Females: The Nature of Women in Society.* London, 1978.

——. *Perceiving Women.* London, 1972.

Arensberg, Conrad. *The Irish Countryman: An Anthropological Study.* 1937; repr. New York, 1968.

Atkinson, Clarissa. *The Oldest Vocation: Christian Motherhood in the Middle Ages.* Ithaca, N.Y., 1991.

——. "'Your Servant, My Mother': The Figure of Saint Monica in the Ideology of Christian Motherhood." In Atkinson, Constance H. Buchanan, and Margaret R. Miles, eds., *Immaculate and Powerful: The Female in Sacred Image and Social Reality,* 139–72. Boston, 1985.

Baillie, Michael. "Marker Dates: Turning Prehistory into History." *Archaeology Ireland* 2 (1988): 154–55.

Bakhtin, Mikhail. *The Dialogic Imagination: Four Essays by M. M. Bakhtin.* Ed. Michael Holquist. Austin, Tex., 1981.

Barber, Elizabeth Wayland. *Women's Work: The First 20,000 Years.* New York, 1994.

Barrière, Bernadette. "The Cistercian Convent of Coyroux in the Twelfth and Thirteenth Centuries." *Gesta* 31 (1992): 76–82.

Bates, Daniel, et al., eds. "Kidnapping and Elopement as Alternative Systems of Marriage." *Anthropological Quarterly* 47.3 (1974).

Baumgarten, Rolf. *Bibliography of Irish Linguistics and Literature, 1942–71.* Dublin, 1986.

Beauvoir, Simone de. *The Second Sex.* New York, 1949.

Bennett, Judith. *Women in the Medieval English Countryside: Gender and Household in Brigstock before the Plague.* Oxford, 1987.

Benoit, F. *L'héroisation équestre.* Aix-en-Provence, 1954.

Berman, Constance H. "Men's Houses, Women's Houses: The Relationship between the Sexes in Twelfth-Century Monasticism." In Andrew MacLeish, ed., *The Medieval Monastery,* 43–52. St. Cloud, Minn., 1988.

Bhreathnach, Máire. "The Sovereignty Goddess as Goddess of Death?" *ZCP* 39 (1982): 243–60.

Binchy, D. A. "Distraint in Irish Law." *Celtica* 10 (1973): 22–71.

——. "The Fair of Tailtiu and the Feast of Tara." *Ériu* 18 (1958): 113–38.

——. "The Legal Capacity of Women in Regard to Contracts." In Rudolf Thurneysen, D. A. Binchy, et al., *Studies in Early Irish Law,* 207–34. Dublin, 1936.

——. "Secular Institutions." In Myles Dillon, ed., *Early Irish Society,* 52–65. Dublin, 1954.

Bitel, Lisa. " 'Conceived in Sins, Born in Delights': Stories of Procreation from Early Ireland." *Journal of the History of Sexuality* 3 (1992): 181–202.

——. *"In Visu Noctis:* Dreams in Early Medieval Hagiography and Histories, 500–900." *History of Religions* 31 (1991): 39–59.

——. *Isle of the Saints: Monastic Settlement and Christian Community in Early Ireland.* Ithaca, N.Y., 1990.

——. "Sex, Sin, and Celibacy in Early Christian Ireland." *PHCC* 7 (1987): 65–95.

——. "Women's Donations to the Churches in Early Ireland," *JRSAI* 114 (1984): 5–23.

——. "Women's Monastic Enclosures in Early Ireland: A Study in Female Spirituality and Male Monastic Mentalities." *Journal of Medieval History* 12 (1986): 15–36.

Blair, J., and Richard Sharpe, eds. *Pastoral Care before the Parish.* Leicester, 1992.

Bloch, Marc. *Feudal Society.* Chicago, 1961; repr. 1968.

Blumberg, Rae Lesser. "Rural Women in Development: Veil of Invisibility, World of Work." *International Journal of Intercultural Relations* 3 (1979): 447–72.

Boserup, Ester. *Women's Role in Economic Development.* Aldershot, U.K., 1986.

Boswell, John. *The Kindness of Strangers: The Abandonment of Children in Western Europe from Late Antiquity to the Renaissance.* New York, 1988.

Bowen, Charles. "Great-Bladdered Medb: Mythology and Invention in the *Táin Bó Cúailnge.*" *Éire-Ireland* 10 (1975): 14–34.

Bradley, John, ed. *Settlement and Society in Medieval Ireland: Studies Presented to F. X. Martin, O.S.A.* Kilkenny, Éire, 1988.

Bray, Dorothy Ann. "The Image of St. Brigit in the Early Irish Church." *ÉC* 24 (1984): 209–15.

——. *"Secunda Brigida:* Saint Ita of Killeedy and Brigidine Tradition." In Cyril J. Byrne et al., eds. *Celtic Languages and Celtic Peoples,* Proceedings of the Second North American Congress of Celtic Studies, 27–38. Halifax, 1989.

Breatnach, Liam. "Canon Law and Secular Law in Early Ireland: The Significance of *Bretha Nemed.*" *Peritia* 3 (1984): 439–59.

——. "Lawyers in Early Ireland." In Daire Hogan and W. N. Osborough, eds., *Brehons, Serjeants, and Attorneys: Studies in the History of the Irish Legal Profession,* 1–13. Blackrock, Éire, 1990.

Bremmer, Jan. "Avunculate and Fosterage." *Journal of Indo-European Studies* 4 (1976): 65–76.

Brown, Peter. *The Body and Society: Men, Women, and Sexual Renunciation in Early Christianity.* New York, 1988.

Brundage, James. *Law, Sex, and Christian Society in Medieval Europe.* Chicago, 1987.

Bynum, Caroline. *The Resurrection of the Body in Western Christianity, 200–1336.* New York, 1994.

Byrne, Cyril J., et al., eds. *Celtic Languages and Celtic Peoples,* Proceedings of the Second North American Congress of Celtic Studies. Halifax, 1989.

Byrne, Francis J. *Irish Kings and High-Kings.* London, 1973.

Cadden, Joan. *The Meanings of Sex Difference in the Middle Ages: Medicine, Science, and Culture.* Cambridge, 1993.

Cameron, Averil. "Virginity as Metaphor: Women and the Rhetoric of Early Christianity." In Cameron, ed., *History as Text: The Writing of Ancient History,* 184–205. London, 1989.

Carey, John. "The Location of the Otherworld in Irish Tradition." *Éigse* 19 (1982): 36–43.

———. "Notes on the Irish War-Goddess." *Éigse* 19 (1983): 263–75.

———. "Sequence and Causation in *Echtrae Nerai.*" *Ériu* 39 (1988): 67–74.

———. "Time, Space, and the Otherworld." *Proceedings of the Harvard Celtic Colloquium* 7 (1987): 1–27.

Carney, James. *Studies in Early Irish Literature and History.* Dublin, 1955.

Caulfield, Mina Davis. "Equality, Sex, and Mode of Production." In Gerald D. Berreman, ed., with Kathleen M. Zaretsky, *Social Inequality: Comparative and Developmental Approaches,* 201–19. New York, 1981.

Charles-Edwards, Thomas. *Early Irish and Welsh Kinship.* Oxford, 1993.

———. "The Pastoral Function of the Church in the Early Irish Laws." In J. Blair and Richard Sharpe, eds., *Pastoral Care before the Parish,* 63–80. Leicester, 1992.

———. "Review Article: The Corpus Iuris Hibernici." *Studia Hibernica* 20 (1980): 141–62.

———, et al., eds. *Lawyers and Laymen: Studies in the History of Law Presented to Professor Dafydd Jenkins on His Seventy-fifth Birthday.* Cardiff, 1986.

Cherry, Stella. *A Guide to Sheela-na-Gigs.* Dublin: National Museum of Ireland, 1992.

Clark, Rosalind. "Aspects of the Morrígan in Early Irish Literature." *Irish University Review* 17 (1987): 223–36.

———. *The Great Queens: Irish Goddesses from the Morrígan to Cathleen Ní Houlihan.* Irish Literary Studies 34. Gerrards Cross, U.K., 1991.

Clarke, Howard B., and Anngret Simms, eds. *The Comparative History of Urban Origins in Non-Roman Europe,* BAR International Series 255. Oxford, 1985.

Clover, Carol. "The Politics of Scarcity: Notes on the Sex Ratio in Early Scandinavia." In Helen Damico and Alexandra Hennessey Olsen, eds., *New Readings on Women in Old English Literature,* 100–134. Bloomington, Ind., 1990.

Coleman, Emily R. "Infanticide in the Early Middle Ages." In Susan Stuard, ed., *Women in Medieval Society,* 47–70. Philadelphia, 1976.

———. "Medieval Marriage Characteristics: A Neglected Factor in the History of Medieval Serfdom." *Journal of Interdisciplinary History* 2 (1971): 205–21.

Colman, Rebecca. "The Abduction of Women in Barbarian Law." *Florilegium* 5 (1983): 62–75.

Condren, Mary. *The Serpent and the Goddess: Women, Religion, and Power in Celtic Ireland.* New York, 1989.

Cosgrove, Art, ed. *Marriage in Ireland.* Dublin, 1985.

———. *New History of Ireland.* Vol. 2: *Medieval Ireland, 1169–1534.* Oxford, 1993.

Crawford, W. H. "Women in the Domestic Linen Industry." In Margaret MacCurtain and Mary O'Dowd, eds., *Women in Early Modern Ireland,* 255–64. Edinburgh, 1991.

Cullen, Nuala. "Women and the Preparation of Food in Eighteenth-Century Ireland." In Margaret MacCurtain and Mary O'Dowd, eds., *Women in Early Modern Ireland,* 265–75. Edinburgh, 1991.

Dalarun, Jacques. "Regard des clercs." In Michelle Perrot and Georges Duby, gen. eds. *Histoire des femmes en occident.* Vol. 2: *Le Moyen Age,* ed. Christiane Klapisch-Zuber, 31–54. Paris, 1991.

Damico, Helen, and Alexandra Hennessey Olsen, eds. *New Readings on Women in Old English Literature.* Bloomington, Ind., 1990.

Damsholt, Nanna. "The Role of Icelandic Women in the Sagas and in the Production of Homespun Cloth." *Scandinavian Journal of History* 9.2 (1984): 75–90.

Davies, Wendy. "Celtic Women in the Early Middle Ages." In Averil Cameron and Amelie Kuhrt, eds., *Images of Women in Antiquity,* 153–57. Detroit, 1983.

——. "The Place of Healing in Early Irish Society." In Donnchadh Ó Corráin, et al., eds., *Sages, Saints, and Storytellers: Celtic Studies in Honour of Professor James Carney,* 43–55. Maynooth, Éire, 1989.

——. *Small Worlds: The Village Community in Early Medieval Brittany.* London, 1988.

——, and Paul Fouracre, eds. *The Settlement of Disputes in Early Medieval Europe.* Cambridge, 1986.

Demyttenaere, Albert. "The Cleric, Women, and the Stain: Some Beliefs and Ritual Practices Concerning Women in the Early Middle Ages." In Werner Affeldt and Ursula Vorwerk, eds., *Frauen in Spätantike und Frühmittelalter: Lebensbedingungen, Lebensnormen, Lebensformen,* 141–65. Berlin, 1990.

Doan, James. "Sovereignty Aspects in the Roles of Women in Medieval Irish and Welsh Society." *PHCC* 5 (1985): 87–102.

——. *Women and Goddesses in Early Celtic History, Myth, and Legend.* Northeastern University Working Papers in Irish Studies 87—4/5. Boston, 1987.

Doherty, Charles. "Exchange and Trade in Early Medieval Ireland." *JRSAI* 110 (1980): 67–89.

——. "Monastic Towns in Early Medieval Ireland." In H. B. Clarke and Anngret Simms, eds. *The Comparative History of Urban Origins in Non-Roman Europe.* Oxford, 1984.

——. Some Aspects of Hagiography as a Source for Irish Economic History." *Peritia* 1 (1982): 300–328.

Douglas, Mary. *Purity and Danger.* New York, 1966.

Duby, Georges. "Youth in Aristocratic Society: Northwestern France in the Twelfth Century." In Duby, *The Chivalrous Society,* 112–22. Berkeley, 1977.

Dumézil, Georges. "Le trio des Macha." *Revue de l'Histoire des Religions* 146 (1954): 5–17.

Dumville, David. "Echtrae and Immram: Some Problems of Definition." *Ériu* 27 (1976): 73–94.

——. "The World of the *Síd* and the Attitude of the Narrator in *Táin Bó Fraích.*" *Studia Celtica Japonica* 7 (1995): 21–25.

Dunn, James H. "Síle-na-gCíoch." *Éire-Ireland* 12 (1977): 68–85.

Dunn, Vincent A. *Cattle-Raids and Courtships: Medieval Narrative Genres in a Traditional Context.* New York, 1989.

Edwards, Nancy. *The Archaeology of Early Medieval Ireland*. Philadelphia, 1990.

Erler, Mary, and Maryanne Kowalski, eds. *Women and Power in the Middle Ages*. Athens, Ga., 1988.

Fell, Christine. *Women in Anglo-Saxon England*. London, 1984.

Fleischer, Manfred P. "Are Women Human? The Debate of 1595." *Sixteenth-Century Journal* 12 (1981): 108–22.

Flint, Valerie. *The Rise of Magic in Early Medieval Europe*. Princeton, 1991.

Ford, Patrick K. "Celtic Women: The Opposing Sex." *Viator* 19 (1988): 417–38.

——, ed. *Celtic Folklore and Christianity*. Santa Barbara, Calif., 1983.

Fox, Robin. *The Tory Islanders: A People of the Celtic Fringe*. Cambridge, 1978.

Frisch, Rose E. "Population, Food Intake, and Fertility." *Science* 199 (1977): 22–30.

Garlick, Barbara, et al., eds., *Stereotypes of Women in Power: Historical Perspectives and Revisionist Views*. Philadelphia, 1994.

Gilchrist, Roberta. *Gender and Material Culture: The Archaeology of Religious Women*. London, 1994.

——. "Women's Archaeology? Political Feminism, Gender Theory, and Historical Revisionism." *Antiquity* 65 (1991): 495–501.

Good, James. "The Mariology of the Blathmac Poems." *Irish Ecclesiastical Record* 104 (1956): 1–7.

——. "The Mariology of the Early Irish Church." *Irish Ecclesiastical Record* 100 (1963): 73–79.

Goody, Jack. *The Development of the Family and Marriage in Europe*. Cambridge, 1983.

——, and Joan Buckley. "Implications of the Sexual Division of Labor in Agriculture." In J. Clyde Mitchell, ed., *Numerical Techniques in Social Anthropology*, 33–47. Philadelphia, 1980.

Gravdal, Kathryn. "Chrétien de Troyes and the Medieval Romance of Sexual Violation." *Signs* 17.3 (1992): 558–85.

Green, Miranda. *Symbol and Image in Celtic Art*. London, 1989.

Guyonvarc'h, Christian-J. *Textes mythologiques irlandais*. Rennes, 1980.

Gwynn, Aubrey, and R. Neville Hadcock. *Medieval Religious Houses: Ireland (with an Appendix to Early Sites)*. London, 1970.

Gwynn, E. J. "Senbriathra Fithail." *RC* 46 (1929): 268–71.

Hall, Dianne P. "Gender and Sanctity in the Hagiography of Early Medieval Irish Women." M.A. thesis, University of Melbourne, 1992.

Hamlin, Ann, and Chris Lynn, eds. *Pieces of the Past: Archaeological Excavations by the Department of the Environment*. Belfast, 1988.

Hamp, Eric. "Irish *Síd* 'Tumulus' and Irish *Síd* 'Peace'," *ÉC* 19 (1982): 141.

Hastrup, Kirsten. "The Semantics of Biology: Virginity." In Shirley Ardener, ed., *Defining Females: The Nature of Women in Society*, 49–65. London, 1978.

——. "The Sexual Boundary—Purity: Heterosexuality and Virginity." *Anthropological Society of Oxford* 5 (1974): 137–47.

Hennessy, William. "The Ancient Irish Goddess of War." *RC* 1 (1870–72): 32–55.

Herbert, Máire. "Celtic Heroine? The Archaeology of the Deirdre Story." In Toni O'Brien Johnson and David Cairns, eds., *Gender in Irish Writing*, 13–22. Philadelphia, 1991.

——. *Iona, Kells, and Derry: The History and Hagiography of the Monastic Family of Columba.* Oxford, 1988.

——. "The Universe of Male and Female: A Reading of the Deirdre Story." In Cyril J. Byrne, et al., eds. *Celtic Languages and Celtic Peoples.* Proceedings of the Second North American Congress of Celtic Studies, 54–64. Halifax, 1989.

Herlihy, David. "Land, Family, and Women in Continental Europe, 701–1200." *Traditio* 18 (1962): 89–120.

——. "Life Expectancies for Women in Medieval Society." In R. T. Morewedge, ed., *The Role of Women in the Middle Ages,* 1–22. Albany, 1975.

——. *Medieval Households.* Cambridge, Mass., 1985.

——. *Opera Muliebria: Women and Work in Medieval Europe.* New York, 1990.

Hillgarth, Jocelyn. "Ireland and Spain in the Seventh Century." *Peritia* 3 (1987): 1–16.

Hirschon, Renée. "Open Body, Closed Space: The Transformation of Female Sexuality." In Shirley Ardener, ed. *Defining Females: The Nature of Women in Society,* 66–87. London, 1978.

Hollis, Stephanie. *Anglo-Saxon Women and the Church: Sharing a Common Fate.* Woodbridge, Suffolk, 1992.

Hughes, Diane Owen. "From Brideprice to Dowry in Mediterranean Europe." *Journal of Family History* 3 (1978): 262–96.

Hughes, Kathleen. *The Church in Early Irish Society.* Ithaca, N.Y., 1967.

——. *Early Christian Ireland: An Introduction to the Sources.* Ithaca, N.Y., 1973.

Hunt, Lynn, ed. *The Invention of Pornography: Obscenity and the Origin of Modernity.* New York, 1993.

Huston, Nancy. "The Matrix of War: Mothers and Heroes." In Susan Rubin Suleiman, ed., *The Female Body in Western Culture: Contemporary Perspectives,* 119–38. Cambridge, 1986.

Jackson, Kenneth H. *The Oldest Irish Tradition: A Window on the Iron Age.* Cambridge, 1964.

Jacobsen, Grethe. "Pregnancy and Childbirth in the Medieval North: A Topology of Sources and a Preliminary Study." *Scandinavian History Journal* 9 (1984): 91–111.

Jacquart, Danielle, and Claude Thomasset. *Sexuality and Medicine in the Middle Ages.* Princeton, 1988.

Jenkins, Dafydd, and Morfydd E. Owen, eds. *The Welsh Law of Women: Studies Presented to Professor Daniel A. Binchy.* Cardiff, 1980.

Jenkins, Richard P. "Witches and Fairies: Supernatural Aggression and Deviance among the Irish Peasantry." *Ulster Folklife* 23 (1977): 33–56.

Jerman, J. A. "The 'Sheela-na-Gig' Carving of the British Isles: Suggestions for a Re-classification, and Other Notes." *County Louth Archaeology and History Journal* 20 (1981): 10–24.

Jesch, Judith. *Women in the Viking Age.* Woodbridge, Suffolk, 1991.

Jochens, Jenny. "The Church and Sexuality in Medieval Iceland." *Journal of Medieval History* 6 (1980): 377–91.

——. "Consent in Marriage: Old Norse Law, Life, and Literature." *Scandinavian Studies* 58 (1986): 142–76.

——. "The Illicit Love Visit: An Archaeology of Old Norse Sexuality." *Journal of the History of Sexuality* 1 (1991): 357–92.

Johnson, Penelope. *Equal in Monastic Profession: Religious Women in Medieval France.* Chicago, 1991.

Karras, Ruth Mazo. "Concubinage and Slavery in the Viking Age." *Scandinavian Studies* 62.2 (1990): 141–62.

Kelleher, John V. "The Pre-Norman Irish Genealogies." *Irish Historical Studies* 16 (1968): 138–53.

Kelly, Fergus. *Guide to Early Irish Law.* Dublin, 1987.

Kelly, Joseph F. T. "Christianity and the Latin Tradition in Early Medieval Ireland." *Bulletin of the John Rylands University Library of Manchester* 68.2 (1986): 410–33.

Kelly, Patricia. "The *Táin* as Literature." In J. P. Mallory, ed., *Aspects of the Táin,* 69–102. Belfast, 1992.

Kent, Susan, ed. *Domestic Architecture and the Use of Space: An Interdisciplinary and Cross-Cultural Study.* Cambridge, 1990.

Kerlouegan, François. "Essai sur la mise en nourriture et l'éducation dans les pays celtqiues d'après le témoignage des textes hagiograophiques latins." *ÉC* 12 (1968–69): 101–46.

Killeen, J. F. "The Debility of the Ulstermen—a Suggestion." *ZCP* 33 (1974): 81–86.

Kus, Susan, and Victor Raharijaona. "Domestic Space and the Tenacity of Tradition among Some Betsileo of Madagascar." In Susan Kent, ed., *Domestic Architecture and the Use of Space: An Interdisciplinary and Cross-Cultural Study,* 21–33. Cambridge, 1990.

Laiou, Angeliki, ed. *Consent and Coercion to Sex and Marriage in Ancient and Medieval Societies.* Washington, D.C.: Dumbarton Oaks, 1993.

Laqueur, Thomas. *Making Sex: Body and Gender from the Greeks to Freud.* Cambridge, Mass., 1990.

——. "Orgasm, Generation, and the Politics of Reproductive Biology." *Representations* 14 (1986): 1–41.

Larkin, Emmet. "The Devotional Revolution in Ireland, 1850–75." *American Historical Review* 77.3 (1972): 625–52.

Lears, T. J. Jackson. "The Concept of Cultural Hegemony: Problems and Possibilities." *American Historical Review* 90.3 (1985): 567–93.

Ledermann, Rena. "Contested Order: Gender and Society in the Southern New Guinea Highlands." *American Ethnologist* 16 (1989): 230–47.

LeGoff, Jacques. "The Symbolic Ritual of Vassalage." In LeGoff, *Time, Work, and Culture in the Middle Ages,* 237–88. Chicago, 1980.

Le Roy Ladurie, Emmanuel. *Montaillou: The Promised Land of Error.* Repr. New York, 1979.

Lewin, Ellen. "By Design: Reproductive Strategies and the Meaning of Motherhood." In H. Homans, ed., *The Sexual Politics of Reproduction,* 123–38. Aldershot, U.K., 1988.

Leyser, Karl J. *Rule and Conflict in an Early Medieval Society: Ottonian Saxony.* London, 1979.

Lucas, A. T. "Cattle in Ancient and Medieval Irish Society." *O'Connell School Union Record.* Dublin, 1958.

——. *Cattle in Ancient Ireland.* Kilkenny, Éire, 1989.

——. "The Plundering and Burning of Churches in Ireland, 7th to 16th Century." In Étienne Rynne, ed., *North Munster Studies*, 16–54. Limerick, 1967.

Lynn, C. J. "Deer Park Farms, Glenarm, Co. Antrim." *Archaeology Ireland* 1.1 (1987): 11–15.

——. "Early Christian Period Domestic Structures: A Change from Round to Rectangular." *Irish Archaeological Forum* 5 (1978): 29–45.

——. "An Early Christian Period Site in Ballybrolly, County Armagh." *UJA* 46 (1983): 47–51.

——. "A Rath in Seacash Townland, County Antrim." *UJA* 41 (1978): 55–74.

——. "Two Raths at Ballyhenry, County Antrim." *UJA* 46 (1983): 67–91.

Lysaught, Patricia. *The Banshee: The Irish Supernatural Death-Messenger.* Dublin, 1986.

Mac Cana, Proinsias. "Aspects of the Theme of King and Goddess in Irish Literature." *ÉC* 7 (1955–56): 76–114, 356–413; 8 (1958–59): 59–65.

——. *Celtic Mythology.* Repr. Feltham, Middlesex, 1986.

——. "Conservation and Innovation in Early Celtic Literature." *ÉC* 13 (1971): 61–118.

——. "*Laíded, Gressacht,* Formalized Incitement." *Ériu* 43 (1992): 69–92.

——. *The Learned Tales of Medieval Ireland.* Dublin, 1980.

——. "The Sinless Otherworld of *Immram Brain.*" *Ériu* 27 (1976): 95–115.

——. "Women in Irish Mythology." *Crane Bag* 4.1 (1980): 7–10.

MacCormack, Carol, and Marilyn Strathern, eds. *Nature, Culture, and Gender.* Cambridge, 1980.

MacCurtain, Margaret, and Mary O'Dowd, eds. *Women in Early Modern Ireland.* Edinburgh, 1991.

Mac Eoin, Gearóid. "The Dating of Middle Irish Texts." *Proceedings of the British Academy* 69 (1982): 109–37.

Mac Niocaill, Gearóid. "Orality and Literacy in Some Middle-Irish King-Tales." In Stephen N. Tranter and Hildegard L. C. Tristram, eds., *Early Irish Literature— Media and Communication,* 149–83. Tübingen, 1989.

Mallory, J. P., ed. *Aspects of the Táin.* Belfast, 1992.

Manning, Conleth. "Archaeological Excavation of a Succession of Enclosures at Millockstown, Co. Louth. *PRIA* 86 C (1986): 135–81.

Mathieu, Nicole-Claude, ed. *L'Arraisonnement des femmes: Essais en anthropologie des sexes.* Cahiers de l'homme: Ethno.-géog.-ling. n.s. 24. Paris, 1985.

McAll, Christopher. "The Normal Paradigms of a Woman's Life in the Irish and Welsh Law Texts." In Dafydd Jenkins and Morfydd E. Owen, eds., *The Welsh Law of Women: Studies Presented to Professor Daniel A. Binchy,* 7–22. Cardiff, 1980.

McCone, Kim. "Brigit in the Seventh Century: A Saint with Three Lives?" *Peritia* 1 (1982): 107–45.

——. *Pagan Past and Christian Present in Early Irish Literature.* Maynooth, Éire, 1990.

McCormick, Finbar. "Dairying and Beef Production in Early Christian Ireland." In T. Reeves-Smyth and F. Hamond, eds., *Landscape Archaeology in Ireland,* BAR 116, 253–68. Oxford, 1968.

McKinnon, Catharine. *Only Words*. Cambridge, Mass., 1993.

McLeod, Glenda. *Virtue and Venom: Catalogs of Women from Antiquity to the Renaissance*. Ann Arbor, Mich., 1991.

McLeod, Neil. *Early Irish Contract Law*. Sydney Series in Celtic Studies 1. Sydney, 1992.

McNamara, Jo Ann. "Chaste Marriage and Clerical Celibacy." In Vern Bullough and James Brundage, eds. *Sexual Practices and the Medieval Church*, 14–21. Buffalo, 1982.

——. "Living Sermons: Consecrated Women and the Conversion of Gaul." In John A. Nichols and Lillian Thomas Shank, eds., *Medieval Religious Women*, vol. 2: *Peaceweavers*, 19–37. Kalamazoo, Mich., 1987.

——. "Muffled Voices: The Lives of Consecrated Women in the Fourth Century." In John A. Nichols and Lillian Thomas Shank, eds., *Medieval Religious Women*, vol. 1: *Distant Echoes*, 11–30. Kalamazoo, Mich., 1984.

——, and Suzanne Wemple. "The Power of Women through the Family in Medieval Europe, 500–1100." In Mary Erler and Maryanne Kowalski, eds., *Women and Power in the Middle Ages*, 83–101. Athens, Ga., 1988.

Melia, Daniel. "Law and the Shaman Saint." In Patrick Ford, ed., *Celtic Folklore and Christianity*, 113–28. Santa Barbara, Calif., 1983.

Müller, Wolfgang P. "Lucretia and the Medieval Canonists." *Bulletin of Medieval Canon Law* n.s. 19 (1989): 13–32.

Murphy, Gerard. *Saga and Myth in Ancient Ireland*. Dublin, 1961.

Murray, Alexander. *Germanic Kinship Structure: Studies in Law and Society in Antiquity and the Early Middle Ages*. Toronto, 1983.

Mytum, Harold. *The Origins of Early Christian Ireland*. London, 1992.

Nagy, Joseph F. "Fenian Heroes and Their Rites of Passage." In Bo Almqvist et al., eds., *The Heroic Process: Form, Function, and Fantasy in Folk Epic*, 161–82. Dun Laoghaire, Éire, 1987.

——. *The Wisdom of the Outlaw: The Boyhood Deeds of Finn in Gaelic Narrative Tradition*. Berkeley, 1985.

Ní Chatháin, Proinséas. "Swineherds, Seers, and Druids." *Studia Celtica* 14–15 (1979–80): 200–211.

Nichols, John A., and Lillian Thomas Shank, eds. *Medieval Religious Women*. Vol. 1: *Distant Echoes*. Kalamazoo, Mich., 1984. Vol. 2: *Peaceweavers*. Kalamazoo, Mich., 1987.

Ní Dhonnchadha, Máirín. "*Caillech* and Other Terms for Veiled Women in Medieval Irish Texts." *Éigse* 28 (1994–95): 71–96.

——. "The Guarantor List of *Cáin Adomnáin*, 697." *Peritia* 1 (1982): 178–215.

——. "*Inailt*, Foster-Sister, Fosterling." *Celtica* 18 (1986): 185–91.

——. "The *Lex Innocentium*: Adomnán's Law for Women, Clerics, and Youths, 697 A.D." In Mary O'Dowd and Sabine Wichert, eds., *Chattel, Servant, or Citizen*, 53–76. Belfast, 1995.

Noonan, John T. *Contraception: A History of Its Treatment by the Catholic Theologians and Canonists*. Cambridge, Mass., 1965.

Ó Bróin, Tomás. "What Is the 'Debility' of the Ulstermen?" *Éigse* 10 (1963): 286–99.

——. "The Word *Noínden*." *Éigse* 13 (1969–70): 165–76.

Ó Catháin, Séamas. "Hearth-Prayers and Other Traditions of Brigit: Celtic Goddess and Holy Woman." *JRSAI* 122 (1992): 12–34.

Ó Cathasaigh, Donál. "The Cult of Brigid: A Study of Pagan-Christian Syncretism in Ireland." In James J. Preston, ed., *Mother Worship: Theme and Variations*, 75–94. Chapel Hill, N.C., 1982.

Ó Cathasaigh, Tomás. "The Eponym of Cnogba." *Éigse* 23 (1989): 27–38.

———. "The Semantics of *Síd*." *Éigse* 17 (1977–78): 127–54.

———. "The Sister's Son in Early Irish Literature." *Peritia* 5 (1986): 128–60.

Ó Coileáin, Seán. "Oral or Literary: Some Strands of the Argument." *Studia Hibernica* 17/18 (1977–78): 7–35.

———. "The Structure of a Literary Cycle." *Ériu* 25 (1974): 88–125.

Ó Corráin, Donnchadh. "Dál Cais—Church and Dynasty." *Ériu* 24 (1973): 52–63.

———. "The Early Irish Churches: Some Aspects of Organisation." In Ó Corráin, ed., *Irish Antiquity*. Cork, 1981.

———. *Ireland before the Normans*. Dublin, 1972.

———. "Irish Law and Canon Law." In Proinséas Ní Chatháin and Michael Richter, eds., *Irland und Europa: Die Kirche im Frühmittelalter*, 157–66. Stuttgart, 1984.

———. "Irish Regnal Succession: A Reappraisal." *Studia Hibernica* 11 (1971): 7–39.

———. "Legend as Critic." In Tom Dunne, ed., *The Writer as Witness: Literature as Historical Evidence*, 23–38. Cork, 1987.

———. "Marriage in Early Ireland." In Art Cosgrove, ed., *Marriage in Ireland*, 5–24. Dublin, 1985.

———. "Nationality and Kingship in Pre-Norman Ireland." In T. W. Moody, ed., *Nationality and the Pursuit of National Independence*. Belfast, 1978.

———. "Women in Early Irish Society." In Ó Corráin and Margaret MacCurtain, eds., *Women in Irish Society: The Historical Dimension*, 1–10. Westport, Conn., 1980.

———, et al., eds. *Sages, Saints, and Storytellers: Celtic Studies in Honour of Professor James Carney*. Maynooth, Éire, 1989.

———, Liam Breatnach, and Aidan Breen. "The Laws of the Irish." *Peritia* 3 (1984): 382–438.

———, and Margaret MacCurtain, eds. *Women in Irish Society: The Historical Dimension*. Westport, Conn., 1980.

Ó Cuív, Brian. "Varia II: Lost Legends of Mis and Dubh Ruis." *Celtica* 1 (1950): 352–33.

O'Curry, Eugene. *Lectures on the Manners and Customs of the Ancient Irish*. 3 vols. Dublin, 1873.

O'Dwyer, Peter. *Mary: A History of Devotion in Ireland*. Dublin, 1988.

O'Flaherty, Wendy Doniger. *Women, Androgynes, and Other Mythical Beasts*. Chicago, 1980.

O Hehir, Brendan. "The Christian Revision of *Eachtra Airt Meic Chuind ocus Tochmarc Delbchaime Ingine Morgain*." In Patrick K. Ford, ed., *Celtic Folklore and Christianity*, 159–79. Santa Barbara, Calif., 1983.

O'Leary, Philip. "Contention at Feasts in Early Irish Literature." *Éigse* 20 (1984): 115–27.

———. "*Fír Fer*: An Internalized Ethical Concept in Early Irish Literature?" *Éigse* 22 (1987): 1–14.

——. "The Honour of Women in Early Irish Literature." *Ériu* 38 (1987): 27–44.

O'Loan, J. "Livestock in the Brehon Laws." *Agricultural History Review* 7 (1959): 65–74.

O'Rahilly, T. F. *Early Irish History and Myth.* Dublin, 1946; repr. 1976.

——. "On the Origins of the Names Érainn and Ériu." *Ériu* 14 (1943): 7–28.

Ó Riain, Pádraig. "Boundary Association in Early Irish Society." *Studia Celtica* 7 (1972): 12–29.

——. "A Study of the Irish Legend of the Wild Man." *Éigse* 14 (1972): 179–206.

Ó Ríordáin, Seán P. "Excavations at Cush, Co. Limerick." *PRIA* 45 C (1939–40): 83–181.

——. "Lough Gur Excavations: Three Marshland Habitation Sites." *JRSAI* 79 (1949): 126–45.

Ó Sé, Micheál. "Old Irish Buttermaking." *JCHAS* 54 (1949): 61–67.

——. "Old Irish Cheese and Other Milk Products." *JCHAS* 53 (1948): 82–87.

Parker, Roszika. *The Subversive Stitch: Embroidery and the Making of the Feminine.* London, 1984.

Parson, John Carmi. "Family, Sex, and Power: The Rhythms of Medieval Queenship." In Parson, ed., *Medieval Queenship,* 1–11. New York, 1993.

Patterson, Nerys. *Cattle-Lords and Clansmen: Kinship and Rank in Early Ireland.* Harvard Studies in Sociology. Cambridge, 1991.

Petersen, William. "A Demographer's View of Prehistoric Demography." *Current Anthropology* 16 (1975): 227–46.

Power, Nancy. "Classes of Women Described in the *Senchas Már.*" In Rudolf Thurneysen and D. A. Binchy et al., *Studies in Early Irish Law,* 81–108. Dublin, 1936.

Power, Patrick. *Sex and Marriage in Ancient Ireland.* Dublin, 1976.

Price, Sally. *Co-Wives and Calabashes.* 2d ed. Ann Arbor, 1993.

Puhvel, Jaan. *Comparative Mythology.* Baltimore, 1987.

——. *Myth and Law among the Indo-Europeans.* Berkeley, Calif., 1970.

Rader, Rosemary. *Breaking Boundaries: Male/Female Friendship in Early Christian Communities.* New York, 1983.

Rees, Alwyn, and Brinley Rees. *Celtic Heritage.* London, 1961.

Rosaldo, M. Z., and Louise Lamphere, eds. *Woman, Culture, and Society.* Stanford, Calif., 1974.

Rosenthal, Joel T., ed. *Medieval Women and the Sources of Medieval History.* Athens, Ga., 1990.

Ross, Anne. "The Divine Hag of the Pagan Celts." In Venetia Newall, ed., *The Witch Figure,* 139–64. London, 1973.

——. *Pagan Celtic Britain.* London, 1967.

Ross, Margaret Clunies. "Concubinage in Anglo-Saxon England." *Past and Present* 108 (1985): 13–28.

——. "Women and Power in the Scandinavian Sagas." In Barbara Garlick et al., eds., *Stereotypes of Women in Power: Historical Perspectives and Revisionist Views,* 105–19. New York, 1992.

Roubin, Lucienne. "Espace masculin, espace feminin en communautés provençales." *Annales, E.S.C.* 26.2 (1970): 537–60.

Rousselle, Aline. *Porneia: On Desire and the Body in Antiquity.* Oxford, 1988.

Ruether, Rosemary, ed. *Religion and Sexism: Images of Women in the Jewish and Christian Traditions.* New York, 1974.

Russell, Josiah Cox. *Late Ancient and Medieval Population Control.* Philadelphia, 1985.

Ryan, John. *Irish Monasticism: Its Origins and Early Development.* Dublin, 1931.

Rynne, Étienne. "A Pagan Celtic Background for Sheela-na-gigs?" In Rynne, ed., *Figures from the Past: Studies on Figurative Art in Christian Ireland in Honour of Helen M. Roe,* 189–202. Dublin, 1987.

Salisbury, Joyce E. "Latin Doctors of the Church on Sexuality." *Journal of Medieval History* 12 (1986): 279–90.

Sanday, Peggy Reeves, and Ruth Gallagher Goodenough, eds. *Beyond the Second Sex: New Directions in the Anthropology of Gender.* Philadelphia, 1990.

Schulenberg, Jane T. "Saints' Lives as a Source for the History of Women, 500–1100." In Joel T. Rosenthal, ed., *Medieval Women and the Sources of Medieval History,* 238–320. Athens, Ga., 1990.

——. "Strict Active Enclosure and Its Effects on the Female Monastic Experience (ca. 500–1100)." In John A. Nichols and Lillian Thomas Shank, eds., *Medieval Religious Women,* vol. 1: *Distant Echoes,* 51–86. Kalamazoo, 1984.

——. "Women's Monastic Communities, 500–1100: Patterns of Expansion and Decline." In Judith M. Bennett et al., eds., *Sisters and Workers in the Middle Ages,* 208–39. Repr. Chicago, 1989.

Sellner, Edward B. "Brigit of Kildare—a Study in the Liminality of Women's Spiritual Power." *Cross Currents* 39 (1989): 402–19.

Shahar, Shulamith. *Childhood in the Middle Ages.* London, 1990.

Sharpe, Richard. "Churches and Communities in Medieval Ireland." In J. Blair and Richard Sharpe, eds., *Pastoral Care before the Parish,* 81–109. Leicester, 1992.

——. "Some Problems Concerning the Organisation of the Church in Early Medieval Ireland." *Peritia* 3 (1984): 230–70.

——. "*Vitae Sanctae Brigidae:* The Oldest Texts." *Peritia* 1 (1982): 81–106.

Simms, Katherine. "Guesting and Feasting in Gaelic Ireland." *JRSAI* 108 (1978): 67–100.

——. "The Legal Position of Irishwomen in the Later Middle Ages." *Irish Jurist* n.s. 10 (1975): 96–111.

Sims-Williams, Patrick. "Some Celtic Otherworld Terms." In A. T. E. Matonis and Daniel F. Melia, eds., *Celtic Language, Celtic Culture,* 57–81. Van Nuys, Calif., 1990.

Siskind, Janet. "Kinship and Mode of Production." *American Anthropologist* 80.4 (1978): 860–72.

Sjoestedt, Marie-Louise. *Gods and Heroes of the Celts.* London, 1949.

Slotkin, Edgar M. "Medieval Irish Scribes and Fixed Texts." *Éigse* 17 (1978–79): 437–50.

——. "*Noínden:* Its Semantic Range." In A. T. E. Matonis and Daniel F. Melia, eds., *Celtic Language, Celtic Culture,* 137–50. Van Nuys, Calif., 1990.

Smith, Roland M. "Fithal and Flann Fína." *RC* 47 (1930): 30–38.

——. "The *Speculum Principum* in Early Irish Literature." *Speculum* 2 (1927): 411–45.

Smyth, A. P. *Celtic Leinster: Towards an Historical Geography of Early Irish Civilization, A.D. 500–1600.* Blackrock, Éire, 1982.

Solterer, Helen. "Figures of Female Militancy in French Literature." *Signs* 16.3 (1991): 522–49.

Sørensen, Preben Meulengracht. "Murder in the Marital Bed: An Attempt at Understanding a Crucial Scene in *Gíslasaga*." In John Lindow et al., eds., *Structure and Meaning in Old Norse Literature: New Approaches to Textual Analysis in Literary Criticism*, 235–63. Odense, Denmark, 1986.

Stacey, Robin. *The Road to Judgment: From Custom to Court in Medieval Ireland and Wales*. Philadelphia, 1994.

Stokes, Whitley. "The Ancient Irish Goddess of War: Corrections and Additions." *RC* 2 (1873–75): 489–92.

Stout, Matthew. "Ringforts in the South-west Midlands of Ireland." *PRIA* C 91 8 (1991): 201–43.

Tabet, Paola. "Fertilité naturelle, reproduction forcée." In Nicole-Claude Mathieu, ed., *L'arraisonnement des femmes: Essais en anthropologie des sexes*, 61–146. Cahiers de l'Homme: Ethno.-Géog.-Ling., n.s. 24. Paris, 1985.

Tewkin, Owsei. *Galenism: Rise and Decline of a Medical Philosophy*. Ithaca, N.Y., 1973.

Thurneysen, Rudolf. "Allerlei Keltisches. 7 Göttin *Medb*." *ZCP* 18 (1929): 108–10; 19 (1933): 352.

——, and D. A. Binchy, et al. *Studies in Early Irish Law*. Dublin, 1936.

Tierney, J. J. "The Celtic Ethnography of Posidonius." *PRIA* 60 C (1959–60): 189–275.

Trindade, W. Ann. "Irish Gormlaith as a Sovereignty Figure." *ÉC* 23 (1966): 143–56.

Valente, Roberta. "Gwydion and Aranrhod: Crossing the Borders of Gender in *Math*." *Bulletin of the Board of Celtic Studies* 35 (1988): 1–9.

Van Baal, Jan. "The Part of Women in the Marriage Trade." *Bijdragen* (Leiden) 126.3 (1970).

Wallace, P. F. "The Archaeology of Viking Dublin." In Howard B. Clarke and Anngret Simms, eds., *The Comparative History of Urban Origins in Non-Roman Europe*, BAR International Series 255, 103–45. Oxford, 1985.

——. "The Origins of Dublin." In B. G. Scott, ed., *Studies on Early Ireland*. Belfast, 1981.

Walsh, Katherine. "Scholarship and the Natural Sciences in Early Medieval Ireland." *Studies* 74 (1985): 207–19.

Watt, John. *The Church in Medieval Ireland*. Dublin, 1972.

Wemple, Suzanne Fonay. *Women in Frankish Society: Marriage and the Cloister, 500 to 900*. Philadelphia, 1981.

Williams, B. B. "Excavations at Ballyutoag, County Antrim." *UJA* 47 (1984): 37–49.

Wilson, Stephen. "The Myth of Mothering a Myth: The Historical View of European Child-rearing." *Social History* 9 (1984): 181–98.

Wogan-Brown, Jocelyn. "Saints' Lives and the Female Reader." *Forum for Modern Language Studies* 27 (1991): 314–32.

Wood, Charles T. "The Doctor's Dilemma: Sin, Salvation, and the Menstrual Cycle in Medieval Thought." *Speculum* 56 (1981): 710–27.

Index